Sons of the Mountains

In Garb of old Gaul, wi' the fire of old Rome,
from the heath-cover'd mountains of Scotia we come,
Where the Romans endeavour'd our country to gain,
But our Ancestors fought, and they fought not in vain.

We're tall as the oak on the mount of the vale,
Are swift as the roe which the hound doth assail,
As the full moon in Autumn our shields do appear,
Minerva would dread to encounter our spear.

As a storm in the ocean when Boreas blows,
So we are enrag'd when we rush on our foes;
We Sons of the Mountains, tremendous as rocks,
dash the force of our foes with our thundering strokes.

Quebec and Cape Breton, the pride of old France,
In their troops fondly boasted till we did advance;
But when our claymores they saw us produce,
Their courage did fail, and they sued for a truce.

Sir Henry Erskine, c.1763

Sons of the Mountains

The Highland Regiments in the French and Indian War, 1756-1767

Volume Two

Ian Macpherson McCulloch

PURPLE MOUNTAIN PRESS
Fleischmanns, New York

FORT TICONDEROGA
Ticonderoga, New York

ROBIN BRASS STUDIO
Toronto, Ontario

Sons of the Mountains: The Highland Regiments in the French and Indian War, 1756-1767
Volume Two of Two Volumes

First edition 2006

Published in the United States by

Purple Mountain Press, Ltd.
P.O. Box 309, Fleischmanns, New York 12430-0309
845-254-4062, 845-254-4476 (fax), purple@catskill.net
www.catskill.net/purple

and

Fort Ticonderoga
P.O. Box 390, Ticonderoga, New York 12883-0390
518-585-28210, 518-585-2210 (fax), fort@fort-ticonderoga.org
www.fort-ticonderoga.org

Published in Canada by

Robin Brass Studio, Inc.
rbrass@sympatico.ca
www.rbstudiobooks.com

International Standard book numbers
United States
ISBN-10: 1-930098-75-8
Canada
ISBN-13: 978-1-896941-49-3
ISBN-10: 1-896941-49-4

Library of Congress Control Number 2006903644

Title page illustration courtesy of Osprey Publishing, UK.

Manufactured in the United States of America on acid-free paper.

Contents

PART ONE

Regimental Officers Registers

The officers of the three Highland regiments listed on the following pages are presented in order of their regimental seniority during the Seven Year's War (SYW), i.e. NOT alphabetically; nor by the date of original commissions in the Army; nor by their rank achieved in other regiments once transferred or promoted later in their careers. An asterisk by a name denotes an officer actually serving in the regiment when it was sent overseas, (or in the case of the 2nd/42nd, 77th or 78th Regiments of Foot, those officers who were original members at the time of the battalion/regiment's actual raising). A number in square brackets [1] behind a name is to assist the reader in keeping track of the many officers who shared the same name (for example, in Fraser's Highlanders, there are four John Frasers, six Alexander Frasers and seven Simon Frasers). Please note that "dd" is a term used in the Commission and Succession books meaning "discharged dead."

The two junior regiments were styled the First and Second Highland Battalions initially, then assigned the numbers 62nd and 63rd Regiments of Foot. These numbers were short-lived as they were adjusted upwards to 77th and 78th respectively when fourteen second battalions of existing senior regiments in the British army were established as regiments in their own right. For easy reference and clarity in the registers, I have used their final number designators of 77th and 78th Foot throughout. The Royal Highland Regiment was, initially, the 43rd Regiment of Foot in the order of battle before dropping down a number to the 42nd Foot. I have inserted Crawford's and Sempill's in brackets behind those officers who were senior enough to have served under those Colonels of the regiment in its earliest years in order to avoid confusion with the 43rd Foot (Kennedy's) which served during the SYW.

Finally, these registers would not have been possible without the sterling assistance of colleagues Robert Andrews and John Houlding, whose intimate knowledge of the 18th century British army officers' corps is second to none. I must also mention the invaluable assistance of Dr William Forbes, Marie Fraser of the Clan Fraser Society of Canada, Dr. Ruby Campbell, seannachie of Clan Campbell, and Alan Gray who assisted greatly in my understanding of the intricate genealogical linkages that bound these three regiments so closely together by blood and marriage. Any mistakes that remain below, however, are solely mine. If descendants of any the officers listed herein have any additional information or corrections they wish to bring to my attention, then they are strongly encouraged to contact the author via the publisher so that their biographical data can be revised and updated for future editions.

42nd Foot (The Royal Highland Regiment)

Lieutenants-Colonel

Francis Grant* (1717-1782)
Ensign: 17 July 1739, Independent Highland Company (IHC), Campbell of Carrick's;
Capt: 18 June 1743, 43rd Foot (Crawford's);
Major: 1 October 1745, 42nd Foot;
Lt. Col: 17 December 1755, 42nd Foot;
Col: "*in America*", 12 January 1758; "*in the Army*", 19 February 1762; 9 July 1762, 90th Foot (Light Infantry); half-pay 11 July 1763; 6 November 1768, 63rd Foot;
Maj-Gen: 30 April 1770;
Lt.-Gen: 29 August 1777.

Born 10 August 1717, the 3rd living son of Sir James Grant of Grant, and Anne Colquhoun of Luss. By the time he went to North America, his father had died and his oldest living brother, Ludovic, was the Laird of Grant. Francis was one of three "original" officers of the 42nd still remaining 17 years after its inception in 1739, the other being Gordon Graham of Drainie and John MacNeil (see below). Commissioned as a second lieutenant in one of the six Independent Companies of the Watch, Grant was promoted lieutenant when his company was amalgamated in 1739 with the other five and four new ones to form the 43rd Regiment of Foot (Earl of Crawford's). By the time of the '45, Grant had risen to the post of regimental second-in-command of the Regiment. Promoted lieutenant-colonel in January 1756, he took the first division to North America in April and arrived in New York, 16 June 1756. He was made a "*Colonel in America*" early in 1758 and slightly wounded at Ticonderoga, 8 July 1758, leading the left wing of the army. For the 1760 campaign against Montréal, he was placed in charge of the vanguard comprising the brigaded grenadiers and light infantry of Amherst's army. He spent the winter with both battalions of the 42nd in Montréal until ordered to march both to Staten Island and take command of all troops assembling there for General Monckton's expedition against Martinique. Grant, now a "Brigadier-in-America" commanded the 2nd Brigade consisting of both battalions of the 42nd, the 77th (Montgomery's) and the 2nd/1st Foot (*The Royal*). He was appointed Colonel of the 90th Foot in July 1762, a newly-raised regiment sent over from Ireland for the Havana campaign, and thus officially handed over command of the 1st/42nd to Gordon Graham (see below). When Grant's 90th Foot was disbanded at the peace, he returned to England where he married Catherine Sophia Cox 17 March 1763, granddaughter of the Duke of Buckingham and daughter of Joseph Cox of Stanford Vale. This union produced 3 sons and 3 daughters. Died a Lt. General and Colonel of the 63rd Foot in 1781. He was buried at St Peter's Church in Farnborough, Hampshire, England. His gravestone reads: "*Sacred to the memory of Lieut. General Francis Grant, fourth son of Sir James Grant of Grant Bar. in whom the grave and active soldier the affectionate husband and father and friend were conspicuously united. He quitted this mortal life for a happy immortality universally lamented Dec*r *29th 1781 aged sixty-three.*"

Commission Books [hereafter *CBs*]; *Succession Books* [hereafter *SBs*]; *British Army Lists* [hereafter *BALs*]; Stewart, *Sketches*, I-II, *in passim*; F.C. Richards, *The Black Watch at Ticonderoga* [hereafter *Black Watch*], in Vol. X, Proceedings of the NY State Historical Association (1910), *in passim*; *MHP*, 50.

Facing page: LORD JOHN MURRAY (1711-1787). Colonel of the 42nd Foot (Royal Highland Regiment) for over 40 years, he was a younger son of the 1st Duke of Atholl by his second wife. Lord John began his military career as an ensign in the 3rd Foot Guards and by 1738 was a captain. In 1743 Lord John was aide-de-camp to King George II. In 1745 Murray was appointed Colonel of the 42nd and held that post until he died in 1787.
(Courtesy Trustees of the Black Watch Museum, Perth)

Gordon Graham,* of Drainie [Drynie] (c.1720-c.1785)

Ensign: 30 October 1739; 43rd Foot (Crawford's);
Lieut: 24 June 1743, 43rd Foot;
Capt: 3 June 1752, 42nd Foot;
Capt-Lt: 4 October 1746, 42nd Foot;
Major: 17 July 1758, 42nd Foot;
Lt. Col: "in the Army," 12 January 1762: 9 July 1762, 42nd Foot; retired 12 December 1770.

Gordon Graham joined the regiment as an ensign on its formation in 1739 and rose to the rank of captain by 1747, before retiring onto the half-pay list in 1749. He came off half-pay in June 1752, buying the captaincy of John MacLeod, yʳ of MacLeod, and, when the regiment sailed for North America in 1756, was the senior serving captain and regimental paymaster. He was brother-in-law to Lt. Henry Munro, 77th Foot (whose sister Anna was married to Gordon's younger brother George) as well as Lt. John Sutherland, 42nd Foot (see below). When the three Additional Companies were added to the regiment's establishment in 1757, Graham made the case for a second major to be appointed within the regiment, similar to the war time establishments of the two new Highland battalions, the 77th and 78th Foot. In a memorial he sketched out his previous service: "*Your Memorialist hath…upwards of twenty-five years, twelve of which as Captain in the above Regiment, and is now the eldest in that rank. That he hath served in Flanders and elsewhere during all the last war, some part of which he was employed as Major of Brigade, and had a Commission as such from General St. Clair in the Expedition under his command in the year 1746.*" *Drainie* was supported in his request by Lt-Col. Francis Grant and Major General James Abercromby. His request was overtaken by events and he was promoted major on the death of Duncan Campbell after the battle of Ticonderoga where he was slightly wounded. His arguments for a second major bore fruit, for John Reid, the next captain in seniority, was promoted second major next year on 1 August 1759. *Drainie* handed over his 1st/42nd duties to Reid however as he was made the major-commandant of the 2nd/42nd shortly afterwards. It had arrived, sickly and poorly-equipped from its grueling ordeal in the Caribbean. *Drainie* spent the better part of the winter of 1759/60 reorganizing, re-clothing, re-equipping and training the battalion. During the winter of 1760/61, he clashed with Francis Grant over who really commanded the 2nd/42nd and lost out to the latter. The following year he assumed command of the 1st/42nd on Francis Grant's departure to take up his

appointment as the new Colonel of the 90th Foot, while John Reid (see below) replaced him a major-commandant of the 2nd/42nd and John MacNeil (see below) replaced Reid as the new major of the 1st/42nd. He returned home to Scotland in January 1764 with a leave granted until 16 July 1766 but did not return to America and was listed as AWOL for some time. He rejoined the regiment when it returned to Ireland in 1767, after an absence of three years. He retired three years later in December 1770.

CBs; *SBs*; *BALs*; Stewart, *Sketches*, I-II, *in passim*; Richards, *Black Watch*, *in passim*; "List of the Officers of the 42nd or Royal Highland Regiment according to seniority dated December 29th, 1762," *BL*, Add. MSS. 21634: f.178c; *WO* 1/1.; *NAC*, MG 23, series K34 (Frederick Mackenzie Papers) Order Book, 1761-62.

Majors

Duncan Campbell,* 9th of Inverawe, (1702-1758)

Ensign: 24 April 1725, Independent Highland Coy (IHC), Campbell of Carrick's;
Lieut: 5 January 1728, IHC, half-pay, 6 August 1739; exchanged on promotion;
Capt: 25 December 1744, Additional Coy, 43rd Foot (Sempill's);
Major: 17 December 1755, 42nd Foot.

Born 22 November 1702, the eldest son and heir of Archibald Campbell, 8th of Inverawe and Janet McLean. Married Jean Campbell 20 March 1732, daughter of Colonel Alexander Campbell of Finab. His son, Lieutenant Alexander Campbell (see below) served in the regiment at the same time. Duncan began his military career as an ensign in one of the six original IHCs that were later amalgamated in 1739 to form "The Black Watch," or 43rd Foot. Duncan went out as a lieutenant on half-pay at that time, retiring to his estate at Inverawe. Five years later, he raised one of the three Additional Companies added to the 43rd Foot during the '45 Jacobite Uprising. His company was disbanded at the peace but he remained on strength as one of the peacetime company commanders and purchased the majority from Francis Grant when the latter was promoted lieutenant-colonel. When the regiment was ordered to North America in January 1756, *Inverawe* was already in Scotland recruiting the Second Division to bring it up to war establishment. He brought it over to America in August 1756 and was wounded two years later at the regiment's first major engagement, the battle of Ticon-

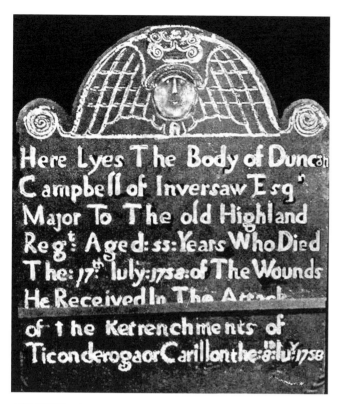

GRAVESTONE OF DUNCAN CAMPBELL OF *IN-VERAWE*, (1702-1758). His gravestone reads: *"Here lyes the Body of Duncan Campbell of Inverawe, Esquire, Major to the old Highland regiment, aged 55 years, who died the 17th July, 1758, of the Wounds he received in the Attack of the Retrenchment of Ticonderoga or Carrillon, on the 8th July, 1758."*

(Courtesy, Fort Ticonderoga Museum)

deroga, 8 July 1758. His right arm shattered, he was transported back to Fort Edward where his arm was amputated. He died nine days after the battle, his final resting place (after several moves), the Union Cemetery in Hudson Falls, New York. An account of his death, burial and reburials can be found in: William H. Hill, *Old Fort Edward*, Privately Printed, Fort Edward, 1929, pp. 163-164.the Union Cemetery in Fort Ann, NY. His gravestone reads: *"Here lyes the Body of Duncan Campbell of Inverawe, Esquire, Major to the old Highland regiment, aged 55 years, who died the 17th July, 1758, of the Wounds he received in the Attack of the Retrenchment of Ticonderoga or Carrillon, on the 8th July, 1758."* The tale of Major Campbell meeting the "weird" or ghost of his foster brother before the battle at Ticonderoga (who foretold of his death back in the Highlands) has been immortalized by Robert Louis Stevenson in his ballad *"A Legend of the West Highlands."*

CBs; *SBs*; *BALs*; Stewart, *Sketches*, I-II, *in passim*; Richards, *Black Watch, in passim;* Lord Archibald Campbell, *Records of Argyll*, 140.

John [Robertson] Reid,* of Straloch (1721-1807)

Lieut: 8 June 1745, Lord Loudoun's Highlanders; half-pay, 4 January 1748/9;
Capt-Lt: 20 June 1751, 42nd Foot;
Capt: 3 June 1752, 42nd Foot;
Major: 1 August 1759, 42nd Foot;
Lt. Col: "in the Army," 3 February 1762; half-pay 31 March 1770;
Col: "in America," 29 August 1777; 7 April 1780, 95th Foot; half-pay 31 May 1783; 27 November 1794, 88th Foot (Connaught Rangers);
Maj-Gen: 19 October 1781;
Lt.-Gen: 12 October 1793;
General: 1 January 1798.

Born 13 February 1721, at Inverchroskie, Scotland, the eldest son of Alexander Robertson of Straloch, known locally as *"Baron Reid."* John, and his younger brother, Alexander (see below), adopted the more distinctive surname Reid early in life. He and his brother were first cousins to Capt. John Small (see below) and kinsmen of brothers Lt. John Robertson, (see below) and Capt. James Robertson of Lude, 77th Foot. John received his early education in Perth and subsequently studied law at Edinburgh University for two years. During the '45, he left to become a lieutenant in Lord Loudoun's 64th Foot in June 1745 and was taken prisoner at Prestonpans the following year. The following spring he rejoined his regiment, and on 25 March 1746 was responsible for capturing a significant Jacobite treasure landed at Tongue Bay, intended as a payroll for Bonnie Prince Charlie's army. From 1747 to 1748, Reid served in Flanders with Loudoun's Highlanders and took part in the defense of Bergen-op-Zoom but on the reduction of his regiment at the peace exchanged to half-pay. He purchased a captain-lieutenant's commission in the 42nd in 1751 and a captaincy the following year. He acquired a reputation as a very fine musician and composer, and according to Stewart of Garth was acknowledged to be *"one of the most accomplished flute players of the age."* It was during the years just prior to the Regiment leaving for North America that he composed the music for his *"Highland March,"* written for two violins or flutes and a violoncello. In later years, words were added to the music and it became known as *"The Garb*

JOHN REID, (1721-1807) finished the war as Major to the 42nd Regiment of Foot and brought the regiment back to Ireland in 1767. He retired in 1770 to enjoy and improve his American estates, but the Revolution broke out and he was dispossessed of everything. In 1779-80 he raised the 95th Foot at his own expense. He was considered one of the most accomplished flautists of his day and his composition *Garb of Old Gaul* **remains the slow march of the Black Watch today.** (Print after a painting from *A Military History of Perthshire*)

of Old Gaul," and to this day remains the Slow March of the Black Watch. Four years later, he was the second senior captain when the regiment sailed for New York. He fell ill prior to the 1758 Ticonderoga campaign, Abercromby thus left him at Fort Edward and ordered him "*to take upon you the charge of said Fort, and all duties incumbent upon you as Commandant thereof, until you have my orders for so doing, or until you shall be superceded by an officer of Higher Rank, bearing His Majesty's Commission. Given under my Hand and Seal at Fort Edward the 22nd*

Day of June, 1758." Reid was promoted major of the 1st Battalion the following summer for the 1759 Ticonderoga and Crown Point campaign. For the 1760 expedition against Montréal, he commanded the 1st/42nd, as Colonel Francis Grant was detached "*on command*" leading the army's vanguard and Major Gordon Graham had been transferred to the command of the 2nd/42nd. While in garrison at Montréal for the winter 1760-61, Reid heard that other Highland officers of his seniority and station, such as Robert Keith and John Campbell of Dunoon (see 78th Register), were being allowed to raise their own regiments in Scotland. Eager for a chance at promotion to lieutenant-colonel, Reid wrote to his father to help solicit the Duke of Atholl's support in raising "*a battalion of real hardy Highlanders*" for the King's service. If the offer was ever made to London, it must have been turned down, for Reid continued as the acting-commanding officer of the 1st/42nd Foot when it deployed to the Caribbean as part of General Robert Monckton's 1762 expedition against Martinique. While the regiment prepared for this expedition encamped at Staten Island for the latter part of 1761, Reid married Susanna "Sukie" Alexander, the daughter of James Alexander, Surveyor-General of New York and New Jersey. She was the sister of William Alexander who claimed the earldom of Stirling as male representative of his cousin, last holder of that title. Reid was wounded twice at the storming of Mount Tartenson in January 1762, one "*a violent contusion on One Thigh which for several days and threaten'd a mortification*" and another potentially serious one when a French musket ball struck him waist high in his pocket, but luckily was stopped by "*a bunch of keys and some Spanish Dollars.*" Reid was rewarded for gallantry on the day with the rank of brevet lieutenant-colonel, and recovered from his wounds in time to take part in the Havana expedition later that summer. On its surrender, he returned sickly to New York and spent the year of 1763 recovering his health on his American estates though still nominally in command of the regiment as Lt. Colonel Graham (see above) had returned home to Scotland on sick leave. The following year, Reid acted as Col. Henry Bouquet's second-in-command for the 1764 Muskingum expedition to chastise the Ohio Indian tribes. He brought the regiment home to Ireland in 1767 and retired in 1770, ostensibly to enjoy and improve his American estates but the Revolution broke out and he was dispossessed of everything. In 1779-80, despite having lost his family estate of Straloch to creditors, he raised at his own expense the 95th Foot when Spain joined France as allies of the American colonists.

In January 1781, the regiment was instrumental in preventing Jersey, one of the Channel Islands off France, from falling into enemy hands. At the 1783 peace, when the 95th was disbanded, Reid had already been a major-general for two years. Ten years later, in 1793, he was promoted lieutenant-general and, the following year, appointed Colonel of the 88th Foot (Connaught Rangers). In 1803 he was promoted general. He died four years later on 6 February 1807 and was buried at St. Margaret's Church, Westminster. His fortune, recouped in large measure from an inheritance left to him by his first cousin, John Small, (see below) allowed him to bequest all of it to his old *alma mater*, Edinburgh University, with the proviso that part of it should go to founding and maintaining a Chair in Music, and the balance going towards *"the general interest and advantages of the University."* He added that he would like an annual concert given on or near his birthday, at which should be performed *"one solo for the German flute, hautboy, or clarinet, also one march, and one minuet, with accompaniments by a select band, in order to show the taste of music about the middle of the last century, when they were by me composed, and with a view to keep my memory in remembrance."* Every year the concert is a major fixture in the university's schedule.

CBs; SBs; BALs; Stewart, *Sketches,* I-II, *in passim;* Richards, *Black Watch, in passim;* "General John Reid, 1721-1807," in *A Military History of Perth shire, 1660-1902,* [hereafter *MHP*], Marchioness of Tullabardine, ed., (Perth, 1908), 387-95; "List of the Officers of the 42nd or Royal Highland Regiment according to seniority dated December 29th, 1762," *BL,* Add. MSS. 21634: f.178c.

John McNeil* (1728-1762)

Ensign: 6 August 1742, 43rd Foot (Crawford's);
Lieut: 1 October 1745, 43rd Foot;
Capt-Lt: 3 June 1752, 42nd Foot;
Capt: 16 December 1755, 42nd Foot;
Major: 9 July 1762, 42nd Foot.
Born 1728 in the Western Isles of Scotland. Joined the 43rd Foot as an ensign and was present in London when some of the Highlanders mutinied and decided to return to Scotland. He fought at Fontenoy and throughout the Flanders campaign. He was the first cousin of Lt-Col. William Farquhar, commanding the 44th Foot who writing Amherst on 29 August 1759 from Niagara, represented that his cousin *"had met with many disappointments, having been 18 years in the Service, and purchased all his Commissions, and having Captain Reid given a company from half-pay, contrary to Lord John Mur-*

ray's promise to Farquhar." He recommended his cousin for the second majority in the 42nd Foot, but Reid won out. MacNeil participated in all the North American campaigns and was finally promoted major at Havana *"in room of"* Gordon Graham promoted to lieutenant-colonel July 1762. His promotion was short-lived, for a few weeks later, he died of fever, and was replaced by Alan Campbell (see below).

CBs; SBs; BALs; Stewart, *Sketches,* I-II, *in passim;* Richards, *Black Watch, in passim.*

Allan Campbell* (1723-1794)

Ensign: 25 December 1744, Additional Company, 43rd Foot (Crawford's);
Lieut: 1 December 1746, 43rd Foot;
Capt-Lt: 16 December 1752, 42nd Foot;
Capt: 13 March 1755, 42nd Foot;
Major: 20 June 1759, *"Acting";* 15 August 1762, 2nd/42nd Foot; half-pay, 18 March 1763; full pay, 27 March 1770, 36th Foot;
Lt. Col: *"in the Army,"* 25 May 1772; 26 January 1778, 36th Foot;
Col: *"in the Army,"* 17 November 1780;
Maj-Gen: 28 September 1787.

Allan Campbell was born 1723 in Ardchattan, Argyle, 6th of seven sons from the second marriage of Patrick Campbell of Barcaldine and Lucy Cameron, daughter of Lochiel. He was a younger brother to Colin of Glenure (*Red Fox* of Robert Louis Stevenson fame and, allegedly, murdered by James Stewart of Appin). He was thus the uncle of Ensign George Campbell (see below) as well as uncle to three 77th officers, Major Alex Campbell, Capt. Mungo Campbell and Lt. John Campbell *Melfort* (see respective registers below). Alan was commissioned an ensign in one of the three Additional Companies added to the regiment in December 1744 and received *"no pay whilst Youngest"* i.e. most junior. His company was captured at the Battle of Prestonpans guarding the baggage train though he was exchanged the following year. During the Uprising, three brothers served as lieutenants in Lord Loudoun's Highlanders. In August 1746, he purchased a lieutenancy from Kenneth Sutherland in the 43rd Foot and on the 1752 Atholl Roll is shown as one of the two grenadier lieutenants in Robert Campbell of Finab's company. He was commanding the grenadiers when the regiment went to North America in 1756. Fought at Ticonderoga, 8 July 1758, and the following summer, 20 June 1759, was *"appointed Major to the Battalion of Grenediers* [sic] *for the Campaign"* against Ticonderoga and Crown Point. He fought at Martinique and Havana in 1762 and was promoted when Major John MacNeil died 15 August 1762 of fever. He commanded the 390-strong composite force of Highlanders from the 42nd and 77th that fought under Henry Bouquet's leadership at Bushy Run, August 1763. Bouquet singled Alan and his Highlanders out for praise on the first night of the two day-affair, stating: *"I cannot sufficiently acknowledge the constant assistance I have recev'd from Maj Campbell nor do sufficient Justice to the Troops for their cool and steady Behaviour."* With peace declared, Campbell as the junior major realized he would have to exchange to half-pay unless he could purchase the senior major's commission from John Reid. Unable to muster the funds Reid demanded, the unsung hero of Bushy Run bitterly exchanged to half-pay. He returned to the Army six years later as the major of the 36th Foot. In 1778, he was commanding the 36th Foot as its lieutenant-colonel, promoted a "brevet" colonel two years later and finally promoted major-general, 28 September 1787. He died unmarried, 13 November 1794, in London.

CBs; *SBs*; *BALs*; Stewart, *Sketches*, I-II, *in passim*; Richards, *Black Watch*, *in passim*; "List of the Officers of the 42nd or Royal Highland Regiment according to seniority dated December 29th, 1762," *BL* Add. MSS. 21634: f.178c.

Captains

Thomas [Graham] Graeme,* of Duchray, (1721-1773)

Ensign: 30 June 1741, 43rd Foot (Crawford's);
Lieut: 6 August 1746, 43rd Foot;
Capt: 15 February 1756, 42nd Foot;
Major: 31 March 1770, 42nd Foot;
Lt. Col: 12 December 1770, 42nd Foot; retired, 7 December 1771.

The eldest son of Alexander Graeme of Rednock and Duchray, and Margaret Stirling. Also older brother of Capt. John Graeme (see below). On the 1752 Atholl Roll, he is shown as one of the two grenadier lieutenants in Robert Campbell of Finab's company. Promoted captain in 1756, he took his company to North America with the First Division. Wounded at Ticonderoga, 8 July 1758. Fought in all the major campaigns of the regiment. Returned to Ireland with the 42nd in 1767 and married Sarah Blamire, sister of well-known English

Thomas Graeme *Duchray* (1721-1773). Graeme commanded his company throughout the Seven Years' War and was wounded at Ticonderoga, 8 July 1758. After 14 years as a captain he spent nine months as the Major in 1770 and another nine months in 1771 as the Lieutenant-Colonel before retiring at the age of 50. He died two years later in 1773. (Courtesy, Trustees of the Black Watch Museum, Perth)

poetess, Susanna Blamire. Land grant records dated 4 March 1765, show *Thomas Graeme, Capt. in 42nd Regt. Requested 10,000 acres. Granted 5,000"* in Vermont. After 14 years as a Black Watch captain, he spent nine months as the second-in-command in 1770, and, another eight months the following year as the commanding officer, before retiring at the age of 50. He died two years later in 1773 without children, his estates of Duchray and Rednock passing to his younger brother, John.

CBs; *SBs*; *BALs*; Stewart, *Sketches*, I-II, *in passim*; Richards, *Black Watch*, *in passim*; PRO, Journal of the Commissioners for Trade and Plantations, Vol.12., January 1764 - December 1767; "List of the Officers of the 42nd or Royal Highland Regiment according to seniority dated December 29th, 1762," *BL* Add. MSS. 21634: f.178c.

James Abercrombie* (c.1722-1775)
2nd Lieut: 15 May 1742; 1st Foot (*The Royal*);
Lieut: 11 June 1744, 1st Foot (*The Royal*);
Capt: 16 February 1756, 42nd Foot;
Major: 25 July 1760, 78th Foot (Fraser's Highlanders);
half-pay 24 December 1763;
Lt. Col: 27 March 1770, 22nd Foot.

His birth date and actual parentage remain unknown, perhaps an indication that he was a natural son. He was certainly related to Major General James Abercromby of Glassaugh for, in his will written at the latter's estate of Glassaugh in 1765, he named him *"his friend and relation"* as well as executor and beneficiary. *Glassaugh* was Lt-Colonel, commanding the 1st Foot in Ireland, when young James was commissioned a 2nd lieutenant in the same regiment May 1742. Lt-Colonel Abercromby may also have assisted his "relation" purchase his initial commissions while soldiering in Flanders with his regiment. In September/October 1746, he was with the expedition that went against the French port of L'Orient. He is the *"Jemmy Abercromby"* of the 1st Foot who was thanked in a 1747 letter by David Hume (later a famous Scottish philosopher) written in London. Hume was a close friend of *Glassaugh* and had participated in the same expedition. In February 1754, James sold several Banff shire properties to his kinsman, Colonel Abercromby of Glassaugh (Over and Nether Auchinderrin, Hilton of Auchiderrin, Aldekarn, Littlefield and Mills), all located about one mile north of Abercherder in the parish of Marnoch, south of Banff. Two years later, in 1756, James was given command of one of the two companies added to the 42nd before it deployed to North America. He traveled as a staff officer with his kinsman, Major General Abercromby, the designated second-in-command to Lord Loudoun. James served as an ADC to three successive Commanders-in-Chief in North America: John Campbell, Lord Loudoun; his kinsman, Abercromby; and Major-General Sir Jeffery Amherst. James must have acquired some engineer training during his Flanders campaigns as he has left several very fine maps of the North American theatre. Fluent in French, James was also utilized by his successive commanders for all French correspondence with the Marquis de Vaudreuil and other senior ranking French officials. He was instrumental in communicating and finalizing the terms of surrender with Governor General Vaudreuil for the surrender of New France at Montréal in September 1760. He was gazetted to the 78th Foot (Frasers' Highlanders) as major, 25 July 1760, and was commanding a company at Québec when the regiment was disbanded in 1763; retired on half pay. (see 78th register for his time as acting regimental commandant). He returned to duty on 27 March, 1770 when gazetted lieutenant-colonel of 22nd Foot. He took his battalion to Dublin, Ireland on garrison duties in October 1773 and was ordered two years later to take the 22nd Foot back to America. On his arrival in Boston he was immediately appointed Adjutant-General to the army, 3 May 1775. According to Major-General James Grant, he was severely wounded by friendly fire while leading one of the grenadier battalion's up the slopes of Breed's Hill [Bunker Hill] at Boston, and died a week later on 24 June 17, 1775.

CBs; SBs; BALs; Stewart, *Sketches,* I-II, *in passim;* Richards, *Black Watch, in passim;* "List of the Officers of the 42nd or Royal Highland Regiment according to seniority dated December 29th, 1762," *BL* Add. MSS. 21634: f.178c; *JGP.*

John Campbell* [1], of Strachur, (1727- 1806)
Ensign: 1 May 1745, 43rd Foot (Sempill's); transferred on promotion to Loudoun's Highlanders;
Lieut: 8 June 1745, Loudoun's Highlanders;
Capt-Lt: 1 October 1747, Loudoun's Highlanders;
Capt: 1 October 1747, Loudoun's Highlanders; half-pay, 1748; rejoined 9 April 1756, 42nd Foot;
Major: 11 July 1759, 17th Foot;
Lt. Col: *"in the Army,"* 1 February 1762; 1 May 1773, 57th Foot;
Col: *"in the Army,"* 1 May 1777; appointed 2 November 1780, 57th Foot, until death, August 1806;
Brigadier: "in the Army," 1777-1778 and Commander, Staten Island;
Maj-Gen: 19 February 1779;
Lieut Gen: "in America," 28 September 1781; 28 September 1787;
Gen: 26 January 1797.

Son of Colin Campbell, of Strachur and Ardgartan (1695-1743), and Mary Lamont, presumably the daughter of Mungo Campbell of Hundleshope. The family estates of Strachur are located on the eastern shore of Loch Fyne and in Gaelic mean *"Glen of the Heron."* He started his military career at the age of 18 as an ensign in the 43rd Foot, but transferred to a new-raising regiment commanded by his life-long patron and kinsman, John Campbell, Lord Loudoun. Strachur exchanged to half-pay in 1749 as a captain, but returned to active duty in 1756 when he was given command of one of the two companies added to the 42nd before it deployed to North America. Wounded slightly in the breast at Ticonderoga, 8 July 1758, he was made major to the 17th

Foot (Forbes) after the battle and took part in the capture of Montréal, 1760. His battalion was ordered to garrison Fort Stanwix for the winter of 1760/61. His regiment went to the Caribbean in October 1761 and he was made lieutenant-colonel "in the Army" while commanding his regiment at Martinique and Havana in 1762. After a disastrous, sickly campaign, his unit returned to garrison duties in the Mohawk River Valley. He took his regiment back to England in July 1767. He was made commanding officer of the 57th Foot in May 1773 when the incumbent officer, Thomas Townsend died. Campbell returned to America in May 1776 with the 57th as part of Cornwallis' army. They initially landed at Cape Fear, North Carolina but moved north to take part in the various battles for Long Island and the capture of Paulus Hook. When the army moved to Philadelphia in 1777, Campbell was left in command of Staten Island with the local rank of brigadier general. In November 1778, he was ordered to Western Florida to command all British troops in the colony. He was promoted major-general "in the Army" February 1779 and arrived via Jamaica with 1300 German mercenaries and Loyalist troops of dubious quality to protect the entire Mississippi frontier, as well as the important ports of Mobile and Pensacola. When Spain declared war on England, Baton Rouge, Natchez and Mobile quickly fell. After a spirited defense of Pensacola against a besieging force of 7000 Spaniards, Campbell surrendered on 8 May 1781 and became a prisoner of war. While in Florida, Campbell was appointed Colonel to the 57th Foot (*The Diehards*) an appointment he proudly held until his death some 30 years later. When he was exchanged out of captivity, he went to Halifax, Nova Scotia, replacing General Guy Carleton, 1st Baron Dorchester, as Commander-in-Chief in North America, a post he retained until retiring in 1787 at 70 years of age. While at Halifax, he presented new colours to the 42nd Foot, one of the highlights of his career. He did not waste the opportunity to reminisce about his own service, "*a man of stern and proud disposition and very methodical, though not without a sense of humour.*" Campbell returned to Scotland in 1787 and was promoted to the rank of lieutenant-general the same year, and to general, 26 January 1797. He died at Strachur House, unmarried, on 28 August 1806.

CBs; SBs; BALs; Stewart, *Sketches,* I-II, *in passim;* Richards, *Black Watch, in passim;* "John Campbell," *DCB;* "John Campbell" in *Burkes Peerage and Baronetage,* 107th ed., vol. I, 187; "John Campbell" in William M. MacBean, *Biographical Register of Saint Andrew's Society of the State of New York.* Vol. I, [hereafter *SAS*],(1756-1806) (New York, 1922); "List of the Officers of the 42nd or Royal Highland Regiment according to seniority dated December 29th, 1762," *BL* Add. MSS. 21634: f.178c; *Scots Magazine,* vii, 298.

James Stewart, y^r of Urrard, (c.1727-c.1790)

Ensign: Lord Loudoun's Highlanders;
Lieut: Lord Loudoun's, half-pay 1749; Dutch-Scots Brigade, discharged 22 April 1757;
Capt: 18 July 1757, 42nd Foot; resigned 5 May 1762.

Born at Urrard House which was in the centre of the battlefield at Killiecrankie, Scotland, the same building from which Viscount Claverhouse (Bonnie Dundee) was shot and killed in 1689. James started his career as an ensign in Lord Loudoun's Highlanders in the '45 Uprising. Went out on half-pay as a lieutenant in 1749 and joined the Dutch-Scots Brigade. Resigned as lieutenant in Stewart's Regiment when offered the captaincy of one the three Black Watch Additional Companies authorized in July 1757. Wounded at Ticonderoga, 8 July 1758 whilst commanding Captain Abercrombie's company. Participated in the capture of Forts Ticonderoga and Crown Point the following year and commanded his company during the capture of Montréal in 1760. He fought at Martinique and then resigned his commission. His company orderly books from 1759 to 1761 are preserved at the Black Watch Archives at Balhousie Castle, Perth, Scotland and are a valuable insight into the everyday workings of the 42nd during the Seven Years' War as well as its dress and equipment.

CBs; SBs; BALs; Stewart, *Sketches,* I-II, *in passim;* Richards, *Black Watch,* in passim;; James Ferguson, *Papers Illustrating the History of the Scots Brigade in the Service of the United Netherlands 1572-1782,* Vol. II., (1698-1782) [hereafter *DSB*] (Edinburgh, 1899), 426; "List of the Officers of the 42nd or Royal Highland Regiment according to seniority dated December 29th, 1762," *BL* Add. MSS. 21634: f.178c.

James Murray, [later of Strowan] (1734-1794)

Lieut: 1749, Saxon Grenadier Guards;
Capt: 20 July 1757; 42nd Foot; exchanged 3rd Foot Guards;
Capt-Lt: 3 November 1769, 3rd Foot Guards;
Lt. Col: 3 November 1769, "*by brevet*"; 18 April 1770, 3rd Foot Guards (& Captain);
Col: appointed 25 December 1777, new-raising 77th Highlanders; half-pay 8 May 1783; 1 November 1783; Lt-Col Commandant, 78th/72nd Foot; appointed Col. 72nd Foot, 26 May 1786;
Maj-Gen: 20 November 1783;
Lt.-Gen: 1793.

Born at Tullibardine, Scotland, 19 March 1734, the 2nd son of Lord George Murray and Amelia Murray, heiress of Strowan and Glencarse. At the age of fifteen, he was commissioned a lieutenant in the Saxon Grenadier Guards, joining his regiment two years later after completion of his studies at Utrecht. His first action was against the forces of Frederick the Great at the commencement of the Seven Years' War and he was taken prisoner with the Saxon army that capitulated at Pirna on the Elbe in October 1765. He was released on parole the following year and his uncle, James, the 3rd Duke of Atholl, secured for him the command of one of the three 42nd Additional Companies authorized in July 1757. He was wounded at Ticonderoga, 8 July 1758, commanding Captain John Reid's company. On the request of Lord John Murray, his godfather and half-uncle, he was given command of the 2nd/42nd's grenadier company and led them during the capture of Montréal 1760 and at Martinique where he was severely wounded February 1762. Doctors, unable to recover the musket ball which passed through a lung and lodged under his scapula, gave him only a few days to live but, to the surprise of all, he recovered and was on his feet in a few weeks. He was never able to lie down afterwards, *"and during the thirty-two years of his subsequent life, he slept in an upright posture, supported in his bed by pillows."* He was invalided back to Scotland where he spent more than six years on sick leave. He rejoined the 42nd at Londonderry in 1769, but exchanged the following year into the prestigious 3rd Foot Guards [later the Scots Guards] as a captain-lieutenant. He obtained promotion the following year to captain and lieutenant-colonel and in 1772 was elected the Member of Parliament for Perth, a riding he held for 22 years (1773-1794). During this period he was governor successively of Upnor Castle in 1775 and Fort William in 1780. At the outbreak of the American Revolution, Murray offered to raise a Highland regiment, but was turned down. Two years later, the 4th Duke of Atholl went directly to the King in London and secured a Colonel's commission for him while he was commanding the Scots Guards in New Jersey. Murray returned from America in 1778 and his newly-raised 77th (Duke of Atholl's) Highlanders were sent to garrison Ireland and dispersed by companies to police Irish towns. In 1783, as the war overseas was winding down, they were brought back to England and the Highlanders fully expecting to be disbanded and sent home. However, a parsimonious government, without consulting Murray, decided to let it be known that they were to be shipped to India which predictably provoked a violent mutiny

in Portsmouth. The Athollmen publicly denounced Murray as a traitor and dishonourable chief who had sold them out to the East India Company. Understandably hurt and angered by such accusations, the irascible Colonel wanted to go after the ringleaders but the government wishing no trouble, ordered his 77th immediately disbanded. The soldiers returned to the Highlands singing derisively:

> *There have been traitors you may see,*
> *In Forty-Five and Eighty-three,*
> *But let Murray still branded be,*
> *And all good men abhor him!*

It was said the mutiny added *"half a score to his looks,"* but unfazed, Murray raised another regiment as its lieutenant-colonel commandant. Originally numbered the 78th Foot, it was subsequently renumbered the 72nd [later the Seaforth Highlanders]. He was appointed its Colonel in 1786 and remained so until his death. In 1793 he was promoted lieutenant-general and, in March of the following year, felt obliged to resign his seat in Parliament due to ill health and died a few days later on 18 March 1794.

CBs; *SBs*; *BALs*; Stewart, *Sketches*, I-II, *in passim*; Richards, *Black Watch*, in passim; John Prebble, *Mutiny: Highland Regiments in Revolt 1743-1804*, (Harmondsworth, 1975), 211-59; "Lieutenant-general James Murray of Strowan 1734-94," *MHP*, 411-14; "List of the Officers of the 42nd or Royal Highland Regiment according to seniority dated December 29th, 1762," *BL* Add. MSS. 21634: f.178c.

Thomas Stirling, y^r of Ardoch (1733-1808)
Ensign: 30 September 1747, 1st Marjoribanks, Dutch Scots Brigade; half-pay 1753; 31 October 1756, 1st Marjoribanks, Dutch Scots Brigade;
Lieut: 20 July 1757, Marjoribank's, Dutch Scots Brigade
Capt: 24 July 1757, 42nd Foot;
Major: 12 December 1770, 42nd Foot;
Lt. Col: 7 September 1771, 42nd Foot; retired 21 March 1782.
Col: 19 February, 1779, "by brevet" and ADC to King; appointed 13 February 1782, 1st/71st Foot; appointed 13 January 1790, 41st Foot;
Brigadier: 1776;
Maj-Gen: 20 November 1782; half-pay 4 June 1784;
Lt.-Gen: 3 May 1796;
General: 1 January 1801.

Born in St. Petersburg, Russia, 8 October 1733, the 2nd son of Sir Henry Stirling, 3rd Baronet of Ardoch, and Anne Gordon, the 3rd daughter of Admiral Thomas Gordon, a native of Aberdeen, Admiral of the Russian Fleet and the Governor of Cronstadt. Thomas was commissioned originally as an ensign in the Dutch service, 30 September 1747. He exchanged to half-pay in 1753. He returned to active duty as an ensign in the 1st Battalion of Colonel Marjoribank's' Regiment, 31 October 1756, and the following year was promoted lieutenant. When three Additional Companies were raised as reinforcement companies to Lord John Murray's 42nd Highland Regiment of Foot, Stirling was recommended by the Duke of Atholl as a prospective company com-

Thomas Stirling, y^r of Ardoch (1733-1808). Stirling successfully led a company-sized expedition down the Ohio to take possession of Fort de Chartres on the Mississippi in 1765-66. He was made Lieutenant Colonel in 1771 and took the 42nd Foot to America during the War for Independence. Although seriously wounded in 1779, in 1782 he became Colonel of the 71st regiment. General Sir Thomas Stirling died 8 May 1808. (Courtesy, Trustees of the Black Watch Museum, Perth)

mander when another officer, Mercer, turned the command down. Stirling duly raised the requisite number of men for the Watch and was gazetted a captain, 24 July 1757. Stirling sailed for North America in November of the same year, but did not arrive with the other two companies. His transport ship was blown so far off its intended course for New York, it ended up off the island of Antigua in the Caribbean. Served with the 42nd in Amherst's 1759 expedition against Forts Ticonderoga and Crown Point, and the 1760 campaign against Montréal. Was wounded at the storming of Morne Tartenson on Martinique, 24 January 1762, but was sufficiently recovered to serve in the capture of Havana later that year, where he fell ill with fever. Stirling went home for a prolonged recovery, and two years later, in August 1765, successfully led a company-sized expedition down the Ohio to take possession of Fort de Chartres on the Mississippi. In 1767, he left America for garrison duty in Ireland and Scotland. In 1770, after 13 years in the rank of captain, Stirling was gazetted major to the regiment. The following year, he was promoted to lieutenant colonel commanding the battalion and took it overseas on the outbreak of the American Revolution. He commanded it for three years of the war. Acting as a brigade-commander, he was badly wounded at Springfield, New Jersey in 1779 and invalided home and replaced by Major Charles Graham, (see below) the son of Gordon Graham. Stirling was made Colonel "*by brevet,*" 19 February 1779, and an *aide-de-camp* to His Majesty, King George III. Stirling was appointed Colonel of the 71st Highland Regiment of Foot, 13 February 1782, and was promoted Major General, 20 November 1782. He exchanged to half-pay when the 71st was disbanded, 4 June 1784, but returned to active status when appointed Colonel of the 41st Regiment of Foot, 13 January 1790, and created a baronet. After General James Murray's death in 1794, he purchased his old comrade-in-arms' estate of Strowan. He was promoted lieutenant-general, 3 May 1796. On 26 July 1799, on the death of his older brother, William, Stirling succeeded to the baronetcy of Ardoch and, two years later, achieved the rank of full general (1 January 1801). He died unmarried 8 May 1808.

CBs; *SBs*; *BALs*; Stewart, *Sketches*, I-II, *in passim*; Richards, *Black Watch*, in passim;; *DNB*, XVIII, 1270-1271; *WO* 34/55: f. 58.; "General Sir Thomas Stirling of Ardoch and Strowan," in *MHP*, 407-10; "List of the Officers of the 42nd or Royal Highland Regiment according to seniority dated December 29th, 1762," *BL* Add. MSS. 21634: f.178c.

Francis Maclean* (1717-1781)
Ensign: Dutch Scots Brigade;
Lieut: 21 June 1750, Gordon's, Dutch Scots Brigade;
Capt: 15 July 1758, 2nd/42nd Foot;
Major: *"in the Army,"* 25 March 1759; 22 January 1761, 97th Foot:
Lt. Col: 13 April 1762, 97th Foot;
Col: *"by brevet,"* 28 August 1777; appointed 16 December 1777, 82nd Foot;
Brigadier: *"in America,"* 1778.

Born in 1717, Francis was the son of Captain William Maclean of Blaich and Anne Kinloch. He was a cousin to Captain Sir Allan Maclean of Brolas, 77th Foot, 21st clan chieftain (see 77th Register). He started his military career in the Dutch-Scots Brigade and fought at Bergen op Zoom where he was taken prisoner and praised by Marshal Lowendahl, the French commander for his bravery. He was the oldest and most experienced of the seven company commanders selected for the newly-raised 2nd/42nd Foot in the summer of 1758. The second battalion was sent as part of General Hopson's 1759 expedition to capture Martinique and Guadeloupe, Maclean wounded on the latter island. He replaced Major Anstruther as an *"acting"* commandant and was brevetted a major in the Army by Major-General Barrington. He brought the remnants of the 2nd/42nd to Albany in July 1759 and was replaced as commandant by the more senior, Gordon Graham (see above). He served with the 2nd Battalion until after the capture of Montréal 1760, whereupon he learned he was promoted major to the new-raising 97th Foot. He returned to England to train his new unit which participated in the expedition against Belle-Isle. In 1762, he was promoted lieutenant-colonel *"in the Army"* and was one of several officers handpicked to join Lord Loudoun and Colonel Simon Fraser for service in the Portuguese army fighting against Spain and France. By the end of 1762, the competent Maclean was appointed Governor of Almeida and latterly was accorded the rank of major-general in the Portuguese army. He was subsequently made Governor of the province of Estremadura and the capital city of Lisbon, a post he held for ten years. In 1774, a Scottish lady visiting the city in 1774 noted *"General Maclean, Govr of Lisbon and commander in chief of the land forces… is indeed a fine highland looking fellow, and tho' not now a boy is still a great favourite with the Ladies."* In 1778, he returned to the British army, his country then at war with its American colonies. He was made Colonel of the 82nd Foot raised for service in North America, given the rank of

Brigadier General and sent to command at Halifax, Nova Scotia. From there, he mounted the successful expedition against Castine, Maine in June 1779 where he successfully fended off an American counter attack and siege, before returning to Halifax. He died from illness two years later, 4 May 1781, and was buried in a vault beneath St Paul's Anglican Church in Halifax.

CBs; *SBs*; *BALs*; Stewart, *Sketches*, I-II, *in passim*; Janet Schaw, *Journal of a Lady of Quality. . .*, E.W. Andrews, ed., (New Haven, 1939), 238; J.P. Maclean, *Highland Settlements*, 392-3; *Miscellaneous Correspondence*, Vol. II, [August 1758], 867; "Francis MacLean," *DCB*; *DSB*, II, 403, 420.

Archibald Campbell* [1] (c.1730-1761).
Ensign: 8 June 1745, 64th Foot (Lord Loudoun's);
Lieut: 7 December 1745, 64th Foot (Lord Loudoun's); half-pay, 1749; full pay, 27 December 1755, 53rd/51st Foot (Napier's); transferred on promotion;
Capt: 16 July 1758, 2nd/42nd Foot; 18 August 1759, exchanged to 87th Foot (Keith's Highlanders);
Major: 20 December 1760, 87th Foot.
Younger brother to John Campbell, the Laird of Achalader and 2nd son of John Campbell and Catherine, daughter of Ewen Cameron of Lochiel. Thus, first cousin to Capt. Allan Campbell (see above), Capt Allan Cameron *Glendessary*, 77th Foot and to Lt. Donald Cameron *Fassifern* of the 78th Foot (see respective Registers below). One of the seven company commanders selected for the newly-raised 2nd Battalion of the 42nd Foot in summer 1758 which was then sent as part of General Hopson's 1759 expedition to capture Martinique and Guadeloupe. Exchanged to 87th Foot (Keith's Highlanders) and won a battlefield promotion to major for rescuing Lord Howard of Walden from a strong detachment of the enemy. He was killed at the battle of Fallinghausen, 1761.

CBs; *SBs*; *BALs*; Stewart, *Sketches*, I-II, *in passim*; *Miscellaneous Correspondence*, II, (August 1758), 867; *Highland Clans and Regiment*; Margaret Olympia Campbell, *Memorial History of the Campbells of Melfort*, (London, 1882), 45.

Alexander Sinclair* (1732-1760)
Ensign: 28 August 1753, 2nd/ 1st Foot (The Royal);
Lieut: 3 January 1756, 53rd/51st Foot (Napier's);
Capt: 17 July 1758, 2nd /42nd Foot.

Alexander Sinclair was born in Scotland in 1732 and was commissioned ensign in the 2nd/1st Foot (*The Royal*) 28 August 1753. He was commissioned lieutenant in the new-raising 53rd [51st] Foot on 3 January

1756. Two years later, he was one of the seven company commanders selected for the newly-raised 2nd Battalion of the 42nd Foot in the summer of 1758 and promoted captain, 17 July 1758. His company was then sent as part of General Hopson's 1759 expedition to capture Martinique and Guadeloupe. He is shown sick at Perth, 13 November 1758, prior to his departure to the West Indies with his company in December 1758. Amherst recorded him as having died at Guadeloupe in 1759 though the Commission Book for the 42nd shows Lieutenant Kenneth Tolmie promoted Captain vice Sinclair *"discharged dead"* 27 July 1760.

CBs; SBs; BALs; Stewart, *Sketches*, I-II, *in passim; WO* 25/209; *O14; Miscellaneous Correspondence,* II, (August 1758), 867.

William Murray,* y[r] of Lintrose (1737-1777)
Ensign: 31 December 1755, 34th Foot;
Lieut: 26 September 1757, 1st/34th Foot;
Capt: 18 July 1758, 2nd/42nd Foot;
Major: 11 September 1771, 42nd Foot;
Lt. Col: 5 October 1777, 27th Foot.

Born in Scotland, 30 November 1737, oldest son of John Murray of Lintrose and Amelia Murray, daughter of Sir William Murray, 3rd B[t] Ochtertyre and Katherine Fraser, daughter of Hugh Fraser, 9th Lord Lovat. Started his military career in the 34th Foot and was promoted to the command of one of the seven new companies in the new-raising 2nd Battalion of the 42nd Foot in summer 1758. Part of General Hopson's 1759 expedition to capture Martinique and Guadeloupe, his company was one of two blown off course and thus participated in the attack on Fort Louis, Guadeloupe with the fleet's Marine battalion. Participated in the capture of Montréal, 1760, and the 1762 Caribbean campaigns at Martinique and Havana. Fought at Bushy Run, August 1763 and commanded three companies at Carlisle the winter of 1763-64. Went on Col. Bouquet's 1764 Muskingum expedition and on return was commandant of Fort Pitt for the winter of 1764-65 as well as the following year 66-67. Listed as a participant in the peace talks with Shawnee, Delaware and Iroquois Indians at Fort Pitt, 9-10 June 1766. George Croghan reported that he was approached by Chiefs of the several nations on the news that the 42nd, and in particular, fort commandant William Murray, would be leaving North America. They said: *"It is of the greatest Consequence to us, that a good man Should Command at this place; the Present Commanding officer Captain Murray Our Father, has always Treated Our People Sivilly, and Since you was there last year, we have never had the least difference with him nor his Peo-*

ple, and we hear that he is to go away Soon we therefore desire you to Write to the General, that he may be continued here Longer." Returned to Ireland in 1767 and became the regiment's major in 1771. Fought during the Revolution and transferred to take command of the 27th Foot (Enniskillens) in 1777. On 2 November 1777, however, Murray died of fever at Philadelphia and was buried in the Christ Church graveyard beside Minerva Grant, the wife of his long-time friend and fellow officer, Major William Grant *Rothiemurchus.* (See below).

CBs; SBs; BALs; "List of the Officers of the 42nd or Royal Highland Regiment according to seniority dated December 29th, 1762," *BL* Add. MSS. 21634: f.178c; Stewart, *Sketches*, I-II, *in passim;* Richards, *Black Watch, in passim;* 'Return of Officers who commanded at Fort Pitt," *BL,* Add. MSS. 21651, f.107; *Miscellaneous Correspondence,* II, (August 1758), 867.

John Stewart,* y[r] of Stenton
Ensign: (and Adjutant) 1749, 1st Stewart's, Dutch-Scots Brigade; resigned 29 January 1758;
Capt: 20 July 1758, 2nd /42nd Foot; retired, 7 September 1771.

Born in the parish of Caputh, Perthshire, he was persuaded to leave school by Gordon of Glenbucket and carried arms in the Atholl Brigade of the Jacobite Army during the rebellion. Lord John Murray wrote to his brother the Duke of Atholl from London, 22 July 1758, to express his displeasure that Stewart had been nominated as one of the seven company commanders for the newly-raised 2nd/42nd Foot. *"There is one of your recommendations, Lieutenant John Stewart in the Dutch for a Company, who was in the late Rebellion. I wish you had not named him as he is the only one of that denomination in the Regiment under my command; which the King has been pleased to honour with the Title of Royal Highland Regiment, and I am sure will be very disagreeable to the Corps, and if you think proper to write of it to the Duke of Argyle, and propose Lieutenant John Murray instead, I don't doubt it may be done."* Stewart retained his new commission however, and participated in General Hopson's 1759 expedition to capture Martinique and Guadeloupe. In summer 1760, he was left behind at newly-built Fort Ontario in command of 150 Highlanders of the 1st and 2nd/42nd who were too sick to proceed on Amherst's campaign against Montréal. He fought at Martinique and Havana in 1762, and again at Bushy Run in August 1763. He was fort commandant at Fort Ligonier from 3 March 1764 to 14 September 1764 and participated with the regiment on Bouquet's Muskingum expedition to chastise the Ohio Indians. He retired 7 September 1771.

CBs; SBs; BALs; "List of the Officers of the 42nd or Royal Highland Regiment according to seniority dated December 29th, 1762," *BL* Add. MSS. 21634: f.178c; *Miscellaneous Correspondence,* II, (August 1758), 867; *BALs;* Stewart, *Sketches,* I-II, *in passim; DSB;* "Return of Officers who commanded at Fort Ligonier," *BL,* Add. MSS. 21651, f.114; Richards, *Black Watch, in passim.*

Alexander [Robertson] Reid* (c.1730-1762)

Ensign: Majoribank's, Dutch-Scots Brigade;
Lieut: 1750, 2nd Drumlanrig's, Dutch-Scots Brigade; pensioned 30 October 1757;
Capt: Dutch-Scots Brigade, retired 30 April 1758; commissioned 21 July 1758, 2nd /42nd Foot.

Younger brother of John [Robertson] Reid and first cousin of John Small (see below). A Dutch-Scots Brigade veteran and one of the seven company commanders selected for the newly-raised 2nd/42nd Foot in summer 1758 sent as part of General Hopson's 1759 expedition to capture Martinique and Guadeloupe in 1759. Died of fever on a ship off Havana, 2 August 1762.

CBs; SBs; BALs; "List of the Officers of the 42nd or Royal Highland Regiment according to seniority dated December 29th, 1762," *BL* Add. MSS. 21634: f.178c; Stewart, *Sketches,* I-II, *in passim;* Richards, *Black Watch, in passim; DSB; Miscellaneous Correspondence,* II, (August 1758), 867.

William Grant,* y^r of Rothiemurchas [1] (1723- c.1787)

Ensign: 20 May 1745, 43rd Foot (Sempill's);
Lieut: 22 November 1746, 43rd Foot;
Capt: 23 July 1758, 42nd Foot;
Major: "*in the Army,*" 23 July 1772; 5 October 1777; 42nd Foot;
Lt. Col: "*in the Army,*" 29 August 1777; retired 25 August 1778.

First son of Patrick Grant, 4th of Rothiemurchus, and his second wife, Rachel Grant of Tullochgorm. First cousin to Major James Grant of the 77th Foot (see 77th Register) and older brother of Lt. Lewis Grant, 42nd (see below). Wounded serving in grenadier company at Ticonderoga, 8 July 1758. As the senior lieutenant of the regiment, he was promoted captain after the battle of Ticonderoga "*in room of Gordon Graham promoted.*" Participated in the 1759 campaign against Forts Ticonderoga and Crown Point, the capture of Montréal in 1760 and the Caribbean campaigns against Martinique and Havana, 1762. Fought at Bushy Run, August 1763 and commanded at Fort Pitt from 22 January 1764 to 24 Sep-

tember 1764. Went on Col. Bouquet's 1764 expedition to Muskingum to punish the Ohio Indians. Was commanding the 42nd grenadier company when it sailed for America in 1776. Already a major in the Army since July 1772, he was promoted to lieutenant-colonel in the Army in August 1777 and subsequently made major of the 2nd Battalion of the 42nd Foot two months later. Grant became despondent when his wife Minerva died from fever in fall 1777 at Philadelphia, and subsequently lost his desire to soldier and retired from the army in August 1778.

CBs; SBs; BALs; "List of the Officers of the 42nd or Royal Highland Regiment according to seniority dated December 29th, 1762," *BL* Add. MSS. 21634: f.178c; Stewart, *Sketches,* I-II, *in passim;* Gruber, *JPAW,* 517; Richards, *Black Watch,* 58; "*Return of Officers who commanded at Fort Pitt,*" *BL,* Add. MSS. 21651, f.107.

Robert Arbuthnot* (c.1730-1758)

2nd Lieut: 9th Marines (Powlett's); half-pay 22 May 1747;
Lieut: 2 June 1747, Drumlanrig's, Dutch-Scots Brigade;
Capt: 19 July 1758, 42nd Foot; died, 14 December 1758.

A former Marine officer and a Dutch-Scots veteran who was given his commission in the newly-raised 2nd Battalion of the 42nd Foot, then died suddenly 14 December 1758 just before sailing to the Caribbean. Replaced at the last minute by David Haldane (see below).

CBs; SBs; BALs; Stewart, *Sketches,* I-II, *in passim; Miscellaneous Correspondence,* II, (August 1758), 867.

David Haldane,* 3rd of Aberuthven (c.1722- 1777?)

Ensign: unknown;
Lieut: 31 December 1754, 51st Foot; appointed adjutant, 18 May to 25 August 1756; exchanged to 2nd/19th Foot, 25 August 1756; transferred on promotion;
Capt: 14 December 1758, 42nd Foot; exchanged, 28 April 1762, "brevet major" to 100th Foot (Campbell's Highlanders); half-pay 18 November 1763; removed from list 10 March 1777.

Born c. 1722, the son of John Haldane, 2nd of Aberuthven and Anne Ross, daughter of David Ross of Inverchasley, later Lord Ankerville. His name appears in a disposition of lands, dated 16 December 1743, in favour of Captain George Haldane (3rd Foot Guards, his first cousin, once removed). In this document he is designated "*Ensign David Haldane of Aberuthven.*" A David Haldane is shown on the passenger list of the

Everly Transport arriving in Halifax in 1749 as a member of the Governor Edward Cornwallis' staff. The entry reads: *David Haldane, Lieutenant, 1 Male Servant, Total 2 - Colonel Murray's* David Haldane appears as one of five signatories along with Edward Cornwallis, requesting the establishment of one of the earliest Masonic Lodges in Canada. While in Halifax, he was commissioned lieutenant in William Pepperell's new-raising 51st Foot and his name appears on a list of officer's who surrendered at Fort Oswego in 1756. On the disbandment of that regiment, in which he had also served as adjutant, and his release from captivity, he exchanged to the new 2nd Battalion of the 19th Foot. In 1758, as forces were gathering for an expedition against Martinique and Guadeloupe under General Hopson, he secured the last captain's position in the newly-raised 2nd/42nd Foot, when one of its seven company commanders, Robert Arbuthnot, suddenly died in London before boarding ship (see above). His cousin, Brigadier George Haldane, the Governor-designate of Jamaica, who was participating in the same expedition, may have been instrumental in securing him the promotion. David served at the capture of Montréal 1760, and Martinique in 1762. In April 1762, he was appointed brevet-major to the 100th Foot (Campbell's Highlanders) to replace the major-commandant, Colin Campbell of Kilberrie, (see below) who was accused of murdering one of his own officers. He reverted to the rank of captain at the Peace and exchanged to half-pay, 18 November 1763. In subsequent petitions for land grants dated 22 April 1765 Haldane is shown as a 42nd captain on half pay, requesting 10,000 acres and eventually granted 5,000 acres in what is now Vermont. He appears, however, to have taken up residence in Princeton, New Jersey as PRO documents show a *"Captain Haldan of Princetown"* who, with others, was charged with high treason in August 1774, not long before the outbreak of the American Revolution. His removal from the Army List, effective 10 March 1777, was probably due to rebel sympathies.

CBs; *SBs*; *BALs*; "List of the Officers of the 42nd or Royal Highland Regiment according to seniority dated December 29th, 1762," *BL* Add. MSS. 21634: f.178c; Stewart, *Sketches*, I-II, in passim; *PRO*, Journal of the Commissioners for Trade and Plantations, Vol. XII, January 1764 - December 1767, 818; *PRO*, Home Office Papers, 1773-5; J.A.L. Haldane, *The Haldanes of Gleneagles*, (Edinburgh, 1929), 291-2.

Peter Daly (c.1735-c.1790)
Ensign: 16 February 1756, 27th Foot (Enniskillen);
Lieut: 21 July 1758, 27th Foot; transferred on promotion;

Capt: 11 July 1759, 42nd Foot; exchanged 4 December 1759, 55th Foot; retired, 28 May 1768.

Came to North America as an ensign in the 27th Foot (Enniskillen) and was promoted lieutenant in the same regiment after the battle of Ticonderoga, 8 July 1758. He was made captain *"in room of"* John Campbell [1] but he only remained in the regiment less than six months. He exchanged to the 55th Foot, 4 December 1759. Retired 28 May 1768.

CBs; *SBs*; *BALs*; Stewart, *Sketches*, I-II, *in passim.*

Archibald "Sheriff" Campbell,* [2] (1729-1762)
Ensign: 6 August 1746, 43rd Foot (Sempill's);
Lieut: 28 July 1757, 42nd Foot;
Capt: 4 December 1759, 42nd Foot.

Second son of Archibald Campbell of Stonefield, the *"sheriff depute of Argyll"* for 47 years and hence the son's nickname, given the number of officers in the regiment with the same name. One of ten officers who exchanged from half-pay to bring the regiment up to its wartime establishment of two lieutenants per company prior to its departure to North America. Wounded at the battle of Ticonderoga, 8 July 1758 and was commanding the light infantry company of the 1st Battalion during the 1760 expedition down the St Lawrence against Montréal. Died of fever at sea in the Caribbean, 4 June 1762.

CBs; *SBs*; *BALs*; Stewart, *Sketches*, I-II, *in passim*; *NAS*, GD 87/1 f.82; *Scots Magazine*, xxxix, 455.

John Campbell,* [2] of Glendaruel, (1729-1795)
Ensign: 25 September 1745, 43rd Foot (Sempill's);
Lieut: 16 May 1748, 43rd Foot;
Capt-Lt: 2 August 1759, 42nd Foot;
Capt: 26 July 1760, 42nd Foot; exchanged 25 March 1762, 27th Foot (Enniskillens); half-pay 1771;
Major: 2 July 1773, "in America";
Lt. Col: 29 August 1777, "in America";
Col: 20 November 1782, "in America."

Born in Glendaruel, Strathclyde in 1729, the 2nd son of Duncan Campbell of Lochhead and Elizabeth Campbell, daughter of the Rev. Alexander Campbell, Minister of Glenaray. John Campbell is erroneously described as *"younger of Glenfalloch"* by Stewart of Garth; *"of Lochend"* on Lord Loudon's 1747 list; and *"younger of Glenlyon"* on Loudoun's 1752 List. He joined the regiment as an ensign in Duncan Campbell of Inverawe's Additional Company raised in 1745. He was promoted lieutenant in room of John Campbell, "*yr of Glenlyon*," the latter purchasing a captaincy and creating the vacancy. *Glendaruel* was the third most senior lieutenant of the 42nd Foot when it sailed for North America in 1756. "*Slightly wounded in the arm*" at Ticonderoga, 8 July 1758, he was promoted Capt-Lt. "*in room of*" Robert Gray who transferred to the 55th Foot and full captain on James Abercrombie's promotion to major in the 78th Foot. On the regiment's return from Havana, he was stationed at Trois Rivieres where, in 1763, he went out on half-pay. He remained in North America and married Anne-Marie, the daughter of Corne St Luc in Trois Rivieres, Québec. He returned to Ireland with his regiment in August in 1767 and went out on half-pay in 1771. He gained the support of the Duke of Argyll in his bid to return to Canada as the Superintendent of Indians for Québec and was named to the post 3 July 1773 by Sir Guy Carleton who was eager to reduce the Johnson's family's monopoly and influence in the department. Campbell was active in resisting the American invasion in 1775 and led a sortie which captured Ethan Allan of "Green Mountain Boys" fame. He was shortly thereafter captured himself and sent to New York. Released the following year he and his deputy, Alexander Fraser, a former 78th officer (see 78th Register) was placed in charge of the western Indians on the Burgoyne campaign, but as neither could speak any Indian languages "Gentleman Johnny" deemed them to be "*of no weight*" in Indian councils. His ranks of major through colonel were later deemed to be honorary courtesy titles only and he received neither rank nor pay as a regular officer. Died as Superintendent of Indian Affairs in Québec 23 June 1795.

CBs; *SBs*; *BALs*; Stewart, *Sketches*, I-II, *in passim*; Abercromby to Stanwix, 12 August 1751, *AB* 531; Richards, *Black Watch*, 64-65, "John Campbell," *DCB*, IV, 129-131.

Kenneth Tolmie* (1724-1809)
Ensign: 24 June 1746, 43rd Foot (Sempill's);
Lieut: 23 January 1756, 42nd Foot;
Capt: 27 July 1760, 42nd Foot; resigned, 29 April 1762.

Born 1 April 1724, on the Isle of Skye, the son of William Tolmie, Commissioner to Norman MacLeod, 19th Chief of MacLeod. Had some former training as an engineer officer, perhaps acquired while serving in Flanders, as he was detached to the Royal Engineers to command one of the "*four companys of workmen from the Regulars, consisting each of 1 officer, 1 serjt, 1 Corpll & 25 men*" for the 1758 Ticonderoga campaign. The following year, after the capture of Crown Point, he was appointed, 25

September 1759, "*Overseer for the work on the fort and to receive his directions from Lieut Col. Eyre.*" He also took over the secondary duty of regimental paymaster from Capt. Gordon Graham who was promoted major-commandant to the the 2nd/42nd Foot. Fought in all battles and campaigns of the regiment. Promoted to the command of a company, 27 July 1760, at Fort Ontario. Resigned after the capture of Martinique, April 1762.

CBs; *SBs*; *BALs*; Stewart, *Sketches*, I-II, *in passim*; Richards, *Black Watch*, *in passim*; *MOB*, 436-7.

William Cockburn (c.1728-1762)
Ensign: 29 May 1745, 1st Foot (The Royal);
Lieut: 22 January 1755, 2nd/1st Foot (The Royal);
Capt-Lt: 16 July 1758, 15th Foot (Amherst's); transferred on promotion;
Capt: 16 September 1760, 42nd Foot.

Came to North America as a lieutenant with the 2nd/1st Foot (The Royal) and landed with it at Louisburg, June 1758. Transferred to 15th Foot on promotion to captain-lieutenant after the Louisburg landings. Fought at the battle of the Plains of Abraham, 1759 and Sillery, 1760. Transferred from the 15th Foot on promotion to captain in the 42nd after the capture of Montréal "*in room of*" James Abercrombie promoted. Killed two years later at the storming of Morne Tartenson on Martinique, 24 January 1762.

CBs; *SBs*; *BALs*; Stewart, *Sketches*, I-II, *in passim*; Richards, *Black Watch*, *in passim*.

John [Graham] Graeme* [2], (1723-1790)
Ensign: 25 July 1750, 42nd Foot;
Lieut: 25 January 1756, 42nd Foot; appointed QM, 19 February 1756; resigned QM, 13 October 1761;
Capt: 14 February 1762, 42nd Foot; half-pay, 24 October 1763; full-pay, 25 December 1765; retired 28 January 1771.

Born in Scotland, 1723, the 2nd son of Alexander Graham of Rednock and Duchray, and Margaret Stirling. He was the younger brother of Captain Thomas Graeme of the 42nd Foot (see above) and is often confused with his cousin , Capt-Lt John Graeme , y^r of Inchbrakie (see below) who was killed at Bushy Run, 1763. Wounded at Ticonderoga, 8 July 1758. Fought in all major campaigns and served as the senior QM until his resignation on 13 October 1761 at Staten Island. He was promoted captain after William Cockburn was killed at the storming of Morne Tartenson on Martinique, January 1762. He was wounded a second time at Bushy Run, August 1763 and exchanged to half-pay, 24 October 1763. He returned to active service as a captain on 25 December 1765 however, and returned with the regiment to Ireland in 1767. He married Christian Murray, only daughter of Robert [Macgregor] Murray of Glencarnoch, 6th chieftain of the proscribed Macgregor clan – "*The Children of the Mist*." Both of her brothers were killed in North America in 1758, John Murray, a lieutenant with the 78th Foot (Fraser's Highlanders) at Louisburg (see 78th Register), and James Murray, captain-lieutenant of the 55th Foot (Howe's) at Ticonderoga. He died 14 October 1790.

CBs; *SBs*; *BALs*; "List of the Officers of the 42nd or Royal Highland Regiment according to seniority dated December 29th, 1762," *BL* Add. MSS. 21634: f.178c; Stewart, *Sketches*, I-II, *in passim.*

Alexander Macdonald (c.1735-c.1790)
Capt: 28 October 1760, IHC; amalgamated, 6 June 1761, 100th Foot (Campbell's Highlanders); exchanged 28 April 1762, 42nd Foot; half pay, 24 October 1763; full-pay, 26 May 1769, 22nd Foot;
Major: 10 March 1777, 2nd/71st Foot (Fraser's Highlanders);
Lt-Col: 25 October 1779, 2nd/71st Foot; retired 31 December 1781.

A captain of an Independent Company raised to serve in the Channel Islands which was then amalgamated into the 100th Foot (Campbell's Highlanders) commanded by a former Black Watch officer, Colin Campbell of Kilberrie (see below). Macdonald served at St. Helier on Jersey, before being sent to the Caribbean to participate in Monckton's 1762 Martinique expedition. When his commanding officer killed Capt John McKaarg, one of his brother company commanders, Macdonald exchanged into the 42nd to fill a vacancy left by Capt David Haldane of the 42nd (see above), the latter officer brevetted major in the 100th and made "acting" commandant while Major Campbell awaited trial. Macdonald served in the 2nd/42nd until its disbandment and exchanged to half-pay, 24 October 1763. He returned to active service as a captain in the 22nd Foot in May 1769. Eight years later, he transferred on promotion to major of the new-raising 2nd/71st Foot (Fraser's Highlanders) and fought with them in all engagements. He transferred to the First Battalion as its lieutenant-colonel in October 1779.

CBs; *SBs*; *BALs*; "List of the Officers of the 42nd or Royal Highland Regiment according to seniority dated December 29th, 1762," *BL* Add. MSS. 21634: f.178c; Stewart, *Sketches*, I-II, *in passim.*

Archibald Campbell, [3] of Glendaruel (1720-1762)
Lieut: 28 July 1757; 42nd Foot;
Capt: 29 April 1762, 42nd Foot.

Archibald was born in 1720, the eldest son of Duncan Campbell of Lochhead and his wife Elizabeth Campbell, eldest daughter of Rev. Alexander Campbell, minister of Glenaray. Came to North America in summer 1758 with the three Additional Companies. Participated in the campaigns to capture Forts Ticonderoga and Crown Point in 1759, and, in the capture of Montréal 1760. He was the elder brother of John Campbell of Glendaruel (see above) who succeeded him after his death on 3 June 1762. The record of his death was cited in *Scots Magazine*, September 1762, as follows: "*Death.– In the passage from Martinico to the Havannah* [sic], *Captain Archibald Campbell of Glendaruel, of a yellow fever. June 3rd.*"

CBs; *SBs*; *BALs*; "List of the Officers of the 42nd or Royal Highland Regiment according to seniority dated December 29th, 1762," *BL* Add. MSS. 21634: f.178c; Stewart, *Sketches*, I-II, *in passim*; *Scots Magazine*, xxiv, 507.

James Abercromby, yʳ of Glassaugh, (1740-1804)
Ensign: 25 December 1756, 44th Foot (Abercromby's); transferred on promotion;
Lieut: 26 March 1758, 35th Foot (Otway's); transferred on promotion;
Capt: 5 May 1762, 42nd Foot; half-pay, 24 October 1763; full pay, 15 May 1765, 3rd Foot (Burton's); 9 June 1786, North British Invalids Company;
Major: "*in the Army,*" 29 August 1777;
Lt-Col: "*in the Army,*" 19 February 1783;
Col: 1 March 1794, [shown as "Invalids"].

Born 1740 in Banffshire, Scotland, 3rd son of Major General James Abercromby of Glassaugh, Commander-in-Chief in North America (1758-1759), and Mary Duff of Dipple. "*A List of Commissions Granted by The Rᵗ Honble The Earl of Loudoun*" states that James jⁿʳ who had come over with his father in the summer of 1756, was appointed to his father's regiment, the 44th Foot, "*in the Place of Ensigne Rodes of this Country who grew weare of the Service and Resigned,*" effective 25 December 1756. He was promoted lieutenant in the 35th Foot on 26 March and served at the siege of Louisburg, 1758 and the siege of Québec, 1759. After the capture of Martinique, 1762,

James Abercromby, yʳ of Glassaugh, 1740-1804. The third son of Major General James Abercromby of Glassaugh, commander in chief in North America (1758-1759) came to America with his father in the summer of 1756 and was appointed an ensign in the 44th Foot in December of that year. As lieutenant in the 35th Foot, he took part in the siege of Louisbourg in 1758 and in the siege of Québec in 1759. After the capture of Martinique in 1762, he was made Captain in the Black Watch. He exchanged to half-pay in 1763 and died in 1804. (Courtesy, J. Robert Maguire)

he transferred on promotion into the 42nd "*in room of*" James Stewart of Urrard who retired. As one of the junior captains at the 1763 peace, James, jⁿʳ went out on half-pay but returned to the army as a full pay captain in the "The Buffs" or 3rd Foot (Burton's). He received promotions to major and lieutenant-colonel "in the Army" during the American Revolution indicating that he served as a staff officer vice a regimental officer. He received command of an Invalid company in Scotland and became a Colonel, 1 March 1794. He died in 1804.

CBs; SBs; BALs; "List of the Officers of the 42nd or Royal Highland Regiment according to seniority dated December 29th, 1762," BL, Add. MSS. 21634: f.178c; Stewart, Sketches, I-II, in passim; Pargellis, MA, 332.

Alexander Turnbull* (c.1735-1804)

Ensign: 3 June 1752, 42nd Foot;
Lieut: 27 January 1756, 42nd Foot;
Capt-Lt: 15 February 1762, 42nd Foot;
Capt: 4 June 1762, 42nd Foot; half-pay, 24 October 1763; full pay 3 May 1764, 35th Foot;
Major: "*in the Army*," 29 August 1777; retired 5 February 1778.

Of the Turnbulls of Stracathro in Angus-shire. Went to North America with the first division of his regiment in 1756. Assigned with his platoon to the defense of Sir William Johnson's residence in fall of 1756. Fought in all major engagements. Turnbull, according to the New York *Gazette*, had a near escape with Indians on Amherst's 1759 campaign Ticonderoga: "*Mr. Turnbull, …and four of the Light Infantry of Lord John Murray's Royal Highland Regiment, went out yesterday in a whaleboat to fish about the islands in the lake; but while they were fishing they perceived three whaleboats and a bark canoe coming out altogether from the 2nd island, and making towards them. At first, Mr. Turnbull thought they were some of our own people; but when they came nearer he soon discovered them to be enemies; on which he and his men made the best of their way for the shore, and the enemy pursued them very hard, especially the bark canoe, in which were 12 or 14 Indians, but our people happily got to shore before them, and ran up through the woods. The Enemy followed them for 4 miles, but could not take any of them prisoners. They all 5 came safe home in camp about 8 o'clock the day after; but without either coat, breeches, shoes, or hose.*" Wounded at the storming of Morne Tartenson on Martinique, 16 January 1762, and promoted captain lieutenant afterwards in room of John Graham promoted. Promoted captain at the siege of Havana "*in room of*" Archibald Campbell dead. Went out on half-pay 24 October 1763. Almost immediately returned as a full-pay captain in the 35th Foot (Fletcher's), 3 May 1764. Promoted major in the Army in 1777 and retired February 1778. He died in 1804.

CBs; SBs; BALs; "List of the Officers of the 42nd or Royal Highland Regiment according to seniority dated December 29th, 1762," BL Add. MSS. 21634: f.178c; Stewart, *Sketches, I-II, in passim;* July 16, 1759, Weyman's New York *Gazette* (No. 22).

Robert Menzies (c.1730-1762)

Lieut: 2 August 1757, 42nd Foot;
Capt: 9 July 1762, 42nd Foot.

Son of James Menzies and Janet Stevenson of Edinburgh and younger brother of Sir John Menzies. An Additional Company officer who came to North America in the summer of 1758. He fought in all subsequent campaigns of the regiment and was promoted captain at Havana, 9 July 1762, "*in room of John McNeil promoted.*" He died a few weeks later of fever, 17 August 1762.

CBs; SBs; BALs; "List of the Officers of the 42nd or Royal Highland Regiment according to seniority dated December 29th, 1762," BL, Add. MSS. 21634: f.178c; Stewart, Sketches, I-II, in passim.

Alexander MacIntosh,* y^r of Culclachy (c.1729-1776)

Ensign: Dutch-Scots Brigade;
Lieut: 29 January 1756, 42nd Foot;
Capt: 24 July 1762, 42nd Foot; half-pay 24 October 1763; full pay, 25 December 1770, 10th Foot.

Second son of John MacIntosh of Culclachy and Janet MacIntosh of Aberarder. A Dutch-Scots officer who resigned to join the 42nd to bring it up to its wartime establishment of two lieutenants per company. Wounded at Ticonderoga, 8 July 1758 and again at the storming of Morne Tartenson on Martinique, 16 January 1762. Promoted captain at Havana "*in room of James Macdonald discharged dead,*" and went out on half-pay as a junior captain, 24 October 1763. In 1770, returned to America on full pay with the 10th Foot. Killed in action at Fort Washington, 16 November 1776.

CBs; SBs; BALs; "List of the Officers of the 42nd or Royal Highland Regiment according to seniority dated December 29th, 1762," BL, Add. MSS. 21634: f.178c; Stewart, Sketches, I-II, in passim.

James Gray* (c.1730-1795)

Ensign: 23 May 1746, Lord Loudoun's Highlanders; half-pay, 4 January 1748/9;
Lieut: 30 January 1756, 42nd Foot;
Capt-Lt: 24 July 1762, 42nd Foot;
Capt: 2 August 1762, 42nd Foot; resigned, 1 February 1763.
Major: 1777, King's Royal Regiment of New York [Provincials]; retired 1783.

Son of William and Janet Gray of Lairg in Sutherland. His older brother John came to North America with General Oglethorpe's 42nd Foot as an ensign, the same year James was commissioned an ensign in Lord Loudoun's Highlanders. James served in Scotland until 1749 and exchanged to half-pay. His brother John, who remained in America, joined Captain Paul Demere's South Carolina Independent Company and was with Braddock at the Monongahela in 1755. James was recalled to duty in 1756 after the Massacre (his brother John survived) and joined the 42nd as a full-pay lieutenant prior to its embarkation for America. Served in all major campaigns and did engineer's duty in 1759 and 1760. In spring 1760, still a lieutenant, he was actively lobbying for a commandant's sinecure after the war with Lord Loudoun: "*As the wars in America is at an end, and no more hope of Preferment, I must use the freedom once more to ask your Lordship's interest. Promotion or Rank in the Army I can not expect. But as your Lordship must know in a short time, how the affairs of this Country must go, If any thing Could be done for me about the Forts, it would be of greater Service to me than Continuing all my lifetime a Subaltern. I am very well known to General Amherst and I am Certain your Lordship's Recommendation would get me some Employment. . . .*" Promoted captain at Havana in 1762, but resigned due to ill health. Chose to remain in North America, settling and marrying in Essex County, New Jersey. In 1771, he moved to Stone Hook, five miles from Albany and rented a farm from Stephen Schuyler. On the outbreak of the Revolution, he was offered command of a regiment of Continental troops as well as an appointment as Chief Engineer on the expedition against Canada which he declined. Instead, he and Sir John Johnson, son of Sir William Johnson, decided to raise a Loyalist regiment from the Highland and Loyalist tenantry of the Mohawk Valley, but before they could do so, Gray was arrested by Schuyler's militia and imprisoned at Albany. On 9 May 1777, he escaped with 200 other men north to Montréal where he became the Major to the first provincial regiment raised during the Revolution: the King's Royal New Yorkers commanded by Sir John Johnson. In 1785 he returned to Britain to take care of his father and his estate. He died 17 May 1795.

CBs; SBs; BALs; Stewart, Sketches, I-II, in passim; "James Gray" from Collections of the New Jersey Historical Society, Vol. X.

John Small* (1726-1796)

2nd Lieut: 2 June 1747, Drumlanrig's, Dutch-Scots Brigade;
Lieut: Dutch-Scots Brigade; resigned; 11 April 1756, 42nd Foot; appointed Brigade-Major "*in America,*" January 1762-1764;
Capt-Lt: 6 August 1762; 42nd Foot;
Capt: 6 August 1762, 42nd Foot; half-pay, 24 October 1763; full pay 30 April 1765, 21st Foot (Royal North British Fuzileers); appointed Brigade-Major in America, June 1775;
Major: 13 June 1775, Major-commandant, 2nd/84th Foot (Royal Highland Emigrants [RHE]);

Lt. Col: 17 November 1780, "Lt. Col. Commandant," 2nd/RHE;
Col: 18 November 1790;
Maj-Gen: 3 October 1794.

Born 1726 in Strathardale, Atholl, Scotland, third son of Patrick Small of Leanoch and Magdalene Robertson, sister of Alexander "Baron Reid" Robertson. He was thus the first cousin of John and Alexander Reid (see both above) and a kinsman to the brothers Lt. John Robertson (see below) and Capt. James Robertson of Lude, 77th Foot (See 77th Register). In 1747 he joined the Dutch-Scots Brigade as a 2nd lieutenant in the Earl of Drumlanrig's regiment of the Dutch-Scots Brigade in 1747. In 1756, Small came off half-pay of the Dutch-

John Small (1726-1796). A cameo painted on ivory of Major John Small in the uniform of the 84th Foot (Royal Highland Emigrants). During the Seven Years' War, he held a variety of staff appointments, including brigade-major in the Martinique 1762 and Muskingum 1764 campaigns. He commanded the 2nd Battalion RHE during the Revolution but was employed as a staff officer most of the time. He died a Major General in 1796. (Courtesy, National Archives of Canada)

Scots service to become a lieutenant in the 42nd Foot. He was involved in the Oswego, Montréal, Ticonderoga, and West Indies campaigns. As a senior lieutenant, Brigadier Francis Grant had him appointed his Major of Brigade for the Martinique campaign, 1762. In August 1762, he was promoted to captain and the following year, with the reduction of the regiment, Small went on half pay in October 1763. He stayed on however and served as Colonel Bouquet's Major of Brigade on half-pay for the 1764 Muskingum expedition. Small was sent as the bearer of Bouquet's success back to England where in recognition of the victory and Small's own dedication to service met with the King's pleasure and he was placed back on full pay as a captain in the 21st Foot (Royal North British Fusileers) effective 30 April 1765. At this time, land grant records dated 22 April 1765 show: "*John Small, Captain in 21st Regt. Requested 10,000 acres. Granted 5,000*" in Vermont. Small served with the 21st Foot in America until 1775 when he received an unofficial commission from General Gage to raise the Young Royal Highlanders at his own expense. A short-lived unit, it was rolled into the Royal Highland Emigrants (84th Foot) as its 2nd Battalion with Small as its major-commandant. Small however, an experienced staff officer and former brigade major from the last war, spent the greatest part of his time in New York on staff duty. While in New York, Small participated in the battles of Lexington and Breed's Hill (Bunker Hill) in 1775. At the latter, he commanded a composite battalion of grenadiers which attempted to storm the hill three times and suffered overwhelming casualties. He was immortalized by American painter Trumbull who painted Small pushing up the firelock of a British grenadier about to bayonet Dr. Warren lying wounded on the ground. One anecdotal story that offers an explanation of Small's miraculous escape at Bunker Hill is that his old friend, General Israel Putnam, a fellow Mason and staff colleague from the Siege of Havana, was in the American entrenchments and told his sharpshooters to spare Small with the words: "*For God's sake do not shoot that man for he is like a brother to me!*" In 1777-78, Small personally took charge of an expedition to attack St. John and Machias from Halifax, Nova Scotia. In 1778, Small was assigned as brigade-major to General Pigot's force in the campaign to capture Rhode Island. His skills as a staff officer brought him promotion to lieutenant-colonel commandant of his RHE battalion in 1780. Went out on half pay in 1785 and supervised the move of his disbanded regiment to land grants in Nova Scotia. Through his political connections to the Crown, he was eventually promoted major general in 1794 and appointed Lieutenant-Governor of Guernsey in the Channel Islands. Small died 17 March 1796 at St Peter's Port, Guernsey, aged 70 years. He left a small fortune to his first cousin and childhood friend, John Reid (see above).

CBs; SBs; BALs; "List of the Officers of the 42nd or Royal Highland Regiment according to seniority dated December 29th, 1762," *BL* Add. MSS. 21634: f.178c; Stewart, *Sketches*, I-II, *in passim; PRO,* Journal of the Commissioners for Trade and Plantations, Vol. 12, January 1764 - December 1767; *MHP;* Stacey, "Major John Small, 1726-1796" *DCB;, JSAHR,* 102-4; *DSB,* 413; *NAC,* MG 23, series K34 (Frederick Mackenzie Papers) Order Book, 1761-62.

Charles Forbes, 2nd Auchernach (1730-1794)
Ensign: 23 April 1746, 2nd/1st Foot;
Lieut: 16 February 1756, 2nd/1st Foot; transferred on promotion;
Capt-Lt: 15 August 1762; 42nd Foot;
Capt: 15 August 1762, 42nd Foot; half-pay 24 October 1763; full-pay 11 September 1765, 66th Foot; exchanged 20 June 1766, 22nd Foot; retired 20 May 1773.

A memorial by Forbes to Amherst sketches his early career: "*Your Memorialist has been a Commissioned Officer above fifteen years; that he was present at the Battle of Culloden, served the Campaign 1747 in Flanders, has been in America ever since the Battalion has been ordered abroad, and had the Honour to serve at the Siege of Louisburgh under your Excellency's Command.*" At the siege of Havana, 1762, Forbes was promoted "*by reason of his gallant action in the final assault on the Moro, having lead the troops forward with enthusiasm.*" He was made captain-lieutenant "*in room of John Small promoted,*" 15 August 1762, and later in the day, full captain "*in room of Alan Campbell, promoted major.*" Fought at Bushy Run, August 1763, and was fort commandant at Fort Ligonier from September–December 1763 before exchanging to half-pay, 24 October 1763. He returned to duty with the 66th Foot as a captain in September 1765, and then exchanged the following year into the 22nd Foot. He retired May 1773.

CBs; SBs; BALs; "List of the Officers of the 42nd or Royal Highland Regiment according to seniority dated December 29th, 1762," *BL* Add. MSS. 21634: f.178c; Stewart, *Sketches*, I-II, *in passim; BL,* Add. MSS. 21651: f. 114; *DSB,* II, 414.

Daniel Shaw
Ensign: Dutch-Scots Brigade;
Lieut: 26 August 1756, 2nd/34th Foot; transferred on promotion;

Capt: 17 August 1762, 2nd/42nd Foot; half-pay 24 October 1763; full-pay, 10 June 1768, 62nd Foot; half-pay, 7 September 1771, 62nd Foot; full-pay, 6 November 1772; retired 28 April 1774.

Commissioned in 34th Foot (Cavendish's), an English regiment, and served at the taking of Belleisle, 1761. He arrived at Havana in June 1762 and two months later found himself as "eldest lieutenant" and a Gaelic speaker, transferred on promotion to the 42nd Foot "*in room of Robert Menzies,*" discharged dead. Was listed with the sick at Long Island in spring 1763 and exchanged to half-pay in 1763. A petition he submitted requesting land grants in Prince Edward Island for himself and his two sons claimed he "*was upon constant Service during the last two wars; was in the following sieges and battles, vizt: at the Battles of Fontenoy and La Felt [Laffeldt], at the Sieges of Bergen op Zoom, when it was stormed; at the burning of the shipping in St. Malo, at the taking of Cherbourg; at St. Cas; at the Siege of the Moro and conquest of Havannah, and served with your Majesty's 34th and 42nd Regiments in the West Indies and North America until the 2nd Battalion of the 42nd Regiment was sent to England in November 1762 and was reduced 18 March, 1763.*" He rejoined the army from half-pay in 1768 as a captain in the 62nd Foot, exchanged to half-pay in 1771, rejoined the following year, and then retired just before the outbreak of the American Revolution.

CBs; SBs; BALs; "List of the Officers of the 42nd or Royal Highland Regiment according to seniority dated December 29th, 1762," *BL* Add. MSS. 21634: f.178c; Stewart, *Sketches*, I-II, *in passim.*

John Campbell, [3] y^r of Melfort (1730-1790)
Lieut: 30 July 1757, 77th Foot; appointed adjutant, 77th Foot, 11 July 1759; resigned adjutancy, 1 February 1763; transferred on promotion;
Captain: 1 February 1763, 42nd Foot; half-pay, 24 October 1763;
Major: c. 1779, Argyll (Western) Fencibles.

Son and heir of Archibald Campbell and Annabel Campbell, sister of John Campbell of Barcaldine. Nephew of Major Allan Campbell, 42nd Foot (see above) and first cousin of Major Alex Campbell and Captain Mungo Campbell of the 77th Foot (see 77th Register). Came to North America as a lieutenant in one of the 77th's Additional Companies. Participated in all major campaigns of Montgomery's Highlanders, including the capture of Montréal in 1760. Transferred to the 42nd Foot on promotion to captain while recu-

John Campbell, *Melfort* (1730-1790). A portrait by an unknown artist of Captain John Campbell *Melfort* in the uniform of the 42nd Foot, c.1762. He originally came to North America as a lieutenant in the 77th Foot (Montgomery's). A full color portrait of him appears on the cover of this volume. (Courtesy, Trustees of the Black Watch Museum, Perth)

perating at New York after the grueling Caribbean campaign. Out on half-pay, October 1763. Was second-major in the Argyll (Western) Fencibles along with first major, Hugh Montgomerie, (another former 77th officer - see Register), when that regiment mutinied at Edinburgh in October 1779. Considered a popular officer amongst the men, it was Melfort's calm actions along with support from Montgomerie that quelled the disturbances. He married his cousin in 1767, Colina, daughter of John Campbell of Achalader and Isabella Campbell, daughter of Patrick Campbell of Barcaldine. He died at Bath in 1790 at the age of 60.

CBs; *SBs*; *BALs*; "List of the Officers of the 42nd or Royal Highland Regiment according to seniority dated December 29th, 1762," *BL* Add. MSS. 21634: f.178c; Stewart, *Sketches*, I-II, *in passim*.

Captains-Lieutenant

John Campbell,* [4] (1717- 1758)
Ensign: 1 May 1745, 43rd Foot (Sempill's);
Lieut: 4 October 1746, 43rd Foot;
Capt-Lt: 16 February 1756, 42nd Foot.

Born on Duneaves estate, on the River Lyon in Perthshire, son of Duncan Campbell, (youngest brother of John Campbell, 2nd of Duneaves) and Janet Robertson. Older brother of Alexander Campbell [4] (see below) and foster-brother to John Campbell, jnr of Glenlyon, Major of Marines and former Black Watch officer. Joined the 43rd Foot (Crawford's) as a "sentinel" or private soldier in 1740 and three years later, was one of three Highlanders selected to perform a display of Highland weaponry in London at the special request of King George II. According to Stewart of Garth: "*They performed the broadsword exercise, and that of the Lochaber axe, or lance, before his majesty, the Duke of Cumberland, Marshal Wade and a number of general officers assembled for the purpose in the great gallery at St. James. They displayed so much dexterity and skill in the management of their weapons, as to give perfect satisfaction to his majesty. Each got a gratuity of one guinea, which they gave to the porter at the palace as they went out.*" John fought at Fontenoy in 1745 as a private and was given a battlefield commission to ensign "for gallantry." He was sent to Scotland where he served as ensign "*with no pay while junior*" in one of the Regiment's additional companies raised in the Highlands during 1745. Ten years later, as the senior lieutenant prior to the regiment being ordered to North America, he received the captain-lieutenancy without purchase and subsequently commanded the absentee Colonel's company for two years overseas. At the battle of Ticonderoga, 8 July 1758, Campbell led his company from the front, the only group of men to penetrate the French defensive works. Inside, he did deadly slaughter with his broadsword before being bayoneted and killed by French grenadiers led by General Montcalm.

CBs; *SBs*; *BALs*; Stewart, *Sketches*, I-II, *in passim*.

Robert Gray,* yr of Skibo, (1729-1776)
Ensign: 6 June 1745, 43rd Foot (Sempill's);
Lieut: 7 August 1747, 43rd Foot;
Capt Lt: 22 July 1758, 42nd Foot; transferred on promotion;
Capt: 2 August 1759, 80th Foot (Gage's Light Infantry);

exchanged 13 September 1760, 55th Foot; Major: "in the Army," 23 July 1772; 55th Foot; died, 14 April 1776.

Only son of George Gray, 6th of Skibo, and Isobel Munro. Joined the regiment as a 16-year old ensign. Wounded at Ticonderoga, 8 July 1758, and promoted Captain-Lt. in room of John Campbell of Duneaves killed at the same battle. Transferred the following year into Gage's Light Infantry on promotion to captain. Participated in Amherst's 1760 expedition to capture Montréal and exchanged into the more senior 55th Foot on the day of the French town's capitulation. In 1763, he was second-in-command to Capt. James Dalyell's relief force sent to Detroit and was severely wounded in the shoulder at the battle of Bloody Run, 1763. He was appointed ADC to Major-General Amherst "*in room of*" Capt. Dalyell killed at Bloody Run. He returned to America with the 55th Foot during the American Revolution and while ashore at Halifax, Nova Scotia, fell ill and died 14 April 1776. He was buried the next day in the churchyard of St Paul's Anglican church.

CBs; *SBs*; *BALs*; Stewart, *Sketches*, I-II, *in passim*.

James Grant* (1718-1778)

Ensign: 7 October 1746, 43rd Foot (Sempill's); adjutant 42nd Foot, 26 June 1751;
Lieut: 24 January 1756; 42nd Foot;
Capt-Lt: 28 July 1760; resigned adjutancy, 1st /42nd Foot, 27 August 1760;
Capt: 8 October 1761, 80th Foot; half-pay, 1 November 1764; full-pay, 1 January 1766, 47th Foot; retired, 29 October 1768.

A kinsman of Lt. Colonel Francis Grant. Commissioned 1746 and appointed adjutant 26 June 1751. He was wounded at the battle of Ticonderoga, 8 July 1758, and left the regiment on promotion to captain in the 80th Foot (Gage's Light Infantry) in 1761. Went on half-pay in November 1764. He returned to active duty as a captain in the 47th Foot in January 1766, but retired two years later after his regiment returned to Ireland. He became Town-Major of Limerick and died in 1778.

CBs; *SBs*; *BALs*; "List of the Officers of the 42nd or Royal Highland Regiment according to seniority dated December 29th, 1762," *BL* Add. MSS. 21634: f.178c; Stewart, *Sketches*, I-II, *in passim*.

John [Graham] Graeme, y^r of Inchbrakie, (c.1730-1763)

Ensign: 25 July 1758, 42nd Foot;
Lieut: 31 July 1760, 42nd Foot;
Capt-Lt: 5 August 1762, 42nd Foot;
Capt: "in the Army," 1 February 1762.

Third son of Patrick Graeme, 7th of Inchbrakie and Janet Pearson of Kippenross. First cousin of the brothers Captains Thomas and John Graham of Duchray, also serving in the 42nd Foot (see above). Stewart of Garth and successive historians have incorrectly labeled this John as *Duchray's* younger brother (probably because the British army lists spelt his name Graham). One of eight young gentlemen volunteers of the 42nd sent to Robert Rogers' Ranging School in October 1757. Promoted ensign after the Battle of Ticonderoga, 8 July 1758, "*in room of Duncan Campbell promoted.*" Fought in all major campaigns. Killed by Indians at Edge Hill, during the battle of Bushy Run, 4 August 1763. By contrast, Captain John Graham, Duchray's younger brother, was wounded at the same battle but shortly thereafter went out on half-pay as the most junior company commander, married and fathered several children.

CBs; *SBs*; *BALs*; "List of the Officers of the 42nd or Royal Highland Regiment according to seniority dated December 29th, 1762," *BL* Add. MSS. 21634: f.178c; Stewart, *Sketches*, I-II, *in passim*.

Patrick Balneavis,* y^r of Eradrour, (1739-c.1790)

Ensign: 28 January 1756, 42nd Foot;
Lieut: 1 April 1758, 42nd Foot;
Capt-Lt: 23 August 1763; 42nd Foot; retired 31 March 1770.

Born in 1739, son of Henry Balneavis of Eradrour and Helen Campbell, daughter of John Campbell of Glenlyon. Nephew of Major John Campbell, yr of Glenlyon, of the Marines, a former 42nd officer (1745-48) and Lieutenant Archibald "Roy" Campbell, 78th Foot. (see 78th Register). Commissioned ensign in the regiment just prior to its departure for North America. Promoted lieutenant 1 April 1758 in room of Sir James Cockburn who transferred to the 48th Foot. Was wounded three months later at Ticonderoga, 8 July 1758. Participated in all major campaigns and was wounded again at Martinique in 1762, and a third time at Bushy Run, 1763. Promoted in room of Capt. Lt. John Graeme killed at Bushy Run. Listed as a participant in peace talks with Shawnee, Delaware and Iroquois Indians at Fort Pitt, 9-10 June 1766. Retired in March 1770.

CBs; *SBs*; *BALs*; "List of the Officers of the 42nd or Royal Highland Regiment according to seniority dated December 29th, 1762," *BL* Add. MSS. 21634: f.178c; Stewart, *Sketches*, I-II, *in passim*; Croghan to Gage, 15 June 1766, *Clements Library*, Gage Papers, American Series, Vol.52; Reel 10.

Lieutenants

George Farquharson* (1725-1758)

Ensign: 14 October, 1745, 43rd Foot (Crawford's);
Lieut: 29 March 1750; 42nd Foot.

The older brother of Alexander Farquharson (see below). Killed at Ticonderoga, 8 July 1758.

CBs; *SBs*; *BALs*; Stewart, *Sketches*, I-II, *in passim*.

Colin Campbell,* of Kilberrie, (1728-c.1790)

Ensign: 1 November 1739, 43rd Foot (Crawford's);
Lieut: 8 June 1745, Lord Loudoun's Highlanders; half-pay, 4 January 1749; 9 February 1750-1, 42nd Foot;
Capt: 27 April 1756, 2nd/1st Foot (The Royal); exchanged 27 August 1756, 2nd/4th Foot; 20 August 1759, 38th Foot;
Major: 4 May 1761, 100th Foot (Campbell's Highlanders); cashiered 20 August 1762.

The eldest son and heir of Capt. Dugald Campbell of Kilberrie and Elizabeth, eldest daughter of Dugald of Kilberry and Barbara Campbell, daughter and heir of Dugald Campbell of Lagg. Went to America with the regiment with the First Division where he learned that he had been promoted captain in the 2nd/1st Foot (The Royal) and returned immediately to Britain. On his arrival he exchanged into the 2nd/4th Foot in August 1756 to avoid returning to North America a second time. Three years later however, his battalion was sent to fight at Martinique as part of General Hopson's 1759 expedition. His unit was left to form part of the garrison of Guadeloupe and later in the summer of 1759, he exchanged into the 38th Foot which was stationed further north on the island of Barbados. In 1761, chafing to get away from the West Indies, he was given the opportunity to command a new-raising regiment that was created by amalgamating some Independent Companies raised in Scotland and he was given the rank of major-commandant. Known as the 100th Foot (Campbell's Highlanders), his unit was at first posted on Jersey, the largest of the Channel Islands off the coast of France. By late 1761, however, he was sent back to the Caribbean with his regiment to join General Monckton's expeditionary force assembling at Bridgetown, Barbados for a descent on Martinique. After the surrender of the island, he was arrested for assaulting and killing one of his own company commanders, Capt. John McKaarg, outside the latter's tent. Imprisoned and relieved of his command on General Monckton's orders, Kilberrie was replaced by Captain David Haldane of the 42nd Foot (see above). Campbell was subsequently found guilty of manslaughter and cashiered from the Army, 20 August 1762. Fiercely disputing his innocence in the affair, he privately published a book in London wherein he characterized his victim as an embezzler, debtor and a scoundrel, and included all court martial transcripts and proceedings. Campbell concluded his narrative by claiming to have been wrongly convicted and relieved of his command. In 1764 he brought a lawsuit against General Monckton, the courts exonerating his commander of any wrongdoing and accusing Campbell of maliciously and frivolously attempting to slander the good name of a general officer. Monckton wisely decided not to bother with a counter-suit and accepted an appointment as governor of Berwick-upon-Tweed in 1765 and was promoted lieutenant-general in 1770. Kilberrie died 24 years later, aged 76, at Edinburgh, and was buried at St. Cuthbert's Church.

CBs; *SBs*; *BALs*; Stewart, *Sketches*, I-II, *in passim*; The Newgate Calendar; *Scots Magazine*, lx., 72.

James Campbell* [1] (1725-c.1780)

Ensign: 14 October 1745, 43rd Foot (Crawford's);
Lieut: 3 June 1752, 42nd Foot; superseded 15 May 1757.

On 24 April 1757, Francis Grant reported to Lord Loudoun that he "*not heard from Lieutenant James Campbell since we left Ireland, which makes me think he has given up all thoughts of joining the Regiment.*" Loudoun subsequently informed the Duke of Cumberland that Campbell had "*remained in Irland when the Regt came out and has never Acknowledged the Orders I sent him from London by HRH Orders.*" Campbell was therefore superseded, and Loudoun promoted Archibald Lamont, "*Eldest Ensigne*" serving in America in his place (see below).

CBs; *SBs*; *BALs*; Stewart, *Sketches*, I-II, *in passim*; Francis Grant to Lord Loudoun, Schenectady, 24 April 1757, (*LO* 3455).

Sir James Cockburn,* 3rd B^t. of that Ilk, (1722-c.1795)

Ensign: 24 June 1746, 43rd Foot (Sempill's);

Lieut: 15 March 1755, 42nd Foot; transferred on promotion;

Capt: 22 March 1758, 48th Foot;

Major: 4 March 1769, 48th Foot;

Lt. Col: "in the Army," 29 August 1777; retired 26 February 1780.

The only son of Sir William Cockburn and Helen Lermonth. Inherited his father's baronetcy in 1754. Transferred to the 48th Foot before the battle of Ticonderoga and fought at the plains of Abraham, 1759. Was severely wounded at the battle of Sillery outside Québec, 28 April 1760. He married Mary Rochead of Masterton, 8 April 1764, and had one son. Promoted major of the 48th Foot in 1769, and brevetted lieutenant-colonel "in the Army" August 1777, during the American Revolution. He retired in February 1780.

CBs; *SBs*; *BALs*; Stewart, *Sketches*, I-II, *in passim*; Burkes Peerage, ed.104 (London, 197), 558.

Hugh [Ewan] Macpherson,* (1730-1758)

Ensign: 20 August 1751, 42nd Foot;

Lieut: 26 January 1756, 42nd Foot.

Fourth son of Alexander Macpherson of Culcherine, a cadet family of the Macphersons of Breakachy, and, Isabel Campbell, daughter of Hugh Campbell, a cadet of the family of Ardkinglas. Went to North America with the first Division and was killed at the battle of Ticonderoga, 8 July 1758.

CBs; *SBs*; *BALs*; Stewart, *Sketches*, I-II, *in passim*; Douglas' *Baronetage of Scotland*, (1798) reprinted in Alexander Macpherson, *Glimpses: Genealogy of the Macphersons*, 493-503.

Alexander Campbell,* 10th of Inverawe (c.1728-1760)

Ensign: 4 September 1754, 42nd Foot;

Lieut: 28 January 1756, 42nd Foot; exchanged 21 July 1759, Argyllshire Fencibles.

Second son of Duncan Campbell, 9th of Inverawe (see above) and Jean Campbell, daughter of Alexander Campbell of Finab. His elder brother, Lt. Dougald Campbell had been commissioned a lieutenant in the 21st Foot (North British Fusileers) and had died in 1756 at Gibraltar. Succeeded to the estate of Inverawe on his father's death though was seriously wounded himself at the battle of Ticonderoga, 8 July 1758, and invalided back to Scotland. Exchanged into Argyllshire Fencibles as a lieutenant the following summer, but died from wound complications several months later in Glasgow, 8 February 1760.

CBs; *SBs*; *BALs*; Stewart, *Sketches*, I-II, *in passim*; Richards, *Black Watch, in passim*; Scots Magazine (February, 1760); *Burkes Peerage, Baronetage and Knightage*, 107th ed., Vol. I., (2003), 188.

William Baillie of Torbreck,* (c.1730-1758)

Ensign: 1747, Lord Loudoun's Highlanders; half-pay 1748;

Lieut: 10 April 1748, Drumlanrig's, Dutch-Scots Brigade; 31 January 1756, 42nd Foot.

Briefly served as an ensign during the '45 and went on half-pay at the peace. Commissioned a second lieutenant in Drumlanrig's Regiment of the Dutch-Scots Brigade; resigned to take up British commission in the 42nd Foot to bring it up to its wartime establishment of two lieutenants per company. Killed at Ticonderoga, 8 July 1758.

CBs; *SBs*; *BALs*; Stewart, *Sketches*, I-II, *in passim*.

Hugh Arnot* (1732-c.1800)

Ensign: 1745, 64th Foot (Lord Loudoun's Highlanders);

2nd Lt: 30 December 1754, 15th Marines;

Lieut: 6 December 1755, 58th Marines; exchanged 9 April 1756, 42nd Foot; transferred on promotion;

Capt: 27 December 1757, 80th Foot; exchanged 16 August 1760, 46th Foot; retired 12 November 1767.

Eldest of five sons of James Arnot of Dalquhatswood, in the parish of Loudoun, near Galston, Ayrshire, the Factor to John Campbell, 4th Earl Loudoun. Hugh started his military career as an ensign in Lord Loudoun's Highlanders during the '45 and exchanged to half-pay in 1748. He joined the Marines in 1754 and was serving in the West Indies when he transferred to the 42nd Foot the spring of 1756 as one its two grenadier lieutenants. His company commander, Capt. Alan Campbell, remarked that "*Mr. Arnot* [is] *one of my Lieuts who was last year in the Marines and on the Jamaica Station.*" During his education and early military career, Hugh must have acquired some drafting skills, for in the winter of 1757/58 he offered Lord Loudoun his "*small but willing service, in that of copying Plans.*" A few weeks later, General James Abercromby recommended Arnot to Loudoun for a captaincy in the new-raising 80th Foot (Gage's Light Infantry) stating that Lt. Arnot "*is a well behaved & deserving young man and if there is any room in this corps I see no objection in preferring him for a company.*" Loudoun knew the Arnot family well, William Arnot having lent his Lordship large sums of money on several occasions. Arnot transferred to the new regiment, his commission dated 27 December 1757. He fought at

Ticonderoga with the 80th Foot and left a compelling journal and several maps of that experience. In 1760, after the fall of Montréal and the defeat of the French in North America, he decided to transfer out of a very junior regiment which was in danger of disbanding. He secured a captaincy in the 46th Foot (General Thomas Murray's) and retired in November 1767 when his regiment returned to Ireland from North America. He died insane.

CBs; SBs; BALs; Stewart, Sketches, I-II, in passim; see journal and letters by Arnot, in Westbrook, "Like Roaring Lions...," BFTM; Richards, Black Watch, in passim.

John Sutherland* [1] (c.1728-1758).
Ensign: IHC? 1745;
Lieut: 10 April 1756, 42nd Foot.

John was the 2nd son of John Sutherland of Little Tarbol by his second wife, Christian Mackenzie, and brother-in-law to Lt. Henry Munro of the 77th Foot (see 77th register) and Captain Gordon Graham of Drainie (see above). One of ten lieutenants who came off of half-pay to bring the regiment up to its wartime establishment of two lieutenants per company prior to its departure to North America. Killed at the battle of Ticonderoga, 8 July 1758.

CBs; SBs; BALs; Stewart, Sketches, I-II, in passim.

James Campbell* [2] (c.1728-c.1796)
Ensign: 24 January 1756, 42nd Foot;
Lieut: 14 December 1756, 42nd Foot; transferred on promotion;
Capt: 3 September 1762, IHC; half-pay 31 January 1763; 14 April 1778, Western Regiment of Fencible Men, [WRFM];
Major: 9 June 1779, WRFM; captain's half-pay, 21 April 1783.

The first 42nd officer to be promoted within the regiment while serving in North America, Lord Loudoun noting in his own hand that Campbell was the *"Eldest Ensigne in the Regt."* He replaced Colin Campbell of Kilberrie who had returned to Britain earlier in the year on promotion to captain in the 1st Foot. He participated in all major campaigns of the regiment and, after the siege of Havana 1762, returned home to Scotland to command a newly-raised Independent Highland Company (IHC). His command lasted only a few weeks and he went out on half-pay as a captain in January 1763. He returned to duty in April 1778 as a captain in the Western Regiment of Fencible Men and was promoted its major the following year. He went out on his regular captain's half pay when the Fencibles were disbanded 21 April 1783. Not on the half-pay list after 1796.

CBs; SBs; BALs; "List of the Officers of the 42nd or Royal Highland Regiment according to seniority dated December 29th, 1762," BL Add. MSS. 21634: f.178c; Stewart, Sketches, I-II, in passim.

Archibald Lamont* (c. 1728-c.1800)
Ensign: 25 January 1756, 42nd Foot;
Lieut: 15 May 1757, 42nd Foot; half-pay; 2 September 1775, 60th Foot; half-pay, 21 January 1777.

Promoted lieutenant in May 1757 *"in room of James Campbell"* who never joined the regiment in North America, despite being repeatedly ordered to do so by Lord Loudoun. Served throughout all campaigns with the regiment and went out on half pay 16 March 1764 before the projected expedition to the Muskingum. Returned to active duty in September 1775 as a lieutenant in the new-raising 3rd Battalion of the 60th Foot (Royal Americans) but exchanged two years later onto half-pay, 21 January 1777.

CBs; SBs; BALs; Stewart, Sketches, I-II, in passim.

David Milne (1735-1762)
Ensign: 30 September 1747, Marjoribank's, Dutch-Scots Brigade;
Lieut: 19 July 1757; 42nd Foot.

Started his military career as an ensign in the Dutch-Scots Brigade and is usually shown erroneously as "Mills" on the British Army Lists [BALs]. Commissioned a lieutenant, July 1757, in one of the three Additional Companies authorized for the 42nd and sent to North America spring 1758. Fought in all major campaigns. Wounded at Ticonderoga, 8 July 1758 and wounded seriously again at the storming of Morne Tartenson, Martinique, 16 January 1762. Died, 8 August 1762, on a hospital ship off of Havana.

CBs; SBs; BALs; Stewart, Sketches, I-II, in passim.

Simon Blair (c.1740-1762)
Ensign: 5 May 1756, 57th Foot (renumbered 55th [Perry's]); exchanged 9 July 1756, 16th Foot; transferred on promotion;
Lieut: 20 July 1757, 42nd Foot.

Born in Atholl, Scotland and started his military career in 1756 as an ensign in the 57th /55th Foot). Exchanged into the 16th Foot two months later. Promoted to lieutenant the following year in one of the three Additional Companies authorized for the 42nd and sent to North America spring 1758. Fought in all major campaigns. Died of fever at Havana, September 1762.

CBs; *SBs*; *BALs*; Stewart, *Sketches*, I-II, *in passim.*

David Barclay (c.1740-1762)
Cornet: Sir Robert Rich's Dragoons; half-pay 1748-9;
Lieut: 25 July 1757, 42nd Foot.

Served during the War of Austrian Succession as a cornet in Sir Robert Rich's Dragoons and exchanged to half-pay in 1748. Returned to active duty as an Additional Company officer sent to the 42nd Foot in the spring of 1758. He participated in all major campaigns of the regiment and was killed at the storming of Morne Grenier on Martinique, 24 January 1762.

CBs; *SBs*; *BALs*; Stewart, *Sketches*, I-II, *in passim.*

Alexander Mackay (c.1740-1772)
Lieut: 1 August 1757; 42nd Foot;
Capt-Lt: 31 March 1770, 42nd Foot.

One of eleven children of Robert *"The Tutor of Farr"* Mackay and the great-grandson of Lord Reay. His brothers were Major Samuel Mackay, 60th and Captain John Mackay, 31st Foot, and he was brother-in-law to Lt. John Gray of the 101st Foot (Johnstone's Highlanders). Was an Additional Company officer who came over in the spring of 1758 and participated in all major campaigns of the regiment. Captured by the French on Lake Champlain in October 1759 but returned to the regiment the following month in a major prisoner exchange. He returned with the cadre of the 2nd/42nd Foot in October 1762 and spent 1763 in Britain. He returned to the regiment in 1764 and participated in Bouquet's Muskingum expedition. Listed as a participant in peace talks with Shawnee, Delaware and Iroquois Indians at Fort Pitt, 9-10 June 1766. He returned to Ireland with the regiment in 1767 and was promoted captain-lieutenant in March 1770. He died two years later on 23 November 1772.

CBs; *SBs*; *BALs*; "List of the Officers of the 42nd or Royal Highland Regiment according to seniority dated December 29th, 1762," *BL* Add. MSS. 21634: f.178c; Stewart, *Sketches*, I-II, *in passim*; Croghan to Gage, 15 June 1766, *Gage Papers*, American Series, Vol. 52, Reel 10.

John Campbell, [5] (c.1735-1762)
Lieut: 15 July 1758, 42nd Foot.

An Additional Company officer who arrived in time to participate in the battle of Ticonderoga, 8 July 1758, where he was wounded. He served in all major campaigns of the regiment, contracted fever at the siege of Havana 1762 and died in a New York hospital, 1 October 1762.

CBs; *SBs*; *BALs*; Stewart, *Sketches*, I-II, *in passim.*

Alexander McLean* (c.1740-1762)
Ensign: Dutch Scots Brigade,
Lieut: 16 July 1758, 2nd/42nd Foot; appointed adjutant 2nd/42nd Foot, 7 October 1758; resigned, 20 March 1759; transferred on promotion;
Capt: 20 August 1759, 87th Foot (Keith's Highlanders);
Major: 14 July 1761, 87th Foot; exchanged, 26 April 1762, 88th Foot (Campbell's Highland Volunteers).

Started his military career in the Dutch-Scots brigade. Commissioned lieutenant in the 2nd/42nd Foot, summer 1758, and fought in Martinique and Guadeloupe. Severely wounded, 4 February 1759, at Basse Terre, Guadeloupe, while leading a platoon of light infantry and as a result, had his arm amputated.In March 1759 he was promoted captain in the new-raising Keith's Highlanders back in Scotland which was destined for service in Germany. He was promoted major after the battle of Fallinghausen in July 1761 and was killed the following year at Brucher Muhl in Germany, 21 September 1762.

CBs; *SBs*; *BALs*; Stewart, *Sketches*, I-II, *in passim*; *Miscellaneous Correspondence*, II, (August 1758), 867.

George Sinclair* [1] (c.1740-1759)
Lieut: 17 July 1758, 42nd Foot.

Commissioned lieutenant in the 2/42nd Foot, summer 1758, and fought in Martinique. Died of wounds, 1 June 1759, sustained during the Martinique/Guadeloupe campaign 1759.

CBs; *SBs*; *BALs*; Stewart, *Sketches*, I-II, *in passim*; *Miscellaneous Correspondence*, II, (August 1758), 867.

John Murray* (c.1735-c.1790)
Lieut: 18 July 1758, 2nd/42nd Foot; transferred on promotion;
Capt: 26 September 1759, 87th Foot (Keith's Highlanders);
Major: 24 May 1763, 87th Foot; retired 31 March 1770.

Son of Lord Edward Murray. Commissioned lieutenant in the 2nd/42nd Foot, summer 1758, and never came to America, listed as *"Recruiting in Scotland."* Transferred to 87th Foot (Keith's Highlanders) on promotion to captain September 1759 and went to Germany. Promoted major, 24 May 1763, and retired 31 March 1770.

CBs; *SBs*; *BALs*; Stewart, *Sketches*, I-II, *in passim*; *Miscellaneous Correspondence*, II, (August 1758), 867.

Gordon Clunes* (c.1740-c.1814)
Lieut: 19 July 1758, 2nd/42nd Foot; transferred; 26 August 1759, 87th Foot (Keith's Highlanders);
Capt-Lt: 20 December 1760, 87th Foot;
Capt: 25 April 1762, 87th Foot; half-pay 24 May 1763.

Commissioned lieutenant in the 2/42nd Foot, summer 1758, and never came to America, listed as *"Recruiting in Scotland."* Transferred to 87th Foot (Keith's Highlanders) and fought in Germany. Wounded at the battle of Camphen, 15 October 1760. Promoted captain in April 1762 and out on half-pay May 1763.

CBs; *SBs*; *BALs*; Stewart, *Sketches*, I-II, *in passim*; *Miscellaneous Correspondence*, II, (August 1758), 867.

James Fraser,* 7th Belladrum, (1732-1808)
Lieut: 20 July 1758, 2nd/42nd Foot; transferred on promotion;
Capt-Lt: 8 October 1759, 87th Foot (Keith's Highlanders);
Capt: 20 December 1760, 87th Foot; half-pay, 24 May 1763; full-pay, 8 January 1779, Northern Regiment of Fencible Men; exchanged 8 April 1779, 2nd /71st Foot (Fraser's Highlanders); retired 24 June 1782.
Major: "in the Army," 29 August 1777.

James Fraser, 7th Belladrum, son of James Fraser, 6th Belladrum & Isobel Fraser of Fairfield. Commissioned lieutenant in the 2nd/42nd Foot, summer 1758, and never came to America, listed as *"Recruiting in Scotland."* Transferred to 87th Foot (Keith's Highlanders) on promotion to captain-lieutenant and fought in Germany. Promoted captain December 1760, he was wounded the following year at the battle of Falling-hausen, 15/16 July, 1761. He went out on half-pay in May 1763 but returned to active duty with the Northern Regiment of Fencible Men, January 1779. A few months later he exchanged into the 2nd Battalion of the 71st Foot (Fraser's Highlanders) and spent the rest of the war in North America. He retired in June 1782. In 1794 James Fraser of Belladrum was convinced by Archibald Campbell Fraser of Lovat (1736-1815) to come out of retirement to help raise the Fraser Fencibles, serving as Colonel until 1797, when he was replaced by Lovat's eldest son John Simon Frederick Fraser (1765-1803). James Fraser of Belladrum died 28 May 1808.

CBs; *SBs*; *BALs*; Stewart, *Sketches*, I-II, *in passim*; *Miscellaneous Correspondence*, II, (August 1758), 867.

John Robertson,* yʳ of Lude, (c.1740-1773)
Lieut: 21 July 1758, 42nd Foot;
Capt-Lt: 23 November 1772, 42nd Foot.

Second son of John Robertson of Lude and Charlotte Murray, daughter of William Murray, 2nd Lord Nairne. Brother of Captain James Robertson of Lude, 77th Foot (see 77th Register) and a kinsman of Major John [Robertson] Reid, 42nd Foot and Captain John Small, 42nd Foot (see both above). Commissioned lieutenant in the 2nd/42nd Foot, summer 1758, and fought in Martinique and Guadeloupe. One of two officers wounded in the fighting on Guadeloupe before being sent with the remnants to Albany for garrison duties winter 1759/60. On his return to Martinique in 1762 with the regiment, he was wounded again storming the ridge known as Morne Tartenson, Martinique on 16 January 1762. One of the few officers to remain in the regiment at the 1763 peace. He participated in the 1764 Muskingum expedition and returned with the regiment to Ireland in 1767. Promoted captain-lieutenant in 1772 and died the following year on 1 May 1773.

CBs; *SBs*; *BALs*; Stewart, *Sketches*, I-II, *in passim*; *Miscellaneous Correspondence*, II, (August 1758), 867.

John Grant (1731-1793)
Lieut: 22 July 1758, 2nd/42nd Foot; exchanged onto half-pay, 24 April 1764;
Capt: 25 September 1778; Royal Garrison Battalion; half-pay, 25 October 1783; full-pay, 13 September 1786, North British Invalid Company; exchanged 13 July 1791, Guernsey Invalid Company.

Born in 1731, the son of the Factor for Ludovic Grant, the Laird of Grant. Commissioned lieutenant in William

Murray's company in the 2nd/42nd Foot, summer 1758, and fought in Martinique and Guadeloupe before being sent with the survivors to Albany for garrison duties winter 1759/60. Participated in the capture of Montréal, 1760. Went to the Caribbean where he served as one of the 42nd's light infantry officers at Martinique and Havana. Out on half-pay in 1763. During the American Revolution, he returned to active duty September 1778 with a provincial corps, the Royal Garrison Battalion. Went out on half-pay in October 1783 but soon secured a captaincy of a North British Invalid Company, no doubt through the influence of the Laird of Grant. Five years later he transferred to the command of the Guernsey Invalid Company. His unpublished memoirs, written in later life, exist in manuscript form at the Alexander Turnbull Museum in Wellington, New Zealand.

CBs; *SBs*; *BALs*; Stewart, *Sketches*, I-II, *in passim*; Miscellaneous Correspondence, II, (August 1758), 867; John Grant, *Journal of John Grant, 2nd Battalion 42nd Regiment, covering service from 1758 to 1761. Register House*, Series RH 4/77 (Microfilm).

George Leslie* (c.1735-1762)

Lieut: 23 July 1758, 2nd/42nd Foot.

Commissioned lieutenant in the 2nd/42nd Foot, summer 1758, and was wounded in the fighting for Marne Tortenson above Fort Royal on Martinique in January 1759. Was sent with the survivors to Albany, New York to recuperate over the winter of 1759/60. On his return to Martinique in 1762, he was wounded a second time, storming the same hill, Morne Tartenson, on 24 January 1762. Died of wounds and fever at Havana, 11 August 1762.

CBs; *SBs*; *BALs*; Stewart, *Sketches*, I-II, *in passim*; Miscellaneous Correspondence, II, (August 1758), 867.

Duncan Campbell,* 2nd Barbreck (*Barr Breac*, later 8th Lochnell) (c.1740-1837)

Ensign: 26 January 1756, 42nd Foot;
Lieut: 23 July 1758, 42nd Foot; half-pay 16 August 1764;
Capt: 14 June 1775, 2nd/84th (RHE); half-pay 2 February 1784;
Major: -
Lt-Col: 30 October 1793, 98th Foot (Argyllshire Highlanders);
Col: 3 March 1796, 98th Foot (Argyllshire Highlanders);
Brigadier: 23 February 1797;
Maj-Gen: 29 April 1802;
Lt-Gen: 25 April 1808;
General: 12 August 1819.

Born in Argyll, grandson of Sir Patrick Campbell, 7th of Lochnell, who commanded one of the original six independent companies of the "Black Watch." Son of Colonel Dugald Campbell of Ballimore, 8th of Lochnell, and the nephew of Major John Campbell of Ballimore, 78th Foot (see 78th Register). His father's and uncle's brother, Colin Campbell of Ballimore, was killed at Culloden, 1746, with the loyal Argyllshire Militia. Went to North America as an ensign with the Second Division and promoted lieutenant after the battle of Ticonderoga, 8 July 1758, "*in room of William Grant, promoted.*" Wounded at Bushy Run, 1763, and exchanged to half-pay in August 1764. On the death of his father in 1765, he became the Laird of Lochnell. During the American Revolution he was commissioned a captain in the 2nd/84th Foot (Royal Highland Emigrants) with whom he served the remainder of the war, exchanging to half-pay February 1784. Nearly a decade later, his kinsman John Campbell, 5th Duke of Argyll, asked him to raise a regiment of 1100 men, the 98th Argyll Highlanders, of which he was appointed Lt-Colonel commandant. Three years later he was appointed its colonel, 3 March 1796. It was subsequently re-numbered the 91st Foot in 1798. He died with the rank of General, 19 April 1837, a military career spanning some 81 years.

CBs; *SBs*; *BALs*; Stewart, *Sketches*, I-II, *in passim*.

Adam [Stewart] Stuart* (c.1740-c.1818)

Lieut: 24 July 1758, 42nd Foot; appointed QM, 5 August 1758, 2nd /42nd Foot; half-pay lieutenant 24 October 1763; resigned QM, 15 March 1764.

Commissioned lieutenant in the 2nd/42nd Foot, summer of 1758 and appointed the battalion QM as well. Fought in Martinique and Guadeloupe the following winter before being sent with the survivors to Albany for the winter of 1759/60. He served during all the major campaigns and was the only surviving QM at Havana. He embarked for Britain in October 1762 and remained there, exchanging to half-pay as a lieutenant retaining his appointment as QM. He resigned the QM position a year later in favour of the Lt-Colonel's son, Charles Graham, 15 February 1764.

CBs; *SBs*; *BALs*; Stewart, *Sketches*, I-II, *in passim*; Miscellaneous Correspondence, II, (August 1758), 867.

Donald Campbell,* (c.1735-1761)

Ensign: 5 May 1756, 42nd Foot;
Lieut: 24 July 1758, 42nd Foot; retired, 13 June 1761.

Born in Taynuilt, Argyll, the son of Donald Campbell, baillie of Muckairn. Promoted lieutenant after the battle of Ticonderoga, 8 July 1758, *"in room of Robert Gray, promoted."* He participated in the capture of Forts Ticonderoga and Crown Point in 1759 and Montréal in 1760. After spending the winter in Montréal 1760-61, he was asked to leave the regiment for non-payment of debts. He resigned 8 March 1761, though the official records state 13 June 1761. On his return to London, an impecunious Campbell turned his hand to forgery. His amateurish attempt to impersonate the well-known Captain Quinton Kennedy of the 44th and pass a false note was detected at the offices of regimental agent, John Calcraft. He was arrested and tried at the Old Bailey on 8 August 1761 with *"falsely forging, and counterfeiting, a certain bill of exchange, with the name Peter Dacey there unto subscribed, for the payment of one hundred pounds; and for publishing the same, with intent to defraud John Calcraft , Esq."* He was found guilty as charged, sentenced to death and hanged 5 October 1761.

CBs; SBs; BALs; Stewart, *Sketches*, I-II, in passim; Richards, *Black Watch*, 54n; *The Proceedings of the Old Bailey,* 16 September 1761, t.17610916-34.

George Grant* (c.1740-1788)
Lieut: 25 July 1758, 42nd Foot; exchanged onto half-pay, 10 December 1768.

Commissioned lieutenant in the 2nd/42nd Foot, summer 1758, and fought in Martinique and Guadeloupe. Sent with the survivors to Albany for garrison duties winter 1759/60. Listed as a participant in peace talks with Shawnee, Delaware and Iroquois Indians at Fort Pitt, 9-10 June 1766. Exchanged out of the regiment onto half-pay in December 1768. He died 10 June 1788.

CBs; *SBs*; *BALs*; Stewart, *Sketches*, I-II, in passim; Croghan to Gage, 15 June 1766, *Gage Papers*, American Series, Vol.52; Reel 10; *Miscellaneous Correspondence*, II, (August 1758), 867.

James McIntosh (c.1738-1763)
Ensign: 10 December 1756, 42nd Foot;
Lieut: 25 July 1758, 42nd Foot.

First gentleman volunteer to be promoted after the regiment arrived in North America. Lord Loudoun's annotation by his name on a list of granted commissions states that McIntosh was *"very uesfull* [sic] *in Recruiting last Spring."* He was involved in a serious quarrel with Ensign George Maclagan (see below) shortly thereafter, in which the latter officer was placed under arrest by Lt.

Colonel Grant. The remainder of the regiment's subalterns sided with McIntosh, refusing to do duty with Maclagan. Maclagan subsequently resigned and was replaced by Peter Grant (see below). Promoted lieutenant after the Battle of Ticonderoga, 8 July 1758, *"in room of George Farquharson, killed."* Participated in all major campaigns of the regiment and was killed at the battle of Bushy Run, 5 August 1763.

CBs; *SBs*; *BALs*; Stewart, *Sketches*, I-II, *in passim*; Pargellis, *MA*, 281.

Robert Robertson*
Lieut: 26 July 1758, 2nd/42nd Foot.

Son of the Laird of Wester Straloch. Commissioned lieutenant in the 2nd /42nd Foot, summer 1758, and fought in Martinique and Guadeloupe. Sent with the survivors to Albany and died in the hospital July 1759.

CBs; *SBs*; *BALs*; Stewart, *Sketches*, I-II, *in passim*; *Miscellaneous Correspondence*, II, (August 1758), 867.

John Smith (1732-1783)
Ensign: 15 May 1757, 42nd Foot;
Lieut: 26 July 1758, 42nd Foot;
Capt-Lt: 14 January 1775, 42nd Foot;
Capt: 14 January 1775, 42nd Foot.
Major: *"by brevet,"* 1783.

John Smith was born in Scotland in 1732 and joined the 42nd Foot as a gentleman volunteer c. 1756 while it was still stationed in Ireland and preparing to go overseas. He was commissioned ensign 15 May 1757 prior to the regiment departing New York for Halifax, Lord Loudoun personally noting on a List of Commissions that he was *"Son of Cornet Smith of MG Cholmondly's"* a cavalry regiment stationed in Ireland. Smith was wounded the following year at the battle of Ticonderoga, 8 July 1758, and two weeks later was promoted to lieutenant *"in room of Lieutenant Hugh Macpherson, killed."* Smith served on all subsequent campaigns of the regiment: Ticonderoga and Crown Point 1759, Montréal 1760, the Caribbean 1762. He was with the remains of his regiment that marched with Bouquet to relieve Fort Pitt and fought at Bushy Run in August 1763. On the downsizing of the 42nd Foot to a peacetime establishment in October 1763, he was retained as one of the more senior and veteran lieutenants of the regiment and was entrusted with the command of Fort Ligonier 25 December 1763-2 March 1764. In the fall of 1764, Smith participated in Bouquet's Muskingum expedition to chastise the Ohio Indians. In 1765, he served as Captain Thomas Stirling's (See above) second-in-command on the expedition down the Illinois to secure Fort de Chartres and its dependencies for the British Crown. On his return from the expedition, Smith was hard-pressed financially, as were his brother officers, but he kept his commission and returned with the 42nd to Ireland in 1767. He was made captain-lieutenant in January 1775 and was promoted captain six months later, August 1775. He died a brevet-major while serving at Paulus Hook, New Jersey, 26 July 1783. His obituary reads:"*New York, July 30, 1783. Last Friday evening died at Powles-Hook, Major John Smith, of the 42d, or Royal Highland Regiment, and on Sunday his remains were interred there with military honours. During a service of twenty-nine years, his conduct as an officer and a gentleman, was uniformly such as acquire him the greatest respect and esteem of that regiment in particular, and of numerous acquaintances, who now sincerely regret the loss of so valuable a friend.*" His tombstone was made from the base of the equestrian statue of King George II pulled down on Bowling Green in New York City. His epitaph reads: "*In Memory of//Major JOHN SMITH//of the//XLII nd or Royal Highland Reg//Who died 25 July 1783//In the 48th year of his Age//This Stone is erected//By the OFFICERS of that Reg//His//Bravery Generosity Humanity//During an honourable service//of 29 Years//Endeared him to the Soldiers//To his Acquaintance & Friends.*" When Jersey City was graded, the slab was removed to a New Jersey residence and used as a stepping stone. In 1874, it was presented to the New-York Historical Society.

CBs; *SBs*; *BALs*; Stewart, *Sketches*, I-II, *in passim*; *Officers of the Black Watch 1725 to 1952*, (Perth, 1952, [revised edition]); *BM*, Add. MSS. 21651: f. 114; Pargellis, *MA*, 362; *Royal Gazette*, New York, Wednesday, July 30, 1783.

Peter Grant (c.1735-1762)
Ensign: 16 May 1757, 42nd Foot;
Lieut: 27 July 1758, 42nd Foot.

A gentleman volunteer carrying arms in the regiment who was assisted by his kinsman, Lt Col. Francis Grant to secure the vacated ensigncy of George Maclagan. A note by Lord Loudoun reads: "*Payed £ 50 to cary Ensign McLagon home who had Sufferd himself to ill use the regt refused to do Duty with him and he resigned his Commission.*" Wounded at Ticonderoga, 8 July 1758. Promoted lieutenant after the Battle of Ticonderoga, 8 July 1758, "*in room of William Baillie, killed.*" Died of wounds at Martinique, 17 April 1762.

CBs; *SBs*; *BALs*; Stewart, *Sketches*, I-II, *in passim*; *Officers of the Black Watch 1725 to 1952*, (Perth, 1952, [revised edition]).

Duncan Stewart, y^r of Derculich (c.1732-1758)
Ensign: 17 July 1757, 42nd Foot;
Lieut: 28 July 1758, 42nd Foot.

Son of Robert Stewart of Derculich and cousin to Ensign Patrick Stewart, yr of Bonskied (see below). One of the three ensigns appointed to the three Additional Companies raised in 1757. Arrived at Fort Edward in time to fight at the battle of Ticonderoga, 8 July 1758. Promoted lieutenant 28 July 1758, "*in room of John Sutherland, killed*" at the battle but died of his own wounds on the day his promotion was published in orders.

CBs; *SBs*; *BALs*; Stewart, *Sketches*, I-II, *in passim*; *Officers of the Black Watch 1725 to 1952*, (Perth, 1952, [revised edition]).

Simon Fraser (c.1735-c.1796)
Ensign: 10 December 1756, 4th/60th Foot (Royal Americans);
Lieut: 28 July 1758, 42nd Foot.

Commissioned ensign initially in the Royal Americans, he transferred to the 42nd Foot on promotion to lieutenant "*in room of Duncan Stewart, discharged dead*" after the battle of Ticonderoga, 8 July 1758. Fraser participated in all major campaigns of the regiment and exchanged to half-pay, 24 October 1763.

CBs; *SBs*; *BALs*; Stewart, *Sketches*, I-II, *in passim*; *Officers of the Black Watch 1725 to 1952*, (Perth, 1952, [revised edition]).

Alexander Farquharson (c.1738-1762)
Ensign: 22 July 1757, 42nd Foot;
Lieut: 29 July 1758, 42nd Foot.

Younger brother of Lt. George Farquharson (see above). One of the three ensigns of the three Additional Companies raised in 1757. Promoted Lieutenant after the battle of Ticonderoga, 8 July 1758, "*in room of Hugh Arnotte, pref'd (80th Foot).*" Died of fever at Havana, 25 July 1762.

CBs; *SBs*; *BALs*; Stewart, *Sketches*, I-II, *in passim*; *Officers of the Black Watch 1725 to 1952*, (Perth, 1952, [revised edition]).

John Campbell,* [6] (c.1740-c.1800)
Lieut: 15 September 1758, 2nd/42nd Foot; half-pay, 24

October 1763; full-pay 25 December 1763; retired 12 July 1773.

Commissioned lieutenant in the 2nd/42nd Foot, summer 1758, and fought in Martinique and Guadeloupe. Sent with the survivors to Albany for garrison duties in the winter of winter 1759/60. Fought in all subsequent campaigns of the regiment including Bushy Run, August 1763. Went out on half-pay 24 October 1763 but was still serving with the regiment as late as summer 1764. Returned to active duty with the regiment 25 December 1765 and returned with the regiment to Ireland in 1767. He retired in 1773.

CBs; *SBs*; *BALs*; Stewart, *Sketches*, I-II, *in passim*; *Officers of the Black Watch 1725 to 1952*, (Perth, 1952, [revised edition]; *Miscellaneous Correspondence*, II, (August 1758), 867.

George Sinclair [2] (1739-c.1800)
Lieut: 30 December 1758; 2nd/42nd Foot; exchanged 26 July 1760 to 85th Foot (Craufurd's *Royal Voluntiers*)
Capt-Lt: 12 February, 1762, 85th Foot (Craufurd's);
Capt: 12 June 1762, 85th Foot; half-pay, 24 May 1763; full-pay, 28 February 1766, 65th Foot;
Major: "in the Army" 29 August 1777;
Lt-Col: "in the Army" 19 February 1783; retired 9 May 1789.

George Sinclair was born in Scotland in 1739 and commissioned lieutenant in the 2nd/42nd Foot, 30 December 1758. He does not appear to have gone to America and exchanged June 1760 to become a lieutenant in the new-raising 85th Foot (Craufurd's *Royal Voluntiers*). He was replaced on the 42nd Foot's officer establishment, 30 July 1760, by Ensign Archibald Campbell [6]. Sinclair was promoted captain-lieutenant in the 85th Foot, 12 February 1762, and captain in the same regiment, 2 June 1762. Exchanged onto half pay, 24 May 1763, and remained there until exchanged to an active service captaincy in the 65th Foot, 28 February 1766. He was made major in the army August 1777 and lieutenant colonel in the army, February 1783. He retired as a captain of the 65th Foot in May 1789.

CBs; *SBs*; *BALs*; Stewart, *Sketches*, I-II, *in passim*; *Miscellaneous Correspondence*, II, (August 1758), 867.

William Brown* (c.1740-c.1793)
Ensign: 16 July 1758, 42nd Foot;
Lieut: 20 March 1759, 42nd Foot; transferred on promotion;
Capt: 9 November 1762, 82nd (Invalid) Foot; exchanged

1771, Hull Invalid Company; transferred, 1775, to Berwick Invalid Company; exchanged, 3 November 1770 to 59th Foot;
Brevet-Major: 29 August 1777;
Brevet Lt.-Col. 19 February 1783.

Joined as an ensign in the newly-raised 2nd Battalion in the summer of 1758 and saw service at Martinique and Guadeloupe 1759. On his return to Martinique in 1762, he was wounded at the storming of Morne Tartenson on 24 January 1762 and invalided back to England where he was promoted and placed in the 82nd Regiment (Invalid) of Foot. He exchanged 1771 into the Hull Invalid Company and was made captain of the new-raising Invalid Company in Berwick-upon-Tweed in 1775. In 1777, he was the Duke of Atholl's choice for the lieutenant-colonelcy of the new-raising 77th Foot during the American Revolution (Atholl Highlander's), and Brown discharged the duties of battalion commander for one month, but Lord Barrington refused to make the appointment official on the ground's that Brown could not be promoted two steps in rank at once. To mollify Captain Brown for his disappointment, the Duke procured for him the Governorship of Upnor Castle and the brevet rank of major "in the Army." Brown returned to active duty three years later with the 59th Foot in November 1779, and was made a brevet lieutenant-colonel in February 1783.

CBs; *SBs*; *BALs*; "List of the Officers of the 42nd or Royal Highland Regiment according to seniority dated December 29th, 1762," *BL* Add. MSS. 21634: f.178c; Stewart, *Sketches*, I-II, *in passim*; *Miscellaneous Correspondence*, II, (August 1758), 867; *MHP*, 71n.

Thomas Fletcher,* of Lindertis (c.1730-1780)
Ensign: 17 July 1758, 2nd/42nd Foot;
Lieut: 1 June 1759; 2nd/42nd Foot; half-pay, 24 October 1763;
Capt: Honorable East India Company Army (HEIC);
Major: HEIC.
Lt-Col: HEIC

Born in Forfar (now Ayrshire). Joined as an ensign in the newly- raised 2nd Battalion in the summer of 1758 and saw service at Martinique and Guadeloupe 1759. Participated in the 1760 capture of Montréal and returned to the Caribbean in 1762. He exchanged to half-pay in 1763 and joined the East India Company's army where he rose to the rank of full Colonel. He was killed in action at the battle of Conjeveram, 10 September 1780, fighting against the overwhelming forces of the Tippo Sultan. His estate of Lindertis was sold the same year to John Wedderburn.

CBs; *SBs*; *BALs*; "List of the Officers of the 42nd or Royal Highland Regiment according to seniority dated December 29th, 1762," *BL* Add. MSS. 21634: f.178c; Stewart, *Sketches*, I-II, *in passim*; *Miscellaneous Correspondence*, II, (August 1758), 867.

John Elliot (1736-c.1790)
Ensign: 22 November 1756, 27th Foot; transferred on promotion;
Lieut: 2 August 1759, 42nd Foot; transferred 14 February 1760, 2nd/1st Foot (The Royal); exchanged to the 1st/1st Foot, 1764; exchanged 2nd/1st Foot; appointed QM, 18 November 1768; retired 6 June 1770.

Born in Ulster in 1736, John Elliot entered the army in 1756 as an ensign in the 27th Foot (Enniskillens) and arrived in North America the summer of 1757. Was wounded at the battle of Ticonderoga, 8 July 1758, and promoted the following year into a vacant lieutenancy in the 2nd/42nd Foot which had just arrived from Guadeloupe; exchanged into the 2nd/1st Foot (The Royal), 14 February 1760, while garrisoning New York. At the peace, he exchanged into the 1st/1st Foot (The Royal) and was appointed QM to the 2nd Battalion on 18 November 1768. He retired, 6 June 1770.

CBs; *SBs*; *BALs*; "List of the Officers of the 42nd or Royal Highland Regiment according to seniority dated December 29th, 1762," *BL* Add. MSS. 21634: f.178c; Stewart, *Sketches*, I-II, *in passim*.

Elbert Herring* (1737-c.1790)
Ensign: 3 April 1758, 42nd Foot;
Lieut: 14 November 1759, 42nd Foot.

Elbert Herring, older brother of Ensign Peter Herring (see below), was born in New York, 7 April 1737. He was one of the original ensigns that came to North America with the regiment and participated in all major campaigns. He was promoted lieutenant, 14 November 1759, "*in room of*" Robert Robertson who died of fever contracted while serving at Guadeloupe. Herring participated in the capture of Montréal 1760 and went with the regiment to the Caribbean in 1762. After the surrender of Havana and the regiment's return to New York in October 1762, he retired, 7 December 1762.

CBs; *SBs*; *BALs*; Stewart, *Sketches*, I-II, *in passim*.

John Leith, of Leith Hall (1731-1763)
Ensign: 27 July 1758, 42nd Foot;
Lieut: 4 December 1759, 42nd Foot; half-pay 24 October 1763.

A gentleman volunteer promoted ensign after the battle of Ticonderoga, 8 July 1758, "*in room of James McIntosh promoted.*" Participated in all campaigns of the regiment and exchanged to half-pay, 24 October 1763. Killed in a duel at Aberdeen, 25 December 1763. His silver mounted powder horn is on display at Leith Hall.

CBs; *SBs*; *BALs*; "List of the Officers of the 42nd or Royal Highland Regiment according to seniority dated December 29th, 1762," *BL*, Add. MSS. 21634: f.178c; Stewart, *Sketches*, I-II, *in passim*.

Archibald Campbell [4] (c.1738-c.1789)
Ensign: 22 November 1756, 1st/1st Foot (The Royal); transferred on promotion;
Lieut: 14 February 1760,

Archibald Campbell was commissioned Ensign in the 1st Battalion of the 1st or Royal Regiment of Foot, 22 November 1756 and became Lieutenant in the 42nd Foot, vice Elliot to 1st Foot, 14 February 1760. He was retained in the reductions of 1763 but exchanged to half-pay on the 77th Foot (Montgomery's) list, 17 March 1764. He is not found in the records after 1789.

CBs; *SBs*; *BALs*; "List of the Officers of the 42nd or Royal Highland Regiment according to seniority dated December 29th, 1762," *BL* Add. MSS. 21634: f.178c.

Alexander Donaldson* (c.1735-1795)
Ensign: 18 July 1758, 2nd/42nd Foot; appointed adjutant, 2nd/42nd Foot, 20 March 1759;
Lieut: 8 May 1760, 42nd Foot; after 1763 served as Lieut. on ensign's pay;
Capt: 31 March 1770, 42nd Foot; transferred on promotion;
Major: 19 December 1777, 76th Foot (Macdonald's Highlanders); retired 10 August 1780.

Joined as an ensign in the newly-raised 2nd/42nd in the summer of 1758 and saw service at Martinique and Guadeloupe, 1759. Served on all major campaigns and, as the experienced adjutant of both the 1st and 2nd battalions of the regiment, talked down mutinous soldiers at Fort Pitt in August 1764 prior to the Muskingum expedition. Was listed as a participant in peace talks with Shawnee, Delaware and Iroquois Indians at Fort

Pitt, 9-10 June, 1766. Married Anne, daughter of Lt. Col. Gordon Graham of Drainie, his commanding officer (see above) in May 1773 and thus became brother-in-law to Charles Graham (see below). After the outbreak of the American Revolution, he was promoted first major of the new raising 76th Foot (Macdonald's Highlanders) in 1777, *"an officer admirably calculated to command and train a body of young Highlanders"* according to Stewart of Garth as he was *"a native of the country and having served nineteen years as adjutant and captain in the 42nd regiment, he had full knowledge of their characteristics and habits."* The newly-designated commanding officer, Lt. Colonel John Macdonell of Lochgarry, a former Fraser Highlander (see 78th Register) had been captured by the Americans at sea while returning from America to Scotland. Donaldson spent a year in command of the regiment at Fort George, but became ill from a growing tumour on his back. Daily command thus passed to the arrogant John Sinclair, Lord Berrisdale. When the ailing Donaldson marched the regiment down to the Lowlands, his Highlanders mutinied over outstanding pay matters and other petty grievances nursed during his absence at a town near Edinburgh. Through his consultations and persuasion the men returned to duty after being promised their bounty money and that they were ***not*** bound for the West Indies. When the 76th sailed for New York, their well-liked, but very ill senior Major remained behind. Shortly afterwards, Donaldson retired 10 August 1780, selling his majority to the Honorable Captain Needham (Lord Kilmory). Died 1795.

CBs; *SBs*; *BALs*; Stewart, *Sketches*, I-II, *in passim*; Croghan to Gage, 15 June 1766, *Clements Library*, Gage Papers, American Series, Vol. 52, Reel 10.

Archibald Campbell, [5] (c.1740-1774)
Ensign: 24 July 1758, 42nd Foot;
Lieut: 26 July 1760, 42nd Foot; half-pay, 24 October 1763.

Probably the younger son of Duncan Campbell, (brother to John Campbell, 2nd of Duneaves) and Janet Robertson. Archibald's older brother, John Campbell [4], commanded the Colonel's company (see above) and Archie probably served in it as a gentleman volunteer until a vacancy occurred. Promoted ensign after the battle of Ticonderoga, 8 July 1758, *"in room of George Rattray, killed"* and subsequently to lieutenant, 26 July 1760, at Fort Ontario to replace the one-armed Alexander MacLean, 2nd/42nd who left to join the 85th Foot in Germany on promotion to captain. Participated in all

campaigns of the 1st/42nd and exchanged to half-pay, 24 October 1763. On his return to Scotland, he married Margaret Small, daughter of Capt. James Small, Factor to the forfeited Robertson estates of Struan, at Edinburgh, 5 February 1764. His eldest son, Archibald, born 12 March 1769, became Major-General Sir Archibald Campbell (1769-1843) and the Lieutenant-Governor of New Brunswick, Canada (1831-37). The father is shown "dd" from the British Army half-pay list 17 December 1774.

SBs; *BALs*; Stewart, *Sketches*, I-II, *in passim*.

Patrick Sinclair* (1736-1820)
Ensign: 21 July 1758, 2nd/42nd Foot;
Lieut: 27 July 1760, 42nd Foot; exchanged, 24 October 1761, 15th Foot (Amherst's);
Capt: 13 April 1772, 15th Foot; half-pay 8 January 1773; full-pay, 1 April 1780, 1st/84th Foot (RHE);
Major: "in the Army," 12 June 1782; half-pay, 1 June 1784;
Lt-Col: "in the Army," 12 October 1793;
Col: "in the Army," 26 January 1797;
Maj-Gen: 25 September 1803;
Lt-Gen: 25 July 1810.

Born 1736, at Lybster, Scotland, the son of Alexander Sinclair and Aemilia Sinclair. He would appear to have had some naval training and sailing experience prior to joining the new-raising 2nd/42nd as an ensign in July 1758. He fought at Martinique and Guadeloupe as part of General Hopson's 1759 expedition and, while at Fort Ontario, Oswego, was promoted lieutenant *"in room of Lt Murray"* July 1760. During the army's descent down the St Lawrence, Sinclair was captain of the snow *Mohawk* at the capture of Fort Levis. He remained detached "on command" with his ship while the 42nd went on to capture and subsequently garrison Montréal 1760-61. He exchanged into the 15th Foot, 24 October 1761, and remained on the lakes until 1767 commanding various vessels. He was the first Briton to sail a ship on Lake Huron and Lake Michigan and was ordered by Colonel John Bradstreet to construct a stockade fort on the Huron River (Port Huron, Michigan) which he was permitted to name Fort Sinclair. He returned with the 15th Foot to England in 1767 and was promoted captain April 1772. He went out on half-pay the following year and returned to his family estate at Lybster in Inverness-shire from whence he lobbied for a job on the Great Lakes in any capacity. His efforts bore fruit, for he was appointed lieutenant-governor and superintendent of Michilimackinac, 7 April 1775, though it took him four years to reach his new post because of the American War of Independence. Once there, Sinclair constructed a new fort, re-located the town and gave large quantities of gifts to the western Indians to keep them loyal. He incurred huge cost overruns, was officially investigated, but cleared of any wrongdoing. During his time there, he purchased a captaincy in the 2nd /84th Foot and went out on half-pay in 1784 and returned to England. On his arrival, his creditors had him thrown into Newgate Prison for debt. After obtaining sufficient funds for his release, he promptly sued Governor Frederick Haldimand for 50,000 pounds to pay off the costs associated with Fort Michilimackinac and won his case. It was a pyrrhic victory however, as he was subsequently impoverished by the hefty legal bills required to clear his name and credit. He retired to Lybster, a half-pay officer, and despite subsequent promotions to lieutenant-colonel (1793), colonel (1797), and major-general (1803), he declared bankruptcy in 1804 and died destitute 30 June 1820, a lieutenant-general (1810) and still drawing a salary as the lieutenant-governor of Michilimackinac.

CBs; SBs; BALs; Stewart, *Sketches*, I-II, *in passim*; "Patrick Sinclair," *DCB*; H.B. Eaton, "*Lieutenant-General Patrick Sinclair: An Account of His Military Career.*" *JSAHR*, Vol. 56 (Autumn, Winter 1978), 128-142, 215-232; 57 (Spring 1979), 45-55.

Lewis Grant [1] (c.1726 -1813)
Ensign: 23 July 1758, 42nd Foot;
Lieut: 29 July 1760; 42nd Foot; retired 24 October 1763.

Third son of Patrick Grant, 4th Rothiemurchus and his second wife, Rachel Grant of Tullochgorm, and younger brother of Captain William Grant (see above). A sergeant in his brother's company, he was promoted ensign after the battle of Ticonderoga, 8 July 1758, "*in room of Patrick Stewart, killed*." Fought in all major campaigns and was promoted lieutenant while at Fort Ontario. Exchanged to half-pay in 1763. Outlived all his brothers, dying at Inverdruie, 19 November 1813, aged 86.

CBs; SBs; BALs; Stewart, *Sketches*, I-II, *in passim*.

Allan Grant (c.1740-1799)
Ensign: 26 July 1758, 42nd Foot;
Lieut: 1 August 1760, 42nd Foot; half-pay, 24 October 1763.

Promoted ensign after the battle of Ticonderoga, 8 July 1758,

"*in room of Donald Campbell promoted.*" Fought in all major campaigns of the regiment. Went out on half-pay 1763.

CBs; SBs; BALs; Stewart, *Sketches*, I-II, *in passim*.

John [Mac] Gregor (c.1725-c.1800)
Sgt-Major: 42nd Foot;
Ensign: 22 July 1758; 42nd Foot;
Lieut: "*in the Army,*" 28 July 1760; 27 August 1760, 42nd Foot; (appointed adjutant, 27 August 1760, resigned 22 October 1761); transferred, 22 October 1761, 60th Foot (Royal Americans); half-pay, 24 October 1763; full pay, 27 August 1777, 42nd Foot;
Capt: 22 March 1780, 2nd/42nd Foot; retired 20 June 1782.

Born 14 December 1732 in Balquhidder, Scotland, the grandson of "Rob Roy" [MacGregor] Campbell and 4th son of Coll [MacGregor] Campbell and Margaret [MacGregor] Campbell of Kerletter. Promoted ensign after the battle of Ticonderoga, 8 July 1758, "*in room of George Campbell, pref'd (80th Foot).*" An experienced soldier, Gregor was promoted lieutenant and appointed adjutant, 27 August 1760, in room of James Grant, but resigned his adjutancy in 22 October 1761, in favour of a kinsman, William [Mac] Gregor. He exchanged to half-pay, 24 October 1763, and returned to Scotland where he married a daughter of John MacAlpin of Edinburgh. On 18 June 1768, he married for a second time in Balquhidder parish, one Catherine Murray. On the outbreak of the American Revolution he returned as a full-pay lieutenant in the 42nd Foot, and before leaving, erected a tombstone to his father Coll [Macgregor] Campbell in the Balquhidder cemetery whereon he styled himself "*Lieut. John Gregory.*" While serving in North America, he was made a captain in the new raising 2nd/42nd on 22 March 1780. He retired 20 June 1782.

CBs; SBs; BALs; Stewart, *Sketches*, I-II, *in passim*.

Archibald McNab (c.1740-1762)
Ensign: 29 July 1758, 42nd Foot;
Lieut: 13 June 1761, 42nd Foot.

Promoted ensign after the battle of Ticonderoga, 8 July 1758, "*in room of*" Peter Grant promoted. Fought at all major campaigns of the regiment. Promoted lieutenant while the regiment was at Crown Point, en route to Staten Island. Died of fever in a New York hospital, 15 October 1762.

CBs; SBs; BALs.

Archibald Campbell [6] (c.1740-1777)

Ensign: 7 April 1758, Roger's Rangers (Burbank's); commissioned 21 July 1758, 42nd Foot;
Lieut: 30 July 1761, 42nd Foot; half-pay, 24 October 1763; full pay, 1770, 26th Foot.

One of eight young gentlemen volunteers of the 42nd sent to Robert Rogers' Ranging School in October 1757. Served as an ensign in Captain Burbank's ranger company. Promoted ensign after the battle of Ticonderoga, 8 July 1758, *"in room of Norman McLeod, pref*[erre]*'d (80th Foot)."* As ranger commissions did not count for seniority in the Army, Campbell's seniority dated to his 42nd commission. Commissioned a lieutenant while both battalions were at Fort Ontario, Oswego preparing for the 1760 expedition against Montréal. He served at Martinique and the siege of Havana in 1762 and exchanged to half-pay on 24 October 1763. He returned to active duty with the 26th Foot (Cameronians) in 1770 and was killed in action at Peekskill, NY, on 17 March 1777.

CBs; SBs; BALs; Stewart, *Sketches,* I-II, *in passim.*

Charles Menzies (c.1740-c.1800)

Ensign: 28 July 1758, 42nd Foot;
Lieut: 8 October 1761, 42nd Foot; half-pay, 24 October 1763; full pay, 15 August 1775, 35th Foot (Fletcher's); transferred on promotion;
Capt: 24 May 1780, 1st/71st (Fraser's Highlanders); retired 22 March 1784.

One of eight young gentlemen volunteers of the 42nd sent to Robert Rogers' Ranging School in October 1757. Promoted ensign after the battle of Ticonderoga, 8 July 1758, *"in room of"* John Smith promoted. Made lieutenant at Staten Island prior to the Caribbean campaign of 1762, and exchanged to half-pay at the peace. Commanded Fort Bedford from April to July 1764 whilst a half-pay officer. He returned to duty with the 35th Foot at the outbreak of the American Revolution in 1775, transferred on promotion to captain into the 71st (Fraser Highlanders) in May 1780. He retired 22 March 1784.

CBs; SBs; BALs; Stewart, *Sketches,* I-II, *in passim;* "Return of Officers who commanded at Fort Bedford," *BL,* Add. MSS. 21651, f.109.

Burke Bingham (c.1738-c.1790)

Ensign: 27 April 1756, 28th Foot (Bragg's); transferred on promotion;
Lieut: 24 October 1761, 42nd Foot; exchanged 24 April 1762, 48th Foot; retired 21 June 1764.

Came to North America as an ensign in the 28th Foot and fought at the battle of the Plains of Abraham, 13 September 1759 and Sillery, 28 April 1760; went to the Staten Island in the fall of 1761 where forces were marshaled for General Monckton's 1762 expedition against Martinique. Transferred to the 42nd on promotion to lieutenant *"in room of"* Patrick Sinclair. He served at the capture of Martinique, 1762, then exchanged to the 48th Foot in April 1762. He resigned, 21 June 1764.

CBs; SBs; BALs; Stewart, *Sketches,* I-II, *in passim.*

Neil McLean* (c.1740-c.1800)

Ensign: 15 September 1758, 42nd Foot;
Lieut: 14 February 1762, 42nd Foot; half-pay 24 October 1763; full-pay, 19 January 1771, 21st Foot (Royal North British Fuzileers); transferred on promotion;
Capt-Lt: 10 August 1777, 9th Foot;
Capt: 11 August 1778, 9th Foot; retired 21 January 1784.

Commissioned an ensign in the new-raising 2nd/42nd, Maclean replaced the no-show James McDuff and fought at Martinique and Guadeloupe in 1759. He took part in the capture of Montréal, 1760 and, in 1762, returned to Martinique where he was promoted lieutenant *"in room of Alexander Turnbull promoted."* He exchanged to half-pay 24 October 1763 and returned to active duty with the 21st Foot (Royal North British Fuzileers) in 1771. In 1777 he transferred to the 9th Foot on promotion to captain-lieutenant, and was promoted the following year to captain. He retired at the peace in 1784.

CBs; SBs; BALs; Stewart, *Sketches,* I-II, *in passim;*

John Fraser (c.1735-c.1795)

Sgt: 48th Foot;
Ensign: 10 March 1760, 48th Foot;
Lieut: 25 March 1762, 42nd Foot; exchanged 9 August 1762, back to 48th Foot;
Capt: 12 December 1770, 48th Foot; retired 30 April 1771.

Sergeant John Fraser of the 48th Foot was appointed an ensign in his regiment, *"having distinguished himself in the field"* as a light infantry soldier in the irregular winter warfare that raged at Québec 1759-60. Fraser had been recommended by his colonel as *"qualified in every respect, to act up to the dignity of an Officer."* He transferred from the 48th to the 42nd Foot on promotion to lieutenant after the capture of Martinique, March 1762. Served only four months as a lieutenant in the 42nd, then exchanged back to his old regiment at Havana in August. In 1770, he was promoted captain in the 48th and retired the following year.

CBs; SBs; BALs; Stewart, *Sketches*, I-II, *in passim*; Knox's *Journal*, II, 357.

Daniel Robertson* (c.1733-1810)
Surgeon's Mate: April 1754, 42nd Foot;
Ensign: 26 July 1760, 42nd Foot;
Lieut: 29 April 1762, 42nd Foot; on half-pay, 24 October 1763;
Capt-Lt: 14 June 1775, 1st/84th Foot (Royal Highland Emigrants); half-pay 1 June 1784; appointed Fort-Major of Mackinac 1782-87;
Capt: 27 February 1776, 84th (RHE); half-pay, 1 June 1784; full-pay, 27 February 1793, 60th Foot;
Major: *"in the Army,"* 18 November 1790;
Lt-Col: *"in the Army,"* 1 March 1794;
Col: *"in the Army,"* 1 January 1798.

Born in Dunkeld, Scotland, c.1733. Enlisted as a surgeon's mate in the 42nd in 1754 and came to North America with the First Division aboard the transport *Charleston*. Commissioned an ensign in Montréal, he participated in all the campaigns of the regiment. While garrisoned at Montréal, he married the 19 year-old Marie-Louise Reaume, widow of Joseph Fournerie de Vezon and thus gained entry into one of the most prominent French Canadian families involved in the fur trade. Married life was short as he was sent to the Caribbean in 1761-62, and also fought at Bushy Run in August 1763. As a junior lieutenant, he went out on half-pay in October 1763 and returned to Montréal where he soon rose to social prominence as a local magistrate, medical practitioner, and land owner. Between 1763 and 1773, Robertson fathered six children, two of whom died in infancy. His wife died in 1773. With the outbreak of the Revolution he was appointed a major in the Montréal militia but was soon offered the captain-lieutenancy in the 1st/84th Foot (Royal Highland Emigrants) summer 1775. He enlisted a company of ex-Fraser Highlanders, Montgomery Highlanders and Black Watch soldiers and was ordered to garrison Fort St. John's on the Richelieu River guarding the approaches to Montréal. Besieged by American general Richard Montgomery, a fellow Scot and former captain in the 17th Foot, the fort surrendered on 3 November

1776 and Robertson was taken to Connecticut as a prisoner of war, but exchanged the following year. In September 1779, he was appointed commandant of the small post at Oswegatchie (Ogdensburg, NY) and supervised Indian raids from there on the Mohawk Valley. In 1782, he was handpicked by Governor General Haldimand to be commandant of Fort Mackinac at Michilimackinac and assumed command on 18 September. He oversaw the completion of the fort which experienced costly overruns under Capt. Patrick Sinclair, a former brother officer (see above). Robertson was placed on half-pay in 1784 while still the commandant and was relieved 1787. Robertson returned to Montréal and between 1787 and 1806 amassed over 5000 acres of land near Chatham Township on the east bank of the Ottawa River by purchasing the grants of disbanded soldiers of the 84th Foot. He worked to attract settlers and develop his properties and, by 1804, had established 43 families in the Argenteuil region of Québec. Promoted "Major in the Army" in 1790 and "Colonel in the Army" by 1 January 1798. During this period he switched from half-pay of the 84th to half-pay of the 60th Foot (Royal Americans). His social prominence also increased with his election as an honorary member of the prestigious Beaver Club of Montréal in 1793, and his appointments as justice of the peace in 1799 and school commissioner in 1805. By 1804 he was colonel of the Argenteuil battalion of militia. He died in Montréal on 5 April 1810 at the age of 77.

CBs; SBs; BALs; Stewart, *Sketches*, I-II, *in passim*; "Daniel Robertson," *DCB*.

John McIntosh (c.1735-c.1790)
Ensign: 4 December 1759; 42nd Foot;
Lieutenant, 15 May 1762; 42nd Foot; adjutant, 2 November 1768;
Capt-Lt: 16 August 1775; 42nd Foot; resigned adjutancy, 20 March 1776;
Captain: 5 October 1777, 42nd Foot; retired, 20 September 1779.

A gentleman volunteer promoted from the ranks while the regiment was in winter quarters at Fort Edward. McIntosh served in all major campaigns of the regiment and was promoted lieutenant May 1762 after the capture of Martinique and before the siege of Havana. He fought at Bushy Run, 1763 and was with the 1764 Muskingum expedition to subdue the Ohio Indians. He returned with the regiment to Ireland in 1767 and was appointed the adjutant the following year for the next eight years. He was promoted to command the

Colonel's company as captain-lieutenant and resigned his adjutancy the following year in March 1776. After the regiment arrived for service in America, he was promoted captain October 1777. Wounded at the battle of Harlem Heights on 16 September 1776, McIntosh retired prematurely on 20 September 1779 following Lt-Colonel Stirling's refusal to grant him leave to return to Scotland to take care of his personal affairs.

CBs; SBs; BALs; Stewart, *Sketches,* I-II, *in passim;* Clinton's General Orders 9/22/79.

Alexander [Mac] Gregor (c.1735-1762)
Ensign: 5 December 1759, 42nd Foot;
Lieut: 4 June 1762, 42nd Foot.

A gentleman volunteer promoted from the ranks while the regiment was in winter quarters in upstate NY. He participated in the capture of Montréal 1760 and was promoted lieutenant at the siege of Havana, June 1762. He died of fever four months later in a New York hospital, 1 October 1762.

CBs; SBs; BALs; Stewart, *Sketches,* I-II, *in passim.*

James Eddington (1739-1802)
Ensign: 2 March 1757, 1st/1st Foot (The Royal); exchanged 1757, 2nd/1st Foot; transferred on promotion;
Lieut: 9 July 1762, 42nd Foot; resigned 10 February 1770;
Capt: Honorable East India Company Army, (HEIC);
Major: HEIC;
Lt-Col: HEIC.

Commissioned ensign in the 1st/1st Foot (The Royal) 2 March 1757 and exchanged the same year into the 2nd Battalion of the Royal destined for North America service. He fought at Louisburg, 1758 and accompanied his regiment on Amherst's 1759 expedition to take Ticonderoga and Crown Point. He was wounded at the battle of Etchoe in Col Montgomery's 1760 campaign against the Cherokees in the Carolinas. He was gazetted lieutenant July 1762 in the 42nd at Havana *"in room of Robert Menzies promoted"* and, by 1765, was in command at Fort Loudoun. He was handpicked as one of four officers suitable for the Stirling Expedition in 1765, sent to take possession of Fort de Chartres in the Illinois country. Eddington returned with the Royal Highland Regiment to Ireland in 1767, but left the British army, 10 February 1770 to start a second military career in the service of the Honorable East India Company army. He rose to the rank of lieutenant-colonel and died in 1802.

CBs; SBs; BALs; Stewart, *Sketches,* I-II, *in passim;* "Edington" WO 34/47: ff. 17-18; "Eidingtoun" WO 25/209; WO 25/209: f. 159; "The Towns of Windham County," *Vermont Historical Gazetteer,* Vol. V, (Brandon, 1891).

George Campbell [1] (c.1730-1769)
Ensign: 8 May 1759, 42nd Foot;
Lieut: 24 July 1762, 42nd Foot; half-pay 24 October 1763; full-pay, 4 May 1767, 30th Foot.
Lieut: HEIC
Capt.: HEIC
Lt. Col.: King's American Regiment, 7 June 1777;
Half pay: 10 October 1783;
Colonel in the army, 12 October 1793;
Major General, 25 October 1795.

Second son of Lauchlan Campbell of Islay, and Martha (or Murella) Campbell. His father was the well-known Campbell laird who was promised 1000 acres in New York colony for every Highland family he brought over from Scotland in 1737, with the caveat that land would not be granted until they were physically on the ground. Campbell paid for the transportation of over 83 families, a total of 423 persons, but Governor Clarke reneged on his pledge and Campbell was left virtually destitute. The father returned to Scotland during the '45 and commanded a company of Argyllshire Militia and returned to America in 1747 where he died shortly afterwards. Donald, the eldest of his three sons, petitioned Lord Loudoun for some assistance on the latter's arrival in 1756 as Commander-in-Chief, the result being all three sons eventually obtained commissions in the British army ; Donald (60th Foot); James (48th Foot) and George (42nd). In 1763, 10,000 acres were granted to the three brothers in the present township of Greenwich, Washington County, NY. George, the second eldest of the three brothers was last to be commissioned and came across from an ensigncy in Roger's Rangers into the 42nd at Fort Edward, his seniority in the British army dating from 8 May 1760. He was promoted lieutenant at the siege of Havana in July 1762 *"in room of James Gray promoted."* He exchanged to half-pay 24 October 1763, but returned to active duty on 4 May 1767 as a lieutenant with the 30th Foot (Lord Loudoun's) at Gibraltar and retired two years later at Gibraltar, 26 May 1769. He then entered the service of the Honourable East India Company and was commissioned Lieutenant in the 1st Sepoy Regiment, Madras Infantry,

7 or 17 July 1770 [Sir Duncan Campbell has his commission as Ensign on 7 July, but as George Campbell had already held a commission as a Lieutenant, it would seem logical for him to have been commissioned at that same rank]. George Campbell may have been made Captain, 1st Sepoy Regiment, Madras Infantry, 26 April 1777. When the American War for Independence broke out in 1775, Campbell left India and returned to America. He was appointed Lieutenant Colonel of the King's American Regiment, 7 June 1777. On 25 December 1782, the KAR was placed on the strength of the regular Army as the Fourth American Regiment. The KAR was shipped to Saint John Nova Scotia [now New Brunswick] where after land grants were distributed, it was disbanded, 10 October 1783. Campbell returned to India. While on half-pay, Campbell was promoted Colonel in the army, 12 October 1793, and Major General, 25 October 1795. He died at Madras, 5 June 1799, aged 63 while still on the half pay of the King's American Regiment of Foot and was buried in St. Marys Cemetery, Fort St. George.

CBs; SBs; BALs. Todd Braisted and Nan Cole.

Thomas Cunnison (c.1740-1762)
Ensign: 6 February 1759, 42nd Foot;
Lieut: 17 April 1762, 42nd Foot.

A gentleman volunteer with the 2nd/42nd Foot at Martinique and Guadeloupe, he was promoted ensign 6 February 1759 *"in room of William McLean killed."* He participated in the capture of Montréal 1760 and was promoted lieutenant after the capture of Martinique 1762 *"in room of Peter Grant, discharged dead."* Died of fever at Havana, 26 July 1762.

CBs; SBs; BALs.

Archibald Cameron (c.1738-c.1795)
Ensign: 9 July 1760, 15th Foot; 1761, 28th Foot
Lieut: 25 July 1762, 42nd Foot; half-pay, 24 October 1763; full-pay, 26 December 1770, 2nd /1st Foot (The Royal); Irish half-pay, 3 March 1772.

A gentleman volunteer who came over originally with the 78th Foot (Fraser's Highlanders) and distinguished himself during the fighting at the battle of Sillery, 28 April 1760. Promoted ensign into the 15th Foot (Amherst's) on the recommendation of General James Murray. He exchanged into the 28th Foot (Braggs) the following year and went with that regiment to fight in

the Caribbean. He transferred to the 42nd on promotion to lieutenant at Havana *"in room of Alexander Farquharson, dd"* and went out on half-pay at the 1763 peace. He returned to active duty as a lieutenant in December 1770 with the 2nd/1st Foot but went out two years later on Irish half-pay, 3 March 1772.

CBs; SBs; BALs.

Thomas Keating (c.1740-1797)
Ensign: 1 November 1761, 2nd/1st Foot (The Royal); transferred on promotion;
Lieut: 26 July 1762, 42nd Foot; half-pay 24 October 1763;
Capt: -
Major: *"in the Army,"* 23 April 1783;
Col: 12 October 1779; half-pay, as Lt-colonel, 27 April 1783.

Commissioned ensign in the 1st/1st Foot. The same year, he transferred to the 2nd Battalion of the Royal, earmarked for North American service. He fought at Louisburg, 1758, and accompanied his regiment on Amherst's 1759 expedition to take Ticonderoga and Crown Point. He transferred to the 42nd on promotion to lieutenant in July 1762 at Havana and exchanged to half-pay at the peace. He returned to active service during the American Revolution as the Colonel of the 88th Foot, a special unit raised in October 1779 in Worcestershire to garrison Jamaica. Keating's rank was temporary only and when his unit was disbanded he was placed on lieutenant-colonel's half pay. He died in 1797 with the rank of lieutenant-colonel *"in the Army."*

CBs; SBs; BALs; Stewart, *Sketches,* I-II, *in passim.*

John Charles St. Clair (c.1740-1762)
Ensign: 30 July 1758, 42nd Foot;
Lieut: 15 January 1762, 42nd Foot.

A gentleman volunteer promoted ensign after the battle of Ticonderoga *"in room of"* Alexander Farquharson promoted. He was promoted lieutenant *"in room of"* David Barclay who was killed 24 January 1762. St. Clair died four months later of fever at sea off of Martinique, 15 May 1762.

CBs; SBs; BALs; Stewart, *Sketches,* I-II, *in passim.*

Nathaniel McCulloch (c.1735-1771)
Ensign: 23 July 1759, 42nd Foot;
Lieut: 2 August 1762, 42nd Foot.

A gentleman volunteer promoted from the ranks at Lake George Camp, NY, "*in room of Phineas Macpherson, discharged dead.*" Participated in the Caribbean campaigns in 1762 and fought at the battle of Bushy Run August 1763. On 25 May 1764, as the 42nd prepared to march westwards on the Muskingum expedition, Lt-Colonel John Reid informed Bouquet that "*Lieut McCullack chuses to serve the Campaign, in hopes that something might turn out to his Advantage, and will act as Qr Master to the Regiment.*" McCulloch's services were rewarded with a return to active duty, his seniority in the regiment dated 16 August 1764. He was commandant at Fort Bedford the winter of 1764/65. He was granted 2000 acres in Hebron, Washington County, NY, on 3 May 1765 but never appears to have taken up residence there. He returned with the regiment to Ireland in 1767 and died there, 16 December 1771.

CBs; SBs; BALs; Stewart, *Sketches*, I-II, *in passim;* "Return of Officers who commanded at Fort Bedford," *BL*, Add. MSS. 21651, f.109.

John Sutherland [2] (c.1740-1762)
Ensign: 27 July 1760; 42nd Foot;
Lieut: 8 August 1762; 42nd Foot; dd 9 September 1762.

A gentleman volunteer promoted while the regiment was encamped at Oswego prior to the Montréal campaign, 1760. Promoted lieutenant at the siege of Havana but died a few weeks later of fever on a hospital ship.

CBs; SBs; BALs; Stewart, *Sketches*, I-II, *in passim.*

Charles Grant (c.1738-c.1800)
Ensign: 28 July 1759, 42nd Foot;
Lieut: 8 August 1762, 42nd Foot;
Capt: 20 March 1776, 42nd Foot; retired, 26 August 1785.

A gentleman volunteer, initially "carrying arms" with the 77th Foot (Montgomery's), under the protection of Major James Grant. He was captured by the French at Fort Duquesne, September 1758 along with his patron, and exchanged the following year. Major Grant secured an ensigncy for him in the 2nd/42nd which wintered at Albany, NY, 1759-60. He participated in the capture of Montréal the following year, Martinique in 1762 and was promoted lieutenant at Havana in August 1762. Instead of going out on half-pay, he reverted to the rank of ensign but retained his seniority as lieutenant and participated in the 1764 expedition to Muskingum

under Bouquet. He returned with the regiment to Ireland in 1767 and was promoted captain nine years later, March 1776. In 1780, during the American Revolution, he married an American named Miss Hunt, an event frowned on by at least one brother officer, John Peebles (see below). He retired five years later in August 1785.

CBs; SBs; BALs.

Ann Gordon (c. 1737-1787)
Ensign: 3 February 1757, 46th Foot; transferred on promotion;
Lieut: 16 August 1762, 42nd Foot; half-pay, 24 October 1763.

Ann Gordon was son of Adam Gordon of Dalpholly, Sutherland, and brother to Sir William Gordon, B^t of Invergordon married to Helen Gray, daughter of Robert Gray, 5th of Skibo. He was a brother-in-law to Capt-Lt. Robert Gray, 42nd Foot (see above). "Master Ann ," according to the 1743 Kirk sessions of Golspie, "*was accused by two girls in the parish as having fathered their pregnancies, and unable to deny the charges and unwilling to submit to church censure he fled from the country.*" He was commissioned an ensign in the 46th Foot and transferred on promotion into the 42nd at Havana. He was wounded at Ticonderoga, 8 July 1758, the following year at the siege of Niagara, 1759 and yet again at Bushy Run, 5 August 1763. He summed up his own career in a 16 December 1763 letter to Bouquet begging to be excused to go down country from Fort Bedford as he was already on half-pay and had urgent personal business in Albany: "*I have been very unlucky in the Services, my Commission Cost me dear & have Sustain'd losses since in this Country to the amount of 200 pounds S^{tg} by Ship Wreck. Having Spent a good deal of my Youth in the Service, & being in one of the unlucky Corps for Justice in their Promotion, have serv'd five years an Ensign in this Country & now a reduc'd Lieut$^{t.}$ After Seven Years Service in North America, with almost the loss of a limb.*" By 1775, the half-pay Gordon was living at St. Sulpice, near Montréal and contracted cancer of the face. He returned to Britain on two occasions in an effort to find a cure, but was unsuccessful and died 22 August 1787 in Canada, "*a blind and a shocking spectacle.*"

CBs; SBs; BALs; 1743 Kirk Session Records of Golspie in Grant, *Golspie's Story*, (Golspie, 1983).

Samuel Steele (c.1742-c.1810)
Ensign: 30 July 1760, 42nd Foot;
Lieut: 17 August 1762, 42nd Foot; half-pay 24 October

1763; full-pay, 23 February 1765, 34th Foot;
Capt: 1 January 1777, 34th Foot;
Major: 18 November 1790, "in the Army"; retired, 3 September 1792.

A gentleman volunteer from the 80th Foot (Gage's) promoted ensign in the 2nd/42nd while preparing for the expedition against Montréal in 1760. He served at the capture of Montréal, September 1760 and, subsequently, at Martinique in January 1762. Whilst recovering from fever in New York in July 1762, Steel was made ensign to the composite company of "*recover'd men*" formed under the command of Captain Charles Macdonell *Glengarry*, 78th Foot, and sent with Col. William Amherst's expedition to retake St John's, Newfoundland from the French. He distinguished himself for bravery and leadership at the dawn assault on Flagstaff Hill (Signal Hill) on 13 September 1762, taking over command of the company when all other senior officers became casualties. He exchanged to half-pay in October 1763 but returned to active duty in 1765 as a lieutenant in the 34th Foot (Cavendish's) stationed in Western Florida and at Fort de Chartres in the Illinois country. He returned with the regiment to Ireland in 1767 and was promoted captain-lieutenant nine years later in March 1776, and became a full captain the following year. The 34th were dispatched to serve in Québec, Canada, during the American Revolution and Captain Samuel Steele appears briefly as commandant at Fort Chambly on the Richelieu River writing to Governor Frederick Haldimand on 22 September 1782. His regiment remained in Canada until 1787 before returning home. Breveted a major "*in the Army*" in 1790, Steele retired two years later on 3 September 1792. Of interest to Canadian readers, his grand nephew and namesake, Major General Sir "Sam" Steele, was famous as a senior officer of the Royal Canadian Mounted Police, the first commanding officer of Lord Strathcona's Horse , and a divisional commander in World War One.

CBs; SBs; BALs; "Elmes Steele" and "Samuel Benfield Steele" in *DCB*.

William Grant [2] (c.1740-1763?)
Ensign: 14 February 1760, 42nd Foot;
Lieut: 22 October 1762, 42nd Foot.

A gentleman volunteer promoted while the regiment was stationed at Fort Edward and its dependencies. Participated in the capture of Montréal 1760 and went with the regiment to the Caribbean in 1762. Was promoted lieutenant "*in room of*" James Campbell leaving the regiment in New York, 22 October 1763. He may have died soon after for he is not shown in the 1763 BAL.

CBs; SBs; BALs.

James Douglas (c.1740-1762)
Ensign: 31 July 1760, 42nd Foot;
Lieut: 21 August 1762, 42nd Foot.

A gentleman volunteer commissioned ensign while the regiment prepared for the 1760 campaign against Montréal at Oswego summer 1760. Participated in the capture of Montréal, 1760, and Martinique, 1762. Promoted lieutenant at the siege of Havana, 1762, and died in hospital at New York, 15 September 1762.

CBs; SBs; BALs.

Thomas Scott (c.1742-c.1811)
Ensign: 16 September 1760, 42nd Foot;
Lieut: 9 September 1762, 42nd Foot.

A gentleman volunteer commissioned ensign at Montréal "*in room of*" William McIntosh transferring to Keith's Highlanders. He was promoted lieutenant "*in room of John Sutherland, discharged dead*" at Havana in September 1762, and exchanged to half-pay in October 1763. His last appearance in the half pay list in the printed Army Listis in 1811.

CBs; SBs; BALs.

Charles Graham, y^r of Drainie, (c.1742-1800)
Ensign: 17 September 1760, 42nd Foot;
Lieut: 10 September 1762, 42nd Foot; appointed QM 15 February 1764; resigned 3 September 1766;
Capt: 7 September 1771; 42nd Foot;
Major: 25 August 1778; 42nd Foot;
Lt.-Col: 28 April 1782, 42nd Foot;
Col: "*in America,*" 10 November 1790; "in the Army," 12 October 1793; appointed Colonel 5th West Indies Regiment, 30 November 1796-6 August 1800;
Maj Gen: 26 February 1795.

Son of Lt-Col. Gordon Graham of Drainie (see above), commissioned ensign after the capture of Montréal, 1760. Fought in the Caribbean, 1762 and stayed in the regiment after it downsized to a peace establishment.

Despite his appointment to QM, 15 February 1764, he did not serve in that capacity for the 1764 expedition to the Muskingum commanded by Colonel Henry Bouquet. Instead it was performed by half-pay lieutenant Nathaniel McCulloch, which would indicate that Graham was home on leave with his father in 1764. He resigned as QM, 3 September 1766, in Philadelphia, and returned to Ireland in 1767 with the regiment. Appointed to command the grenadier company in August 1776, he was made major of the regiment in August 1778 and immediately re-assigned as the major to the 2nd Battalion of British Grenadiers. He replaced Thomas Stirling as the commanding officer in 1782 and took the regiment to Halifax, Nova Scotia in 1783 where it remained in garrison for the next three years. In 1787, the regiment went to Cape Breton Island and sent two companies to Prince Edward Island. By 1790, he was brevetted a colonel *"in America"* and by 1793, *"in the Army."* He was appointed a brigadier for Sir Ralph Abercromby's expedition against the French and Dutch possessions in the West Indies in September 1794 and promoted major-general the following year. He was appointed Colonel of the 5th West Indies Regiment in November 1796 and was the temporary commander-in-chief at St Vincent from September 1796 to March 1797 in Abercromby's absence. Died in the West Indies, August 1800.

CBs; *SBs*; *BALs*; Stewart, *Sketches*, I-II, *in passim*.

Henry Timberlake (1730-65)
Ensign: 1756, 2nd Battalion, Virginia Regiment;
Lieut: 14 October 1762, 42nd Foot; half-pay, 24 October 1763.

Colonial journalist and cartographer, Henry Timberlake was born in Virginia in 1730 and died in England on September 30, 1765. He joined Virginia's provincial regiment in 1756 and served in several campaigns during the French and Indian War. In November 1761, the Cherokees concluded a truce with Lt Col James Grant who had burned the Middle Towns before Timberlake's provincial battalion could mount their own attack against the Overhill settlements from the north-east. At the peace negotiations, one of the Cherokee chiefs requested that an officer journey to the Cherokee villages on the Little Tennessee River to explain the treaty and provide assurances that the colonists intended to honor it. Ensign Henry Timberlake of the Virginia Regiment volunteered to go. After a twenty-three-day journey down the Holston River, Timberlake presented the

provisions of the peace treaty to Cherokee leaders gathered in the Chota council house. He also visited Citico and Chilhowee, where he was welcomed with considerable celebration and respect. Timberlake left the Overhill country in early March 1762, reach Williamsburg in April. In May he escorted three distinguished Cherokee leaders, including Ostenaco, to London, where they stayed until August. Two months later, at the request of Lord Egremont, Timberlake was promoted lieutenant in the 42nd Foot on 14 October 1762 without purchase as a reward for his services. He never joined the regiment and, a year later, exchanged to half-pay. Timberlake's primary legacy is the journal he kept while living with the Cherokees 1761-62. Published in 1765, the year of his death, the volume contained a thorough and detailed account of eighteenth-century Cherokee life and became a basis for all subsequent anthropological and historical studies of eighteenth-century Cherokees. Timberlake's map, entitled *"A Draught of the Cherokee Country,"* accurately depicted all the Cherokee villages on the lower Little Tennessee River and provided important demographic information about village sizes, populations, and leaders. The journal, simply entitled *Memoirs*, and his map of the Overhill Cherokee country have been reprinted several times.

CBs; *SBs*; *BALs*; Stewart, *Sketches*, I-II, *in passim*; Richards, *Black Watch*, *in passim*; Amherst to Fauquier, 18 October 1762, WO 34/37: f. 269; Samuel C. Williams, ed., Lieutenant Henry Timberlake's *Memoirs*, 1756-1765, (1927).

Alexander Graham (c.1740-c.1785)
Ensign: 29 April 1762, 42nd Foot;
Lieut: 7 December 1762, 42nd Foot; half-pay, 24 October 1763.

A gentleman volunteer commissioned ensign after the capture of Martinique, April 1762, *"in room of Daniel Robertson, promoted."* A few months later he was promoted lieutenant *"in room of Elbert Herring, resigned."* He never joined the regiment in America and exchanged to half-pay, 24 October 1763 while still in Scotland.

CBs; *SBs*; *BALs*; Stewart, *Sketches*, I-II, *in passim*; Richards, *Black Watch*, *in passim*.

James [John] Dow (c. 1725-c.1800)
Ensign: 4 May 1757, 60th Foot (Royal Americans);
Lieut: 24 May 1758, 60th Foot; appointed QM 1st/60th 22 October 1758; resigned QM 24 August 1763; half-pay,

24 August 1763; full-pay, 16 March 1764, 42nd Foot; resigned 13 December 1765.

Was noted by Lord Loudoun in his "List of Commissions" as having "*caryed armes*" and being "*recommended by Lt Col Holden*." Commissioned ensign in the 60th Foot (Royal Americans) in May 1757 and was promoted lieutenant the following year in May 1758. His son Archibald Dow was also a lieutenant in the regiment. James (who periodically appears as "John Dowe" in the BALs) was appointed QM of the 1st/60th Foot, a post he held until his resignation in 1763. He was "*Dangerously Wounded*" at the battle of Bushy Run, 1763 and was sent to Philadelphia to recuperate. Out on half-pay officially on 24 August 1763, his friend Bouquet ensured he was taken on strength of the 42nd Foot, his seniority dated 16 March 1764. By summer 1764 he had recovered enough from his wound to attend to battalion business at Niagara where he was enlisted by Col John Bradstreet as a QM to his expedition west. Dow wrote to Bouquet from Sandusky Bay in October 1764 that he had "*been Uneasie that ever I had the misfortune to leave you, and my worthey old Corps, with whom I lived so long in good Freindship*." Ensign Christie reported to Bouquet in January 1765 that he "*was Relieved from Fort Brewington the 17th December last by Lieut Dow of the 42d Regiment, and Arrived here with my garrison, the first Instant*." Dow retired the following winter, 13 December 1765.

CBs; *SBs*; *BALs*; BL, Add. MSS. 21651:ff.19 &134; Pargellis, *MA*, 365.

George Rigge (c.1740-1782)

Ensign: 6 October 1757, 2nd/33rd Foot (renumbered 72nd Foot in 1758);
Lieut: 19 December 1759, 72nd Foot; exchanged 9 January 1760, 86th Foot; half-pay 19 October 1763; full pay, 2 April 1764, 42nd Foot; half-pay, 20 February 1767; full-pay, 6 October 1779, Captain Aylward's Jersey Invalid Company; half-pay 14 March 1781.

Served in several regiments before coming off half-pay at the end of the Seven Year's War to join the 42nd on garrison duty in western Pennsylvania. He served at Fort Pitt for two years and went out on half-pay when the regiment returned to Ireland in 1767. He returned to active duty in 1779 as a lieutenant in a Jersey Invalid Company during the American Revolution but retired in 1781 and was dead the following year.

CBs; *SBs*; *BALs*.

James Rumsey (c.1740-c.1800)

Lieut: 4 February 1762, Independent Company of Free Negroes; 28 July 1762, 77th Foot; half-pay, 24 December 1763; full-pay (ensign's), 17 March 1764, 42nd Foot; retired 27 August 1766.

Served during the Seven Years War as an officer in an Independent Company of Free Negroes and with the 77th (Montgomery Highlanders) before going out on half-pay 24 December 1763. He returned to active service with the 42nd Foot as a lieutenant on ensign's pay, but with seniority as a lieutenant dated 17 March 1764. He arrived from New York in time to participate on the 1764 Muskingum expedition against the Ohio Indians. The following year he served as the commissary or supply officer for 1765-66 Stirling expedition down the Ohio and Mississippi to take possession of the French forts in the Illinois country. When the expedition finally straggled into New York the summer of 1766, Rumsey retired on 27 August 1766, "*drowned in debt*" and "*obliged to sell out*" according to his commanding officer, Thomas Stirling. His Illinois experience however soon landed him a job and with the trading firm of Baynton, Wharton, and Morgan, [BWM] in Philadelphia and he returned to the Illinois country in 1766 in the capacity of assistant to Morgan. However, difficulties with the military, growing competition from other traders, and charges of unscrupulous business practices brought about a decline in BWM's fortunes by 1767, and the partners went into voluntary receivership with their creditors administering the business. By 1768, Rumsey was putting down his own roots as a merchant. Captain Gordon Forbes, 34th Foot, commanding at Fort de Chartres, reported to General Gage in June 1768 that he had "*given leave to one Mr. Rumsey, Late a Lieutenant in the 42d Regiment (who has the honour of being known to your Excellency) to settle upon a Spot of Ground near Kasakaskies; it has been forfeited to the King ever Since we have been in possession of this Country*." James Rumsey managed affairs for the Illinois branch of BWM during Morgan's leave of absence in 1770 and, although he was a friend of Morgan, he soon left the company to become the fort's commissary as well as the secretary to Lieutenant Colonel John Wilkins, commanding officer of the 18th Foot headquartered at Fort de Chartres.

CBs; *SBs*; *BALs*; Gordon Forbes to Gage, Fort Chartres, June 23, 1768, *Gage Papers*, American Series, vol. 78, 1-4; *SJ*, 22.

Ensigns

George Maclagan* (c.1740-c.1800)
Ensign: 27 January 1756, 42nd Foot; resigned 16 May 1757.

Youngest son of Reverend Maclagan of Little Dunkeld. Eldest brother Alexander, served as lieutenant in Lord Loudoun's Highlanders. Second eldest brother, poet-scholar James Maclagan, served as chaplain to the 42nd Foot (see Volume Two, Part Three). George resigned in spring 1757 after quarrelling with Ensign John McIntosh and being subsequently ostracized by his brother officers. He wrote to his commanding officer, *"I am convinced from several things that have happened to me since I have been in the Regiment that my continuing to serve any longer in it would be disagreeable to the whole corps of officers and likewise being sensible of my own unfitness for a military life I have resolved to quit the Army as soon as I can get leave to resign my commission."* He was replaced by Peter Grant, a volunteer and kinsman of Lieutenant-Colonel Francis Grant. Lord Loudoun, writing to Cumberland, was blunt: *"Ensigne McLagon. . . . Sufferd himself to ill use & the regt refused to do Duty with him and he resigned his Commission."*

CBs; SBs; BALs; Stewart, *Sketches*, I-II, *in passim*; "List of Commissions" quoted in Pargellis, *MA*, 362.

Peter (Patrick) Stewart* (c.1735-1758)
Ensign: 29 January 1756, 42nd Foot.

Younger brother of Alexander Stewart, Laird of Bonskied, and cousin to Lt. Duncan Stewart Derculich (see above). Killed at Ticonderoga, 8 July 1758.

CBs; SBs; BALs; Stewart, *Sketches*, I-II, *in passim*; CA, III, 422.

Normand Macleod,* y^r of Talisker (c.1730-1796)
Private: 1747
Ensign: 30 January 1756, 42nd Foot;
Lieut: 27 December 1757, 80th Foot (Gage's Light Infantry);
Capt-Lt: 4 October 1760, 80th Foot; half-pay, 1 November 1764;
Capt: "by brevet," 25 May 1772.

Born on Skye, Normand MacLeod was the 4th son of Donald, 3rd of Talisker, and Christina, daughter of John MacLeod, 2nd of Contullich. He joined the regiment as a private soldier in 1747 and was commissioned ensign from the ranks 30 January 1756, as the regiment prepared to go overseas to North America. On 27 December 1757, when the regiment was stationed at Schenectady, NY, he exchanged on promotion to lieutenant in the new-raising 80th Foot, or Gage's Light Infantry. He fought at the battle of Ticonderoga, 1758, and was with the expeditions to capture Forts Ticonderoga and Crown Point, 1759 and Montréal, 1760. He was commissioned Captain-Lieutenant of the 80th on 4 October 1760, and served until its reduction in 1764, when he went on half-pay. He was a close friend, fellow Freemason and business associate of Sir William Johnson and lived after the war in New York performing personal commissions for Johnson. MacLeod was appointed a commissary (supply officer) of Indian Affairs at Niagara in 1766 and the following year, commissary of Fort Niagara. With government cutbacks, he lost both positions in 1769 and became a trader at Detroit in partnership with Gregor MacGregor and William Forsyth. During the American Revolution he became a captain in the Detroit militia and accompanied Henry Hamilton's 1778 expedition against Vincennes. He returned to Detroit early in 1779 before Hamilton's garrison was captured by George Rogers Clarke and his small force. MacLeod was an astute businessman and well-respected by all those who knew him. Johnson commented that he had *"great Esteem for Capt MacLeod who is a Worthy Man and one I am always disposed to Serve."* Governor Frederick Haldimand referred to him as *"a Gentleman for whom I have a particular regard."* He died at Montréal in 1796, a wealthy fur trader holding substantial stock in the Northwest Company.

CBs; SBs; BALs; Stewart, *Sketches*, I-II, *in passim*; "Normand MacLeod," DCB.

George Campbell* [2] (c.1738-1763)
Ensign: 31 January 1756; 42nd Foot; transferred on promotion;
Lieut: 28 July 1758, 80th Foot.

The fifth son of John (*Ian Dhu*) Campbell of Barcaldine, Factor to the Earl of Breadalbane's estate and therefore the youngest brother of Major Alexander Campbell and Captain Mungo Campbell, both of the 77th Foot (see 77th register); cousin of Lt "Jack" Campbell of Melfort (see above) and Lt. Colin Campbell, 35th Foot; and the nephew of Major Allan Campbell, 42nd Foot (see above). Slightly wounded on the 1758 Ticonderoga expedition while serving with Gage's Light Infantry, his uncle Allan Campbell reported to his half-brother John that his son *"had had a narrow escape at the French end of the Lake, having had a scratch along the face with a Musket ball."* He added: *"Col. [Gage] has a great regard for him, and very Deservedly for he's a lad of good morals, a good spirit and very fit for his Business."* George participated in Robert Roger's raid against St Francis in September 1759 and his detachment, weak with starvation on the long retreat is to alleged to have eaten the remains of one their own men left on the trail by avenging Indians. He was killed in the action by Seneca Indians on the Niagara Portage, 14 September 1763. Amherst listed him in his 1763 Appendix titled *"Officers Kill'd or Murder'd by the Indians."*

CBs; SBs; BALs; Stewart, Sketches, I-II, in passim; AJ, 1763 Appendix O14: 155; NAS GD 87/1:f.82-89; Mante, History of the Late War in North America.

George Rattray* (c.1740-1758)
Ensign: 19 July 1757, 42nd Foot.

One of the three ensigns of the three Additional Companies raised in 1757. Killed at Ticonderoga, 8 July 1758.

CBs; SBs; BALs; Stewart, Sketches, I-II, in passim; Richards, Black Watch, in passim.

William Maclean* (c.1740-1759)
Ensign: 15 July 1758, 2nd/42nd Foot.

Joined as an ensign in the newly raised 2nd Battalion in the summer of 1758 and was killed at Guadeloupe, 6 February 1759.

CBs; SBs; BALs; Stewart, Sketches, I-II, in passim.

James McDuff
Ensign: superseded, 2nd/42nd Foot.

Son of the Laird of Balaloan. Never joined.

CBs; SBs; BALs.

William MacIntosh* (c.1740-c.1800)
Ensign: 19 July 1758; 2nd/42nd Foot; transferred to 87th Foot (Keith's) on promotion;
Lieut: 28 August 1759, 87th Foot;
Capt: 26 April 1762, 87th Foot; half-pay 24 May 1763; full pay, 16 September 1771, 69th Foot;
Major: *"by brevet,"* 29 August 1777;
Lt-Col: 10 April 1780, 97th Foot; retired 8 September 1783.

Joined as an ensign in the newly raised 2nd/42nd in the summer of 1758 and saw service at Martinique and Guadeloupe 1759. Transferred to 87th Foot (Keith's Highlanders) and fought in Germany. Went out at the peace as a half-pay captain. Back on full pay in 1771 as a captain of the 69th Foot. Promoted brevet major in 1777, he was selected three years later to command the new-raising 97th Foot. Retired in 1783 at the peace.

CBs; SBs; BALs; Stewart, Sketches, I-II, in passim.

John Gordon (c.1740-c.1800)
Ensign: 31 July 1758, 42nd Foot; resigned, 5 December 1759.

A gentleman volunteer promoted after the battle of Ticonderoga, 8 July 1758, who resigned the following December after the successful 1759 campaign to capture Forts Ticonderoga and Crown Point.

CBs; SBs; BALs.

John Cowie (c.1740-1762)
Ensign: 20 May 1759

A volunteer who was commissioned Ensign in the 42nd Royal Highland Regiment of Foot, 20 March 1759. He was commissioned without payment of fees when Ensign William Browne was promoted Lieutenant in the room of Adam Stuart or Stewart. Cowie died at Guadeloupe, either in May 1759 as Amherst recorded under the name of Corrie, or on or about 5 June 1759, when he was replaced in the regimental complement by another *voluntier*, William Angus.

CBs; SBs; BALs.

Phineas Macpherson (c.1735-1760)
Ensign: 1 June 1759, 42nd Foot.

Sergeant-Major promoted from the ranks. Died at Fort Edward, 23 July 1760.

CBs; SBs; BALs.

William Angus
Ensign: 21 June 1759, 42nd Foot; superseded 17 September 1760.

Commissioned to replace John Cowie, who died suddenly. Never joined and was replaced by Charles Graham, son of Drainie (see above).

CBs; SBs; BALs.

Alexander Thomson (c.1735-1761)

Ensign: 29 July 1760, 42nd Foot.

A gentleman volunteer from the 55th Foot commissioned ensign while the regiment prepared for the 1760 campaign against Montréal at Oswego summer 1760. He died of smallpox the following winter at Montréal, 20 February 1761. His effects were sold at vendue, 23 February 1761.

CBs; SBs; BALs.

Matthew Reid (c.1735-1762)

Ensign: 1 August 1760, 42nd Foot; transferred on promotion;
Lieut: 28 February 1761, 40th Foot.

A gentleman volunteer promoted at Fort Ontario. Transferred to the 40th Foot on promotion to lieutenant and died the following year of fever at Havana.

CBs; SBs; BALs.

Patrick Murray (c.1740-c.1793)

Ensign: 9 March 1761, 42nd Foot; transferred on promotion;
Lieut: 21 September 1762, 1st/60th Foot; half-pay, 24 August 1763; full-pay, 25 December 1770, 1st/60th Foot; transferred on promotion;
Capt: 28 September 1775, 4th/60th Foot;
Major: 6 October 1784, 4th/60th Foot; retired 1793.

A nephew of Brigadier General James Murray and gentleman volunteer *"carrying arms"* promoted 9 March 1761 *"in room of"* Alexander Thomson *"dd"* while the regiment was in garrison at Montréal. He transferred on promotion to lieutenant in the 1st/60th (Royal Americans) after the surrender of Havana, 1762, and exchanged to half-pay, 24 August 1763. He returned on full pay, 25 December 1770, with the 1st/60th and served with it until the outbreak of the American Revolution. He was promoted captain in the new-raising 4th/60th Foot, 28 September 1775, and made its major 6 October 1784. His MSS entitled *"Memoir of Major Patrick Murray Who Served in the 60th from 1770 to 1793"* included a "History of the Services of the First Battalion" which is reprinted in Appendix II of Lewis Butler's *Annals of the King's Royal Rifle Corps*, Vol.1 - "The Royal Americans," (London, 1913). His own memoir indicates he retired in 1793, and is confirmed by him not appearing in the BALs after 1794.

CBs; SBs; BALs; Lewis Butler, *The Annals of the King's Royal Rifle Corps*, Vol. I. - "The Royal Americans," (London: 1913), 288-97; 353-4.

Lewis Grant [2] (1740-1762)

Ensign: 13 June 1761, 42nd Foot;

A gentleman volunteer promoted ensign at Crown Point while the regiment was *enroute* to Staten Island. He died of fever at the siege of Havana, 31 August 1762.

CBs; SBs; BALs; "List of the Officers of the 42nd or Royal Highland Regiment according to seniority dated December 29th, 1762," *BL,* Add. MSS. 21634: f.178c.

Thomas Hall (c.1740-c.1790)

Ensign: 22 October 1762, 42nd Foot;
Lieut: 10 February 1770, 42nd Foot; retired 1 March 1773.

A gentleman volunteer promoted after the siege of Havana while the regiment recuperated on Long Island. He fought at Bushy Run, 4-5 August 1763 and participated in the 1764 Muskingum expedition against the Ohio Indians. He returned with the regiment to Ireland in 1767 and was promoted lieutenant there in February 1770. Three years later he retired, March 1773.

CBs; SBs; BALs; "List of the Officers of the 42nd or Royal Highland Regiment according to seniority dated December 29th, 1762," *BL,* Add. MSS. 21634: f.178c.

Peter Herring (1738-1787)

Ensign: 7 December 1762, 42nd Foot;

The younger brother of Elbert Herring (see above) and born 17 December 1738 at New York city. Promoted after the capture of Martinique, in room of Alexander Graham promoted. Fought at Havana and Bushy Run, and took part in the 1764 Muskingum expedition against the Ohio Indians. It appears he did not return to Ireland with the regiment in 1767 as he retired 25 March 1768 in America. He committed suicide in 1787.

CBs; SBs; BALs; "List of the Officers of the 42nd or Royal Highland Regiment according to seniority dated December 29th, 1762," *BL,* Add. MSS. 21634: f.178c.

John Hamilton

Ensign: 13 February 1762, 121st Foot; exchanged 10 December 1762, 42nd Foot.

Must have either died or, never joined, for he is not shown in the 1763 or subsequent British Army Lists.

CBs; *SBs*; *BALs*; Stewart, *Sketches*, I-II, *in passim*; Richards, *Black Watch*, *in passim*.

John Peebles

Surgeon's Mate: 2nd Virginia Regiment, 1758-1759; 77th Foot, 1759-1763;
Ensign: 23 August 1763, 42nd Foot;
Lieut: 31 March 1770, 42nd Foot;
Capt-Lt: 5 October 1777, 42nd Foot;
Capt: 18 August 1778, 42nd Foot; retired 2 February 1782.

Born 11 September 1739, in Irvine, Ayrshire, son of John Peebles and Mary Reoch. Received a good general education and some rudimentary medical training for he was appointed as a surgeon's mate to the Second Battalion of the Virginia Regiment in 1758 at the age of 19. The following year he transferred into the 77th Foot (Montgomery's Highlanders) as the surgeon's mate where he served with some distinction. He was singled out for bravery in tending wounded during the fighting to retake St John's Newfoundland from the French in August 1762. The following year in autumn 1763, he was granted permission to join Col Henry Bouquet's expedition to relieve Fort Pitt during Pontiac's uprising as a gentleman volunteer. He distinguished himself again at the battle of Bushy Run where he was severely wounded. Sir Jeffery Amherst conferred a battlefield promotion upon him in recognition of his gallantry and he spent the winter in New York recovering. By next winter, he was fit enough to command at Fort Ligonier from 2 December 1764 to the summer of 1765. He returned with the regiment to Ireland in 1767, served a stint as the regimental QM, and was serving as captain-lieutenant commanding the Colonel's company when it was told off for North American service at the outbreak of the American Revolution. He succeeded his close friend, Charles Graham, as grenadier captain in August 1778, and fought at every major engagement, recording everything in a series of journals which have been published as *John Peeble's American War* edited by Ira Gruber. He attempted to resign in 1781, but was not permitted to do so by Brigadier-General Thomas Stirling, the commanding officer (see above). When Stirling was replaced the following year by Peeble's long time colleague, Major Charles Graham, Peebles' wish was instantly granted. He sold his commission and returned to Irvine, Ayrshire in Scotland where he married Anna Hamilton, had one daughter, Sarah, and became a sur-

veyor for the port of Irvine in the customs service. He served in the Ayrshire Militia throughout the wars of the French Revolution as a captain and major in the Irvine Volunteers. He died in 1823 at the age of 84.

CBs; *SBs*; *BALs*; Ira Gruber, *John Peebles' American War - The Diary of a Scottish Grenadier, 1776- 1782* (Mechanicsburg, PA, 1998); "Return of Officers who commanded at Fort Ligonier," *BL*, Add. MSS. 21651: f.114.

John Rutherfurd [Rutherford] (1746-1830)

Ensign: 23 August 1763, 42nd Foot;
Lieut: 25 March 1769, 42nd Foot; Capt-Lt: 18 August 1778, 42nd Foot; appointed adjutant, 2nd/42nd Foot, 1777; resigned 31 August 1779;
Capt: 31 December 1780, seniority retroactive to, 18 August 1778, 42nd Foot.

John was born in 1746 at Scarborough, Yorkshire, the 2nd son of Thomas Rutherfurd of Mossburnford and inherited the lands of Mossburnford in Roxburghshire, Scotland on his older brother's death. He accompanied Lt. Charles Robertson, 77th Foot, (see 77th Register) and Sir Robert Davers from Detroit as a gentleman volunteer on an exploration of the St. Clair River to Lake Huron in 1763, when the party was attacked and taken prisoner by Indians on 6 May 1763. The 17-year-old Rutherfurd was adopted by an Ottawa Indian family, but other members of his party were not so fortunate. Robertson and Davers were both killed during the attack and afterwards two soldiers of Montgomery's Highlanders were tortured and killed. Rutherfurd eventually escaped with the assistance of a sympathetic Frenchman but not before witnessing first-hand some of the actions and atrocities around Detroit. He sent a candid account of his experiences in 1763 in a letter home to his uncle, Sir John Nisbet, which was later published as *John Rutherfurd's Captivity Narrative*. On his arrival at Niagara, 17 September 1763, Rutherfurd learned that he had been commissioned ensign in the 42nd Foot effective 23 August 1763. He returned with the regiment to Ireland in 1767 and was promoted lieutenant 31 March 1770. and Captain Lieutenant and Captain, 18 August 1778. He died at the age of 84 and his son placed a memorial to him in the Rutherfurd Aisle of Jedburgh Abbey.

CBs; *SBs*; *BALs*; Rutherford, *John Rutherford's Captivity Narrative, 1763* in *The Siege of Detroit in 1763* M. Quaife, ed., (Chicago, 1958), 219-274.

Daniel Astle (1744-c.1810)
Ensign: 22 October 1762, 74th Foot; half-pay, 1763; full-pay 29 November 1765, 62nd Foot; transferred 42nd Foot, 13 December 1765; transferred on promotion
Lieut: 25 March 1769, 46th Foot.
Capt-Lt: 3 July 1772, 46th Foot;
Capt: 23 August 1775, 46th Foot, retired, 13 April 1778.

An English half-pay officer who rejoined the Army in 1765, first serving in the 62nd Foot, but transferring after one month to the 42nd stationed at Fort Pitt on the frontier. He returned with them to Ireland in 1767 and, two years later transferred into the 46th Foot. He eventually commanded a company of the 46th Foot but retired just before the outbreak of the American Revolution.

CBs; SBs; BALs.

Richard Nicholls Colden (c.1745-1777)
Ensign: 27 August 1766, 42nd Foot; retired, 15 May 1772.

Grandson of the Lieutenant-Governor of New York, Dr. Cadwallader Colden, and eldest son of Alexander Colden, Postmaster and Surveyor-General of New York, and Elizabeth Nicholls. Commissioned ensign, vice James Rumsey who sold out in order to pay his debts (see above). Colden went to Ireland in 1767 with the regiment and retired five years later, still an ensign. It was at this time he probably married Harriet Betham of the Isle of Man and became a brother-in-law to Captain William Bligh of the HMS *Bounty*. He returned to New York and was the Loyalist Postmaster of New York during the War of Independence when he died suddenly in 1777 leaving a widow and two small infant sons. Harriet Colden solicited Benjamin Franklin's protection for her infant sons, natives of New York in 1783 from the Isle of Man, citing the death of her husband, Richard and the distresses and calamities of war had caused her to leave America in 1778. She asked for his intercession to ensure that they could return and be received under the protection of the Governor of New York and possess their rights of inheritance.

CBs; SBs; BALs.

Chaplains

For detailed biographies of all 42nd chaplains see Part Three: "Specialist Officers."

The Reverend Adam Ferguson
Appointed 30 April 1746; resigned 1757.

The Reverend James Stewart
Appointed 20 December 1757, 2nd/42nd Foot; resigned, 20 August 1759.

The Reverend Lauchlan Johnson
Appointed 20 August 1759, 42nd Foot; died of fever at Havana, 1762.

The Reverend Adam Ferguson
Re-appointed 10 August 1762; resigned 15 June 1764.

The Reverend James Maclagan
Appointed 15 June 1764.

Adjutants

James Grant (see above)
Appointed 26 June 1751, 42nd Foot; resigned 1st/42nd Foot, 27 August 1760;

John [Mac] Gregor (see above)
Appointed 1st/42nd Foot, 27 August 1760; resigned 22 October 1761.

William [Mac] Gregor
Appointed 1st/42nd Foot, 22 October 1761; resigned 5 September 1762; half-pay, 24 October 1763.

Alexander McLean (see above)
Appointed 2nd/42nd Foot, 7 October 1758; resigned 20 March 1759;

Alexander Donaldson (see above)
Appointed 2nd/42nd Foot, 20 March 1759; replaced William Gregor, 1st /42nd as the sole adjutant, 42nd Foot; resigned 2 November 1768.

John McIntosh (see above)
Appointed 2 November 1768; resigned 20 March 1776.

Quarter Masters

John Graeme (see above)
Appointed QM, 19 February 1756; resigned 1st/42nd Foot, 13 October 1761.

Colin Macpherson
Appointed QM, 13 October 1761.

Sergeant-Major of the 1st/42nd appointed QM, 1st/42nd Foot, at Staten Island camp *"in room of"* John Graeme, 13 October 1761. Died 9 September 1762, on a hospital ship off Havana.

CBs; SBs; BALs, SOB.

William Munro (c.1730-1786)
Appointed QM, 10 September 1762.

Sergeant-Major of the 1st/42nd appointed QM, 1st/42nd Foot, 10 September 1762, to replace Colin Macpherson who died of fever. Exchanged to half-pay, 24 October 1763. Died 15 October 1786.

CBs; SBs; BALs, SOB.

Adam Stewart (see above)
Appointed QM, 2nd/42nd Foot, 15 August 1758; resigned, 42nd Foot, 15 February 1764.

Charles Graham (see above)
Appointed QM, 42nd Foot, 15 February 1764; resigned 3 September 1766.

Duncan Campbell
Appointed QM, 42nd Foot, 3 September 1766.

Surgeons

David Hepburn (c.1725-1786)
Appointed surgeon, 26 June 1751; 6 August 1758, surgeon, 1st/42nd Foot; half-pay, 10 April 1764.

According to Lord Loudoun's List of Officers prepared December 1744, Hepburn was initially the surgeon's mate to Dr George Munro, 42nd Foot, and brother of Sir Robert Munro of Fowlis, both of whom were killed at Falkirk, January 1746. His name is spelled "Hebburne" on the list but, by June 1751, he had obviously undergone formal medical training and passed his examinations, for he was commissioned the regimental surgeon, 26 June 1751. He went with the First Division to North America in 1756. Shown on a return of surgeons at Havana, August 1762 as *"ill in camp"* Exchanged to half-pay, 10 April 1764, and replaced by Alexander Potts, 3rd/60th Foot (Royal Americans). Died 1786.

CBs; SBs; BALs; "List of the Officers of the 42nd or Royal Highland Regiment according to seniority dated December 29th, 1762," *BL,* Add. MSS. 21634: f.178c.

Robert Drummond (c.1730-c.1788)
Appointed surgeon, 6 August 1758, 2nd/42nd Foot; half-pay, 24 October 1763.

Came over with the Second Battalion to North America as their surgeon, commissioned 5 August 1758, 2nd/42nd Foot and served at Martinique and Guadeloupe in 1759. He returned in 1762 and is shown on a return of surgeons at Havana, August 1762, as *"ill in camp."* He survived, and spent 1763 administering to the sick of both battalions on Long Island. Exchanged to half-pay, 24 October 1763.

CBs; SBs; BALs; "List of the Officers of the 42nd or Royal Highland Regiment according to seniority dated December 29th, 1762," *BL* Add. MSS. 21634: f.178c.

Alexander Potts (c.1740-c.1807)
Appointed surgeon, 8 November 1762, 3rd /60th Foot (Royal Americans); half-pay, 24 August 1763; exchanged full-pay, 10 April 1764, 42nd Foot; resigned 11 September 1777; appointed surgeon, American Hospital, 11 September 1777; half-pay, 25 December 1783.

Surgeon of the disbanded 3rd Battalion, 60th Foot (Royal America) who exchanged to full pay with the 42nd while it was stationed at Fort Pitt. He accompanied the regiment on the Muskingum expedition in August 1764 and is shown on the regimental rolls as returning to Ireland with the regiment in July 1767. He resigned from the regiment during the American Revolution to take up the post of Surgeon to the American Hospital. He shows in later printed army lists as Surgeon to the Hospital in West Indies. He is not in *BAL 1806.*

CBs; SBs; BALs; 42nd Regimental Return, Cork, Ireland, dated 3 September 1767.

Surgeon's Mates

Daniel Robertson (see above)
Appointed 10 November 1758; resigned 26 July 1760.

James Murdoch
Appointed 26 July 1760.

Served as the surgeon's mate on Stirling's 1765-66 expedition to the Illinois country to take possession of Fort de Chartres. May have been the author of one of two surviving journals of that expedition which are now preserved in the museum collections at Balhousie Castle. Captain Stirling noted in his own personal journal that he dictated daily to Murdoch during the trips down the Ohio and Mississippi.

CBs; *SBs*; *BALs*; "List of the Officers of the 42nd or Royal Highland Regiment according to seniority dated December 29th, 1762," *BL* Add. MSS. 21634: f.178c.

77th Foot (Montgomery's Highlanders)

Colonel, The Honorable Archibald Montgomery* (1726-1796)
Ensign: 28 September 1743, 54th [43rd] Foot
Cornet *en seconde*: 15 March 1744, 2nd Dragoon's (North British Dragoons)
Capt: 16 October, 1744, 36th Foot;
Major: 28 June 1751, 36th Foot;
Lt-Col: 4 January 1757, 77th Foot;
Col: 21 January 1758, "in America"; 19 February 1762, "in the Army"; appointed 51st Foot, 24 June 1767; appointed 2nd Dragoons, 2 December 1795;
Maj-Gen: 25 May 1772;
Lt-Gen: 29 August 1777;
General: 12 October 1793.

Born 18 May 1726, 3rd son of the 9th Earl of Eglinton, and Susanna Kennedy, (daughter of Sir Archibald Kennedy, 1st B^t of Culzean) Archibald was educated at Eton and the University of Geneva. He entered the British Army as a cornet in the North British Dragoons and later transferred into Lord Robert Manner's 36th Foot. He was serving as the major of the 36th Foot when chosen by the Duke of Argyll to command the 77th Foot as lieutenant-colonel commandant (4 January 1757). With the help of influential friends, he quickly raised a regiment of 10 companies composed of 105 all ranks each. Later four "Additional Companies" were added, three in 1758, and a fourth in 1759. Montgomery was a Lowland Scot of Norman descent, but according to Stewart of Garth, "*peculiarly well qualified from his con-nections and personal character for the command of a Highland regiment,*" as two of his sisters were married to influential Highland chieftains, Sir Alexander Macdonald of Sleat and the Laird of Abercairney. Montgomery spoke Gaelic, "*mixed much with the people, and being a high-spirited young man, with considerable dash of romantic enthusiasm in his composition, and with manners cheerful and affable, he made himself highly acceptable to the Highlanders.*" He took the regiment to North America in July 1757, landing at Charles Town, South Carolina on 3 September 1757 and the following year was sent northwards and assigned to General John Forbes' expedition sent against Fort Duquesne (Pittsburgh). He was present at the capture of the abandoned Fort Duquesne in November 1758 and commanded his regiment during Amherst's 1759 successful campaign against Ticonderoga and Crown Point. Montgomery was selected the following year by Amherst to lead a force of some 1300 men to South Carolina to subdue the Cherokees who had unleashed retaliatory raids and attacks all along the Carolina frontier after the expulsion of the French from the Ohio valley the year before. His force withdrew in July after devastating the lower Towns and the principal Middle Town, Etchoe, but was unable to penetrate further because of difficult terrain, mounting casualties, lack of supplies and strict orders from Amherst to return to New York as soon as possible. Arriving at Albany, September 1760, his six companies were too late to participate in the conquest of New France and were re-directed to garrison Halifax, Nova

Scotia. Montgomery cited severe rheumatism and asked for leave to return to England on extended leave which was granted by Amherst. There is no record of Montgomery ever returning to rejoin his regiment in North America before it was disbanded in 1763 and he was placed on half-pay. He was elected MP for Ayrshire (1761-1768) on his return and acted as Royal Equerry to Queen Charlotte, 1761-1769. He was given numerous appointments including the Governorships of Dunbarton Castle (1774-1782) and Edinburgh Castle (1782-1796), Deputy Ranger of Hyde Park and St. James' Park in London (1766-1768), and Colonel of the 51st Regiment of Foot, 24 June 1767. In October 1769, he succeeded his murdered older brother, Alexander, 10th Earl of Eglinton, and in 1776, was chosen as one of the sixteen Scottish representative peers. He was made a Major-General in 1772 and a Lieutenant-General in 1777. He died a full General and Colonel of the Scots Greys, (2nd Dragoons), 30 October 1796.

"General Return of the Names, Country, Age and Service of the Officers of the First Highland Battalion Commanded by the Honble Archibald Montgomery," LOC, James Grant Papers, Microfilm no. 48, [hereafter *General Return, 1757*]; *"Proposed List of Officers for 1st Highland Battalion* [1756],"[hereafter *1756 Officers List*], *Ibid.*; CBs; SBs; BALs; Stewart, *Sketches,* I-II, *in passim*; *"Montgomery, Archibald, 11th Earl of Eglinton, 1726-1796," DNB,* XIII: 749-750; *Burkes Peerage,* Valentine II: 617-18.

Majors

James Grant [1],* 4th of Ballindalloch, (1725-1806)
Ensign: 7 September 1741, 1st Foot (*The Royal*);
Lieut: 2 April, 1744, 1st Foot (*The Royal*);
Capt: 24 October 1744, 1st Foot; transferred on promotion;
Major: 5 January 1757, 77th Foot;
Lt-Col: 26 July 1760, 40th Foot
Col: *"in America"*; "in the Army," 25 May 1772; appointed 11 December 1775, 55th Foot; appointed 9 November 1791, 11th Foot;
Maj-Gen: 29 August 1777;
Lt-Gen: 20 November 1782;
General: 3 May 1796.

Born in 1720 at Ballindalloch, Scotland, 2nd son of Colonel William Grant, 1st of Ballindalloch, commander of one of the six Independent Highland Companies [IHC] that later became the Black Watch. A first cousin to Lt. Col. Francis Grant, Capt. William Grant and Lt. Lewis Grant, all of the 42nd Foot (see 42nd Register).

Commissioned ensign in the 1st Foot (*The Royal*) in 1741, he was a lieutenant of grenadiers by 1744. Grant soldiered in Flanders during the War of Austrian Succession and survived the Battle of Fontenoy, 1746. When two new Highland regiments were announced for service in North America in 1757, he actively lobbied for one of the lieutenant-colonelcies, supported in his memorial by Sir Ludovic Grant, the older brother of Lt. Colonel Grant commanding the Black Watch. He transferred from the 1st Foot when he secured the senior majority in Montgomery's Highlanders and went with them to Charles Town, South Carolina in September, 1757. Once there he complained of the 77th being no more than *"the Charles Town Guards."* Personally dissatisfied with his raw untrained unit, Grant wished to be *"a little nearer the Army"* in New York stating he was more than ready *"to give up my Pretentions to the Plaid."* The ambitious Grant yearned for a lieutenant-colonelcy in any permanent or more senior regiment of the line. When the 77th Foot was allocated to Brigadier John Forbes' expedition against Fort Duquesne in 1758, he served the ailing commander as an advisor and staff officer. On 11 September 1758, he was given his first independent command of 800 men to conduct a raid against the French fort, an expedition that went terribly wrong. Instead of surprising and destroying Indian encampments around the fort, Grant's command was surrounded and cut to pieces, and Grant taken prisoner. With more than 300 killed, wounded or captured, General Forbes observed: *"My friend Grant by his thirst for fame, brought on his own perdition, and run a great risque of ours."* Grant's defeat became known throughout North America and Britain and he himself believed his career would *"never outlive this day."* Held as a prisoner of war at Québec, he was eventually released through an exchange of prisoners in late 1759 and on his return to Amherst's command found he was still highly regarded by those in charge. In early 1760, the Cherokees went on the warpath and Grant was appointed second-in-command with the rank of brevet lieutenant colonel to Colonel Archibald Montgomery's southern expedition to the Carolinas. Montgomery later stated that the *"great share of success of his late Expedition"* was due to Grant's *"Merit and Experience."* Grant was rewarded with the lieutenant-colonelcy of the 40th Foot in July 1760. The Cherokees, however, were not subdued, and hostilities continued, necessitating a second expedition in 1761, this time with Grant as the principal commander. Grant's troops methodically destroyed the Cherokee Middle Towns (which earned Grant the Cherokee sobriquet of "Cornpuller") and caused them to sue for peace. He was then ordered to participate in the British attempts against the West Indies, joining General Robert Monckton's forces at Martinique, 9 February 1762, too late to participate in its capture. Grant served at Havana as a Colonel overseeing the siege works being constructed to take Fort Moro and was appointed lieutenant-governor of Havana after its surrender. In February 1763, he returned with the Earl of Albemarle to England to answer charges of financial mismanagement leveled against the Keppel administration. His sickly 40th Foot was sent back to garrison duty in Nova Scotia, once Havana was returned to the Spanish in the 1763 peace treaty. In London, on 21 November 1763, he was appointed Governor of East Florida where he had a stormy seven-year tenure, alienating some constituents because of his refusal to establish a colonial assembly. He returned to his estates in Scotland in 1771 and became MP for Tain in 1773. In December 1775, he was appointed Colonel of the 55th Foot and promoted Major-General in America. Serving under Howe and Clinton, Grant became known as a hardliner, eager, as he put it, *"to give a good Bleeding"* to *"those Bible-faced Yankees."* His advocacy of a torch and sword policy earned him the Americans' undying hatred. He commanded an expedition that captured St Lucia from the French in December 1778 and successfully defended it from counter-attack. He remained the senior military commander in the West Indies, returning to Britain in August 1779 when he fell seriously ill. He retired to his estates to recuperate, was made Lieutenant-General in 1782, and was given the governorships of Dunbarton Castle and Stirling Castle respectively. In 1791, he was given the Colonelcy of the 11th Foot, a more senior infantry line regiment than the 55th, then promoted full General in 1796. He was forced, due to ill health, to resign his seat in Parliament in 1802. He died four years later on his estate at the age of eighty-one.

General Return, 1757; Officers List, 1756; CBs; SBs; BALs; Stewart, *Sketches,* I-II, *in passim; General James Grant of Ballindalloch 1720-1806,* (London, 1930), *in passim;* and Paul David Nelson, *General James Grant: Scottish Soldier and Royal Governor of East Florida,* (Gainesville, 1993), *in passim;* "James Grant," *DNB* VIII: 388-89; *Valentine* I: 379-80.

Alexander Campbell,* y^r of Barcaldine, [1] (1729 - 1777)

Ensign: 1745, Argyllshire Militia
Lieut: Argyllshire Militia;
Capt: 2 June 1747, Independent Company; half-pay 25 December 1750; exchanged 20 June 1753, 1st Foot;

transferred on promotion;
Major: 7 January 1757, 77th Foot;
Lt-Col: 22 March 1761, 95th Foot; half-pay 11 March 1763.
Col: *"in the Army,"* 1777.

Alexander Campbell was the son and heir of John (*Ian Dhu*) Campbell, 5th Barcaldine and Jean Campbell, daughter of David Campbell of Kethick, and started his military career as an ensign in the Argyllshire Militia in 1745, probably in his father's company. His family was a cadet branch of the Breadalbane Campbells, three of his half-uncles - Colin of Glenure, Duncan and Alexander Campbell - all served as lieutenants in Lord Loudoun's Highlanders. His other half-uncle, Allan, three years his elder, served as an ensign in the 42nd Additional Companies during the '45 (See 42nd Register). Alexander's younger brothers were Ensign George Campbell, 42nd Foot, (See 42nd Register) and Captain Mungo Campbell, 77th Foot, (see below). Alexander was made captain of an Independent Company for service in the East Indies in 1747, and exchanged as a captain on half-pay into the 1st Foot, (*The Royal*) in 1753. A regimental colleague of James Grant (see above), he was initially slated to be a captain in the 78th Foot (Fraser's Highlanders), annotated on a 1756 list prepared by James Grant as *"proposed to be removed from Frasers Battalion to this."* He was gazetted second major to the 77th in January 1757 and commanded the regiment for the 1760 Montréal expedition while Col. Montgomery and Major Grant were detached with six companies fighting against the Cherokee. He was promoted Lt. Colonel of the newly created 95th Foot (Burton's) the following year, the latter regiment created from the Independent Companies recently sent to North America to take part in the second expedition against the Cherokees. This expedition was led by his old regimental colleague from the 1st and 77th Regiments, James Grant. In 1763, Alex's 95th Foot was disbanded and he went on half-pay. He married Helen Sinclair on 28 July 1765, the daughter of George Sinclair of Ulbster and 18-year-old niece of his old comrade-in-arms, Captain John Sinclair, senior captain of the 77th. Alex did not inherit his father Barcaldine's estates as his father had sold the family lands to his younger half-brother, Duncan, to pay off debts. In 1774, Alex was made Deputy Governor of Fort George near Inverness and Colonel in the Army, 1777. He died the same year at Bath on 22 April.

General Return, 1757; Officers List, 1756; CBs; SBs; BALs; Stewart, *Sketches,* I-II, *in passim;* "Campbells of Barcaldine" in *Burke's*

Peerage, Peter Townend, ed., 104th edition, (London, 1967), 437; *Scots Magazine*, xxvii, 391.

Alexander Monypenny, of Pitmilly (1726-1801)

Ensign: 3 June 1745; 33rd Foot;

Lieut: 3 May 1749, 33rd Foot; appointed adjutant same day;

Capt: 29 August 1756, 1st /33rd Foot; exchanged 22 February 1757, 55th Foot; transferred on promotion;

Major: 26 July 1760, 77th Foot; transferred, 17 September 1761, 22nd Foot; transferred on promotion;

Lt-Col: *"in the Army,"* 29 April 1762; 1 September 1762, 56th Foot; resigned 3 October 1776.

Born at Pitmilly House near Kingsbarns, Fifeshire, Scotland, the only son of David Monypenny of Pitmilly. Began his career in the 33rd Foot and was wounded at the battle of Maastricht in 1747. He was promoted lieutenant and appointed adjutant to the 33rd Foot, 3 May 1749, and subsequently made a captain in December 1755. He exchanged into the 55th Foot when it was told off for service in North America and was a captain by August 1756. Served as Lord Howe's ADC and brigade major during the 1758 campaign against Ticonderoga. After Howe's premature death, 6 July 1758, he returned to his company, and distinguished himself during the battle after its commanding officer and second-in-command were both killed. After the capture of Montréal 1760, he briefly transferred to the 77th Foot on promotion to major, but never joined, instead exchanging to the majority of the 22nd Foot, a more "senior" and thus safer regiment. He served as Lt. Colonel James Grant's second-in-command on the 1761 expedition against the Cherokees, his diary and journal of that campaign having survived. In 1762, he went to the Caribbean where he served on Lord Albemarle's staff, was promoted lieutenant-colonel *"in the Army,"* 29 April 1762. He succeeded to the title of Laird of Pitmilly upon the death of his father the same year and was appointed to command the 56th Foot (Albemarle's), 1 September 1762. Married Margaret Chamberlain of Dublin, 21 November 1767, his wedding certificate citing him as *"Lieut-Col of 56th Foot,"* and by her had six children, one of whom, David, became 1st Lord Pitmilly. Alex retired 3 October 1776 and befriended Sir Walter Scott in his youth who wrote of him later in life: *"Old Colonel Monypenny was my early friend, kind and hospitable to me when I was a mere boy. He had much of old Withers about him, as expressed in Pope's epitaph –*

> *youth in arms approved!*
> *O soft humanity in age beloved."*

Alexander died a "Colonel in the Army" 1801.

CBs; SBs; BALs; *Burkes' Gentry*, Townend, ed. 18th ed., II, (1969), 450; *Sir Walter Scott's Journal*, Burt Franklin, ed. (New York, 1890); "Monypenny's Order Book & Diary, 1761" in Duane H. King and E. Raymond Evans, eds.: *Journal of Cherokee Studies*, Special Issue, Volume II, Number 3, Summer 1977, 302-319 & 320-331.

John Maunsell (c.1725-1794)

Ensign: 23 May 1742, 39th Foot;

2nd Lieut: 30 April 1746, 39th Foot;

1st Lieut: 25 August 1749, 39th Foot; transferred on promotion;

Capt: 5 January 1750-1, 35th Foot;

Major: 19 September 1760, 77th Foot; transferred 30 September 1761, 35th Foot;

Lt-Col: 31 October 1762, 72nd Foot; transferred 10 December 1762, 27th Foot; half-pay, 2 August 1765; exchanged to half-pay, lt-colonel, 83rd Foot;

Col: "in the Army," 29 August 1777;

Maj-Gen: 19 October 1781;

Lt-Gen: 12 October 1793.

Born in Tipperary, Ireland, John was commissioned ensign in the 39th Foot in 1742 and was promoted lieutenant in 1749. He transferred to the 35th Foot on promotion to captain in January 1750. He fought at the 1757 siege of Fort William Henry and survived the subsequent "Massacre"; was wounded two years later at the battle of the Plains of Abraham outside the walls of Québec, 13 September 1759; was made major to the 77th Regiment, 19 September 1760, and *"never joined"* according to official documents. However, Maunsell did go to Nova Scotia on promotion, joining the 77th in garrison at Halifax [from Québec], 27 October 1760. He remained over the winter and, from surviving correspondence, haggled over the price he had to pay to James Grant for the 77th's majority, indicating to Amherst at the same time that he would like to be transferred to a different regiment. Capt John Gordon tried to negotiate on Grant's behalf to no avail and reported in November 1761 that Maunsell *"is, in reality, the most Shilly Shally, Whistly Wally, Jacky Wagtail that ever my Eyes beheld, he allows himself to be Commanded by the President of the Council, a Provincial Colo. Who has no troops here & Maj Mackellar ye Engineer. He gives our Serjt Major half a dozen Contradictory orders of a morning and at last gives out none at all, times are greatly Chang'd when the Six Companys are wishing for Berkalden [Barcaldine: Major Alex Campbell] to Command, of whom we have had no accots since we Left New York."* The regiment saw the back of Maunsell when the majority in his old regiment, the 35th Foot, opened up, and he sailed off to join them at

Staten Island, his seniority dated 30 September 1761. Made lieutenant-colonel of the 72nd Foot, 31 October 1762, and then exchanged two months later to the 27th Regiment, 10 December 1762, although this post would appear to have been a temporary stop-gap as he was still listed in *BAL November 1763* as major with rank in the army as Lieutenant Colonel. He then went on the Irish half-pay list, 2 August 1765, and sometime in 1767, Maunsell exchanged with William Skinner for the half-pay lieutenant colonelcy of the 83rd Foot. He had married Elizabeth Stillwell Wraxall, widow of Captain Peter Wraxall, NY Independent Companies, in 1763, and bought in 1766 a 76-acre estate at Harlem in northern Manhattan in 1766. He also invested in land in upstate New York and Vermont. After the battle of Lexington, Maunsell not wishing to fight against family and friends of his wife, asked for an alternative post back in Britain and was put in charge of the Commissariat in Kinsale, Ireland. After the war, he and his wife Elizabeth returned to America. As a former British officer, Maunsell had to forfeit much of his properties in the new United States to the worth of some £10,000. However, he did retain his Harlem estate and he had enough resources to buy a residence for himself and his wife in New York City. Maunsell was made Colonel in the Army, 29 August 1777, Major General, 19 October 1781 and Lieutenant General, 12 October 1793. Died 1794 in New York.

CBs; *SBs*; *BALs*; John Gordon to James Grant, 18 November 1761, Halifax, James Grant Papers, *LOC*, Microfilm no. 48 [hereafter *JGP*]; WO 12/6998.

Patrick Sutherland (c.1715-1767)
Ensign: 25 December 1740, 42nd Foot (Oglethorpe's);
Lieut: 12 May 1741, 42nd Foot;
Capt-Lt: 30 July 1745, 42nd Foot;
Capt: 8 November 1745, North Britain Independent Company; 24 April 1747; 42nd Foot (Oglethorpe's); half-pay, 29 May 1749, on disbandment; transferred to full pay 45th Foot, 24 February 1749-50.
Major: 22 March 1761, 77th Foot; half-pay, 24 December 1763;
Lt-Col: Lunenburg Militia, 1753-1766.

Patrick Sutherland was the younger son of James Sutherland of Clyne and Jean Gordon. Both parents were well-connected in the Sutherland hierarchy and descended from the Sutherlands of Duffus, the Earls of Caithness and the Gordon Earls of Sutherland. Patrick joined the army in 1733 and accompanied Oglethorpe's

42nd Regiment of Foot to America in 1739 as a gentleman-volunteer. He first appears in the Army Lists as adjutant *"in room of"* Hugh Mackay, jr, 24 September 1740, of the 42nd Foot, the sole regiment stationed in the fledgling colony of Georgia (not to be confused with the Black Watch which was still numbered 43rd at this time). The commissions of this overseas regiment were badly staffed as Sutherland appears as an ensign in Oglethorpe's correspondence in early 1739 and is mentioned as having a duel with Ensign Leman. He is not shown on the regimental rolls as an ensign until 25 December 1740. In 1745, he obtained leave to return to Scotland during the Rebellion and commanded one of 18 independent Highland companies that were raised by the loyal clans to oppose the invasion of Bonnie Prince Charlie. He commanded the 2nd Sutherland company, which he personally raised and assembled at Dunrobin Castle. His company arrived in Inverness, 8 November 1745, and remained in garrison throughout the '45 rebellion. Though his men saw no action, they did participate in post-Culloden activities, including the rounding up of fugitive Jacobites. On 24 September 1746, Patrick writing from Dunrobin informed Lord Loudoun that he was going to London, as all the companies had been disbanded effective 10 September 1746, *"except Culcairn's and Gunn's which were the first to go to Inverness."* On his return to Georgia, Sutherland was promoted captain, effective 24 April 1747. In 1748, Sutherland successfully petitioned the Board for the Colony of Georgia for further land grants amounting to 1000 acres. He continued his land dealings in Georgia right up until 1764, but it appears he was an absentee landlord. On disbandment of the 42nd (Oglethorpe's) in 1749 he exchanged to half-pay, but shortly thereafter exchanged back to active service with the 45th Foot, 24 February 1750-1, and reported for duty at Halifax, Nova Scotia. In 1752, he was stationed at Pisiquid (Windsor, NS). The following year he served as second-in-command to his Lt Colonel, Charles Lawrence, in the establishment of the German settlement at Lunenburg on the south shore of the colony. When Lawrence returned to Halifax after three months of supervision, he left Sutherland in command at Lunenburg, a post he was to occupy for the next nine years. He purchased waterfront town lots 5, 6 and 7 on Montague Street in Lunenburg in 1756 and owned them until 1762. According to the Diary of the Reverend John Seccombe, minister of Chester, *"Maj'r Patrick Sutherland"* in 1761 also owned the island of *"Great Tancook - six or seven miles from Chester."* In 1756, when the news of two new-raising Highland battalions in Scotland came to his attention, Sutherland actively lobbied for promotion to major with some results. On 16 August 1757, Lord Barrington wrote to the Duke of Cumberland from the War Office:

"Lieutenant Colonel Frazers Battalion has but one Major with it; Mr Campbell [of Dunoon] being at Spa in hopes to recover his Limbs, of which he has almost lost the Use. Captain Sutherland of Warburton's has been proposed by the Duke of Argyll and others as Major **en Seconde** *to that Battalion, which is certainly in great Want of another field officer but I have refused recommending anything of this sort to Lord Loudoun, till I know your R.H.'s pleasure therein."*

Cumberland replied from Germany 28 August 1757:

"My lord Barrington, I have received your Letter of the 16: If Major Campbell of Fraser's Battalion quits, I have no Objection to Captain Sutherland of Warburton's; who is a very proper Man. But I can not allow of three Majors to a Highland Battalion."

It would seem then that Loudoun, Argyll, Barrington and the Duke all thought Patrick was a highly suitable candidate for major. The only fly in the ointment was John Campbell, Captain of Dunoon who lingered on the books while lobbying for his own regiment in Scotland. Meanwhile, Capt. Sutherland distinguished himself at the siege of Louisbourg under Amherst's command several times and afterwards, remained with the 45th Foot in garrison at Louisbourg until 1760. On 22 March 1761, with the direct recommendation of Amherst, Sutherland returned to Lunenburg as the new 1st major of the 77th Foot and the command of the five companies of the regiment while the remainder campaigned in the Caribbean. In 1762, Major Sutherland commanded a small composite battalion consisting of five companies (two 77th composite companies, and three of the Royal Scots) as part of Colonel William Amherst's small force sent to recapture St. John's from the French. On his return to Halifax, Sutherland as the senior 77th officer in North America oversaw the disbandment of the 77th Foot and exchanged to half pay. He died at Lunenburg in 1767.

CBs; SBs; BALs; DCB; "Muster for Louisbourg" dated 12 June 1760, *WO* 12/ 5718, Part 1.

Robert Mirrie (1722-1762)

Ensign: 20 June 1739, 1st Foot;
2nd Lieut: 11 May 1742, 2nd/1st Foot;
1st Lieut: 22 June, 1742, 1st/1st Foot; transferred on promotion;
Capt: 25 June 1747, 2nd/1st Foot; 1756 transferred 2nd /1st Foot, appointed Paymaster, 1757; resigned pay-

master, 22 March 1761; transferred on promotion;
Major: 23 March 1761, 77th Foot.

Born in Scotland in 1722 and started his military career in the 1st Foot (The Royal Regiment). Fought as a lieutenant at Culloden, April 1746, and was promoted to captain the following year. Senior captain of the 2nd/1st Foot at Halifax, Nova Scotia in 1760, he was promoted 2nd Major of the 77th Foot, 22 March 1761 and commanded the nine 77th companies assigned to Lord Rollo's expedition to capture Dominica that were assembled at New York in April 1761. Mirrie Appears in Sir William Johnson's Papers on a list of 77th officers entitled *"Died at Havana,"* 1762. He died of fever 1 July 1762, and was replaced by Captain Samuel Zobel, senior captain of 22nd Foot.

CBs; SBs; BALs.

Samuel Zobel (c. 1724- c.1806)

2nd Lieut: 17 May 1742, 39th Foot;
1st Lieut: 30 April 1746, 39th Foot;
Capt: 5 January 1750/1, 22nd Foot; transferred on promotion;
Major: 1 July 1762, 77th Foot; half-pay 23 December 1763; half-pay, 24 December 1763;
Lt.Col.: brevet *"in the Army,"* 25 May 1772.

Samuel Zobel [Zobell] started his military career in the 39th Foot. At the siege of Havana 1762, he was the senior-serving captain of the 22nd Foot, and when Major Robert Mirrie, 77th Foot, died of fever, Zobel was promoted major to the 77th Foot, 1 July 1762. Whilst recovering on Long Island in late spring of 1763 with the survivors of the nine companies that served at Havana, Zobel received orders that all able-bodied Highlanders were to join Col. Henry Bouquet's relief expedition assembling in Philadelphia to march for Fort Pitt, then under siege by the Ohio Indians. He responded to Sir Jeffery Amherst on 14 June 1763: *"I am sorry to be under the necessity to acquaint Your Excellency my state of health is such as it will be absolutely impossible for me to march with the people. I could not go a mile unless in a [cart] or on horseback if I got the World by it. My disorder still relapsing from time to time which keeps me in the lowest way."* Instead of participating in the 77th's last campaign, Zobel was sent by Amherst back to Britain on 3 September 1763 with his dispatches for Pitt giving details of Pontiac's Indian uprising. Nothing further is known of Zobel, except that he exchanged to half-pay in

December 1763, and nine years later, was given brevet rank as a Lt-Colonel in the Army. He died circa 1806, for he is not listed in the 1807 BAL.

CBs; SBs; BALs; Stewart, *Sketches*, I-II, *in passim*; Zobel to Amherst, Long Island, 14 June, 1763, *WO 34/94*: f. 199; Amherst to Zobel, New York, September 3, 1763, *WO 34/97*: f.99.

Captains

John Sinclair* (1729-1787)
Ensign: Dutch-Scots Brigade;
Lieut: Dutch-Scots Brigade;
Capt: 2 June 1747, Drumlanrig's, Dutch-Scots Brigade; 4 January 1757, 77th Foot; half-pay, 24 December 1763; exchanged 7th Foot, 13 December 1765; retired, 3 June 1774.

Born in 1729, John was the 3rd son of John Sinclair of Ulbster, the hereditary Sheriff of Caithness. He came to the 77th as an experienced half-pay officer of the Dutch Scots Brigade. *The Scots Magazine* in 1747 listing officers of Lord Drumlanrig's Regiment, then raising in Scotland, shows him as *"brother to Ulbster"* (his father had been succeeded by his older brother George) and a captain. Commissioned in Montgomery's Highlanders as the senior captain on 4 January 1757, and according to recruiting documents, raised his men in Sutherland and Caithness. He fought in all the major campaigns of the 77th (Fort Duquesne, 1758; Ticonderoga, 1759; Crown Point, 1759; and, the 1761 Cherokee Expedition) with the exceptions of the capture of Montréal and the subsequent Caribbean campaigns. From late 1760 until the regiment's disbandment in 1763, he and his company garrisoned Annapolis Royal in Nova Scotia. He commanded one of the two composite companies drawn from the five Nova Scotia companies that were sent to recapture St John's, Newfoundland in September 1762 under Colonel William Amherst. Sinclair was passed over for promotion five times. On the departure of the 77th's two original majors on promotion in 1761, Captain John Maunsell (in room of Grant) came in from the 35th and Alexander Monypenny (in room of Campbell), an aide of Amherst, came in from the 55th Foot. Monypenny was almost immediately transferred to the majority of the 22nd Foot and his place taken by Captain Patrick Sutherland, 45th Foot, who was actually already serving in NS. Sinclair was passed over for command a fourth time when Captain Robert Mirrie, the senior captain of the 2nd/1st Foot in Halifax, NS

was promoted 2nd Major of the 77th in order to take eight companies of the regiment to the Caribbean. For Sinclair, it was a blessing in disguise, for Mirrie died of fever at Havana, as did many of the 77th officers, Mirrie being replaced by Captain Samuel Zobel, the senior captain of the 22nd Foot then at Havana. Thus John Sinclair was the senior captain of Montgomery's Highlanders for the entire war and went out on half-pay in December 1763. In 1765, his old comrade-in-arms, Lt-Colonel Alex Campbell, son of Barcaldine, married his 18 year-old niece, Helen Sinclair, after which he returned to active service, exchanging from half pay to captain in the 7th Foot in December 1765. He retired 3 June 1774 at the age of 45. During the American Revolution, he joined the Sutherland Fencibles commanded by his old regimental comrade, Lt. Colonel Nicholas Sutherland (See below) as its senior captain. On the latter's death in 1781, he was made major of the Fencibles and died himself in 1787.

General Return, 1757; Officers List, 1756; CBs; SBs; BALs; Stewart, *Sketches*, I-II, *in passim; DSB*, 389, 425; *WO/1/974*: f. 139; *Caithness Records*, 1767.

The Honorable Hugh Mackenzie* (1724-1762).
Ensign: March, 1742, Dutch-Scots Brigade;
Lieut: January 1745, Dutch-Scots Brigade;
Capt: 2 June 1747, Dutch-Scots Brigade; 6 January 1757, 77th Foot.

The 2nd son of John Mackenzie, 2nd Earl of Cromarty, from his third marriage to Anne Fraser of Lovat, thus a nephew of Colonel Simon Fraser, 78th Foot, and also a brother-in law to Lieutenant Archibald Lamont of that Ilk, 42nd Foot. The 15-year veteran had started his military career in the Dutch-Scots brigade along with his older brother, the Hon. Norman Mackenzie, (who perished at sea taking Highland recruits from Scotland to Holland). He came to the regiment with several recommendations including that of Stewart Mackenzie, the Laird of Macleod and the Laird of Lamond in Argyllshire. In 1757, Hugh raised a company for Montgomery's Highlanders in Glasgow and Ross-shire and was commissioned 6 January 1757. The only 77th captain of three to survive the 14 September action at Fort Duquesne, 1758, though initially reported as killed by Bouquet he was wounded and captured by the French; exchanged 15 November 1759 in time to participate in the capture of Montréal the following year. Sent from Halifax to New York as one of eight companies assigned to Lord Rollo's 2000 man force to capture Dominica as a preliminary to Martinique. *"Capt Hugh*

McKinsey [McKenzie]" appears in Sir William Johnson's Papers on a list of 77th officers entitled *"Died at Havana,"* 1762. In fact, he died at Dominica in September 1761 but was not replaced until 31 December 1761.

General Return, 1757; Officers List, 1756; CBs; SBs; BALs; Stewart, Sketches, I-II, in passim; WO 34/55: ff. 121-122; WO/1/974: f. 139, BP II: 519; O14; SWJP; DSB, II, 404.

The Honorable John Gordon, of Glentanner* (1729-1778)

2nd Lieut: 13 April 1746, 2nd/1st Foot (The Royal Regiment); Lieut: 19 June 1751, 2nd/1st Foot; transferred on promotion; Capt: 7 Jan 1757, 77th Foot; half-pay 24 December 1763; full-pay 5 August 1175' 52nd Foot; Major: "in the Army," 23 July 1772; Lt-Col: "in the army, 29 August 1777; 19 December 1777, 81st Foot.

The Honorable John Gordon was born in Scotland, 19 June 1728, 2nd son of John Gordon, 3rd Earl of Aboyne. He was commissioned 2nd lieutenant in the 2nd/1st Foot (The Royal Regiment), 19 April 1746. He was promoted lieutenant in the same battalion, 19 June 1751. Gordon was made captain in the new-raising Montgomery's Highlanders, 7 January 1757, and raised his company in Edinburgh and Aberdeenshire. He served at the captures of Forts Duquesne [1758], Ticonderoga [1759], and Crown Point [1759]. In March 1760, he went with Col Montgomery's detachment to fight against the Cherokee. On his company's return to garrison Halifax, NS, in November 1761, he was granted three months leave in Britain and while there, married Clementina Lockhart, 18 May 1761. He returned to garrison duties at Halifax and missed the Caribbean campaign. He was placed on half pay when the regiment was disbanded, 24 December 1763. Gordon was made major in the army on 23 July 1772, and returned to active service as captain in the 52nd Foot, 15 August 1775. He was made lieutenant-colonel in the army, 29 August 1777, and was then made lieutenant-colonel to the new-raising 81st Foot (Aberdeenshire Highlanders), 19 December 1777, which was sent to garrison towns in Ireland. While his regiment was still in Ireland, Gordon died 31 October 1778, thus being spared the ignominy of his regiment's mutiny five years later in Portsmouth along with the 77th Foot (Duke of Atholl's Highlanders).

General Return, 1757; Officers List, 1756; CBs; SBs; BALs; Stewart, Sketches, I-II, in passim; WO/1/974: 139; "The Honourable John Gordon," Gordons under Arms.

Alexander Mackenzie, of Balmoir* (1732-1777)

Ensign: Dutch-Scots Brigade;

Lieut: Dutch-Scots Brigade; transferred 2nd/4th Foot, 2 September 1756; transferred on promotion;
Capt: 8 January 1757, 77th Foot; 1763 half-pay; full pay 28 November 1776, 6th Foot;
Major: 27 November 1768; 31st Foot,
Lt-Col: 28 April 1773, 31st Foot.

Alexander Mackenzie was born 1732 in Scotland. Served initially for ten years as an officer in the Dutch-Scots Brigade, then transferred to the British army in 1756 when the 4th Foot (Duroure's) added a second battalion to its war establishment. In 1757, the 15-year veteran transferred to Montgomery's Highlanders and raised his quota of men in Perthshire and Aberdeenshire. Gazetted a captain, 8 January 1757, he served in the Forbes campaign of 1758 and had little regard for the abilities of provincial officers he encountered. When Mackenzie was in command of a 77th detachment at Fort Ligonier the winter of 1758/59, he had difficult relations with Colonel Thomas Lloyd. Mackenzie was in one of four captains that went on Montgomery's campaign to the Carolinas in 1760 where his Colonel characterized him as *"a very good officer."* When directed to proceed from New York to Halifax with his company aboard the *Mercury* transport in November 1760, he was blown by a gale to Newfoundland. His damaged ship finally gained refuge at Providence in the Bahamas where he wintered until sent for by James Grant in South Carolina who was preparing for the second Cherokee expedition. Mackenzie's company arrived in South Carolina April 1761 and marched inland to join Grant's force at Monck's Corner, but Amherst countermanded Grant's orders and directed Mackenzie and his company to rejoin his battalion at New York. There it formed part of an expedition against Dominica. He was wounded at Martinique, 24 January 1762, and exchanged to half-pay, 24 December 1763. He returned to active service as a captain in the 66th Foot, 28 November 1766. He was made Major to the 31st Foot in May 1768 and became the regiment's lieutenant-colonel, 28 April 1773. He died 13 September 1777.

General Return, 1757; Officers List, 1756; CBs; SBs; BALs; Stewart, Sketches, I-II, in passim; WO/1/974: 139; WO 34/77: f. 1 ; WO 34/77: f. 17; WO 34/55: f. 58; Mackenzie to Bouquet, 6 January 1759; printed in BP III: 18-19; Bouquet to Stanwix, 26 April 1759, in BP III: 256-257; AJ; DSB, II, 422.

William MacDonald* (1739-1758)

Capt: 14 January 1757, 77th Foot.

He was recommended by Major Sir James Macdonald, son of Sir Alexander Macdonald of Sleat and, at 18 years of age, was the youngest (and most inexperienced) company commander of the regiment. William raised his company for Montgomery's Highlanders in Edinburgh and Skye in spring 1757, then went with his regiment to Charles Town, SC. Participated in Forbes 1758 campaign in western Pennsylvania and was one of three 77th captains selected to lead a Highland column against Fort Duquesne; killed 14 September 1758 by Indians at the base of Grant's Hill. One of his subalterns described him as *"my worthy, brave, good Captain."*

General Return, 1757; Officers List, 1756; CBs; SBs; BALs; Stewart, *Sketches,* I-II, *in passim; WO/1/974:* f. 139; *BALs;* Robertson to Munro, 24 September 1758, *Ballindalloch Papers.*

George Munro* (1721-1758)

2nd Lieut: 1 January 1747, 2nd Stewart's, Dutch-Scots Brigade; resigned 15 February 1756;
Capt: 15 January 1757, 77th Foot.

The 36-year-old George Munro was the oldest of the company commanders and the eldest son of George Munro of Culcairn, one of the six original company commanders of the Black Watch. His father was murdered by Dugald Roy Cameron at Loch Arkairg in 1746. He was also the nephew of Sir Robert Munro, 6th B[t.] of Foulis, the commanding officer of the 42nd Foot at Fontenoy, who was later killed at Falkirk, 1756. George was thus first cousin to Sir Robert Munro, 7th B[t.] of Foulis. According to a *"General Return of the Names, Country, Age and Service of the Officers of the First Highland Battalion Commanded by the Honble Archibald Montgomery,"* George already had fifteen years of previous military service under his belt. An ink annotation states he served with Lord John Murray's Regiment (42nd Foot), probably as a soldier and non-commissioned officer. He raised his company for Montgomery's Highlanders in Fearran Donull, the traditional lands of the Munros and Macraes, and received his captain's commission dated 15 January 1757. Selected to lead one of the three Highlander columns that marched against Fort Duquesne, he was killed on the morning of 14 September 1758 near the summit of Grant's Hill (Pittsburgh). Lt. Robertson writing to Sir Henry Munro after the battle described him as *"our poor worthy good friend."*

General Return, 1757; Officers List, 1756; CBs; SBs; BALs; Stewart, *Sketches,* I-II, *in passim; WO 1/974:* f. 139; *DSB,* 423; Robertson to Munro, 24 September 1758, *Ballindalloch Papers.*

Roderick MacKenzie* (1733-1762).

Ensign: Dutch-Scots Brigade;
Lieut: 1st Bn, Majoribank's, Dutch-Scots Brigade;
Capt: 17 January 1757, 77th Foot

A veteran of the Dutch Scots brigade, Roderick raised his company for Montgomery's Highlanders in Kintail where the famous castle Eilann Donan stands guard at the mouth of Loch Duich looking west to Skye. His company participated in all campaigns of the regiment up to the capture of Montréal, 1760. In 1760-61, his company was garrisoned at Fort Cumberland on the Chignecto Peninsula between present day Nova Scotia and New Brunswick and thus did not go to the Caribbean with the majority of the battalion in 1761. One of his duties, besides fort commandant, was to round up Acadian settlers who had opposed British forces and had evaded deportation after the fall of Louisbourg in 1758. In October 1761, Mackenzie surprised Acadian refugees at Restigouche and the surrounding countryside, rounding up 700, but was only able to put 325 aboard his ships which were then sent to Halifax. Roderick Mackenzie commanded one of the two Montgomery composite companies sent to recapture St John's Newfoundland from the French which they had seized while British forces were operating at Havana. He died 5 October 1762 of wounds received while storming the heights at Quidi Vidi, St. John's, Newfoundland on 12 September 1762. The Commission Register indicate that he was replaced by James Duff on 19 October 1762. His close friend, Colonel William Amherst, the expedition's commander, according to the Boston *Evening Post* dated 8 Nov. 1762 *"to show respect to Merit ordered a grave stone to be laid on Capt. Roderick MacKenzie of Col. Montgomery's Highland Regiment, who received a mortal wound on the day of landing on Newfoundland."* The inscription reads: *"Here rests Roderick Mc:Kenzie Esq[r] who was a Captain in the 77th: Regiment: He received a mortal wound In gaining from the Enemy the Important Post of Kitty Vitty, on the 13th of September 1762. In Respect to his Virtues, In gratitude to his Valour, Lt: Col. Amherst lays this Stone to his Memory."*

General Return, 1757; Officers List, 1756; CBs; SBs; BALs; Stewart, *Sketches,* I-II, *in passim; WO/1/974:* f. 139; *WO 34/93:* f. 208; *O15/10; O14.*

Sir Allan Maclean, of Morven, Brolas & Coll, (c.1725-1783)

Ensign: Dutch Scots Brigade;
Lieut: Dutch-Scots Brigade;
Capt: IHC 1745-47; 16 July 1757, 77th Foot; resigned,

Major: 25 June 1762, 119th Foot (Prince's Own); half-pay
29 August 1763;
Lt-Col: "in the Army," 25 May 1772.

Born the eldest son of Donald Maclean, 3rd Brolas, by
his second marriage, Sir Allan was the 21st chieftain
and 6th baronet Morven. Styled "The Red Knight of
Duart" in Gaelic, Sir Allan was an experienced officer of
the Dutch-Scots Brigade and was wounded during the
siege of Bergen-op-Zoom. *The Scots Magazine* listing
officers of Lord Drumlanrig's Regiment, then raising in
Scotland, shows him as "*Allan Maclean, Brolus, a captain
of the independent companies.*" When three newly-raised
77th Additional Companies were sent over to North
America to participate in Forbes' campaign against Fort
Duquesne, 1758, Sir Allan, as the most senior and experienced officer, was placed in charge; he participated in
the Ticonderoga and Crown Point campaigns, 1759.
Major Alexander Campbell reported to his father after
the victory at Ticonderoga that "*Sir Allan McLean is
doing very well and is very much esteemed.*" He added,
"*When the Knight gets a little Drunk he swears he scarce
knows the difference in his affections betwixt a Bredalbane
Campbell and a MacLean.*" Sir Allan participated in the
1760 Cherokee Expedition. His wife Una, who had
come over to Charleston during the Cherokee campaign to be with him, died of fever while he was campaigning up-country. He left the regiment on promotion to Major-commandant of the new-raising 119th
Foot which never saw combat but, instead, was used to
supply drafts to the 87th and 88th Regiments of Foot
serving in Germany. At the peace, Sir Allan exchanged
to half-pay to Inchkenneth, one of his smaller islands in
the district of Mull, where he took up residence with
one of his three daughters. In 1772, he was promoted to
lieutenant-colonel in the Army, and the following year
was visited by Samuel Johnson and James Boswell on
their 1773 Tour of the Hebrides. Johnson was delighted
with their reception "*by a gentleman and two ladies of high
birth, polished manners and elegant conversation*" who
"*practiced all the kindness of hospitality and refinement of
courtesy.*" Johnson recorded: "*Sir Allan is the Chieftain of
the great clan of Maclean, which is said to claim second place
among the Highland families, yielding only to Macdonald.
Though by misconduct of his ancestors, most of the extensive
territory which would have descended to him, has been alien-
ated, he still retains the dignity and authority of his birth.*"
Died without a male heir, 10 December 1783.

CBs; SBs; BALs; Stewart, *Sketches*, I-II, *in passim*; Samuel Johnson, *A Journey to the Western Isles of Scotland*, Chapter 30,
"Inchkenneth"; NAS GD 87/1/85.

James Robertson, y^r of Lude, (c.1740-1771)

Capt: 19 July 1757, 77th Foot; half-pay 24 December
1763.

Oldest son of the Laird of Lude, John Robertson, and
Charlotte Murray, daughter of William Murray, 2nd
Lord Nairne. Older brother of Lt. John Robertson, 42nd
Foot Additional Companies. Also a kinsman of Major
John [Robertson] Reid and Lt. John Small, also 42nd
Foot [see 42nd Register for all three officers]. Before
leaving for America, James married his first cousin,
Margaret Murray, 4 April 1758. He would not return to
Scotland for another eight years. Commanded one of
the 77th's three Additional Companies sent to Pennsylvania as reinforcements, spring 1758. Participated in the
1758 capture of Fort Duquesne, subsequently re-named
Fort Pitt by General Forbes. His company and another
were selected to remain behind as garrison troops for
the winter. Robertson was a great help in rebuilding
and re-fortifying Fort Pitt and appears to have had
extensive engineering experience, perhaps gained on
foreign service. Capt Harry Gordon, an engineer with
the Royal Americans described Robertson as "*an officer
of Practise, and great Application to our Bussiness. He told
me he would willingly goe to P.burgh on the Footing of being
paid as Pract^r Eng^r. That Gentleman might be of great Consequence at such a Post – As I am of the Opinion he could be
as useful as any Engineer. ….*" Robertson's company was
left behind at Pittsburgh when the 77th relocated from
Lancaster, PA to Albany, NY to participate in Amherst's
expedition against Ticonderoga and Crown Point. He
did not rejoin his regiment until mid-November 1759
and the following year participated in the capture of
Montréal. In 1761, while *en route* to Dominica in the
Caribbean, his transport was attacked by a French privateer. He and several soldiers were wounded when
they successfully defended their transport against
boarders. Their seriously damaged transport returned
to New York. He commanded the 77th light infantry
company at the battle of Bushy Run, 4-5 August 1763,
and appears to have been the senior 77th officer present. He commanded the remnants of the nine companies that had served in the Caribbean, less those who
transferred to the 42nd Foot in late 1763, and marched
them back to New York via Philadelphia to take ship for
home and disbandment. Robertson's remnant company
however was tasked one last time while in Philadelphia, ordered to protect the Moravian Indians from a
lynch mob comprising displaced Scotch-Irish settlers
from the Pennsylvanian frontier. Robertson's hard-bit-
ten veterans escorted these terrified Christian Indians

as far as Perth Amboy, and earned Benjamin Franklin's glowing praise for their professional demeanor, a sound testament to Robertson's leadership skills. He died 26 July 1771.

CBs; *SBs*; *BALs*; Pennsylvania *Gazette*, 30 July 1767.

Allan Cameron, of Glendessary (c.1730-c.1795)
Capt: 22 July 1757, 77th Foot; resigned 14 September 1760.

Allan Cameron, younger brother of John, 3rd of Glendessary, was a son of Allan, 2nd of Glendessary and Christian, daughter of Sir Ewen Cameron of Lochiel by his wife Jean Barclay, daughter of Col. David Barclay, 17th of Urie. Allan Cameron was appointed captain in the 77th Foot, 22 January 1757, his previous military service unknown. Commanded one of the three Additional Companies sent over spring 1758 to Pennsylvania as reinforcements and participated in the capture of Fort Duquesne, subsequently re-named Fort Pitt by General Forbes. He resigned his commission 14 September 1760 a year after the death of his first cousin, Captain Allan Cameron of Dungallon, 78th Foot (see 78th Register) from fever at the siege of Québec, 3 September 1759. His cousin Dungallon left him his estates and Glendessary joined the St. Andrew's Society of New York in 1760 as he passed through that city to take ship home for Scotland. He was succeeded by his son, Alexander.

CBs; *SBs*; *BALs*; WO 25/209: 226-28.

Mungo Campbell (1728-1777)
Ensign: 18 July 1745, Argyllshire Militia;
Lieut: -
Capt: 15 September, 1758, 77th Foot; transferred 55th Foot, 17 September 1760;
Major: 31 August 1770, 55th Foot; transferred on promotion;
Lt-Col: 15 June 1776, 52nd Foot.

Mungo Campbell was the illegitimate son of John Campbell of Barcaldine and half-brother to the 77th's second Major, Alex Campbell. He was present when his half-uncle, Colin Campbell of Glenure, ("Red Fox") was murdered, and was a principal witness at the famous Appin Murder Trial of Jamie Stewart. Mungo was originally trained as a lawyer, then became a Factor for Barcaldine after Colin's death. As an ensign in the Argyllshire Militia during the '45 he was used by the Commander in Chief in Scotland to ferret out Jacobites in the

Highlands after Culloden. He was granted the last free captaincy in the 77th and came to North America in the summer of 1759, commanding the last Additional company bringing the regiment's total establishment up to fourteen companies. His half-uncle, Major Allan Campbell of the 42nd at Fort Ticonderoga noted to another brother, Duncan of Glenure, that *"Mungo with his Companie arrived here a few days ago."* After the capture of Montréal 1760 and the announced reductions to the Highland regiments, he transferred into the more senior (and less likely to be reduced) 55th Foot. This deal was, no doubt, brokered between his half-nephew, Major Alexander Campbell commanding the 77th Foot (Montgomery was away with six companies, plus Grant, fighting the Cherokees in SC) and Major Alexander Duncan, 55th Foot. Mungo spent some time at Forts Ontario and Fort Brewerton in western NY and mightily impressed one young lady in the wilderness. The well-known Scottish author and poet, Anne McVicar Grant (of Laggan) while traveling to Oswego with her father, Duncan McVicar, an officer of the 55th met *"Captain Mungo Campbell, whose warm and generous heart, whose enlightened and comprehensive mind, whose social qualities and public virtues I should delight to commemorate did my limits permit; suffice it, that he is endeared to my recollection by being the first person who ever supposed me to have a mind capable of culture, and I was ever after distinguished by his partial notice. Here we were detained by a premature fall of snow. Very much disposed to be happy anywhere, I was here particularly so."*
Mungo remained in the 55th Foot for another ten years before promotion to Major. Just after the outbreak of the American Revolution, Mungo was made Lt. Col. commanding the 52nd Foot on 15 June 1776. He was killed the following year – 7 October 1777 - leading an assault on a fort ironically named for a fellow Scot – Montgomery – and the name of his former regiment and commanding officer.

CBs; *SBs*; *BALs*; Stewart, *Sketches*, I-II, *in passim*; Anne [McVicar] Grant, *Memoirs of an American Lady*, Vol I., (New York, 1901 [reprint]), 63; WO 25/209: 226-228.

Alexander MacIntosh* (1725-1780)
2nd Lieut: IHC, 1745-46; 1 January 1749, Dutch-Scots Brigade;
Capt-Lt: 4 January 1757, 77th Foot;
Capt: 15 September 1758, 77th Foot; half-pay, 24 December 1763.

One of two Alexander MacIntoshs that served in the Dutch-Scots Brigade, most likely the one listed in the

Scots Magazine in 1747 listing officers of Lord Drum-lanrig's Regiment, then raising in Scotland. He is shown as "*Alex. McIntosh, a lieut. of the independent companies, brother to the laird* [Captain Aeneas McIntosh, 42nd Foot]." In 1758, while serving as the captain-lieutenant of the 77th in Charles Town, South Carolina, McIntosh was ordered by secret dispatch to report immediately to Admiral Boscawen at Halifax by William Pitt. There he met Robert Macpherson, chaplain of the 78th Fraser's, who recorded in a letter home: "*Capt McIntosh of Montgomerie's is come here from general Forbes, all those gentlemen of that Regt. are alive & hearty.*" By the time Forbes finally reached Fort Ligonier, Macintosh had returned from the successful siege with dispatches from General Abercromby. Appears on the *List of the Officers Recommended by the Honbl. Col. Montgomery* for promotion after Grant's raid *in absentia*. Promoted "*in room of Capt. McDonald Kd . . . Capt. Lieut. Alex. McIntosh Recommended by Lord Eglintoun, has served long in the Dutch Service. . . .*" He fought in all major campaigns thereafter and exchanged to half-pay, 24 December 1763, and died 4 January 1780.

General Return, 1757; Officers List, 1756; CBs; SBs; BALs; Stewart, *Sketches,* I-II, *in passim; WO 34/44:* f.182.

Charles Farquharson* (1716-1762)

Ensign: March, 1744, Dutch Scots Brigade
Lieut: 1748, Dutch-Scots Brigade; 6 January 1757, 77th Foot;
Capt: 16 September 1758; 77th Foot.

The 41-year-old Farquharson was a 15- year veteran of the Dutch-Scots brigade and the senior lieutenant of the regiment at the time of its raising. On a list of proposed officers for the new regiment he is noted as "*Cousin to Invercauld.*" He appears on the *List of the Officers Recommended by the Honbl. Col. Montgomery* after the Fort Duquesne Raid, promoted *in room of Capt. Munro Kd* The Colonel's annotation reads "*Lieut. Farquharson the Eldest Lieut. in the Regiment hath Served long in the Dutch Service, Recommended by Col. Montgomery and a good officer. . . .*" "*Capt Fargison*" also appears in Sir William Johnson's Papers on a list of 77th officers entitled "*Died at Havana,*" 1762.

General Return, 1757; Officers List, 1756; CBs; SBs; BALs; Stewart, *Sketches,* I-II, *in passim; WO 34/44:* f.182.; *SWJP;* Parson Robert Macpherson to William Macpherson, 20 July 1758, *Grand Camp before Louisbourg, LOC,* James Grant Papers, Microfilm no. 46 [hereafter *JGP*].

George Clerke

Ensign: 4 September, 1754, 44th Foot;
Lieut: 3 July 1755; 44th Foot; transferred on promotion;
Capt: 14 September 1760; 77th Foot; half-pay, 24 December 1763; exchanged full-pay, 49th Foot, 27 September 1764; transferred on promotion;
Major: 9 March 1768, 43rd Foot;
Lt-Col: 8 February 1775; retired 28 August 1776.

Went to North America as a young ensign with his regiment, the 44th Foot, as part of the 1755 expedition against Fort Duquesne. Survived the massacre on the Monongahela and was promoted lieutenant, 3 July 1755. Fought at Ticonderoga with the 44th and took part in the capture of Forts Ticonderoga and Crown Point in 1759. After the capture of Montréal and surrender of New France, he exchanged into the 77th Foot on promotion to captain, 14 September 1760, and went with them to Halifax, Nova Scotia to garrison that province. His company and eight others were sent to Dominica in spring 1761 as part of a 2000 man force under Lord Rollo. After falling sick with fever, he was sent to New York for recovery and joined Colonel William Amherst's staff as a "volunteer" for the 1762 expedition to recapture St John's Newfoundland from the French. He fought at Bushy Run in August 1763 then exchanged to half-pay in December 1763. He returned to active service with the 49th Foot as a company commander, then transferred on promotion to major of the 43rd Foot. Clerke was subsequently promoted its lieutenant-colonel in February 1775, but retired the following year, 28 August 1776.

CBs; SBs; BALs; Stewart, *Sketches,* I-II, *in passim;* Ford, *Officers,* 27; "*A List of the General and Staff Officers, etc...serving in NA,*" (New York, 1777), 5.

Nicholas Sutherland* (1738-1781).

Ensign: 63rd (later 60th) Foot (Royal Americans);
Lieut: 8 January 1757, 77th Foot;
Capt-Lt: 15 September 1758, 77th Foot;
Capt: 31 December 1761, 77th Foot; half-pay, 24 December 1763; exchanged, 14 March 1765, 21st Foot (Royal North British Fuzileers);
Maj: 21 February 1772, 21st Foot; transferred on promotion;
Lt-Col: 5 November 1776, 47th Foot.

Natural son of the 17th Earl of Sutherland and Christian Nicol. Young Nicholas went to America as an ensign in the 60th Foot (Royal Americans) and was assigned to the 1st Battalion under Lt. Col. Henry Bouquet. Transferred to the 77th Foot in Charleston, South Carolina, a relative recorded *"Nicholas Sutherland has got a 1st Lieutenancy in the new Highland Regiment, Captain Sinclair, Ulbster's brother has got a Company. Sutherland is in his Company as is Hugh Gordon, Carrol's son 2nd Lt. and Wm. McLean Capernoch's son."* Appears on *The List of the Officers Recommended by the Honbl. Col. Montgomery* after the Fort Duquesne Raid for promotion *"in room of C. Lt. McIntosh…Lieut. Nicholas Sutherland, has Served in the Royal American Reg.t Recommended by Lord Sutherland."* Commanded the Colonel's company during the 1760 Cherokee campaign and was wounded at the Battle of Etchoe Pass. Commissioned captain 31 December 1761, he exchanged briefly to half-pay 24 December 1763. He returned to active service in 1765 as a captain in the 21st Foot (Royal North British Fuzileers) and wrote from Mobile June 13, 1766, *"I am heartily sick of this country. 'Tis the worst I was ever in."* Promoted major to the 21st Foot in February 1772 and then transferred to the 47th Foot as their new lieutenant-colonel in November 1776. Sutherland was one of the negotiating officers for the surrender of John Burgoyne's army at Saratoga. Final terms of surrender were signed on 16 September and the British marched into captivity the following day. Sutherland requested parole on account of illness soon afterwards. George Washington wrote from Valley Forge, *May 12, 1778 "As Lieut. Colo. Southerland, Major Agnew and Lieut. Poe, have only requested to go to Europe on Parole, It does not appear to me, that I can with propriety apply to Genl. Howe for their exchange. This would imply that they were Prisoners of War. Tho' their exchange is certainly the most desirable mode of release, as it would relieve an equal number of our Officers from Captivity, yet I should be happy if a negociation for the purpose should commence on their part."* Sutherland was exchanged in late 1778. When a second battalion of the *Sutherland Fencibles*, a home defense unit was raised in 1779 by William Wemyss of Wemyss (1760-1822), the lieutenant-colonelcy was given to the experienced Nicholas Sutherland a rank he held concurrently with his command of the Fencibles. He died two years later in 1781 at Québec, still on parole, and was replaced by his half-brother James Sutherland of Uppat (c. 1726-1789).

General Return, 1757; Officers List, 1756; CBs; SBs; BALs; Stewart, Sketches, I-II, in passim; WO 34/44:f.182.; Letter dated 12 May 17778, Valley Forge in The Writings of George Washington, Fitzpatrick, ed.; Douglas Gilchrist Papers, SRO GD 153/37, Box 10, Bundle 32.

John Stuart (1740-c.1790)
Ensign: 5 June 1758, 19th Foot;
Lieut: 9 April 1761, 19th Foot; transferred on promotion; Capt: 16 July 1762, 77th Foot; half-pay 24 December 1763; exchanged, 25 December 1770, 37th Foot; retired 2 July 1777.

Born in Scotland, John started his military career with the 19th Foot and came to North America with the British contingent sent to assist in the reduction of Havana, 1762. When disease ravaged the officer corps of the 77th at the siege and Gaelic-speaking Highland officers were actively sought as replacements, Stuart transferred on promotion to captain. He went out on half-pay 24 December 1763 but returned to active service with the 37th Foot in December 1770. He retired 2 July 1777.

CBs; SBs; BALs.

James Grant* [2] (1738-1776)
Surgeon: 27 April 1756, 36th Foot;
Ensign: 12 January 1757, 77th Foot;
Lieut: 19 September 1758, 77th Foot;
Capt-Lt: 6 May 1762, 77th Foot;
Capt: 5 August 1762, 77th Foot; transferred, 17 August 1762, 40th Foot;
Maj: 12 December 1770, 40th Foot;
Lt-Col: 11 December 1775, 40th Foot.

Born in Scotland 1733, the son of Colonel James Grant and Elspeth Grant, James was commissioned surgeon to the 36th Foot in April 1756 at the age of 18. He was persuaded by Major Archie Montgomery, then also of the 36th Foot, to come and join his new raising Highland Battalion as an ensign, with a recommendation from Sir Ludovic Grant of Grant, his commission dated 12 January 1757. Served during the Fort Duquesne campaign on General Forbes' staff as his personal physician and ADC. A letter to Bouquet by Brigade Major Halkett dated 2nd August 1758 noted: *"Lieut James Grant of the Highland regiment, whom the General has a confidence in as a surgeon, to set out immediately for this place…"* Promoted lieutenant in the room of Lt. Roderick Mackenzie killed 14 September at Fort Duquesne, Grant was responsible for staffing the medal struck to commemorate Forbes' victory at Fort Duquesne, 1758 the following spring. Participated in all major campaigns and was made captain-lieutenant in May 1762 following the capture of Martinique. He was promoted captain at the siege of Havana in August 1762, and almost immediately transferred to the 40th Foot commanded by his kinsman and namesake, Lt. Col. James Grant. He was made major to the 40th Regiment, 12 December 1770. He became lieutenant- colonel of the 40th, 11 December 1775, and was killed in action the following year on Long Island.

General Return, 1757; Officers List, 1756; CBs; SBs; BALs; WO 34/44:f.182.

Robert Grant* (1734-1777)

Lieut: 25 January 1757, 77th Foot; appointed QM 11 May 1759; resigned QM on promotion;
Capt: 16 August 1762, 77th Foot; half-pay 24 December 1763; exchanged, 20 July 1764, 40th Foot; transferred on promotion;
Major: 5 March 1775, 24th Foot.

Born in Scotland, 1734, the notation on a 1756 list of potential officers for the new-raising regiment reads "*A Gentleman who it is thought will be very usefull in raising men.*" Commissioned lieutenant 25 January 1757, Grant served in all major campaigns of the regiment. Was appointed QM in room of Alexander Montgomery, 11 May 1759, holding both positions until he was promoted captain in August 1762 at the siege of Havana. Went out on half-pay 24 December 1763, but returned to active service as a captain the following year in Lt. Col. James Grant's 40th Foot. Was made major to the 24th Foot at the outbreak of the American Revolution and was killed in action at the battle of Hubbardton, 7 July 1777. Thomas Anburey recorded: "*Major Grant, of the 24th Regiment, who had the advance guard attacked their picquets, which were soon driven into the main body. From this attack we lament the death of this very gallant and brave officer, who in all probability fell a victim to the great disadvantages we experience peculiar to this unfortunate contest, those of the riflemen. Upon his coming up with the enemy, he got upon the stump of a tree to reconnoitre and had hardly given the men orders to fire, when he was struck by a rifle ball, fell off the tree, and never uttered another syllable…..*"

General Return, 1757; Officers List, 1756; CBs; SBs; BALs; Stewart, Sketches, I-II, in passim; Anburey: Travels Through the Interior Parts of America, Vol. 1, (London, 1789).

William Erving (1734-1791)

Ensign: 5 April 1756, 50th Foot; half-pay, 7 March 1757; full-pay, 24 September 1757, 15th Foot; Lieut: 29 July 1758, 15th Foot; transferred on promotion;
Capt: 18 August 1762, 77th Foot; half-pay 24 December 1763; full-pay, 6 May 1767, 47th Foot; retired, 14 March 1771.

Born 8 September 1734, in Boston, Massachusetts Colony, the 2nd son of John Erving (1693-1786), a native of Kirkwell, Orkney Islands, Scotland, and Abigail Phillips (1702-1759). The Ervings were a well-connected and influential American family. Older brother, John was married in 1754 to Maria Catherine Shirley, daughter of Governor William Shirley. His elder sister Elizabeth married James Bowdoin, founder of Bowdoin College, and his younger sister Sarah was married to Samuel Waldo, a wealthy Boston merchant and son of Colonel Samuel Waldo. William graduated from Harvard in 1753 and, not surprisingly, started his military career by being commissioned ensign in Shirley's 50th Foot, 5 April 1756. He exchanged to half-pay when the 50th was disbanded, 7 March 1757 but returned to active duty as an ensign in the 15th Foot in September the same year. He was made lieutenant in the 15th Foot, 29 July 1758, at the siege of Louisbourg. He participated in the battle of the Plains of Abraham, 1759, and was wounded the following year at the battle of Sillery at Québec, 28 April 1760. He went with his regiment to the Caribbean and purchased a captaincy in the 77th for £1100 while it was still at Havana. Recuperating with his men in New York in early 1763, he was ordered in June 1763 to take a detachment of recovered men of the two Highland battalions to Fort Niagara via Albany and Oswego during the Pontiac Uprising. He only made it as far as Fort Brewerton where he fell ill and was ordered by Amherst back to New York. He went on half-pay when the 77th was disbanded, 24 December 1763, but returned to active service four years later in May 1767 as a captain in the 47th Foot. Four years later, he retired from the army, 14 March 1771, and applied for a land grant. Erving was granted 5,400 acres in New Hampshire in 1775 which is still known today as Erving's Grant and is one of the few unincorporated areas left in the state today. Erving died in Boston, 30 May 1791 and was buried in the churchyard of King's Chapel.

CBs; SBs; BALs; WO 25/209: 15th Foot.

James Duff* (1731-c.1800)

Ensign: 2 June 1747, 2nd Halkett's, Dutch-Scots Brigade; resigned, 30 January 1757;
Lieut: 11 January 1757, 77th Foot;
Capt: 19 October 1762, 77th Foot; half-pay, 24 December 1763; full pay, 28 February 1766; 40th Foot;
Major: "in the Army," 29 August 1777; retired 26 January 1780.

The son of the Laird of Culbin who started his military career in Drumlanrig's Regiment of the Dutch-Scots Brigade as an ensign in 1747. Ten years later, James was a lieutenant in Halkett's Regiment from which he resigned in order to take a commission as lieutenant in the 77th Foot, 11 January 1757. He was promoted captain in the aftermath of the siege of Havana, October 1762, and exchanged the following year to half-pay. He returned to active service in February 1766 as a captain in Lt. Col. James Grant's 40th Foot. He was made a major "in the Army" while serving during the American Revolution, but took his retirement in January 1780.

General Return, 1757; Officers List, 1756; CBs; SBs; BALs; Stewart, Sketches, I-II, in passim; DSB, 412, 423.

Captains-Lieutenant

Archibald Robertson* (1727-1776)

Ensign: January, 1747, Dutch-Scots Brigade;
Lieut: 10 November 1753, Dutch-Scots Brigade, resigned 25 April 1756; 9 January 1757, 77th Foot;
Capt-Lt: 31 December 1761, 77th Foot; transferred on promotion;
Capt: 6 May 1762, 100th Foot; half-pay, 18 November 1763; full-pay, 15 August 1775, 47th Foot.

Started his military career in the Dutch-Scots Brigade as an ensign in June 1747 and was commissioned a lieutenant in the 77th Foot, ten years later, on 9 January 1757. Served in Captain William Macdonald's company during Grant's raid and was one of two officers ordered forward by Grant to burn outbuildings outside the fort in order to lure the French garrison out. He was wounded during the battle on Grant's Hill, but managed to escape with other men of his platoon. As the most senior survivor of the 77th Foot detachment, he collected and took command of the largest group of survivors of the assorted corps and led it back to Loyalhannon Camp assisted by Lt. Henry Munro. He was made captain lieutenant in the 77th Foot, 31 December 1761, "*in room of*" Nicholas Sutherland promoted after the capture of Dominica. Robertson transferred to the 100th Foot (Campbell's Highlanders) as a captain, 6 May 1762, to replace Captain John McKaarg who was murdered by a former Black Watch officer, Major Colin Campbell (see 42nd Register). He was placed on half-pay when the 100th Foot was disbanded, 18 November 1763; he returned to active service in August 1775 as a

captain in the 47th Foot. He was discharged dead on 12 February 1776.

General Return, 1757; Officers List, 1756; CBs; SBs; BALs; Stewart, Sketches, I-II, in passim.

Alexander MacDonald* [1] (1728-c.1800)

Lieut: 17 January 1757, 77th Foot;
Capt-Lt: 5 August 1762, 77th Foot; half-pay 24 December 1763;
Capt: "by brevet," 25 May 1772; full-pay, 14 June 1775, 2nd RHE;
Major: "by brevet," 19 March 1783; half-pay, 2 February 1783;
Lt-Col: "in the Army," 1 March 1794.

Alex was born on the Isle of Skye in 1728. He served as a gentleman-volunteer in Lord Loudoun's Highlanders at the Battle of Bergen-op-Zoom in 1747 and for ten years served as a non-commissioned officer in Drumlanrig's Regiment, Dutch-Scots Brigade. Alex was commissioned a lieutenant in the new-raising Montgomery's Highlanders, 16 January 1757. Served in Captain William Macdonald's company during Grant's raid and was one of two officers ordered forward by Grant to burn outbuildings outside the fort in order to lure the French garrison out. He was seriously wounded during the subsequent battle on Grant's Hill, and was captured by Indians in the aftermath. He was returned to Fort Pitt in January 1760, and rejoined his regiment in time to participate in the capture of Montréal, 1760. He was wounded again at Martinique in 1762 and was made captain-lieutenant at the siege of Havana in August 1762. After the French and Indian War, he went on half pay and took land grants on Staten Island. In 1774, Alex was forced to leave his prosperous farm and family and follow his conscious as a loyal British subject and former King's officer. Alex informed his long time friends and former Highland officers, John Small (ex-42nd Foot) and now Major to the 21st Foot in New York and Captain Nicholas Sutherland, (ex-77th Foot) also 21st Foot, that he had devised a plan to raise a regiment of veteran Highland soldiers who had settled in America. Allegedly he had hundreds of potential subscribers willing to enlist but needed Small's connections to secure the authorization to form the corps. Small, he proposed could be the Commander, and McDonald would be his Major. Small could only get "unofficial" approval but was told by General Gage to go ahead and recruit his corps pending "official" approval coming from England. With this promise, Alex "*traveled through frost snow and ice all the way to the Mohawk River, where there was two hundred men of my own name who had fled from the severity of their landlords in the highlands of Scotland, the Leading men of whom most cheerfully agreed to be ready at a call, but the affair was obliged to be kept a profound secret 'till it was known whether the government approved of the scheme and otherwise I could have enlisted five hundred men in a months time."* In June 1775, he was made senior captain of the 2nd/84th Foot or Royal Highland Emigrants [RHE] and for his activities against the rebels, was convicted *in absentia* and sentenced to death. By 1780, he was writing from Halifax seeking preferment for his five years service noting that he was now a widower with five small children to care for: *"I have been a Voluntier at the Siege of Bergenobdensoome* [Bergen op Zoom] *in the year 1747 Lieut. upon every Active service the last War both in America and the West Indies, a Capt. Lieut. in the Year 1762 a full Captain in 1772 as appears by the List of the Army and of Course believe that I am now the Oldest Captain in the British Army. That I never was reprimanded in the Execution of my duty by any Superior Officer nor do I believe there are any in the world can broach my Character with ungentleman Behaviour....Lastly I have by this unnatural War lost all my property in America and since I came to this Province has lost a Worthy good Wife and left with five Weak Children."* He was made major "by brevet," 19 March 1783 and once again went on half-pay when the RHE were disbanded 2 February 1783. he was promoted lieutenant-colonel "in the Army" in March 1794 and died c.1800.

General Return, 1757; Officers List, 1756; CBs; SBs; BALs; Stewart, Sketches, I-II, in passim; "Letterbook of Captain MacDonald," CNYHS, (1882), 442-3.

Lieutenants

Alexander MacKenzie* (1721-1758)
Ensign: Dutch-Scots Brigade;
Lieut: 7 January 1757, 77th Foot.

Alexander McKenzie, son of Donald MacKenzie, 5th of Kilcoy and Elizabeth MacKenzie of Highfield. Started his military career *"carrying arms"* as a gentleman volunteer in the Dutch-Scots Brigade and was commissioned 2nd lieutenant, 2 June 1747. He was commissioned a lieutenant in Montgomery's Highlanders, 7 January 1757, and was killed in Grant's defeat near Fort Duquesne, 14 September 1758. Lt. Archibald Robertson noted in a letter after the battle that MacKenzie's man-servant *"when he heard his master was killed, ran in among*

the enemy and said he would have his revenge [even] *if they were a million strong."*

General Return, 1757; Officers List, 1756; CBs; SBs; BALs; Stewart, Sketches, I-II, in passim.

Duncan Bayne* (c.1735-1761)
2nd Lieut: 31 July 1756, 45th Company, Marines; transferred on promotion;
Lieut: 10 January 1757, 77th Foot.

Bayne or Bain was a native of Scotland who started his military career as a 2nd lieutenant in the 45th Marine Company, 31 July 1756, and was subsequently commissioned lieutenant in Montgomery's Highlanders. General Amherst recorded that Bain died on Dominique in August 1761 while the date of his actual death, recorded by Lord Rollo, the expedition commander, was 2 August 1761. The Commission Registers, in which his name is spelled Bean, indicate that he was replaced 31 December 1761.

General Return, 1757; Officers List, 1756; CBs; SBs; BALs; Stewart, Sketches, I-II, in passim; WO 34/55: ff. 19-20; WO 25/209: 226-228.

Colin Campbell* (c.1725-1758)
2nd Lieut: Dutch-Scots Brigade;
Lieut: 13 January 1757, 77th Foot.

Started his military career in the Dutch-Scots Brigade as a 2nd lieutenant and was originally slated to serve in the new–raising 78th (Fraser's Highlanders) but was commissioned instead as a lieutenant in the 77th Foot, 13 January 1757. Killed at Fort Duquesne, 14 September 1758.

General Return, 1757; Officers List, 1756; CBs; SBs; BALs; Stewart, Sketches, I-II, in passim.

Joseph Grant* (1710-c.1786)
Sergeant: Lord Loudoun's Highlanders;
Lieut: 22 January 1757, 77th Foot; half-pay, 24 December 1763.

Records indicate that Sergeant Joseph Grant with 27 years of previous military service last served with Lord Loudoun's Highlanders and was *"Brother to Grant of Auchterblair."* At 47 years of age, he was the oldest officer of the regiment, gazetted lieutenant in the 77th Foot, 22 January 1757. It would appear from regimental documents recently discovered in Ballindalloch Castle that

Joseph initially worked as one of the unofficial QMs, his signature appearing on many of the invoices acknowledging receipt of plaids, hose, bonnets and shoes. He apparently served on all major campaigns of the regiment and was placed on half-pay when the regiment was disbanded, 24 December 1763. He disappears from the half pay lists in 1786, for reasons unknown

General Return, 1757; Officers List, 1757; CBs; SBs; BALs.

Cosmo [Cameron] MacMartin,* 8th of Letterfinlay, (1737-1762)
Lieut: 26 January 1757, 77th Foot;

Cosmo [Cameron] MacMartin born 1737, was the eldest son of George [Cameron] MacMartin, 7th of Letterfinlay and Mary MacIntosh. He was recommended for one of the original lieutenant commissions of the 77th Foot by Lord Adam Gordon. He was gazetted 26 January 1757, and served in all major campaigns of the regiment. He was severely wounded in the head at the battle of Etchoe Pass during the 1760 punitive expedition against the Cherokee. In November 1760, Capt Gordon reported to Lt. Colonel James Grant that *"poor Lieut. McMartin is I am afraid past recovery. He is confined to his bed, is often insensible, deaf, dumb and blind. Doctor [Allen] Stuart & James Grant think he is threatened with a mortification of the bowels."* McMartin died in hospital of his wounds at New York, 15 November 1762.

General Return, 1757; Officers List, 1757; CBs; SBs; BALs; WO 34/47: ff. 17-18; John Gordon to James Grant, 18 November 1761, Halifax, JGP; Major Zobel to Amherst, 18 November 1762, New York. WO 34/91: f. 239.

John McNab* (1735-1762)
Lieut: 29 January 1757, 77th Foot.

John McNab was annotated in a list of potential officers for the new-raising regiment as *"Brother to the Laird of MacNab"* and was subsequently commissioned one of the original lieutenants of the 77th Foot, 29 January 1757. He served in all major campaigns of the regiment. *"Lt [John] McNab"* appears in Sir William Johnson's Papers on a list of 77th officers entitled *"Died at Havana,"* 1762 and the Commission Register confirms his date of death, 27 July 1762.

General Return, 1757; Officers List, 1757; CBs; SBs; BALs; Stewart, Sketches, I-II, in passim.

Hugh Gordon* (1739-1762)
Lieut: 31 January 1757, 77th Foot.

The 18-year-old Hugh Gordon was son of Hugh Gordon, 4th of Carrol, Sheriff Depute of Sutherland and Lucia Dunbar, daughter of Ludovic Dunbar of Grange. He was recommended for a commission by Lord Sutherland and is mentioned in a letter as initially being assigned as a 2nd lieutenant to John Sinclair's company when it traveled to North America in 1757. He was killed at Martinique, 24 January 1762.

General Return, 1757; Officers List, 1757; CBs; SBs; BALs; WO 34/55: f.58; O14.

Donald Macdonald* (1738-c.1800)
Lieut: 1 February 1757, 77th Foot; half-pay, 24 December 1763;
Capt: 25 December 1777, 76th Foot (Macdonald's Highlanders); retired, 9 November 1779.

Donald McDonald, recommended by Sir James Macdonald of Sleat, was commissioned lieutenant in the 77th Foot, 1 February 1757, and served on all major campaigns of the regiment. He was placed on half-pay, 24 December 1763, but returned to active service as a captain in the new-raising 76th (Macdonald's Highlanders) during the American Revolution. His newly-designated commanding officer, Lt. Colonel John Macdonell of Lochgarry, a former Fraser Highlander (see 78th Register) had been captured by the Americans at sea while returning from America to Scotland and thus Macdonald spent a year at Fort George near Inverness training his young Highlanders for overseas service in North America. In March 1779, the Highland soldiers were marched south to the Lowlands where they mutinied over outstanding pay matters and a false rumor that they were being sent to the West Indies. The men returned to duty after being promised their bounty money and that they were *not* to be sent to the West Indies. When the 76th finally sailed for New York, Macdonald remained behind for reasons unknown, retiring 9 November 1779.

General Return, 1757; Officers List, 1757; CBs; SBs; BALs; Stewart, Sketches, I-II, in passim.

William Mackenzie* (1711-1758)
Lieut: 3 February 1757, 77th Foot.

Married to Isobel Mackenzie, daughter of John Mackenzie, 4th of Belmaduthy, the 46-year-old William

Mackenzie was one of the original lieutenants commissioned in the 77th Foot, and at 46 years of age, the second oldest after Lt Joseph Grant. He was killed at Fort Duquesne on the morning of 14 September 1758.

General Return, 1757; Officers List, 1757; CBs; SBs; BALs; O14.

Roderick Mackenzie,* y^r of Gairloch, (1735-1758)
Lieut: 5 February 1757, 77th Foot.

Roderick Mackenzie was one of the original lieutenants commissioned in the 77th Foot. He was killed at Fort Duquesne on the morning of 14 September 1758.

General Return, 1757; Officers List, 1757; CBs; SBs; BALs; O14.

Henry Munro* [1] (1727—1782)
Lieut: 7 February 1757, 77th Foot; half-pay 24 December 1763.

The 3rd son of the Reverend John Munro of Halkirk, Caithness and Janet Gunn, heiress of Braemore. Henry's senior brother, John Gunn Munro of Braemore, was major tenant on the property of Navidale in Sutherland at the time of his commissioning in Montgomery's Highlanders. The holder of the wadset on this property was none other than Major James Grant, the senior major of the regiment (see above). Capt. Gordon Graham of Drainie and Lt. John Sutherland, 42nd Foot, (see 42nd register) were his brothers-in-law. Henry was wounded at Fort Duquesne on 14 September 1758 and one of four officers who escaped death or capture during the debacle. He subsequently fought in all the major campaigns of the 77th (Fort Duquesne, 1758, Ticonderoga & Crown Point 1759 and the 1761 Cherokee Expedition) with the exceptions of the capture of Montréal and the subsequent Caribbean campaigns. From late 1760, until the regiment's disbandment in 1763, he served as a company officer in John Sinclair's company garrisoning Annapolis Royal in Nova Scotia. On discharge he settled in the local area, receiving a grant of 2000 acres in 1765. He married Sarah Hooper, daughter of Thomas Hooper, one of the original Massachusetts's settlers in the township, and they had seven children. In 1765, he was elected the first representative of Granville in the province's legislative assembly, a post he resigned two years later. He became a justice of the peace and was commissioned a lieutenant-colonel in the militia in 1776, a position he held until 1782 when he died suddenly of apoplexy. His widow and young family were then taken care of financially by one of his older brothers, Sir George Gunn Munro, of Poytnzfield.

General Return, 1757; Officers List, 1757; CBs; SBs; BALs.

Alexander Macdonald* [2] (1731-1758)
Lieut: 9 February 1757, 77th Foot;

The 26-year-old Alex Macdonald transferred from the 36th Foot on the request of Major Archibald Montgomery of the same regiment and was gazetted a lieutenant 9 February 1757. He was killed at Fort Duquesne on the morning of 14 September 1758.

General Return, 1757; Officers List, 1757; CBs; SBs; BALs.

Donald Campbell* (1741-1782)
Lieut: 11 February 1757, 77th Foot; half-pay, 24 December 1763;
Capt: 19 December 1777, 74th Foot (Argyle Highlanders).

Born in Islay in 1741, the eldest son and heir of James Campbell, the tacksman of Balenabie, and Bethia Campbell, daughter of Charles Campbell of Ardchattan. Donald, 16, was the youngest lieutenant to be gazetted in the 77th Foot. He soldiered at Fort Duquesne 1758 and Ticonderoga and Crown Point in 1759. In a letter dated 27 July 1759 from Ticonderoga, written by his kinsman, Major Alex Campbell (see above), we learn a great deal about young Balenabie's education and situation: "*I shall be obliged to give Balinabys son more money this year, he spends money in good company, as he gott no Education before he left the Country keeping amongst the People I live with, is the only Method I can think of to supply that deficiency he is a very pretty Lad, butt would be lost if I did not take that method, his father may Grudge the money but I do it for the best, and would expect he would do the same by my son, Thirty pounds a year, will enable the boy to live in good Company, and I am Certain, tis better for him to get so much less from his father att the long, and be fitt to keep Gentlemens company than to go home as he would do, Scarce a Companion for a Ploughman, for which I took him into my Charge, he realy could hardly read or write [and] he is much obliged to Capt Roderick MacKenzie in whose Company he has always been.*" Donald "Balenabie" Campbell participated in the 1760 Cherokee expedition as a lieutenant of grenadiers and also fought in the Caribbean. He returned with the remnants of his regiment to recuperate on Long Island in spring 1763 and was well enough to join Bouquet's expedition raised that summer to relieve Fort Pitt upcountry. He personally led a flying column to the relief of Fort Ligonier from Fort Bedford during the Pontiac Uprising. He commanded the 77th grenadiers at the battle of Bushy Run 1763 where he was wounded; went out on half-pay the following year. Nine years later, in September 1773, James Boswell and Samuel Johnson met a Highland gentleman while visiting Skye September 1773, one Donald Campbell *"who had been lieutenant of grenadiers in the Highland regiment raised by Colonel Montgomery, now Earl of Eglintoune, in the war before last."* Boswell claimed, *"From this gentleman I first learnt how very popular the Colonel was among the Highlanders; of which I had such continued proofs, during the whole course of my Tour, that on my return I could not help telling the noble Earl himself, that I did not before know how great a man he was."* Balenabie returned to service in the new-raising 74th Foot (Argyll Highlanders) December 1777 during the American Revolution when offered a captaincy by Colonel John Campbell of Barbreck, a former officer of the 78th Fraser Highlanders (see 78th Register). In August 1778, the 74th sailed for Halifax, Nova Scotia and Balenabie was placed in command of the Light Company. The following year, his light infantry company and the 74th grenadiers were detached to serve at the siege of Charlestown where they acquitted themselves honorably. Captain Campbell died 23 February 1782 while still on detached command, his regiment then in garrison at Penobscot, Maine.

General Return, 1757; Officers List, 1757; CBs; SBs; BALs; Stewart, *Sketches,* I-II, *in passim; NAS* GD 87/1/85 Maj Alex Campbell to his father, Fort Edward Camp, 19 June 1759; Boswell, *Life of Johnson,* Vol. V., (Tour to the Hebrides).

Hugh Montgomerie, y[r] of Coilsfield, (1739-1819)
Lieut: 21 July 1757, 77th Foot;
Capt: 2 June 1762, 78th Foot; half-pay, 24 December 1763; full pay, 4 February 1767, 2nd 1st Foot; retired 27 January 1776;
Major: 14 April 1778, Argyll (Western) Fencibles;
Lt-Col: 6 March 1782, Argyll (Western) Fencibles; half-pay, 14 April 1778;
Col: appointed c. 1793, West Lowland Fencibles.

Son of Alexander Montgomery of Coilsfield, and younger first cousin of the Lt-Colonel Commandant, Archibald Montgomery, (see above) who was initially gazetted a lieutenant, 21 July 1757, in one of the three Additional Companies of the 77th Foot. Hugh participated in the capture of Fort Duquesne (Pittsburgh) in 1758, the capture of Forts Ticonderoga and Crown Point in 1759, and distinguished himself as a light infantry officer in fighting during the 1760 expedition against the Cherokees in 1760. He was too late returning from South Carolina to participate in Amherst's capture of Montréal and thus spent the next two years garrisoning Nova Scotia with the five companies left there for that purpose. In 1762, he exchanged to the 78th Foot (Fraser's Highlanders) on promotion to captain, 2 June 1762. (See rest of entry in 78th Register).

CBs; SBs; BALs; Stewart, *Sketches,* I-II, *in passim.*

James McLean (c.1740-1761)
Lieut: 27 July 1757, 77th Foot.

The youngest of nine children of Allan Maclean, 10th of Ardgour & Anne Cameron, daughter of Sir Ewen Cameron, 17th Lochiel & Isobel Maclean of Duart. Lt James Maclean's older sister Isobel married Donald Maclean, 3rd of Brolas, making him a first cousin of Sir Allan Maclean of Brolas. Came to North America as a lieutenant in his cousin's Additional Company. Participated in all major campaigns including the 1760 expedition against the Cherokees. *Lt James McLane* appears in Sir William Johnson's *Papers* on a list of officers entitled *"Died at Havana,"* 1762. In fact, he was killed in action at sea on 1 June 1761 when Capt. James Robertson's transport, *en route* to Dominica, was attacked by a French privateersman.

CBs; SBs; BALs; SWJP; O14.

Alexander Campbell [2], s[nr], (c.1735-1786)
Lieut: 29 July 1757, 77th Foot; appointed adjutant, 1 February 1763; half-pay, 24 December 1763.

Alexander Campbell was gazetted lieutenant in one of the 77th Additional Companies that arrived at Philadelphia in April 1758. He participated in the capture of Fort Duquesne, 1758, and served in all major campaigns of the regiment. Appointed adjutant *"in room of"* John Campbell of Melfort, February 1763. After fighting at Bushy Run in 1763, he wrote to Bouquet that he would like to continue in a military career with the Royal Americans, but was reluctant to do so unless he could keep his appointment as adjutant, in addition to his rank of lieutenant. Bouquet declined and Campbell returned to Scotland on half-pay. Appointed Chamberlain and Baillie of North and South Kintyre by the Duke of Argyle on 11 November 1767. He died 10 April 1786, still on lieutenant's half pay.

CBs; SBs; BALs; Stewart, Sketches, I-II, in passim; WO 25/209, 77th Foot.

John Campbell, yʳ of Melfort, (1730-1790)
Lieut: 30 July 1757, 77th Foot; adjutant, 77th, 11 July 1759, resigned adjutancy, 1 February 1763; transferred on promotion;
Capt: 1 February 1763, 42nd Foot; half-pay 24 October 1763;
Major: 1778, Western (Argyll) Fencibles.

A cousin of Major Alex Campbell, 77th Foot, and Captain Mungo Campbell, 77th Foot, (see both above). Came to North America as an officer in one of the Additional Companies. Participated in all major campaigns of the regiment, including the capture of Montréal in 1760. Transferred to the 42nd Foot, on promotion. Exchanged to half-pay, 1763. Was second-major in the Argyll (Western) Fencibles along with first Major Hugh Montgomerie, another former 77th officer. When that regiment mutinied at Edinburgh in October 1779, it was the popular Melfort's calm actions, along with Montgomerie's assistance, that quelled the disturbances.

CBs; SBs; BALs; Stewart, Sketches, I-II, in passim.

James Macpherson (1725-c.1790)
Lieut: 31 July 1757, 77th Foot;
Capt: 18 October 1761, 105th Foot; half-pay 31 March 1763; full pay, 1 September 1771, 42nd Foot;
Major: "in the Army," 29 August 1777; retired 5 June 1778.

Son of Alexander Macpherson of Glenfyne and the younger brother of Mary, wife of Duncan Campbell of Glenure (later Barcaldine), the uncle of Major Alexander Campbell (see above). Commissioned as a lieutenant in one of the three Additional Companies, Macpherson arrived in North America, spring 1758, at Philadelphia. Major Alex Campbell reported to his uncle from Ticonderoga, 27 July 1759, that "your Broyr in law Jamie is well." He was commissioned captain in the new-raising 1st Battalion of the 105th Foot in October 1761 and placed on Irish half-pay at its disbandment, 31 March 1763. He returned to active service as a captain in the 42nd Foot in September 1771 and took command of the Light Infantry company during the Philadelphia Campaign and commanded the Army's

advance guard at the battle of Brandywine. Promoted major "in the Army," 29 August 1777. He retired 5 June 1778.

CBs; SBs; BALs; Stewart, Sketches, I-II, in passim; NAS GD 170/1067: f.2.

John Martin (c.1740-c.1811)
Lieut: 26 April 1757, NY Independent Coy (Wraxall's); transferred 77th Foot, 30 March 1758; half-pay, 24 December 1763.

A gentleman volunteer who "caryed armes in the Highland Regiment [42nd Foot]" according to Lord Loudoun and "Was recommended by the Earl of Eglinton & Lord Barrington" and was gazetted a lieutenant, first in Captain Peter Wraxall's New York Independent Company 26 April 1757, then transferred to the 77th Foot, 30 March 1758. He went out on half-pay 24 December 1763 and was on the list of half pay officers for 47 years, his name finally disappearing in 1810.

CBs; SBs; BALs; Pargellis, MA, 334.

Archibald McVicar
Ensign: 16 July 1757, 77th Foot;
Lieut: 15 September 1758, 77th Foot.

McVicar was commissioned ensign in one of three Additional Companies authorized for the 77th Foot, 16 July 1757, and lieutenant, 15 September 1758. He participated in all major campaigns of the regiment and was killed at the Havana 13 July 1762.

CBs; SBs; BALs; Stewart, Sketches, I-II, in passim.

Alexander Grant* (1734-1813)
Ensign: 4 January 1757, 77th Foot;
Lieut: 15 September 1758, 77th Foot.

Born in Inverness-shire, Scotland, 2nd son of Patrick Grant, the 7th Laird of Glenmoriston and Isobel Grant of Craskie. Brother-in-law to Lt Ewan Cameron, 78th Foot. (see 78th Register). Served five years with the Royal Navy as a midshipman, but on 4 January 1757 accepted a commission in Montgomery's Highlanders as its senior ensign. He survived Grant's Raid at Fort Duquesne in September 1758 as he was sent back early during the action by Major James Grant to convey the news of the disaster and to request assistance for the survivors. He was promoted lieutenant after the raid "in room of Charles Farquharson" was who moved up to the captain-lieutenancy. Amherst placed Grant in command of the *Boscawen* sloop, 16 guns, on Lake Champlain during the 1759 campaign against Crown Point, and the following year, gave him a command on Lake Ontario for the 1760 campaign. After the war, Grant was one of several 77th officers who decided to remain in North America, taking up a land grant at Grosse Pointe near Detroit and marrying Therese Barthe, (1758-1810) in 1774. In 1776, Grant became Commander of the Provincial Marine on the Great Lakes during the Revolution, though this appointment was reduced to Lakes Erie, Huron, and Michigan in 1778. He held the appointment until 1812 when he retired with the rank of Commodore. He was appointed a Justice of the Peace in 1786. Grant served on the Land Board of the District of Hesse from 1789 until 1794 and was appointed Lieutenant of Essex County in 1799. As a senior member of the Executive and Legislative Councils of Upper Canada, he became Administrator-President for a year upon the death of Lieutenant-Governor Hunter in 1805. A contemporary observer of Grant described him as "*a large, stout man, not very polished, but very good tempered, (who) had a great many daughters, all very good looking, all very lively, all very fond of dancing and all very willing to get married as soon as possible.*" In fact Grant had 11 daughters and a son with Therese Barthe, his wife of 36 years. He retired as Commodore at the age of 78 but did not long enjoy his retirement, dying on May 8, 1813 at his beloved Castle Grant. Grant is buried in St. John's churchyard, Sandwich, [Windsor] Ontario.

General Return, 1757; Officers List, 1757; CBs; SBs; BALs; Stewart, *Sketches,* I-II, *in passim;* "Alexander Grant," *DCB,* V, 363-64; Gilkison Family Papers: 1786-1910, *Archives of Ontario* MSS. 497; *WO* 34/44: f.182.

Charles Robertson (c.1735-1763)
Midshipman: c.1752, RN;
Lieut: 15 September 1758, 77th Foot;

A former naval officer, Robertson was commissioned a lieutenant in 14th Additional Company of the 77th commanded by Mungo Campbell in 1759. He was known to, and may have been a relative of, Lieutenant Colonel James Robertson, Amherst's Deputy QM General. Capt. Joshua Loring, RN, wrote that "*Lieut: Robertson, who was sent up to relieve Mr. Grant, was a Good Seaman had been a long time in the Navy.*" Charles Robertson was selected by Loring to serve as his First Lieutenant aboard the *Duke of Cumberland* Brig constructed for Amherst's 1759 campaign on Lake Champlain. He subsequently supervised repairs to the captured French

sloops that were put up at Fort Ticonderoga during the winter of 1759/60. Whilst commanding a patrol in March 1760, he discovered more than 100 batteaux abandoned by the French near the fort the previous summer. He participated in the capture of Montréal in 1760 and, when his battalion was sent to garrison Halifax in late September 1760, he was retained by Amherst in order to build two armed sailing vessels at Fort Niagara on Lake Ontario. This would indicate that Robertson may have had previous experience as a shipbuilder as well for he finished the *Huron*, a six-gun schooner in late 1761, but could not get it through the rapids at the head of the Niagara River and had to wait until the following year. The *Huron* became the first British sailing vessel on Lake Erie, and by mid-summer was joined by Robertson's second ship, the sloop *Michigan*, both of which he took to Detroit where they spent the winter. In the spring of 1763, "Captain" Robertson, accompanied by Sir Robert Davers, led a land party to look for a passage up to Lake Huron through the sand bars blocking the St. Charles River. They were ambushed and captured 6 May 1763 at the head of the river. Robertson and Davers were both killed outrightly, then roasted and eaten. John Rutherfurd, a 17-year-old member of the same party was captured, later escaped and commissioned an ensign in the 42nd Foot (See 42nd Register above). Captain Trent writing to Governor Dinwiddie of Virginia wrote: "*They boiled and eat Sir Robert Davers, and we are informed by Mr. Pauley who escaped the other day, that he had seen an Indian with the skin of Captain Robertson's arm for a tobacco pouch!*" Robertson's ships however ensured that reinforcements and much-needed supplies reached the beleaguered garrison of Detroit during the long tense months of Pontiac's rebellion in 1763.

CBs; SBs; BALs; Loring to Amherst, 6 October 1759. *WO* 34/64: f. 168 "Charles Robertson," *DCB;* Macdonald, "Journal of the Siege of Detroit," Clements Library, Gage Papers, American Series; Robertson to Gage, 3 March 1760; *Journal of Captain William Trent,* Alfred T. Goodman, ed., (Cincinnati, 1871), 88; Rutherford, *John Rutherford's Captivity Narrative, 1763* in *The Siege of Detroit in 1763* M. Quaife, ed., (Chicago, 1958), 219-274.

William Hagart* (c. 1725-1792)
Ensign: 6 January 1757, 77th Foot;
Lieut: 16 September 1758; 77th Foot; appointed QM, 16 August 1762; half-pay, 24 December 1763.

William was born circa 1725-30 in Kenmore, Perthshire, and commissioned the second senior ensign in the 77th Foot, "*Recommended by the Duke of Athole and by Col.*

Montgomery." William was promoted to lieutenant after Major Grant's botched raid of 14 September 1758. He participated in all major campaigns of the 77th and was appointed QM at the siege of Havana, 1762, an appointment he retained until the regiment was disbanded in December 1763 and he went out on half-pay. After the war, Hagart applied for, and was granted, 2000 acres of woodland in what is now Vermont to the east of Lake Champlain. In 1765, he went back to Scotland, married Marion Cairns and began a wine importing business in North Leith, the seaside port of Edinburgh. In 1777, when his former commanding officer, Archibald Montgomery (now the 11th Earl Eglinton) and some other friends formed "The Hunter's Club," 25th October, 1777, they proposed the former 77th QM be appointed an honorary member and serve as their Secretary. A prestigious association with restricted membership of noblemen and country gentry *"who shared a common interest in field sports, races, balls and social assemblies,"* the Hunter's Club of Edinburgh later became the Royal Caledonian Hunt. Hagart served as Hunt Secretary until his death, 7 August 1792, when his two sons, William and Henry, succeeded him.

General Return, 1757; Officers List, 1757; CBs; SBs; BALs; Stewart, *Sketches,* I-II, *in passim.*

Lewis Houston* (1741-1802)
Ensign: 8 January 1757, 77th Foot;
Lieut: 16 September 1758, 77th Foot; half-pay, 24 December 1763;
Capt: East Sutherland Volunteers, c.1790-1798

Lewis Houston was *"recommended by Capt. Dougall [Dugald] Campbell, Member for Argyleshire [1754-1764]"* for an ensigncy in the 77th and after Grant's disastrous raid of 13 September 1758, was on *"the List of the Officers Recommended by the Hon*[bl.] *Col. Montgomery...to be Lieutenant.* Houston participated in all of the major campaigns of the regiment and retired on half-pay in 1763. He returned to Scotland and became a gentleman farmer at Helmsdale in Easter Sutherland, a justice of the peace [c.1773] and a captain commanding the Helmsdale Company of the East Sutherland Volunteers until 20 July 1798. Two years later, the celebrated author of *Memorabilia Domestica, or Parish Life in the North of Scotland,* Douglas Sage, described a trip he made to Sutherland in 1800: *"At Helmsdale we lodged under the hospitable roof of Mr. and Mrs. Houston. Mr. Louis Houston was an amiable man. He occupied the small farm of Easter Helmsdale and the places of Scallbisdale and Suisgill in the Parish of Kildonan, both of which he had sublet to small ten-*

ants. The disorder of which in a few years he died had just begun and he was very nervous. Now, for the first time I met with Mrs. Houston, his kind and motherly wife, with whom my acquaintance continued for upwards of twenty years. . ." Houston would appear to have suffered from Parkinson's or some other disorder of the nervous system and was dead by 1803 according to legal documents.

General Return, 1757; Officers List, 1757; CBs; SBs; BALs; Douglas Sage, *Memorabilia Domestica or Parish Life in the North of Scotland;* "Returns of Officers Services," WO 25/760; *Papers on Sutherland Estate Management 1802;* WO 34/44: f.182.

John MacKinnon (c.1735 -1774).
Lieut: 16 September 1758, 77th Foot; half-pay, 24 December 1763.

John, j[nr] was born on the Isle of Skye, eldest son of John MacKinnon of Mishnish and a half-nephew of Lachlan Mhor, the 28th Chieftain. He is reputed to initially have been offered a commission as an ensign in the 42nd Regiment (Black Watch) but no record of this can be found in the Army Lists or 42nd Muster Rolls. He may have been a gentleman-volunteer *"carrying arms"* with the 42nd but his commissioning date indicates he was taken into the 77th Foot as a lieutenant 16 September 1758 and came to America in the summer of 1759 with the 14th Additional Company commanded by Captain Mungo Campbell. Went to fight the Cherokee in 1760 and was subsequently sent to Nova Scotia where his company remained in garrison at Lunenburg and Annapolis Royal for the rest of the war. Probably served in the same 77th company as Lt. Henry Munro whose family's oral tradition claims he was second-in-command at Annapolis Royal, and like Mackinnon, decided to settle in Nova Scotia. When the regiment was disbanded in late 1763, John settled in Yarmouth, Nova Scotia and purchased land there as early as 1762, probably from Acadian residents. Formal grants of land followed in 1767 as a reward for his military services and also for helping to incorporate Yarmouth as a township with the appropriate authorities in Halifax. Records show him receiving 12 shares of land over three divisions, for a total of 3763 acres. John eventually settled at Chebogue, Nova Scotia and cleared some 30 or 40 acres for stock rearing, a venture in keeping with his Highland background. In 1769, he was appointed a justice of the peace. On 7th January 1774, he left Chebogue to visit his brother Ranald who lived at Argyle on the southeastern shore of Nova Scotia but, on his way, drowned in the Tusket Island Sluice. His remains were recovered and buried in the Chebogue cemetery.

CBs; SBs; BALs; Stewart, *Sketches*, I-II, *in passim*; G.S. Brown, *Yarmouth, Nova Scotia*, (Boston, 1888), 177, 268-71.

William McLean* (1740-c.1790)

Ensign: 10 January 1757, 77th Foot;
Lieut: 18 September 1758, 77th Foot; transferred, 24 July 1762, 40th Foot;
Capt-Lt: 1 April 1773, 40th Foot;
Capt: 28 April 1774, 40th Foot; retired 6 May 1776; 8 February 1779, Sutherland Fencibles.

Initially *"Recommended by Lord Sutherland,"* William McLean was son of James McLean of Capernoch, Factor to the estate of Skelbo in Sutherland, and his wife Jean Sutherland, daughter to Captain Robert Sutherland of Langwell, a cadet family of the Sutherlands of Forse. Appears on a *"List of the Officers Recommended by the Hon^bl. Col. Montgomery* for promotion from ensign to lieutenant after Grant's Raid, 14 September 1758. He fought in all major actions of the war and while at the siege of Havana, 1762, transferred into Lt. Col James Grant's 40th Foot , a more senior regiment and not likely to be disbanded at the peace. With a regimental seniority dated 24 July 1762 he was not forced to go on half-pay as were many of his contemporaries of the 77th. He was promoted captain-lieutenant to the 40th in April 1773 and to captain in April 1774. He retired on 6 May 1776, but on his return to Scotland, joined the Sutherland Fencibles as a captain and served until that home defense regiment was disbanded in 1783.

General Return, 1757; Officers List, 1757; CBs; SBs; BALs; Stewart, *Sketches*, I-II, *in passim; WO 34/44/*: f.182.

John McDonald* (1740-1775)

Ensign: 14 January 1757, 77th Foot;
Lieut: 20 September 1758, 77th Foot; half-pay, 24 December 1763.

Born in Scotland, John Macdonald was recommended initially as an ensign for the 77th by Lord Eglinton and gazetted 14 January 1757. He was captured by the Huron Indians and taken to Detroit after Major James Grant's botched raid on Fort Duquesne, 14 September 1758. Appears on *A List of the Officers Recommended by the Hon^bl. Col. Montgomery* for promotion to lieutenant, albeit while in captivity. Described by a brother officer, Lt. Archie Robertson, as *"a pretty young fellow."* On 17 February 1760, two years later, General Amherst reported to William Pitt that *"Lieut. Macdonald of Montgomery's Highlanders, who was taken Prisoner on the Ohio, has been*

given up by the Indians from Detroit with several other Prisoners..." He served in the Caribbean campaigns and went out on half-pay, 24 December 1763. He died 10 April 1775.

General Return, 1757; Officers List, 1757; CBs; SBs; BALs; Stewart, *Sketches*, I-II, *in passim; WO 34/44*: f. 182.; *Pitt's Corr.*, II, 258.

Ranald McKinnon* (1737-1805)

Ensign: 16 January 1757, 77th Foot;
Lieut: 21 September 1758, 77th Foot; half-pay, 24 December 1763; exchanged on promotion;
Capt: 14 June 1775, 84th Foot, (RHE); half-pay, 2 February 1784.

Ranald was born on the Isle of Skye in 1737, 2nd eldest son of John MacKinnon of Mishnish, (a half brother of Lachlan *Mhor*, the 28th Chieftain), and his 2nd wife, Margaret, daughter of John MacKenzie of Kildun. Ranald obtained his ensigncy in Montgomery's Highlanders, 16 January 1757, *"recommended by Lady Margaret McDonald."* He was promoted lieutenant, 21 September 1758, to replace officers killed during Major James Grant's disastrous attack on Fort Duquesne, 14 September 1758 and appears on the *List of the Officers Recommended by the Hon^bl. Col. Montgomery ...to be Lieutenant."* He participated in the 1759 capture of Forts Ticonderoga and Crown Point ,and in March 1760 was dispatched with his Light Company and five other companies of the regiment to South Carolina to fight against the Cherokees. After participating in the successful burning of the Cherokee Lower Towns, Ranald was one of three 77th officers wounded at the battle of Etchoe Pass on 27 June 1760 near present-day Pickens, South Carolina. These officers and 55 other wounded men were the principal reason Col. Montgomery decided to return to Fort Prince George. When his company garrisoning Annapolis Royal in 1763 was disbanded, he and his elder brother, John, decided to stay on in America. On 20 November 1766, he married Letitia Piggott in Halifax and they had 11 children. Ranald was initially employed in accompanying the surveying parties dispatched to the southwest coasts of Nova Scotia and for his services to the Crown, received land grants there which he collectively named Argyle. He was appointed a customs collector on 11 November 1766 and in 1771 a justice of the peace for the District of Argyle, a commission which he held for 40 years. With the outbreak of the American Revolution in 1775, just a year after his older brother's tragic death, Ranald was active in raising men for the Loyalist cause and training recruits for

Ranald Mackinnon (1737- 1805). A portrait of Captain Ranald Mackinnon in the uniform of the 84th Royal Highland Emigrants. Ranald and his older brother, John, served as lieutenants in the 77th Foot (Montgomery's) and when the the regiment was disbanded in 1763 both brothers elected to settle in Nova Scotia. (Courtesy, Yarmouth County Museum & Archives, Nova Scotia)

the 84th Royal Highland Emigrants. Based on his experiences in the previous war, Ranald was commissioned captain of the Light Company on 14 June 1775. He served with distinction in Nova Scotia and with General Henry Clinton's Grand Army in the South. From June 1776 until the close of the war in 1783, he commanded a detachment of three subalterns, three sergeants and 100 rank and file at Fort Edward in Windsor, Nova Scotia. Ranald died 28 April 1805 in Shelburne, Nova Scotia, aged 68. A striking portrait of Captain MacKinnon, 84th Foot survives, painted sometime after the Revolutionary War, it depicts MacKinnon as a white-haired man in full Highland dress, wearing a blue, ridged

highland bonnet with a band of red and white dicing, a back hackle of velvet and cocks feathers, a black gorget above a white shirt, a red, cutaway Highland military jacket with blue facings, epaulettes and lacing of gold braid, a white waistcoat, and kilt of the dark blue and green "Government" tartan. The gold lace on the blue facings of his jacket is arranged in two parallel strips. His right hand rests on the hilt of a basket-hilted broad sword and he carries a Highland dirk. His baldric or sword belt is of black leather. He wears a sporran mounted with a racoon's head and tassels and diced red and white hose (the Menzies tartan) with black brogues. This portrait is the only full length representation of an officer of the 84th. The artist and date of the work are unknown. The uniform and the sideburn whiskers suggest the years 1784 or 1785.

General Return, 1757; Officers List, 1757; CBs; SBs; BALs; Stewart, *Sketches,* I-II, *in passim;* "Ronald Mackinnon," *DCB;* G.S. Brown, *Yarmouth, Nova Scotia,* (Boston, 1888), 268-71.

Archibald Craufurd* (c.1740-1762)
Ensign: 24 January 1757, 77th Foot;
Lieut: 31 December 1761, 77th Foot.

Came to America as an ensign and participated in the capture of Fort Duquesne, November 1758. Promoted lieutenant after the successful capture of Dominica, 31 December 1761. He died the following year after the siege of Havana in a hospital on Long Island, 6 December 1762.

CBs; SBs; BALs; Zobel to Amherst, 9 December 1762, Long Island, *WO* 34/93: f.253; O14.

Allan Stuart (c.1730-1762)
Ensign: Dutch-Scots Brigade; 15 September 1758, 77th Foot;
Lieut: 31 December 1761, 77th Foot.

Started his military career in the Dutch-Scots Brigade and came to North America with the 77th as a gentleman volunteer. Brother of Captain John Stuart who served with the South Carolina Provincials and was saved by Attakullakulla at the Fort Loudoun massacre in 1761. He appears on *A List of the Gentlemen Volunteers recommended to be made Ensigns* after the Fort Duquesne Raid, September 1758: *"Allan Stewart, has served in the Dutch Service, recommended by Co. Montgomery. in room of Lt. Alex. McKenzie."* His ensign's commission was dated 15 September 1758 and he was subsequently promoted lieutenant after the capture of

Dominica, 31 December 1761. He died of sickness after the siege of Havana, 1762, at New York, his final will reading in part: *"I, Lieut. Allan Stuart, of the Hon. Col. Montgomery's Regiment, being at present in bad state of health and therefore inclined to order my affairs....I make Captain Nicholas Sutherland, Capt. Robert Grant, Lieut. John Campbell, and Lieut. William Hagot [Hagart], all of the Regiment that I have the Honor to serve, executors.... And they are to sell all effects and pay all regimental and other debts. Of the rest, they to pay to the best of mothers, Christian Stuart, £50 Sterling, and the rest to my dear beloved spouse, Hester Bonester, and if she die then to my mother, to be paid into the hands of my brother, Henry Stuart."* Also appears in Sir William Johnson's Papers on a list of officers entitled *"Died at Havana."*

CBs; SBs; BALs; SWJP; Will Abstract in *Liber* 24, 246; WO 34/44/f.182; WO 34/91: f.121.

James Grant [3] (c.1740-c.1792)
Ensign: September 1757, 77th Foot;
Lieut: 7 March 1762, 77th Foot; half-pay, 24 December 1763.

James Grant appears on *A List of the Gentlemen Volunteers recommended to be made Ensigns* after the Fort Duquesne Raid as *"a Relation of Major Grant's"* who *"was in the late Action. Recommended by Colo. Montgomery."* Grant was commissioned ensign 7 September 1758 and made lieutenant on 7 March 1762 after the capture of Martinique, January 1762. When the 77th was disbanded the following year, Grant was placed on half-pay and remained there until 1793.

CBs; SBs; BALs; WO 34/44: f.182.

Alexander Grant [2] (c.1740-c.1798)
Ensign: 20 September 1758, 77th Foot;
Lieut: 6 May 1762, 77th Foot; half-pay, 24 December 1763.

Alexander Grant, a kinsman of Major James Grant, came over to North America as a gentleman volunteer. After Grant's Raid he was promoted 20 September 1758, and lieutenant after the capture of Martinique, 6 May 1762. He was placed on half-pay when the regiment was disbanded, 24 December 1763, and remained on half-pay. He does not appear after 1799.

CBs; SBs; BALs.

George Monro* [2] (c.1738-c.1762?)
Ensign: 20 January 1757, 77th Foot.
Lieut: 2 June 1762, 77th Foot
One of the original ensigns commissioned 20 January 1757 and promoted lieutenant at the siege of Havana, June 1762. He disappears from the BALs after 1763 which may indicate he died, though this should have been recorded.

CBs; SBs; BALs.

Alexander Campbell [3], j^{nr} (c.1740-1762)
Ensign: 4 November 1758, 77th Foot;
Lieut: 13 June 1762, 77th Foot.

Alexander Campbell (erroneously recorded as Archibald Campbell in *WO 25/209*, 77th Foot, f.227v] was commissioned ensign in Mungo Campbell's Additional Company in November, 1759. He was promoted lieutenant at the siege of Havana, but died two months later at sea. His name appears on *John Campbell Adjt: Names of the Officers of Colonel Montgomery' Regiment that died since the Regiment left the Havannah, Sunday (3 October 1762)* as well as in Sir William Johnson's Papers on a list of officers entitled *"Died at Havana,"* 1762.

CBs; SBs; BALs; AFP O36/15; WO 34/91: f. 121; O14; SWJP, III, 990-91.

Thomas Mante (c.1730-1785)
2nd Lieut: 25 June 1756, 94th Company, Marines;
1st Lieut: 1 November 1759, 56th Company, Marines; 24 June 1762, 77th Foot; half-pay, 24 December 1763.

Little is known of Mante's origins, though he may have been of Huguenot extraction and apparently received some training as an engineer before his British service. He was transferred from the Marines to the 77th while serving ashore as an Assistant Engineer at the siege of Havana, 1762. In October, 1762, he along with Captain William Erving, 77th Foot, with 13 privates of the 17th, 42nd & 77th Regiment of Foot were invalided back to New York, but they were forced to endure a leaky ship which detoured to Providence in the Bahamas for repairs. Mante was left behind as too sick to travel on 7 December 1762. He eventually made it to New York, and in the summer of 1763 was reunited with Captain Erving and dispatched north with 40 recovered men of the 77th and 42nd to garrison Albany so that fitter men could be sent westwards to quell the western Indian tribes' uprising. Discharged on half-pay in 1763, Mante, a fluent French speaker, volunteered to act as Col John Bradstreet's major of brigade for an expedition to punish the western Lakes Indians and to recover all white captives. As Bradstreet was subsequently castigated for making a premature peace with the Indians and undermining Col Bouquet's southern expedition to the Muskingum for the same purpose, it's not surprising that Bradstreet could not obtain remuneration for Mante, who returned penniless to England. On his return, he published a *Treatise on the Use of Defensive Arms, translated from the French of Joly de Maizeray, with Remarks* (London, 1771) and his now famous *A History of the Late War in North America, and the islands of the West Indies, including the campaigns of MDCCLXIII and MDCCLXIV against His Majesty's Indian enemies* (London, 1772). In 1773, Mante took service with the French government, and with one brief interval, continued that service for about eight years, all the while acting as a British secret agent. In 1779 he was imprisoned for four months on charges of conducting an illegal correspondence with the British government. On his release he was in bad health *"in consequence of having been cut for the stone twice in five months"* he returned to England in 1781. He endeavored fruitlessly to obtain compensation for his services from the British government and lived on the somewhat grudging charity of a brother and the benevolence of his former commanding officer, Archie Montgomery, now the 11th earl Eglinton, the Duke of Richmond and Sir Guy Carleton, the latter to whom he dedicated his System of Tactics, also translated from the French of Joly de Maizeray. His papers, which now reside in the NAC, suggest he augmented his income by writing romantic novels and perhaps other popular works for Thomas Hookham's Circulating Library. He died in 1785.

CBs; SBs; BALs; NAC R4133/0/6-E, in passim.

James Campbell (c.1740-c.1809)

Ensign: 17 September 1760, 77th Foot;
Lieut: 27 June 1762, 77th Foot; half-pay 24 December 1763.

A gentleman volunteer commissioned an ensign after the capture of Montréal in September 1760. He was promoted lieutenant at the siege of Havana and exchanged to half-pay in December 1763. He disappears from the half-pay list in 1810.

CBs; SBs; BALs.

William Lynch (1739-c.1805)

Ensign: 2 August 1759, 27th Foot; transferred on promotion;
Lieut: 27 June 1762, 77th Foot; transferred, 20 September 1762, 27th Foot; half-pay, 7 September 1771, 8th Foot.

Born in Ireland in 1739 and served as a gentleman volunteer with the 27th Foot (Enniskillen) until commissioned an ensign, 2 August 1759. He transferred to the 77th on promotion to lieutenant at the siege of Havana in June 1762 but only remained two months before transferring back to his old regiment in the same rank. He went out on half-pay in September 1771 and died circa 1805.

CBs; SBs; BALs.

James Rumsey (c.1740-177?)

Lieut: 4 February 1762, Independent Company of Free Negroes; 28 July 1762, 77th Foot; half-pay, 24 December 1763; full-pay (ensign's), 17 March 1764, 42nd Foot; retired, 27 August 1766.

James Rumsey first appears in the British army as a lieutenant in a new-raising Independent Company of Free Negroes, 4 February 1762, in the West Indies. This unit was never raised to strength, so when opportunities arose, the officers of the independent companies exchanged into other corps. Rumsey was transferred 27 July 1762 to a lieutenancy in Montgomery's Highlanders. He went out on half-pay 24 December 1763, and returned to active service with the 42nd with as a lieutenant on ensign's pay but with seniority as a lieutenant dated 17 March 1764. (For rest of biography, see 42nd Register.)

CBs; SBs; BALs.

Robert Moore (c.1740-1786)

Ensign: 5 April 1762, 46th Foot; transferred on promotion;
Lieut: 16 August 1762, 77th Foot; half-pay, 24 December 1763.

A gentleman volunteer who was serving with the 46th Foot at the capture of Martinique. He was commissioned ensign 8 April 1762 and transferred to the 77th on promotion to lieutenant 16 August 1762. he went out on half-pay 24 December 1763 and died circa 1786.

CBs; SBs; BALs.

Alexander Menzies (c.1740-1786)
Ensign: 18 September 1758, 77th Foot;
Lieut: 6 September 1762; half-pay, 24 December 1763.

Appears on A *List of the Gentlemen Volunteers recommended to be made Ensigns* after Major Grant's botched raid against Fort Duquesne, 14 September 1758 with the citation *"a Relation of Sr. Robert Menzies, brought a number of recruits to the Regiment. Recommended by Colo. Montgomery."* Commissioned ensign 18 September 1758 and promoted lieutenant after the capture of Havana, 6 September 1762. Exchanged to half-pay 24 December 1763 and does not appear on the list after 1787.

CBs; *SBs*; *BALs*; Stewart, *Sketches*, I-II, *in passim*; WO 34/44: f.182.

John MacKenzie (1730-1775)
Ensign: Dutch-Scots Brigade; resigned; commissioned 19 September 1758, 77th Foot;
Lieut: 21 September 1762, 77th Foot; half-pay, 24 December 1763.

Initially, a gentleman volunteer serving in the ranks of the 77th Foot, MacKenzie had started his military career with the Dutch Scots Brigade. Appears on A *List of the Gentlemen Volunteers recommended to be made Ensigns* after the Fort Duquesne Raid; and is noted as having *"Served in the Dutch Service and was in the late Action. Recommended by Colo. Montgomery.'* He was in the force commanded by Lieutenant Colonel William Amherst for the recapture of St. John's Newfoundland in 1762 and was made lieutenant, 21 September 1762. He exchanged to half pay when the 77th was disbanded, 24 December 1763. He died while still on half-pay, 14 December 1775.

CBs; *SBs*; *BALs*; WO 34/44: f.182.

Alexander Munro (c.1735-c.1790)
Ensign: 21 September 1758, 77th Foot;
Lieut: 28 September 1762, 77th Foot; half-pay, 24 December 1763; full pay, 2 September 1775, 42nd Foot; transferred on promotion;
Capt: 23 January 1778, 83rd Foot; retired, 8 December 1780.

A gentleman volunteer promoted shortly after Major Grant's botched raid against Fort Duquesne, 14 September 1758, where he was wounded but does not appear on A *List of the Gentlemen Volunteers recommended to be made Ensigns* made by Colonel Montgomery after the action. A close kinsman of Captain George Munro who was killed, he is probably the Alexander Monro mentioned in a letter postscript by Lt. Alexander Robertson to Sir Henry Munro of Foulis from Loyalhannon camp after the raid: *"Alexander and Hugh Munro, cadets, were upon all the duties of honor this campaign. I hope they will both be in Commission this season."* Exchanged to half-pay in December 1763 but returned to active service in September 1775 with the 42nd Foot. He was promoted captain in the 83rd Foot in 1778 and retired two years later in 1780.

CBs; *SBs*; *BALs*; Robertson to Munro, Loyalhannon, 24 September 1758, *Ballindalloch Papers*.

Henry Watson (c.1735-1782)
Ensign: 28 June 1762, 77th Foot;
Lieut: 16 November 1762, 77th Foot; half-pay, 24 December 1763; full-pay, 31 October 1776, 41st Foot (Invalids); transferred, 7 June 1780, 99th Foot.

A gentleman volunteer commissioned from the ranks at Havana 1762 and was subsequently promoted to lieutenant in room of Cosmo Mc Martin dd in November of the same year. He fought at Bushy Run, August 1763 under Colonel Henry Bouquet and while serving on convoy duty at Fort Bedford in the spring of 1764 whilst on half-pay, he got into a quarrel with Captain John Stewart, 42nd Foot, in front of the troops. Subsequently he was placed under arrest along with Lt. Thomas Guy of the 60th Foot, both for gross insubordination. Finally Bouquet and Col Reid of the 42nd convinced Stewart to accept the two subalterns' written apologies without the incident going to a general court-martial. Stewart remained bitter towards Watson, writing to Bouquet on 17 May 1764 *"that those two Gentlemen/ particularly Watson/"* were lucky to have had the commanding officers interceding on their behalf for he was *"fully determined to have them brought to Court martial as they most certainly deserved no better treatment from me"* and that he would be obliged if Bouquet could *"order the Said concession to be Made publick to the troups, As those gentlemen, took so Much pains to asperse my character from the beginning."* He returned to active service from half pay as a lieutenant in the 41st Foot (Invalids), 31 October 1776, then exchanged into the 99th Foot, 7 June 1780. He died, still in service, 14 November 1782.

CBs; *SBs*; *BALs*; Stewart to Bouquet, 17 May 1764, Ligonier, *BL*, Add. MSS. 21650: f.208.

Ensigns

Alexander McKenzie* (c.1740-1761)
Ensign: 22 April 1757, 77th Foot.

Alexander McKenzie was commissioned Ensign on 22 April 1757, *"vice Macrah, not to be found"*; (Macrah had been one of the ensigns listed in the new-raising regiment's original intake) Amherst recorded that Ensign McKenzie was drowned off Dominica in October, 1761.

CBs; SBs; BALs; O14; WO 25/209, 77th Foot.

John MacLachlan,* y^r of Kilchoan, (1744-c.1800)
Ensign: 21 July 1757, 77th Foot; transferred on promotion;
Capt-Lt: 17 October 1761, 110th Foot; half-pay, 1 June 1763;
Capt: "in the Army," 25 May 1772; 15 August 1775, 55th Foot;
Major: "in the Army" 1783; retired, 20 December 1786.

Born in 1744, elder son of the Laird of Kilchoan, a cadet branch of the Maclachans of Kilbride. Came to America as an ensign in one of the three Additional Companies and participated in the capture of Fort Duquesne, November 1758. Returned to Europe on promotion to captain-lieutenant of the 110th Regiment of Foot, by-passing the rank of lieutenant. Went out on half-pay in December 1763. When the rank captain-lieutenant was abolished, he was made captain "in the Army," 25 May 1772. On the outbreak of the American Revolution, he returned to active service as a captain in the 55th Foot, 15 August 1775. He was made major "in the Army," 19 March 1783, and retired, 20 December 1786. He returned to his estates near Kilmelford, south of Oban in Argyllshire. Known locally to residents as *"A' Major maol"* ("The Bald Major"), Maclachlan claimed to have been made prisoner by Indians and tied by his hair to a tree during the French & Indian War. By wrenching his hair out by the roots he had then made his painful escape back to the army, but had remained completely bald thereafter. His brother, Captain Peter Maclachlan, brought a Newfoundland dog back from America which was noted for its swimming across the River Euchar, even when in flood.

CBs; SBs; BALs.

James Bain* (1733-c.1794)
Ensign: 7 January 1758; 77th Foot; resigned, 17 September 1760;

Lieut: 11 December 1761; Hopkin's Independent Company (Queen's Royal American Rangers); half-pay, 24 December 1763; full-pay, 2 May 1772, 1st/60th Foot (Royal Americans);
Capt-Lt: 2 May 1778, 1st/60th Foot;
Capt: 25 December 1778, 1st/60th Foot (Royal Americans); half-pay, 10 October 1782; full-pay, 16 April 1788, 2nd/60th Foot.

Born in Scotland in 1733 and commissioned ensign in one of the 77th Additional Companies that came to America in spring 1758. He resigned his commission at Montréal, 17 September 1760, and took a lieutenant's commission in Captain Joseph Hopkins' Independent Company known as The Queen's Royal American Rangers, 11 December 1761. He was placed on half pay when Hopkins' Rangers were disbanded, 24 December 1763. In 1772, he exchanged from lieutenant's half-pay with Francis Pfister to become a lieutenant in the 1st/60th Foot (Royal Americans), 2 May 1772, "in room of" Francis Pfister. He subsequently became captain lieutenant in the 1st/60th, 2 May 1778, and captain, 25 December 1778. He was went out on half pay, 10 October 1782, but returned as captain in the 2nd/60th, 16 April 1788. He is not listed in BAL 1795.

CBs; SBs; BALs; WO 25/209:ff. 226-228.

John Dunnet
Ensign: 16 September 1758, 77th Foot; transferred, 17th Foot, 2 December 1760; transferred on purchase,
Lieut: 20 August 1761, South Carolina Independent Company; half-pay, 17 March 1764.

Born in Caithness, Scotland, he first appears on *A List of the Gentlemen Volunteers recommended to be made Ensigns* after the Fort Duquesne Raid; *"Jno. Dunnet Served in the Regiment Since Raised and was wounded in the late Action, Recommended by Lo. Montgomery. In room of Lt. Colin Campbell."* Transferred to the 17th Foot as an ensign and went with his company to serve in South Carolina on the second Cherokee expedition and to act as ADC to Lt. Colonel James Grant. He then purchased a lieutenancy in Robert Roger's South Carolina Independent Company and went out on half-pay in 1764. He was immediately employed as the first secretary and clerk to the governing Council of the newly-established British colony of East Florida by its newly-appointed Governor, James Grant.

CBs; SBs; BALs; WO 34/44: f.182.

Duncan McVicar (c.1740-1758)
Ensign: 16 September 1758.

Duncan McVicar was commissioned ensign in the 14th Additional Company, but died two months later, 4 November 1758, before coming to America.

CBs; SBs; BALs.

Humphrey MacDonald (c.1730-1766)
Sergeant: 77th Foot;
Ensign: 2 December 1760, 77th Foot;
Lieut: 27 October 1762, 77th Foot; half-pay, 24 December 1763.

Born in England, Sergeant Humphrey Macdonald of the 77th was commissioned an ensign 2 December 1760 at Halifax, Nova Scotia and was promoted lieutenant after the siege of Havana, 27 October 1762. Went out on half-pay 24 December 1763 and died three years later, 23 February 1766.

CBs; SBs; BALs.

Henry Donaldson (c.1740-1773)
Ensign: 11 March 1762, 77th Foot;

A gentleman volunteer commissioned ensign after the successful capture of Martinique, 11 March 1762, and placed on half-pay when the regiment disbanded 24 December 1763. He died on half-pay, 6 December 1773.

CBs; SBs; BALs.

David Balfour (1746-c.1790)
Ensign: 2 June 1762, 77th Foot; transferred, 14 January 1763, 2nd/1st Foot (*The Royal*);
Lieut: 6 June 1770, 2nd/1st Foot; retired 14 November 1770.

Born in Scotland in 1746, Balfour was a gentleman volunteer commissioned ensign, 2 June 1762, at the siege of Havana. He latterly transferred to the 2nd/1st Foot on 14 January 1763 and was subsequently promoted lieutenant in that regiment 6 June 1770. He retired five months later on 14 November 1770.

CBs; SBs; BALs; WO 25/209: ff. 226-228.

Neil Grant*
Sergeant-Major: 77th Foot;
Ensign: 16 August 1762, 77th Foot;

Sergeant-Major Neil Grant of the 77th Foot was commissioned ensign after the capture of Martinique, 6 May 1762, and subsequently to lieutenant at the siege of Havannah, 16 August 1762. He died the following month at New York.

CBs; SBs; BALs; "John Campbell Adj^t: Names of the Officers of Colonel Montgomery' Regiment that died since the Regiment left the Havannah, Sunday (3 October 1762)." WO 34/91: f. 121; O14, WO 34.

Andrew Crawford (c. 1740-c.1804)
Ensign: 4 November 1762, 77th Foot;

A gentleman volunteer promoted ensign after the siege of Havana, 24 November 1762, and exchanged onto half-pay the following year, 24 December 1763. Disappears from half-pay list in 1805.

CBs; SBs; BALs.

Alexander Oreck (c.1740-c.1798)
Ensign: 14 January 1763, 77th Foot; half-pay, 24 December 1763.

Alexander Oreck was the last gentleman volunteer to be commissioned in Montgomery's Highlanders and exchanged to half pay when the regiment was disbanded, 24 December 1763. He was not in the half pay lists for the 77th Foot in 1799.

CBs; SBs; BALs.

Chaplain

Henry Munro* (1730-1801)
Appointed 12 January 1757. See Part Three – "An Unbounded Ascendancy."

Adjutants

Donald Stewart/Stuart* (c.1730-1762)
Sergeant-Major: Scots-Dutch Brigade;
Adjutant: 12 January 1757, 77th Foot; transferred on promotion;
Ensign: 11 July 1759, 27th Foot (Enniskillens); transferred on promotion;
Lieut: 31 July 1762, 90th Foot; exchanged 25 August 1762, 27th Foot.

Donald [he is Daniel in *WO 34/10*: ff. 117-118] Stuart or Stewart, a former sergeant-major in the Dutch-Scots Brigade of ten years service, was the original adjutant of Montgomery's Highlanders with a commission dated 12 January 1757. He transferred to the 27th Foot (Enniskillens) on promotion to ensign, 11 July 1759. He was taken prisoner by the French on Bulwagga Bay across from Crown Point on 31 March 1760 and was repatriated 14 June 1760. He fought at Martinique 1762 and was promoted lieutenant in the 90th Foot (Grant's) while at the siege of Havana, 1762. He exchanged back to the 27th Foot, 25 August 1762, but fell sick and died in Cuba, 25 October 1762.

CBs; *SBs*; *BALs*; Haviland to Amherst, 4 April 1760. *WO 34/51*: f. 15; *WO 34/10*: ff. 117-118.

John Campbell, of Melfort (see above)
Appointed 11 July 1759.

Alexander Campbell* (see above)
Appointed 1 February 1763.

Quartermasters

Alexander Montgomery*
Appointed: 12 January 1757; resigned, 11 May 1759, on promotion ensign, 27th Foot.

A former sergeant in the 36th Foot, Archibald Montgomery's previous regiment before receiving command of his own battalion, Noted as "*served with Lord Loudoun during the Rebellion.*"

Robert Grant* (see above)
Appointed: 11 May 1759.

William Hagart* (see above)
Appointed: 16 August 1762.

Surgeons

Allan Stewart*
Appointed 12 January 1757; resigned, 16 April 1762.

Was recommended to Archibald Montgomery by "*Dr Fordyce of the Guards and is at present Surgeon to Major genl Stewart's Regt in the Dutch Service.*" Had served two years with the Dutch-Scots Brigade as a surgeon when he accepted a commission in the 77th Foot, 12 January 1757.

General Return, 1757; Officers List, 1756; CBs; SBs; BALs; Stewart, *Sketches*, I-II, *in passim; DSB.*

Donald McLean
Appointed 16 April 1762; half-pay, 24 December 1763. Died on half-pay, 2 January 1782.

78th Foot (Fraser's Highlanders)

Colonel Simon Fraser [1], formerly Master of Lovat, (1726-1782)

Lt-Col: (Commandant): 5 January 1757; 78th Foot;
Col: "in America," 22 January 1758; half-pay, 24 December 1763; appointed 25 October 1775, Col. 71st Foot, (Fraser's Highlanders);
Brigadier: Portuguese Army, 1762;
Maj-Gen: 25 May 1772;
Lt-Gen: 29 August 1777.

Born at Kiltarity, Scotland, 19 October 1726, the eldest son and heir of the 11th Lord Lovat. During the '45, the 18- year-old Master of Lovat, though designated the Colonel of the Frasers of Lovat regiment, wisely stayed out of the fray so that command devolved upon Lieutenant-Colonel Charles Fraser, younger of Inverallochy. The latter officer, while lying wounded on the battlefield, was killed on the orders of General Hawley. Simon was imprisoned briefly in Edinburgh Castle, pardoned and took up work as a solicitor, passing the Scottish Bar, 25 July 1750. He became Advocate-Depute and assisted in the prosecution of James Stewart of Aucharn in Appin, who was executed for the murder of Colin Campbell of Glenure, the brother of Major Allan Campbell, 42nd Foot (see 42nd Register). Gazetted lieutenant-colonel commandant on 5 January 1757, Fraser quickly raised over 1000 men which he confessed *"could not have been procured so speedily by any sum of money, without the concurrence and aid of friends, Gentlemen of the country with proper connections."* He took his regiment first, to Ireland and then, to Halifax, Nova Scotia. They were too late to participate in any 1757 campaigning and his regiment was rerouted to winter quarters in Connecticut. Fraser's regiment featured prominently at the Louisbourg landings the following year and, after the successful conclusion of the siege under General Amherst's command, he took his regiment into winter quarters in upstate New York for 1758/59. At 1759 Siege of Québec, Colonel Fraser was wounded in an ambush whilst leading a raiding force of some 300 Highlanders sent to St Michel parish on the southern shore, 26 July 1759. He missed the actions at Montmorency end-month as well as the victory on the Plains of Abraham three months later. An unidentified staff officer, (probably the urbane Capt Hervey Smyth and one of Wolfe's personal ADCs) wrote: *"Col. Fraser has a good deal of the Low Highland cunning. Penurious and not held in esteem in the army, nor did we think him very enterprising."* By comparison, Smyth said of Col. William Howe: *"Mr. Wolfe's pupil, and heir to his good Qualities, in my humble opinion, he alone promises to grace the Trun-*

Simon Fraser, *Lovat* (1726-1782). Colonel Simon Fraser raised and commanded the 63rd /78th Foot during the Seven Years' War. In 1774, the Lovat estates were fully restored to him for his loyal service to the Crown (on payment of £20,983!), a full decade before any other forfeited Jacobite estates were restored. In 1775 he was asked to raise another regiment, and was gazetted Colonel of the 71st Foot (Fraser's Highlanders) on 25 October. He died in London on 8 February 1782, aged 55, having reached the rank of Lieutenant-General in the British army. (Courtesy, National Archives of Canada) *cheon."* Fraser was wounded a second time the following year at the battle of Sillery near Ste-Foy on 28 April 1760, where he commanded the left wing of General Murray's army. He was left in command at Québec as the acting Governor in June 1760 by Murray who led the healthier elements of his army upriver to effect a union with Amherst and Haviland's converging armies on Montréal. During this period, Fraser was installed as a Grandmaster of the first Grand Lodge of Ancient & Accepted Freemasons in Canada. The absent officers list shows Col. Simon Fraser *"gone to England 23rd Octbr. 1760 by General Amherst's leave."* Command of the regiment passed to the first major, James Abercrombie (see below). Fraser proceeded to London from Scotland in the spring of 1761 to take up his seat in the House of Commons as an elected Member of Parliament for Inverness. He became a brigadier-general in 1762 and accompanied Lord Loudoun to Portugal with a British expeditionary force sent to assist their allies against a Spanish invasion; promoted major-general in 1772. Two years later, the Lovat estates were fully restored for his loyal service to the Crown (on payment of £20,983!), a full decade before any other forfeited Jacobite estates were restored. In 1775, Major-General Simon Fraser was asked to raise another regiment, and accordingly was gazetted Colonel of the 71st Foot, 25 October 1775, which consisted of two battalions totaling 2,340 officers and men. He died in London on 8 February 1782, aged 55, having reached the rank of a lieutenant-general in the British army.

CBs; SBs; BALs; Stewart, *Sketches,* II, 20-1; *Muster Roll of Prince Charles Edward Stuart's Army 1745-46,* [hereafter *Muster Roll*],(Aberdeen University Press, 1984); Fraser to Amherst, 25 October 25, 1759. *WO* 34/78: f. 103 and Amherst to Fraser, 24 March 1760. *WO* 34/4: f. 135. *PRO* Northern Ireland, Dobbs Collection; *DOD* 162/77; Fraser's MSS in *JSAHR*, XVIII, (1939), 9.

Majors

James Clephane, of Carslogie (c.1713-1768)
Ensign: Dutch-Scots Brigade;
Lieut: Dutch-Scots Brigade;
Capt: 1740, Dutch-Scots Brigade;
Major: 1 January 1747/48, Stewart's, Dutch-Scots Brigade; retired, 1756; 4 January 1757, 78th Foot; resigned, 15 April 1760.

James was the younger son of Colonel William Clephane, himself a younger son of George of Carslogie, Fifeshire. A major in Major General Stewart's Regiment

of the Dutch Scots Brigade, James was taken prisoner at Sluys in 1747, exchanged shortly afterwards, and put in command of Stewart's Regiment at the garrison of Tournay. Through the influence of his brother-in-law, Rose of Kilravock, he received a major's commission in the 78th Foot and was present at the capture of Louisbourg, 1758; on the 78th's return to upper New York state as part of Amherst's reinforcement for the defeated General Abercromby, the 78th were ordered into winter quarters along the Mohawk Valley. The experienced Major Clephane was put in command of Fort Stanwix from 11 November 1758 until 9 April the following year. He contracted scurvy like many of his soldiers and was eventually *"left sick at New York"* when the regiment proceeded on the 1759 expedition to Québec. In the fall of that year, Clephane depressed by the death of his older brother, John, a physician serving under Sir John Pringle in Flanders, resigned *"finding himself unfit for Service."* He *"gave power to Colonel Young to sell his Majority with the consent of the Commander in Chief,"* the purchaser being Captain John McPherson; 15 April 1760. Three years later, Clephane was elected a member of the Nairn Town Council and in 1765, was unanimously elected Provost of Nairn, an office he held for several years. He died unmarried in May 1768.

CBs; SBs; BALs; Stewart, *Sketches,* II, 20-1; *PRO, WO 64-12;* Fraser to Amherst, Québec, 25 October 1759, *PRO, WO34/78:* f. 103; Amherst to Fraser, New York, 24 March 1760, WO34/4: f. 135; *DSB,* II, 391, 409; Stewart, *Sketches,* II, 20-1.

John Campbell [1], Captain of Dunoon (c.1725-1773)
2nd Lieut: 5 May 1741, 5th Marines, (Wynard's);
1st Lieut: 30 July 1745, 5th Marines, (Wynard's);
Capt: 1 June 1747, Independent Company; half-pay, 25 January 1750; full pay, 10 May 1751, 3rd Foot (The Buffs);
Major: 6 January 1757, 78th Foot; transferred 88th Foot (Campbell's);
Lt-Col: 1 January 1760, 88th Foot; half-pay, 9 May 1763; Col: "in the Army," 25 May 1772.

John Campbell, Captain of Dunoon, was the son of Archibald Campbell of Innellan, Captain of Dunoon, and his first wife, Lillias Campbell, eldest daughter of Walter Campbell, minister of Dunoon. The Campbells of Dunoon derive descent through the Ardentining Campbells from the House of Ardkinglas. John received his education at Glasgow University and first saw service as 2nd Lieut. in the 5th Marine Regiment (1741), and was promoted to 1st Lieut. in 1744. In 1747 he was appointed a captain in an Independent Company of

Foot sent on the expedition to India under Admiral Boscawen 1748-9. He transferred to the 3rd Foot (The Buffs). Gazetted a major in the 78th Foot, 6 January 1757; on Army list for 1759 but *"never joyn'd"* the regiment. Lord Barrington wrote to Cumberland, 16 August 1757, to inform him that *"Lieutenant Colonel Frazer's Battalion has but one Major with it; Mr. Campbell being at Spa* [a town in Belgium] *in hopes to recover his Limbs, of which he has almost lost the Use."* Lord Loudoun recommended Captain Patrick Sutherland of the 45th Foot as a possible second major for Fraser's 78th Foot in room of Dunoon, but Barrington was unwilling to commit. Dunoon was apparently sufficiently recovered in 1758 to start organize the raising of the 88th Highlanders (1758-59) as its major- commandant but later, gazetted lieutenant-colonel commandant on 1 January 1760. The 88th Foot or "Highland Volunteers" greatly distinguished themselves in Germany; Dunoon exchanged to half-pay in 1763; Campbell was promoted colonel "in the Army" in 1772, commanded in Jersey and was appointed lieutenant-governor of Chelsea Hospital in 1773 for his long and meritorious service. Colonel Campbell died in residence at Chelsea Hospital, 24 April 1773.

CBs; *SBs*; *BALs*; Stewart, *Sketches*, II, 20-1; Johnson, *Heraldry of the Campbells,* (Inveraray, 1977); Pargellis, *MA*, 394, 397; *WO* 64-12.

John MacPherson [1] (1709-1770)

Ensign: Dutch Scots Brigade;
Lieut: Dutch-Scots Brigade;
Capt: 30 September 1747, Marjoribanks, Dutch-Scots Brigade; half-pay, 25 March 1752; discharged 24 June 1757; 5 January 1757, 78th Foot;
Major: 15 April 1760, 78th Foot; resigned 5 October 1760.

John was the younger brother of Ewan Macpherson of Cluny who was "out" in the '45, the latter dying in exile in France in 1756. John started his military career in Marjoribank's Regiment in the Dutch-Scots Brigade and was wounded at the siege and capture of Bergen-op-Zoom by the French in 1747. On 24 June 1757, he was discharged from the Dutch service having accepted a captain's commission in the new-raising 78th Foot, dated 5 January 1757. An experienced and well-liked officer, he was also Colonel Fraser's brother-in-law. Served at Louisbourg and was one of four field officers assigned to the garrison of Fort Stanwix, the winter of 1758/59. During the 1759 Québec campaign he was wounded by the same bullet that wounded Colonel

Fraser in an ambush 26 July 1759, near St Michel on the southern shore opposite Québec. He was promoted to major on 15 April 1760 after lengthy negotiations with James Clephane and wounded yet again at the battle of Sillery, 28 April 1760;
He resigned his commission in October 1760 due to ill health and pressing domestic affairs at home. He returned to Britain with his brother-in-law, Simon Fraser, settling at Badenoch to look after the education and business affairs of the young clan chieftain – his nephew, "Duncan of the Kilns." He never married and died in 1770.

CBs; *SBs*; *BALs*; Stewart, *Sketches*, II, 20-1; *PRO* WO 64-12; *DSB*, II, 408, 425; Parson Robert Macpherson to William Macpherson, 4 Aug. 1760, Québec City, *JGP*.

James Abercrombie (1727-1775)

2nd Lieut: 15 May 1742; 2nd/1st Foot (The Royal);
Lieut: 11 June 1744, 1st Foot (The Royal);
Capt: 16 February 1756, 42nd Foot;
Major: 25 July 1760, 78th Foot (Fraser's Highlanders); half-pay 24 December 1763;
Lt. Col: 27 March 1770, 22nd Foot.

A 42nd captain (see 42nd Register) and former ADC to three successive Commanders-in-Chief in North America: John Campbell, Lord Loudoun; General James Abercromby; and Major-General Jeffery Amherst, James Abercrombie was made second major of the 78th Foot 25 July 1760, filling a vacancy created by John Campbell of Dunoon's promotion in Europe six months earlier. When the first major, John MacPherson, decided to retire shortly afterwards, 5 October 1760, and return to Scotland, Abercrombie became the senior major and acting commandant in Colonel Simon Fraser's absence. Writing in 1761, Parson Robert Macpherson described Abercrombie thusly: *"The Major is one of the most entertaining agreeable Gentlemen I ever knew & has been almost all his life in the Army, knows almost every body in it and was present in most of the Actions of the last and present War in both of which he has always acted Engineer with or Educamp* [sic] *to some of the General Officers, and as he has a pretty liberal education and some money of his own, besides a Great run of Luck in Play, to which for some time he was addicted, he was enabled and may be said to have always lived in the high life. He speaks and understands most of the Modern Languages and in short is a very Compleat Gentleman and an excellent commandant of a Reg*[t.] *"* When the regiment was disbanded in 1763, he exchanged to half pay in December 1763. He returned to active duty in March 1770, gazetted lieutenant-colonel of 22nd Foot, and five years later, led it back to North America; he died of wounds on 23 July 1775 sustained from friendly fire (according to Major-General James Grant) at the battle of Breed's Hill [Bunker Hill], 17 June 1775.

CBs; *SBs*; *BALs*; Stewart, *Sketches*, II, 20-1; Richards, *Black Watch*, 51-2, 72; Parson Robert Macpherson to William Macpherson, 24 Dec. 1761, Berthier, *JGP*.

John Campbell [2], (later, of Barbreck) (c.1725-1794)
Cornet: 26 December 1755, 2nd Dragoons (Royal North British);
Lieut: -
Capt: 9 January 1757, 78th Foot;
Major: 5 October 1760, 78th Foot; half-pay, 24 December 1763;
Lt-Col: "by brevet," 25 May 1772; 25 December 1777, 74th Foot (Argyll Highlanders);
Col: 17 November 1780, 74th Foot (Argyll Highlanders).
Maj-Gen: on half-pay, 28 September 1787.

John was the son of Archibald Campbell of Auchatennie (and of Phantillans and of Ballimore) and his first wife Anne, daughter of Dugald Campbell of Nether Rudill. Also the uncle of Lt. Duncan Campbell, 2nd Barbreck, 42nd Foot (see 42nd Register). An ensign in the 2nd Dragoons; gazetted a captain in the 78th Foot on 9 January 9, 1757; served at Louisbourg in 1758; commanded the regiment at battle of Plains of Abraham on September 13, 1759 as Colonel Fraser had not recovered from wounds received at Montmorency; wounded at Sillery, 28 April 1760; promoted to major 5 October 1760 *"in room of"* John Macpherson; was the second major of the regiment and commanding a company at Québec when the 78th was disbanded in 1763 and he exchanged to half-pay. Gazetted lieutenant-colonel on 25 December 1777 and colonel on 17 November 1780 of the 74th Foot (Argyll Highlanders) raised to fight in the American Revolution. He died unmarried, 10 September 1794, having reached the rank of a major-general in the British army.

CBs; *SBs*; *BALs*; Stewart, *Sketches*, II, 20-1; Johnson, *Heraldry of the Campbells*, 28-9; WO 64/12; WO 34/85: f. 136.

Captains

Charles Baillie, yr of Rosehall, (c.1725-1758)
2nd Lieut: 2 September 1756, 21st Foot;
Capt: 10 January 1757, 78th Foot.

The eldest of the six sons of William Baillie of Rosehall,

the Factor to Ross of Balnagowan. Married Janet Mackay, granddaughter of the 3rd Lord Reay and widow of Colin Campbell of Glenure, allegedly murdered by a Stewart of Aucharn in 1752. Janet's sister, Mary, was her new husband's step-mother and her former brothers-in-law served in the other two Highland regiments, Major Alan Campbell of the 42nd and Capt. Mungo Campbell in the 77th (Montgomery's), [see respective Regimental Registers]. Charles was also a nephew of Major Patrick Sutherland of the 77th Foot on his mother's side. A 2nd lieutenant in the 21st Foot, he transferred to the 78th to become one of the original company commanders of the newly-raised 78th Foot. Gazetted the grenadier captain 10 January 1757, he was killed the following year at the Louisbourg landings, 8 June 1758.

CBs; *SBs*; *BALs*; Stewart, *Sketches*, II, 20-1; *Journal of William Amherst* [hereafter *WAJ*]; WO 64/12.

Simon Fraser [2], of Inverallochy (1732-1759)
Ensign: 2 January 1756, 52nd/50th Foot; transferred on promotion;
Capt: 11 January 1757, 78th Foot.

Started his British military career in the new-raising 52nd Foot, which was shortly thereafter re-numbered the 50th Foot. He was the youngest son of Charles Fraser, 7th Inverallochy, and the younger brother of Lt.-Colonel Charles Fraser, j[nr], who had led the Frasers of Lovat at Culloden. One of the original company commanders of the newly-raised 78th Foot, he served at Louisbourg in 1758; was seriously wounded at battle of plains of Abraham on 13 September 1759, and died of his wounds, 15 October 1759.

CBs; *SBs*; *BALs*; Stewart, *Sketches*, II, 20-1; CO 5/51; WO 64/12.

Donald (Donull Gorm) Macdonell, of Benbecula (c.1728-1760)
Ensign: Booth's, *Royal Ecossais*, French Army;
Lieut: Booth's, *Royal Ecossais*;
Capt: Ogilvie's, *Royal Ecossais*; 12 January 1757, 78th Foot.

Second and natural son of Ranald Macdonell, 17th *"Old"* Clanranald, and half brother to the 18th *"Young"* Clanranald. His younger half-brother, William, also served in the 78th Foot. Donull Gorm joined the French Army before the Jacobite rebellion in 1745. He fought at Stirling, was wounded and went into hiding. He surrendered himself after Culloden as a French officer and, as Britain had a cartel with France and Spain for the exchange of prisoners of war, he expected to be treated as a French officer vice a rebel. In his own words, written at Edinburgh Castle, 15 December 1746,: *"I went to France in year 1742 and served as Cadet in Booth's Reg^{mt}. till I got a Company in Drummond's Reg^{mt}.* [Royal Ecossais] *the year 44 and came along with it to Scotland in Novr. 45, and being wounded before Sterling, I returned to my father's country, where I remained till hearing that all my Reg^{mt}. surrender'd themselves prisoners of War at Inverness, after the Battle of Culloden, I was desirous of doing the same, and I surrendered myself to Capt. John Mackdonald as soon as he came to the Country I was in, in July last…."* In 1756, the Duke of Argyll said of him: *"brother to Clanranald was sent into the French Service when a boy, & had a Company several years, which he quitted some months ago upon the late Act of Parliament & took the Oaths to the Government; for these facts, as well as for his Character, he appeals to My Lord Holderness & undertakes on this occasion to raise 100 men."* Accepted as one of the original company commanders of the newly-raised 78th Foot, he replaced Charles Baillie as Captain of Grenadiers at Louisbourg, June 1758 and was wounded on the night of 21 July 1760 in the approach trenches; killed at Ste-Foy on April 28, 1760; Donald *"Gorm"* was not well-liked by the Highlander rank-and-file according to Grenadier Sergeant James Thompson who unabashedly styled him *"a surly cross dog,"* and in his *Memoirs* hints that MacDonnell was intentionally wounded or "fragged" by his own men at the siege of Louisbourg on 21 July 1758: *"Our Captain had a ball passed through his left wrist and nobody could tell how it came and afaith he immediately shifted his position to the other end of the ground."* Markedly, at the battle of Sillery, 28 April 1760, none of Macdonell's volunteers were drawn from the 78th Foot. Oral tradition in the Highlands of Cape Breton, where several Fraser soldiers returned to settle on the eastern Bras Dor Lakes of Cape Breton (Barra MacNeils, MacEacherns, and Clanranald Macdonells) maintains that it was at this 1760 battle that *"the de'il finally got him,"* and that he *"died amongst strangers."* Harper, in his book *The Fraser Highlanders*, did not include Thompson's somewhat satisfied description of his nemesis' gory - *"a stronger body of French overpowered and completely butchered his whole party, and he himself was found cut and hack'd to pieces in a most shocking manner. There was an end of him!"* This was, no doubt, retaliation for *"Donull Gorm's"* ruthless winter raids against the outlying countryside of Québec where he kept the Québecois militiamen and French regulars constantly off balance.

CBs; *SBs*; *BALs*; Stewart, *Sketches*, II, 20-1; "Donald McDonald" PRO, WO64-12; *CU* 49/5; *WAJ*, 29; *GD* 201/4/81; *Muster Roll of Prince Charles Edward Stuart's Army 1745-46*; Harper, *Fighting Frasers*, 101-2, Thompson's *Memoirs*.

John Macdonell [1], y^r of Lochgarry (1722-1790)

Lieut: c. 1747, Ogilvie's, *Royal Ecossais*;
Capt: *en seconde*, Ogilvie's, *Royal Ecossais*;
13 January 1757, 78th Foot; half-pay; full pay, 23 December 1771;
Major: "by brevet," 23 July 1772; 23 November 1775, 1st/71st Foot (Fraser's Highlanders);
Lt-Col Commandant: 15 December 1777, 76th Foot (MacDonald's Highlanders);
Col: "in the Amy," 20 November 1782; half-pay, 8 March 1783.

Eldest son of Donald Macdonell of Lochgarry and Isabel Gordon. His father was a lieutenant-colonel in the French Army, serving in Ogilvie's Regiment of the *Royal Ecossais*, while John was a *capitaine en seconde* in the same regiment. Reputedly, his father followed him to Calais in 1756 when he learned his eldest and most beloved son was returning home to join the British Army. Failing to persuade his heir to reconsider, Lochgarry pronounced the following curse: *"My curse on any of my race who puts his foot again on British shore; my double curse on he, who of my race may submit to the Guelph* (i.e. House of Hanover) *and my deadliest curse on he who may try again to regain Lochgarry."* He then reputedly threw his dirk after his son and never saw him again. John was one of the original company commanders of the newly-raised 78th Foot, recommended by his cousin and chieftain, Alistair *"Rhuadh"* Macdonell, 12th of Glengarry. Lt. Charles Macdonell, younger brother of Glengarry, also served in the 78th (see below). On 18 May 1757, before leaving for North America, John made his cousin Glengarry *"factor and attorney, and executor and legatee"*; fought at Louisbourg and was one of four company commanders stationed at Fort Stanwix during the winter of 1758/59; wounded through both thighs at the battle of Plains of Abraham, 13 September 1759, and given leave by General Monckton *"to go to the Continent for health."* He was wounded again at the battle of Sillery, 28 April 1760, and the absent officers list shows *"Capt. Jno McDonnell gone to England 3rd Octbr.1760 by General Amherst's leave."* Commanded a company when regiment was disbanded in 1763; he exchanged to half-pay, 24 December 1763.

Returned to active duty as a captain in the 20th Foot and was made a major "by brevet," 23 July 1772. He was made major, 23 November 1775, in the new-raising 1st/71st Foot (Fraser's Highlanders) and went with it to North America. He was gazetted lieutenant-colonel commandant of the new-raising 76th Foot (MacDonald Highlanders) 15 December 1777 while serving in America and was recalled to Scotland to take command. Unfortunately, he was captured in transit on the Atlantic by an American privateer, and was later released on parole for the rest of the war. His family estates of Lochgarry were restored in 1784 and he had a fine manor house built on the site of the original house. He died in London, unmarried, 5 October 1790.

CBs; *SBs*; *BALs*; Stewart, *Sketches*, II, 20-1; "John McDonell" *PRO*, WO 64-12; *PRO*, C5/51; "The Macdonells of Lochgarry," *Clan Donald Magazine*, [No.11]; H.C. McCorry, "Rats, Lice & Scotchmen: Scottish infantry regiments in the service of France, 1742-62," *JSAHR*, Vol. LXXIV, No. 297 (Spring 1996), 26.

Thomas Fraser, of Struy (1709-1758)
Capt: 16 January 1757, 78th Foot

Son of Hugh Fraser, 6th Struy and Mary Baillie. One of the original company commanders of the newly-raised 78th Foot; present at the siege of Louisbourg in June 1758, an extant letter written by Col Simon Fraser attests to his physical presence "*From camp near Louisbourg on 10th August 1758,*" he wrote, "*I have just been reading Struy a lecture.*" Struy returned to Boston with his company, but on the forced march through Massachusetts died of "*a Violent Fever.*" The Boston New-Letter (5 October 1758) reported that "*at Springfield on Thursday last, died there, after a short Illness with a fever, Capt. Thomas Fraser, of Colonel Simon Fraser's Highland Regiment. : An elderly Gentleman, whose Death is greatly lamented. . .*" His captaincy was given to James Fraser, the quartermaster (see below), 27 September 1758. An unidentified family member writing to Baillie James Fraser from New York on 2 November 1758, refers to "*the death of my poor Struy.*"

CBs; *SBs*; *BALs*; *Belladrum Papers*; Jeffery Amherst's *Journal*, entry 24 July 1758; WO 64/12; The Boston *News-Letter*, Thursday, October 5, 1758. N°. 2934; The Boston *Weekly Advertiser*, Monday Oct. 2 1758. N°. 59; The Boston *Gazette and Country Journal*, N°. 183, October 2, 1758; Stewart, *Sketches*, II, 20-1.

Sir Henry Seton, 4th B[t] of Abercorn and Culberg (1729-1803)
Lieut: Dutch-Scots Brigade;
Capt: 17 July 1757, 78th Foot; exchanged to 17th Foot, 22 April 1759;

The eldest son of Sir Henry Seton, 3rd Bt. of Abercorn, and Barbara Wemyss of Bogie. A veteran of the Dutch-Scots Brigade, Sir Harry, as he was universally known, commanded one of three newly-authorized Additional Companies that joined the regiment at their Connecticut winter quarters in April 1758. His company accompanied the regiment to Halifax in spring 1758, but remained there in garrison on guard duty, as they were considered not sufficiently trained to participate in the Louisbourg expedition. Selected soldiers, however, were drafted into the 78th light infantry company. Seton remained in Halifax and served on Monckton's staff during the 1758 siege. His company rejoined the battalion on its way back to Boston and marched with the 78th across Massachusetts to spend the winter in Schenectady in the Mohawk River Valley. In April of 1759, Sir Harry transferred out of the 78th into the 17th Foot (Monckton's) which would form part of Amherst's successful 1759 expedition against Ticonderoga and Crown Point. The following year, Sir Harry's new regiment went north to Montréal via Crown Point with Haviland's expedition to take Montréal. In 1761, his company of the 17th was one of two assigned to Lt Col James Grant's 1761 expedition against the Cherokee. On his return, he rejoined Monckton's staff and accompanied that general officer to the Caribbean. After the fall of Havana, Sir Harry exchanged to half-pay in 1763. He resigned his commission, 6 August 1770, and married Margaret Hay of Drumelzier the same year. He died in Borrowstoness in 1803 where he served as Collector of Customs.

CBs; *SBs*; *BALs*; Stewart, *Sketches*, II, 20-1; *Burkes Peerage*.

Alexander Cameron, 4th of Dungallon, (c.1730-1759)
Ensign: Lochiel's Regiment, 1745;
Lieut: -
Capt: 21 July 1757, 78th Foot.

A former Jacobite officer, whose father, Alexander (3rd Dungallon) had been a major in Cameron of Lochiel's regiment and Standard Bearer to the Prince. Alexander, jn[r], served as an ensign in the clan regiment. Commanded one of three newly-authorized Additional Companies that joined the regiment whilst in Connecticut winter quarters April 1758; he was chosen to command a 100-man light infantry company in Halifax for the Louisbourg expedition. His command was drawn from the best and most fit men of the three Additional Companies left at Halifax and assigned to Major George Scott's Provisional Light Infantry Battalion. Was one of four field officers assigned to the garrison of Fort Stanwix , the winter of 1758/59. Dungallon died of a fever on 3 September 1759, ten days before the Battle of the Plains of Abraham and was buried at the Levis camp. His body was later removed and re-interred at Québec, a monument to his memory erected by John Nairne and Malcolm Fraser, brother officers who had served with him in the 78th's light infantry company. His last will and testament bequeathed his *"whole estate heritable and movable to Allan, brother of John Cameron, 3rd of Glendessary."* Young Lieutenant Donald Cameron, (see entry below) a cousin with the newly-arrived 14th Additional Company, wrote to his brother Ewan back in Scotland that he arrived just in time for his funeral: *"I came time Enouch to see him Interd and that was all. Hew Cameron who is now Capt took care of all his things and saw every thing Roped but his Silver hulted Sword and Goold Wach* [sic] *and Ring. I have his Ring at Present till such time as Glendesry calls for it but I hop I will get from Glendeseray which if I do I will send it home to you."*

CBs; *SBs*; *BALs*; Somerled Macmillan, *Bygone Lochaber: Historical & Traditional*, (Glasgow, 1971 [privately printed], 137; Stewart, *Sketches*, II, 20-1.

Thomas Ross, of Calrossie (c.1723-1759)
Capt: 23 July 1757, 78th Foot.

Son of Thomas Ross, 2nd Calrossie, and Isobel Ross of Easterfearn. Commanded one of the three Additional Companies that joined the regiment in April 1758 while in Connecticut; fought at the siege of Louisbourg; a Highland "gentleman volunteer" noted in his journal that on 29 July 1759, *"Capt Ross and Lt Nairn of Colonel Fraser's Regt. fought a duel this morning, very much to the discredit of the former."* Neither was charged under the Articles of War which prohibited dueling. Ross was killed on 13 September 1759 after the actual battle of Plains of Abraham was over, leading Highland skirmishers down along the St Charles River. Malcolm Fraser noted that Ross *"was mortally wounded in the body, by a cannon ball from the hulks, in the mouth of the St Charles, of which he died in great torment, but with great resolution, in about two hours thereafter."*

CBs; *SBs*; *BALs*; Malcolm Fraser's MSS; *PRO*, C5/51; Stewart, *Sketches*, II, 20-1.

Alexander Fraser [1], 6th Culduthel
Capt: 15 September 1758; 78th Foot; resigned 23 October 1761.

Son of Alexander Fraser, 5th Culduthel, and Grizel Abercromby of Birkenbog. Alexander was the heir of his older half-brother, Malcolm Fraser, a captain in the 42nd Foot who was killed while serving as a volunteer at the siege and capture of Bergen-op-Zoom in 1747. Alex was gazetted captain of the 14th Additional company of the 78th in September 1758. Culduthel and his men then spent the next five months in transit, trying to join their regiment in North America. According to Lt. Donald Cameron, son of Fassifern, and one of the company's new subalterns, they *"arrived at Virginia the twentieth of June 1759 after a long and tedious Pasage and from Virginia we ware Ordered for York, and from York up the River to Albonay, where we parted with Captain [Mungo]Campbe[ll]s Componay,* [14th Company, 77th Foot] *then we ware Ordered Down that same River to York again and from York to Luisbrough, and up the River Sant Lawrence to the Sage of Quebeck. We arrived in Camp before Quebeck September the 3"* . . . just in time to take part in the battle of the Plains of Abraham, 13 September, 1759. The following spring, while commanding the grenadier company at the Battle of Sillery, 28 April 1760, Culduthel was wounded in the head. He resigned his commission, 23 October 1761, and returned to Scotland to recover from his wounds. Culduthel was considered one of the finest singers, huntsmen and sportsmen of his day. He died at Beaulieside, near Inverness, 17 November 1778.

CBs; *SBs*; *BALs*; *AFP* O36/15; *WO* 34/87: f. 220.

James Fraser, y[r] of Castleleathers [1] (1708-c.1785)
Lieut: 4 January 1757, 78th Foot; appointed QM, 12 January 1757; resigned QM, 9 June 1758;
Capt.-Lt: 9 June 1758, 78th Foot;
Capt: 27 September 1758, 78th Foot; resigned 13 December 1759.

The 2nd son of Major James Fraser of Castleleathers and Margaret Dunbar of Grangehill, James was born 27 April 1708, in Scotland. He appears to have been an experienced officer or NCO with previous military service abroad. A 1760 letter requesting permission to sell his commission cites 26 years of military service *"of which there were seven campaigns of war,"* an indication that James' career started circa 1734 at the age of 26. He was the regiment's original QM, appointed 12 January 1757, and was promoted to captain, 27 September 1758, to fill the vacancy created by the death of Thomas Fraser of Struy. An unidentified family friend writing to Baillie James Fraser from New York on 2 November 1758, states: *"I have not seen Col. Fraser as yet nor any of his officers except Simon (Fraser) Balnain's son and James Fraser son of Castleleather who got Strui's Company."* He was wounded at the Plains of Abraham, 13 September 1759, and sent to the continent to recover from wounds in October 1759. He resigned his commission, 13 December 1759, after he discovered he was going blind.

CBs; SBs; BALs; Belladrum Papers; WO 34/78: ff. 103/183; Amherst to Fraser, 24 March 1760, WO 34/4: f. 135.

Simon Fraser, [3] yr of Balnain, (1729-1777)
Lieut: Halkett's, Dutch-Scots-Brigade; discharged 1757; 5 January 1757, 78th Foot;
Capt-Lt: 27 September, 1758, 78th Foot;
Capt: 22 April 1759; 78th Foot; transferred, 1 March 1761, 24th Foot;
Major: *"in the Army,"* 15 March 1761; 8 February 1762, 24th Foot;
Lt-Col: 14 July 1768; 24th Foot;
Col: *"in the Army"*
Brigadier: *"in America"*

Born in 1729, he was the 10th son of Alexander Fraser, 2nd of Balnain and, Jean, a daughter of Angus Mackintosh of Kyllachy; papers in National Archives of Scotland list him as *"brother to Dunballoch"*; served with Dutch-Scots Brigade in Flanders and was wounded at the siege and capture of Bergen-op-Zoom by the French in 1747; took his discharge from Halkett's Regiment of the Dutch-Scot's Brigade to accept a lieutenant's commission in the 78th effective 5 January 1757; promoted to captain-lieutenant at Springfield, Massachusetts on September 27, 1758 after the vacancy was created by the death of Thomas Fraser of Struy. He was promoted to captain on 22 April 1759 to replace Captain Craufurd Walkinshaw who returned to Scotland to recover from sickness. Fraser commanded a company of light infantry under Colonel William Howe at the Siege of Québec, 1759, and was the oft-noted officer in the lead boat who spoke French to the enemy sentries on the descent downriver to where the British army landed at Foulon. The absent officers list shows *"Capt. Simon Frazer gone to England 17th Octbr. 1759 by General Monckton's*

Simon Fraser, *Balnain* **(1729-1777). A detail from the painting** *"The Wounding of Brigadier General Simon Fraser at Saratoga, 1777"*. **During the night of 13 September 1759, Simon Fraser was the officer who replied in French to the challenge of enemy sentries during the descent of the St. Lawrence River. After the battle of the Plains of Abraham, Fraser returned to fight in Germany and by 1762 was Major to the 24th Foot and was made its Lieutenant Colonel 14 July 1768. He returned to America during the Revolution and while serving as a brigadier-general in General John Burgoyne's army he was mortally wounded by a sniper at the battle of Saratoga, 7 October 1777 and died the following day. (Courtesy, Library of Congress)**

leave." Once home, he was reassigned to Germany and served on the staff of Ferdinand of Brunswick. Transferred to 24th Foot (Cornwallis') 1 March 1761, and was made major *"in the Army"* two weeks later. He was made major of the 24th Foot 8 February 1762, and lieutenant-colonel 14 July 1768, serving for a time in Gibraltar. In 1770, he served as ADC to Marquis Townshend, the Lord Lieutenant of Ireland and in 1770 was appointed Quartermaster General in Ireland. He returned to America in April 1776 while nominally still lieutenant-colonel of the 24th Foot (according to the 1777 *BAL*). Gazetted a colonel *"in the Army"* on 22 July 1777, he was mortally wounded by a sniper at the battle of

Saratoga, 7 October 1777, while serving as a brigadier-general in General John Burgoyne's army. He died the following day.

CBs; SBs; BALs; PRO, CO 5/51; *NAS* GD 125/22 16: f.7; WO 64/12 ; MacLean, *Scotch Highlanders,* (Glasgow: 1900), 382; *DNB,* 662-63; Stewart, *Sketches,* II, 21, 45; *AFP* O39/26 & 35; *DSB,* II, 389, 420.

Alexander MacLeod (1724-1772)
Lieut: 1745-48, IHC (MacLeod's); 15 January 1757, 78th Foot;
Capt-Lt: 22 April 1759, 78th Foot;
Capt: 4 September 1759, 78th Foot; half-pay, 24 December 1763..

The eldest son of Donald MacLeod of Balmeanach, a tacksman of Torrin and Kinlockslapin (1741-47) in Strath, and later a factor in Skye. Alexander was born about 1724, and was known in Skye and the Isles as *"Sandy Balmeanach."* During the 1745 Jacobite Rising, he was commissioned a lieutenant in Captain John MacLeod's company raised 15 November 1745, one of the 18 Independent Highland Companies. He acted as a messenger between MacLeod of MacLeod and the notorious Simon, Lord Lovat. The latter, in a November 1745 letter to Donald Cameron of Lochiel, calls Sandy a *"little sneaking gentleman."* Perhaps Sandy MacLeod is best remembered as the officer whom Flora MacDonald cleverly hoodwinked in Monkstadt House, Trotternish, on Sunday, 29 June 1746, on the occasion of her arrival in Skye from Benbecula in charge of the Prince. When the Fraser Highlanders were raised for service abroad, Sandy MacLeod obtained a commission as lieutenant in the regiment dated 11 January 1757. He fought with the 78th at all the major sieges and battles; one of eight lieutenants stationed at Fort Stanwix during the winter 1758/59; promoted captain *"in room of"* Captain Alex Cameron of Dungallon who died of fever just prior to the battle of the Plains of Abraham. Wounded at the battle of Sillery on 28 April 1760, he exchanged onto half-pay with the rank of captain in December 1763 and returned to Balmeanach, where he died 7 April 1772, allegedly poisoned by a jealous husband.

CB; SB; BALs; U 49/5; WO 64/12.; MacKinnon, *The MacLeods: The Genealogy of a Clan,* (Edinburgh, 1970) 96; *The Book of Dunvegan,* II, 94; MacKenzie, *History of the Frasers,* 407; Warrand, *More Culloden Papers,* IV, 177; Stewart, *Sketches,* II, 20-1.

Hugh [Ewan] Cameron (c.1730-c.1790)
Lieut: 6 January 1749, Halkett's, Dutch-Scots Brigade;

discharged, 1756; 12 January 1757, 78th Foot;
Capt-Lt: 4 September 1759; 78th Foot;
Capt: 25 September 1759, 78th Foot; half-pay, 24 December 1763; full pay, 25 December 1770, 13th Foot;
Major: *"in the Army,"* 23 July 1772; retired 2 December 1775.

Served with the Dutch-Scots Brigade in Holland. Gazetted a lieutenant on January 12, 1757; listed among the officers who sailed for Louisbourg in 1758; reported wounded in Wolfe's dispatch of 2 September 1759, but recovered from his wounds; promoted captain-lieutenant *"in room of"* Alexander MacLeod just before the battle of Plains of Abraham. Was wounded a second time on 13 September 1759 and promoted to full captain after the battle *"in room of"* Captain Thomas Ross, killed. Was horribly burned in an accidental gunpowder explosion in a blockhouse outside the Québec walls during the French siege of Québec April-May 1760. Was commanding a company when regiment was disbanded in 1763 and exchanged to half-pay. He returned to active service as a captain in the 13th Foot, December 1770 and was made a major *"in the Army,"* 23 July 1772. He retired 2 December 1775.

CBs; SBs; BALs; Knox, *Journals,* III, 142; Stewart, *Sketches,* II, 20-1; *DSB,* II, 404.

Ranald *"Raonall Oig"* Macdonell, 18th of Keppoch (c.1732-1788)
Lieut: 14 January 1757, 78th Foot;
Capt-Lt: 25 September 1759, 78th Foot;
Capt: 17 October 1759; 78th Foot; half-pay, 24 December 1763; full pay, 18 December 1766, 66th Foot; retired 23 June 1775; 26 December 1777, 74th Foot (Argyll Highlanders); retired 20 January 1779.
Major: *"by brevet,"* 23 July 1772.

Oldest legitimate son of Alexander Macdonell, 17th Keppoch, and Jessie Stewart. Styled himself *"Son of Keppoch"* when gazetted a lieutenant in Fraser's Highlanders on 14 January 1757, despite his father having been dead for ten years, a clear indication that he felt that his older "natural" brother, Angus Ban, in exile, was the rightful chieftain and not he. Served at Louisbourg, 1758 and was wounded *"thro' the knee"* at battle of Plains of Abraham on 13 September 1759. The monthly return of November 1759 lists him as having gone *"to continent for recovery."* The hereditary piper of *Clann Dhomhanuill na Ceapaich, Padraig Cambeuil,* (Patrick Campbell) was not happy with Keppoch's decision to serve the British King and his wounding was seen partially as a punishment for renouncing his Catholic religion. An excerpt of a song entitled *"Raonall Oig Macdonnell of Keppoch,"* translates:

We had news about you yesterday, Monday,
It left me heavy-hearted to speak of it:
You were wounded under the belt,
In your fair, fresh, gentle thigh.
How it grieves me, that you were so young,
And that you were won over by love of money
But that is not surprising, as many worthy men
Have abandoned their homeland and become turn-coats

When promoted to captain, 17 October 1759, his older step-brother, Angus Ban, formally wrote out a resignation of the chieftainship in order that Ranald could start the process to reclaim the Keppoch lands. He was back with his regiment by 1762, General Orders dated 3 June 1762 stating that *"Capt Ron^d. McDond. is appointed to command the Grenadier Company."* When regiment was disbanded in 1763, he exchanged onto half-pay. He returned to active service as a captain in the 66th Foot, was made major *"by brevet"* in 1772, and retired in June 1775. He was convinced to come out of retirement and raise a company of Keppoch Macdonells for the new-raising 74th Foot (MacDonald Highlanders) commanded by his old 78th colleague, John Campbell of Barbreck. "Major" Macdonell retired a second time in January 1779 and died nine years later at Keppoch in 1788.

CBs; SBs; BALs; Stewart, *Sketches*, II, 20-1; "Ronald McDonald," WO 64/12; PRO C5/51.

Charles Macdonell (c.1730-1762)

Lieut: Ogilvie's, *Royal Ecossais*, French Army; 19 January 1757, 78th Foot;
Capt-Lt: 17 October 1759, 78th Foot;
Capt: 13 December 1759, 78th Foot.

Fourth son of John Macdonell, 11th of Glengarry, brother of Alasdair Rhuadh, 12th of Glengarry. Served in Ogilvie's regiment of the *Royal Ecossais* of the French army and was described as having *"that which makes a good officer but is excessively undisciplined."* Gazetted a lieutenant on 19 January 1757 and was wounded at battle of Plains of Abraham on 13 September 1759. He was made captain-lieutenant on 17 October 1759, and two months later, was promoted captain effective, 13 December 1759, replacing Capt. James Fraser who retired due to blindness. He was wounded again at the battle of Sillery, 28 April 1760, and returned to Scotland for recovery; on his return to his unit via New York, he was assigned by General Amherst to command a composite company of 86 recovered men of several regiments and pardoned prisoners hastily thrown together and sent to assist in the recapture of St John's, Newfoundland. Macdonell's company sailed from New York in July 1762 and joined up with troops from Halifax and Louisbourg in August under the command of Colonel William Amherst. Macdonell was seriously wounded in the leg leading a dawn attack on Flagstaff Hill (present day Signal Hill) on 13 September 1762, the same day he had been wounded fighting at the plains of Abraham, three years earlier. Col. Amherst in his report of 20 September 1762 to Lord Egremont, wrote: *"Capt M^c. Donell of Col: Fraser's Reg^t. having Sir Jeffery Amherst's leave to go to England, was to have delivered this to your Lordship, his leg is broke. But the wound he received which keeps him here. May I humbly presume my Lord, to recommend this Gentleman to your Lordships' protection, as a real brave, and good Officer."* Macdonell's leg wound turned gangrenous, required amputation and he died on 21 January 1763 at Quidi Vidi in Newfoundland. James Abercrombie, the senior major of the 78th, wrote to General Amherst from Berthier, 18 February 1763, to express his sorrow that *"Captain Charles McDonell died a few days after the amputation… a good and gallant officer."*

CBs; SBs; BALs; WO 34/94: f. 42; "Charles McDonald," WO 64/12; "The Macdonells of Lochgarry," *Clan Donald Magazine*, [No.11]; Stewart, *Sketches*, II, 20-1; McCorry, "Rats, Lice & Scotchmen. . . ." 17-18; AFP U1350 O42/12; AFP U1350 O102/35.

John Fraser, [1] of Culbokie, (c.1727-1795)

Lieut: 24 January 1757, 78th Foot; appointed QM 27 September 1758; resigned QM 15 April 1759;
Capt: 15 April 1760, 78th Foot; half-pay, 24 December 1763; resigned 1 May 1775.

Younger son of William Fraser of Culbokie & 8th Guisachan, and Margaret Macdonald of Ardnable. John was the older brother of Archibald also serving in the 78th Foot [see below]. Gazetted a lieutenant, 24 January 1757, in Captain Simon Fraser's company [original parchment is in the Chateau de Ramsay Museum, Montréal]; appointed quartermaster 27 September 1758; served at Louisbourg; Sergeant James Thompson mentions that he was an accomplished swordsman and fought in a special regimental contest at Schenectady the winter of 1758/59, losing to a Corporal Macpherson of Dungallon's company. Promoted captain 15 April

1760 just prior to the battle of Sillery, 28 April 1760; appointed paymaster of troops in Montréal in 1763; was commanding a company when the regiment was disbanded; retired on half-pay and stayed in Canada. In 1764, he was appointed a judge of the court of common pleas for Montréal District and the following year married Marie-Claire Fleury Deschambault; in 1775, he resigned his commission as a half-pay officer and became a member of the Legislative Council of Québec. Fraser was briefly imprisoned by the Americans during the occupation of Montréal in 1777. At the end of the American Revolution, he helped to relocate his widowed sister-in-law and her young family, and provided financial assistance and guidance to his youngest nephew, Simon Fraser, born 1776 near Bennington, Vermont, who joined the Northwest Company of Montréal as an apprentice clerk. Simon became the fur trader and explorer after whom the Fraser River in British Columbia is named. In 1784, John Fraser became a member of the Executive Council of Lower Canada and a Judge of the Court of the King's Bench in 1792. His Worship, aged 68, died in Montréal on 5 December 1795 and was buried three days later, 8 December 1795, in the Saint-Amable crypt of the Church of Our Lady.

CBs; SBs; BALs; Stewart, *Sketches*, II, 20-1.

Archibald Roy Campbell (1728-1779)
Lieut: 23 January 1757, 78th Foot;
Capt-Lt: 13 December 1759, 78th Foot;
Capt: 29 April 1760, 78th Foot; half-pay, 24 December 1763.

Born in 1728, the youngest son of John Campbell of Fortingall and Glenlyon who died in 1746. "Archie Roy" as he was commonly known, was listed as a captain in the Atholl Brigade and fought at Culloden for the Jacobite army in 1746 at the age of 18. His foster-brother was Captain John Campbell [4], 42nd Foot, killed at Ticonderoga, 8 July 1758 (See 42nd Register). His older brother was Major John Campbell of Glenlyon of the Marines who had served in the 42nd Additional Companies during the '45. Gazetted a lieutenant in Captain John Macdonell's company [original commissioning scroll is in the Fort Ticonderoga Museum], Archie Roy fought at the siege of Louisbourg 1758; one of eight lieutenants stationed at Fort Stanwix during the winter 1758/59; wounded at battle of Plains of Abraham 13 September 1759, wounded again at Sillery, 28 April 1760; promoted captain *"in room of"* Donald Macdonell killed, after the battle of Sillery, 29 April 1760. The following year his company was in garrison at

Berthier, Québec where Parson Robert Macpherson described him thusly: *"Archy Glenlyon is a friendly, Sensible Honest fellow, a good Companion, has great Mother Wit, but is unlucky enough not to have had a liberal education."* Archie Roy was commanding a company when regiment was disbanded in 1763; and exchanged onto half-pay. The London *Gazetteer* and *New Daily Advertiser*, Wed. Dec. 29, 1779, reported that *Capt. Archibald Campbell, of the late 78th regiment of foot"* died of old wounds reopening on 16 December 1779 *"At Armady in Argyllshire, Scotland."*

CBs; SBs; BALs; PRO, C5/51; *Muster Roll* 1745-46; London *Gazetteer and New Daily Advertiser*, 29 December 1779; Stewart, *Sketches*, II, 20-1; Parson Robert Macpherson to William Macpherson, 24 Dec. 1761, Berthier, *JGP.*

Alexander Campbell, (c.1725-1767)
Lieut: 7 May 1757, 78th Foot;
Capt: 5 October 1760, 78th Foot; half-pay; full-pay, 17 August 1764, 62nd Foot.

Stewart of Garth styles him "of Aross," a Campbell castle on the northeast coast of Mull island in Argyll. He had studied to become a minister but was offered a commission as one of the two grenadier lieutenants in the 78th when Donald MacLean *"brother to the Laird of Isle Muck"* declined the commission in his favour - 7 May 1757. He was wounded at the siege and capture of Louisbourg on the same night as Captain Donald *"Gorm"* Macdonell (see above), and wounded again the following year on the plains of Abraham; 13 September 1759. Alex was taken prisoner at the battle of Sillery, 28 April 1760 and made a captain later in the year when *"in room of"* of his kinsman John Campbell moving up to the second majority to replace the departing John Macpherson. Alex bypassed two more senior Fraser lieutenants in the process, a strong indication that he purchased the captaincy on favorable terms from his kinsman. His company was stationed at Berthier, Québec in 1761 and Parson Robert Macpherson has left us this description: *"Sandy Campbell was to have been Chaplain to this Regt. in my place when I expected the Lieutenancy but it had been a thousand pities he had succeeded to his first expectation as His Majesty would have been deprived of one of the Best Officers, I may venture to say, in the British Army; Universally knowing in Antient and Modern Literature without any Idle Pomp, Show or Parade of Learning, he is without Dissparagement to any, the prettyest young fellow in our Corps."* Alex commanded a company when the regiment was disbanded December 1763. He exchanged onto half-pay, but returned to active service almost immediately [17 August 1764] as a captain in the

62nd Foot, then garrisoning Dominica in the West Indies. He died three years later of disease on 9 December 1767.

CBs; *SBs*; *BALs*; Stewart, Sketches, II, 20-1; *WAJ*, AJ; Harper, *Fighting Frasers*, Knox, *Siege*, III; xx: *PRO* C5/51; *WO* 64-12; *CU* 49/5; *DSB*, II, 422; Parson Robert Macpherson to William Macpherson, 24 December 1761, Berthier, *JGP*.

John Nairn (1731-1802)
2nd Lieut: 1st Stewart's Regt., Dutch Scots Brigade;
Lieut: 17 July 1757, 78th Foot;
Capt: 24 April 1761, 78th Foot; half-pay, 24 December 1763; full pay, 14 June 1775, 84th Foot (RHE);
Major: *"in the Army,"* 29 August 1777; 4 October 1780, 53rd Foot;
Lt-Col: *"in the Army,"* 19 February 1783; retired 22 September 1783.

Enlisted at the age of 14 with the Dutch-Scots Brigade in Holland and served in the 1st Battalion of Stewart's Regiment. Came over to North America as a lieutenant with one of the Three Additional Companies in spring 1758; selected as one of the light infantry company's subalterns and, at the Louisbourg landings, took command of one half of the company with Ensign Malcolm Fraser, while the other half company was commanded by Captain Alexander Cameron of Dungallon. After the siege, Nairn was left behind in the army hospital with fever when the regiment sailed for Boston, but was still able to catch up with it in time to march across Massachusetts and New York to Fort Stanwix for the winter. Wounded at the battle of Sillery, 28 April 1760; promoted to captain in April 1761 after borrowing 400 pounds sterling from his patron, General James Murray, Governor of Québec. He was commanding a company at Québec when regiment was disbanded in 1763; retired on half-pay. The previous year, 27 April 1762, Murray had divided his *seigneury* of La Malbaie in two portions and granted half to Nairn and the other to Nairn's best friend, Lieutenant Malcolm Fraser, 78th Foot (see below). Fraser took Mount Murray and Nairn took Murray Bay and built a manor house overlooking the village of La Malbaie. He married in Christiana Emery 20 July 1769 at Québec. Nairne brought some of his Highland soldiers with him to settle the land in 1764, but the Harveys, Warrens, Macleans and Blackburns who accompanied him married local girls, and while a generation later, the new settlers had large families which were Scottish in name, they were *Canadien* in religion, language and customs. On the outbreak of the American Revolution, Nairn was gazetted a captain in the 1st Bn, 84th Foot (Royal Highland Emigrants). Under the command of Henry Caldwell, Captain Nairn played a leading role in the stubborn defense of Québec against the American army of Arnold and Montgomery in 1776/7. Promoted major *"in the Army"* 29 August 1777, he served at Île aux Noix in 1777 and Carleton Island (now in upstate NY) in 1779. At the latter, he supervised the rebuilding of the original fort and guarded American POWs. He transferred from the RHE, 4 October 1780, on promotion to major of the 53rd Regiment of Foot. Nairn was made a lieutenant colonel *"in the Army"* 19 February 1783 and, at war's end retired to his *seigneury* at Murray's Bay. He died 14 July 1802 at Québec.

CBs; *SBs*; *BALs*; Currie, *The Lairds of Glenlyon* (Perth, 1886), 281; *Captain John Nairne's Orderly Book, 8 May 1762 – 31 December 1762* and "A Military Sketch of Colonel John Nairne," 51-52; *MG* 23, G III 23, Vol.6; *DCB*; ; *DSB*, II, 410; Stewart, *Sketches*, II, 20-1; *DSB*, II; *WO* 25/209.

Hugh Fraser, 4th Eskadale, [1] (c.1720-1801)
Ensign: 24 September 1742, 27th Foot (Enniskillens);
Lieut: 4 September 1754, 27th Foot;
Capt: 23 October 1761, 78th Foot; half-pay, 24 December 1763.

Eldest son and heir of Alexander Fraser, 3rd Eskadale, and Isabel Fraser and raised on the Lovat estates. *"Carryed arms"* as a gentleman volunteer in the ranks of General Blakeney's 27th Foot during the Cartegena expedition of 1740 in the West Indies. He survived the catastrophic death rate caused by rampant sickness and was made ensign in 1742. He fought at Culloden with his regiment in 1746 and was promoted lieutenant 4 September 1754. In the summer of 1757, he came to North America with the 27th Foot to participate in the expedition against Louisbourg. When it was aborted, he and his regiment were assigned to Fort Edward for the winter. He fought at the Battle of Ticonderoga in 1758 and returned the following year with his regiment for Amherst's successful expedition against Ticonderoga and Crown Point. He is also the likely author of an anonymous letter fragment relating the aftermath of Ticonderoga in which he refers to a brother named *"Wullie"* who also survived the battle. This may have been William Frazer, snr, a "gentleman volunteer" of the 42nd who attended Robert Roger's Ranging School in autumn 1757 and was commissioned ensign in the 80th Foot (Gage's Light Infantry) 27 December 1757, and promoted Lt. 25 September 1760. William Frazer was killed in the action five years later on the Niagara

Portage, 14 September 1763. In 1760, Hugh marched on Montréal as part of Brigadier Haviland's army and met up with Murray and Amherst's armies on 13 September 1760. The following year he was at Crown Point, the senior or eldest lieutenant with his regiment which was warned off for the Caribbean campaign against Martinique and Guadeloupe. He was exchanged to the 78th Foot on promotion to captain 23 October 1761 and was commanding a company at Québec when the regiment was disbanded in December 1763; retired on half-pay. According to *The Scots Magazine,* Hugh died in Eskadale, Scotland, March 1801.

CBs; SBs; BALs; Scots Magazine, March 1801; *AJ,* Appendix 1763. *"Officers Kill'd or Murder'd by the Indians."* O14: 155.

Hugh Montgomerie (1739-1819)
Lieut: 21 July 1757, 77th Foot;
Capt: 2 June 1762, 78th Foot; half-pay, 24 December 1763; full pay, 4 February 1767, 2nd/1st Foot; retired 27 January 1776;
Major: 14 April 1778, Argyll (Western) Fencibles;
Lt-Col: 6 March 1782, Argyll (Western) Fencibles; half-pay, 21 April 1783;
Col: appointed c. 1793, West Lowland Fencibles.

Son of Alexander Montgomerie of Coilsfield, initially gazetted a lieutenant, 21 July 1757, in one of the three Additional Companies of the 77th Foot, the sister battalion of Fraser's Highlanders. Fought at Fort Duquesne, 1758, participated in the capture of Forts Ticonderoga and Crown Point in 1759 and distinguished himself as a light infantry officer during the 1760 Cherokee campaign in South Carolina. He served in one of the 77th composite companies at the recapture of St John's Newfoundland under Colonel William Amherst in August 1762. He appears to have been promoted captain retro-active to 2 June 1762 in the 78th Foot for he was still listed as a lieutenant in Montgomery's Highlanders on William Amherst's list of officers who participated in the recapture of St John's two months later. Hugh was in command of a company when the regiment was disbanded in 1763; went on half-pay as a captain in the 78th until 1767 when he returned to active service as a captain in the 2nd/1st Foot, his new commission dated 4 February 1767. He retired 27 January 1776. During the American Revolution he returned to military service on the home front as first major to the Argyll (Western) Fencibles and was painted in that regiment's uniform in 1780 by John Singleton Copley. Hugh was MP for Ayrshire from 1784 to

1789, and again in 1796. In 1796, at the age of 57, he succeeded his cousin Archie Montgomery (see 77th Register) to become the 12th Earl of Eglinton and moved from the House of Commons to the House of Lords. Hugh Montgomerie was the *"sodger Hugh"* of Robbie Burns' poem *The Author's Earnest Cry and Prayer*. He became Colonel of the West Lowland Fencibles in 1793 during the Napoleonic War. In 1806 he was created a peer of the realm and took the name Baron Ardrossan. Eglinton continued a program of improvements on the family estates in Ayrshire and commissioned the architect John Paterson, builder of the Glasgow, Paisley and Johnstone Canal, to rebuild Eglinton Castle and to construct a harbor at Ardrossan. Relations between the two deteriorated to the point that Paterson took extended legal action against Eglinton for the recovery of fees which added significantly to the family debt. He died in 1819.

CBs; SBs; BALs; DNB; NAS GD3/9: f.11; Stewart, *Sketches,* II, 20-1.

Alexander Wood (1738-1769)
Lieut: 1757, 85th Foot;
Capt: 28 October 1760, Independent Company, amalgamated into 98th Foot, 1761; exchanged, 21 January, 1763, 78th Foot; half-pay, 24 December 1763; full pay, 14 December 1764; exchanged, 26 June 1765, 65th Foot; half-pay, 30 April 1768.
Born in Ireland in 1738, a 19-year-old Alexander Wood started his military career with the 85th Foot (Craufurd's *Royal Voluntiers*) raised in 1757, but was commissioned captain of an independent company three years later which would indicate a very powerful and influential patron. His independent company was amalgamated the following year into the 98th Foot (Grey's) and fought first at Belleisle off the coast of France before being sent to the Caribbean where it served during the capture of Martinique and the siege of Havana, 1762. Before it was disbanded however, Wood was transferred to a vacancy in the 78th Foot stationed at Québec, based on the strong recommendations of General Robert Monckton, Commander-in-Chief of the 1762 Martinique expedition. Wood exchanged to half-pay when Fraser's was disbanded, 24 December 1763, but returned to active service in December 1764 as a captain in the 62nd Foot which was stationed in the West Indies. Six months later, he exchanged to the 65th Foot before finally exchanging onto half-pay of the 113th Foot in April 1768. He died the following year, 29 October 1769.

CBs; *SBs*; *BALs*; Egremont to Amherst, 24 November 1762, *CKS*, AFP, U1350 O41/38.

Captains Lieutenant

John Craufurd Walkinshaw (1721-1793)

Ensign: 24 January 1740/1, 58th/47th Foot; transferred to cavalry;

Cornet: 23 April 1741/2, 2nd Dragoons (Royal North British);

2nd Lieut: 1 April 1743/4; retired 23 May 1746;

Capt-Lt: 5 January 1757, 78th Foot;

Major (Commandant): 19 October 1761, 115th Foot (Royal Scotch Lowlanders); half-pay, 9 March 1763.

AKA John Walkinshaw-Craufurd of Craufurdland, the 19th Laird - His father, John Craufurd, 18th of Craufurdland married Robina Walkinshaw, daughter and heiress of John Walkinshaw of that Ilk, Laird of Bishoptoun. Upon their marriage, John's father added the name and arms of Walkinshaw to his own. John, jʳ, started his career in the British army as an infantry ensign in 1741/2 but almost immediately transferred to the cavalry, specifically, the 2nd Dragoons (later Royal Scots Greys) whose current Colonel was the Duke of Argyll. Was present with his regiment at the victory of Dettingen in 1743, and also distinguished himself at Fontenoy two years later. He resigned his King's commission a month after the battle of Culloden, April 1746, and, on learning of the conviction and death sentence passed on his boyhood friend, John Boyd, Earl of Kilmarnock, went to London. He insisted on accompanying the ill-fated John Boyd to the scaffold as a last act of comradeship to receive his head and take care of the body on behalf of the Boyd family. He came out of retirement eleven years later during the raising of the 78th Foot, to accept the post of captain-lieutenant commanding Simon Fraser's company and was commissioned 5 January 1757. He was promoted full captain following the death of Charles Baillie at the Louisbourg landings, 9 June 1758. Contracted scurvy while commanding Fort Herkimer in the Mohawk valley the winter of 58/59 and stayed behind in New York with Major Clephane when the remainder of the regiment went to Québec with Wolfe. A monthly return dated 24 October 1759 describes him as having *"gone to continent for recovery of his health."* While back in Scotland on sick leave, he was asked by the Duke of Argyll to raise a new Highland battalion of six companies and made major-commandant of the 115th Foot (Royal Scotch Lowlanders) effective 19 October 1761. His small battalion was embodied at Paisley near Glasgow and was sent as part of the force under the command of Lord Loudoun and Brigadier Simon Fraser to Lisbon, Portugal, where they arrived 6 May 1762. His small battalion was authorized an extra company and was officially disbanded back at Paisley in March 1763. He exchanged to half-pay 9 March 1763 and was made a lieutenant-colonel "in the Army" in 1772. He died unmarried at Edinburgh, aged 72, February 1793. Despite his devotion to his friends, did not seem to share a similar affinity for his own family. In his will, he left his entire estates to Sir Thomas Coutts, the eminent banker. The deed was, however, contested by his aunt, Elizabeth Craufurd and her daughter. The case was eventually won in the House of Lords in 1806, but his aunt died before winning her long legal battle, and the ancient estates passed back to the rightful heir, her daughter.

CBs; *SBs*; *BALs*; *JSAHR*, Vol. 36, (1958) 3-13; Stewart, *Sketches*, II, 20-1.

Donald McBean of Faillie (later 6th Kinchyle) (1728-c.1790)

Lieut: 1 January 1747, Stewart's, Dutch Scots Brigade; 28 January 1757, 78th Foot;

Capt-Lt: 29 April 1760, 78th Foot; half-pay, 24 December 1763;

Capt: "in the Army," 25 May 1772; full pay, 15 August 1775, 10th Foot.

A Dutch-Scots officer gazetted lieutenant in the new-raising 78th Foot, January 1757; fought in all major campaigns and was wounded at Sillery, 28 April 1760; promoted the following day to captain-lieutenant; exchanged to half-pay with rank of captain-lieutenant in December 1763. He was made full captain "in the Army" while still on half-pay. Returned to active service as a captain in the 10th Foot in August 1775 and joined it in Boston that year. He fought in all major engagements of the Revolution with his regiment. He was married first to Ann McBean, who died 17 January 1754 and was buried in Daviot parish near Inverness. Parish documents dated 1781 and 1783 note that Captain McBean was *"late taxman* [tacksman] *Faillie and now in 10th Regiment of Foot."*

CBs; *SBs*; *BALs*; WO 64-12; Stewart, *Sketches*, II, 20-1; *DSB*, II, 411.

Lieutenants

John Cuthbert, of Castlehill, (1729-1758)
Ensign: Dutch Scots Brigade; resigned 25 April 1756; Lieut: 18 January 1757, 78th Foot.

An ensign with the Dutch Scots Brigade in Holland, and son to George Cuthbert of Castlehill and Mary Mackintosh; gazetted one of the two grenadier lieutenants in Captain Charles Baillie's company on 18 January 1757 when Archibald Macdonald declined the commission; he was killed at the Louisbourg landings, 8 June 1758.

CBs; *SBs*; *BALs*; *DSB*, II, 390, 414, 421; Stewart, *Sketches*, II, 20-1.

Roderick MacNeill, yʳ of Barra
Lieut: 20 January 1757, 78th Foot.

Eldest son of the chief of the MacNeills. Married twice: firstly, Anne MacNeil of Vaslan; secondly to Anne MacNeil of Vatersay. Of the MacNeills, the Duke of Argyll predicted, *"Rory McNeil, Laird of Barra, it is believed will go himself, if not, his brother certainly will & either can easily raise men."* The oldest son eventually went, gazetted a lieutenant, 20 January 1757; killed at battle of the Plains of Abraham 13 September 1759.

CBs; *SBs*; *BALs*; *CU* 5/51; *CU* 49/5; "Rory McNeill," *WO* 64/12.

William MacDonell (c.1730-1779)
Lieut: 21 January 1757, 78th Foot; resigned 12 December 1759.

Younger half-brother of Captain *Donull Gorm* Macdonell, the latter who was killed at Ste-Foy, 28 April 1760 (see above); gazetted a lieutenant on January 20, 1757; severely wounded at the battle of the Plains of Abraham; the monthly return of November 1759 lists him as having *"gone to continent for recovery."* He resigned, 12 December 1759, and later became tacksman of Ormiclate in South Uist, and died there in 1779.

CBs; *SBs*; *BALs*; "Willm McDonell," January 21, 1757, *WO* 64/12.

Hector MacDonell (c.1730-1760)
Lieut: 27 January 1757, 78th Foot;
Fourth son of Alexander MacDonell, 1st Boisdale

[brother of Ranald MacDonell, 17th Clanranald] and thus a first cousin to *Donull Gorm* and William Macdonell. Gazetted a lieutenant on 27 January 1757; fought at Louisbourg and the Plains of Abraham 1759; died of wounds on 8 May 1760 received a week earlier at the battle of Sillery, 28 April 1760. He is mentioned in Lt. Malcolm Fraser's *Journal*: *"… Lieutenant Hector McDonald and Ensign Malcolm Fraser died of their wounds, all very much regretted by every one who knew them."*

CBs; *SBs*; *BALs*; Harper, *Fighting Frasers*, 103; "Hector McDonell," *WO* 64/12.

John *"Dubh"* Fraser [2] aka John McTavish, of Garthbeg (c.1701-1775)
Lieut: 30 January 1757, 78th Foot; half-pay, 24 December 1763.

John *"Dubh"* Fraser of Little-Garth was born in Inverness-shire, Scotland. His brother Alexander McTavish was initially proposed as a lieutenant in the new-raising 78th by the Duke of Argyll and described as *"brother to McTavis of Garthbeg who is head of a small tribe"*; but in the end John McTavish of Garthbeg himself took the commission under his real name, John *Dubh* Fraser, which had been proscribed since the '45. He and his brother had fought at Falkirk and Culloden where their *"small tribe"* was considered a sept clan of the Frasers of Lovat. He was nearly sixty years old when he joined the 78th; fought at Louisbourg in 1758; fell sick when the regiment gathered at Louisbourg for the 1759 expedition against Québec under Wolfe. An army return dated 8 October 1759 by General Monckton shows *Lieut Jno. McTavish*, as of 4 June 1759 *"left sick at Louisbourg"* so he did not participate in the siege of Québec and the subsequent battle on the Plains of Abraham. He rejoined his regiment by 1760 and fought at the battle of Sillery, 28 April 1760, but like many others, sickened with scurvy and deteriorated. Governor Murray interceded on his behalf and General Amherst gave permission for the sixty year old lieutenant to be sent home in the fall of 1761, *"as it would be an act of charity to him and his family."* An absent officers list shows him as having *"gone to England 12th Octbr. 1761 by General Amherst's leave."* McTavish was the senior lieutenant cited on list of officers on half-pay after 1763 and he died 2 March 1775. His second daughter married a fellow 78th officer, Lt. Hugh Fraser, and returned with him to North America. (see above)

CBs; *SBs*; *BALs*; *CU* 49/5; Amherst to Murray, 11 August 1761; *WO* 34/3: f.105.

Alexander MacDonell (c.1735-1759)
Lieut: 2 February 1757, 78th Foot.

Second son of Coll MacDonell, 2nd Barrisdale and Catherine Mackenzie of Balmuchie. Gazetted a lieutenant on 2 February 1757; one of eight lieutenants stationed at Fort Stanwix during the winter 1758/59; mortally wounded at battle of Plains of Abraham on September 13, 1759.

CBs; SBs; BALs; WO C5/51.

John [MacGregor] Murray, y^r of Glencarnoch (c.1735-1758)
Lieut: 6 February 1757, 78th Foot.

Oldest son of of Robert [Macgregor] Murray of Glencarnoch, 6th chieftain of the proscribed Macgregor clan - *"The Children of the Mist."* His younger brother, James, was Captain-Lt of the 55th Foot (Howe's) who was killed at Ticonderoga, 8 July 1757. John was killed 15 days later in the siege trenches at Louisbourg where he was serving as a grenadier officer of the 78th Foot. The Duke of Argyll originally proposed him as ensign, with the remark *"has good interest in the highland of Perthshire."*

CBs; SBs; BALs; CU 49/5; WAJ, in passim.

Simon Fraser [4] (1738-1813)
Ensign: Dutch Scots Brigade
Lieut: 30 January 1757, 78th Foot; appointed QM, 16 January 1763; resigned 14 March 1763; half-pay, 24 December 1763;
Capt: 23 November 1775, 1st/71st Foot (Fraser's Highlanders);
Maj: 14 October 1778, 1st/71st Foot;
Lt-Col: *"in the Army,"* 22 August 1783;
Col: appointed 22 August 1794, 133rd Foot; appointed 26 May 1806, 6th West India Regt.;
Lt-Gen: local rank in Portugal, 30 November 1796; *"in the Army,"* 25 September 1803.

Son of a tacksman, born about 1738. Gazetted a lieutenant 30 January 1757; not a captain-lieutenant, as stated by David Stewart of Garth and often confused with Brigadier Simon Fraser [3] Balnain killed at Saratoga; he was wounded at the battle of Sillery, 28 April 1760; retired on half-pay as a lieutenant in 1763. Raised and commanded a company during the American Revolution for the First Battalion of 71st Foot (Fraser's High-

landers), in which he was gazetted the senior captain on 23 November 1775; promoted to major on 14 October 1778. Fraser served in America until 1781 and retired on half-pay when the 71st was disbanded in 1783. During the Napoleonic Wars, he raised the 133rd Foot and was gazetted its colonel on 22 August 1794. He became a major-general the following year and was given the local rank of lieutenant-general 30 November 1796 while commanding a force of British troops stationed in Portugal from 1797-1800. He was, for some years, second-in-command of the forces in North Britain and in 1806 was appointed Colonel of the 6th West India Regiment. He died in Scotland, 21 March 1813.

CBs; SBs; BALs; Succession of Colonels, JSAHR; Stewart, Sketches, II, 20-1, 44; DSB, II, 389, 420.

Simon Fraser [5]
Lieut: 8 February 1757, 78th Foot;

The third of three Simon Frasers to be gazetted lieutenant on the raising of the regiment. This Simon Fraser was styled *"Simon Tenakyle"* by another Fraser officer serving at Ticonderoga 1758. Tearakyle was killed on 18 June 1758 and reputedly left a wife named Jean Gray and three young children behind in Scotland.

CBs; SBs; BALs; Millar, 112.

John MacDougall
Lieut: 10 February 1757, 78th Foot; resigned, 18 June 1757.

Gazetted a lieutenant on February 10, 1757, but resigned before the regiment sailed to North America in favour of John Douglas, commissioned 18 June 1757.

CBs; SBs; BALs; WO 64/12.

Alexander Fraser [2] (1729-1799)
Lieut: 12 February 1757, 78th Foot; half-pay, 24 December 1763.
Capt: 14 June 1775, 1st/84th Foot (RHE).

Gazetted a lieutenant 12 February 12, 1757; one of eight lieutenants stationed at Fort Stanwix during the winter 1758/59; wounded at battle of Plains of Abraham 13 September 1759 and again at Sillery, 28 April 1760; retired on half-pay in 1763. One, of several officers, who decided to stay in Canada after the regiment's disbandment. Purchased the *seigneury* of La Martiniere or Beauchamp, near Québec from Brigadier-General

James Murray, and later, acquired two others. During the American Revolution he was gazetted a captain in the 1st/84th Foot (Royal Highland Emigrants). His last will and testament indicates a close relationship to Alexander Fraser of Strichen, whose grandson inherited the Lovat estates by entail after the death of Archibald Campbell Fraser of Lovat in 1815, without legitimate surviving issue. Alexander died at St. Charles, Québec on 19 April 1799, *"aged about seventy years."*

CBs; *SBs*; *BALs*; CU 5/51.

John Douglas (c.1730-1759)
Ensign: Dutch-Scots Brigade, resigned 30 October 1757; Lieut: 18 June 1757, 78th Foot.

A former subaltern in the 2nd Battalion of Halkett's regiment in the Dutch-Scots Brigade, Douglas was gazetted a lieutenant on 18 June 1757 after John Mac-Dougall's resignation; one of eight lieutenants stationed at Fort Stanwix during the winter 1758/59; wounded at battle of Plains of Abraham 13 September 1759. The monthly return of 24 October 1759 describes him as *"gone to continent for recovery of his wounds."* The Succession Book records his subsequent death the following year on 9 July 1760.

CBs; *SBs*; *BALs*; Stewart, *Sketches*, II, 20-1; *DSB*, II, 410, 424; WO 25/209.

Arthur John Rose, yr of Kilravock (1739-c.1800)
Lieut: Dutch-Scots Brigade; 17 July 1757, 78th Foot; half-pay, 24 December 1763; full pay, 31 October 1779, Pendennis Castle Invalid Company; exchanged, 19 January 1786, Berwick Invalid Company.

Son of Hugh Rose, 15th Kilravock and Katharine Porteous. His brother, 16th Kilravock was married to Betty Clephane, making Major Clephane his brother-in-law. A lieutenant in the Dutch-Scots Brigade in Holland he came over to North America as a lieutenant with one of the three Additional Companies in spring 1758. Gazetted a lieutenant on 17 July 1757, Rose was one of eight lieutenants stationed at Fort Stanwix where his brother-in-law commanded during the winter 1758/59; wounded at the battle of Sillery 28 April 28, 1760; and exchanged as a lieutenant in Captain Archibald Campbell's company to half-pay in 1763 on disbandment. He returned to active duty 16 years later as a lieutenant in the Pendennis Castle Invalid Company and exchanged five years later into an Invalid Company closer to home

at Berwick-on-Tweed. The following year, his former regimental colleague, John Macdonell of Leek (see below) took over command of the company.

CBs; *SBs*; *BALs*; Stewart, *Sketches*, II, 20-1; *DSB*, II, 422.

Alexander Fraser [3], (c.1735-1798)
Ensign: 13 February 1757, 38th Foot; transferred,
Lieut: 22 July 1757, 78th Foot; half-pay, December 1763; full pay, 25 October 1766, 9th Foot;
Capt-Lt: 13 May 1776, 9th Foot; exchanged, 2 August 1776, 20th Foot; transferred on promotion;
Capt: 11 November 1776, 34th Foot; transferred on promotion;
Major: 18 November 1790;
Lt. Col: *"in the Army,"* 1 March 1794; 1 September 1795, 45th Foot.

Started his military career in 1757 as an ensign in the 38th Foot, but transferred on promotion to lieutenant, 22 July 1757, in one of the three Additional Companies authorized for the 78th Foot that summer. He arrived in spring 1758 with his company in time to participate in the 1758 siege of Louisbourg, and fight at Québec under Wolfe in 1759. He was wounded at the Battle of Sillery (Ste-Foy) 28 April 1760. On disbandment of his regiment in 1763, he was a lieutenant of Captain Alexander MacLeod's company and exchanged to half-pay and by 1765 was employed by General Gage as his special emissary to cooperate with Sir William Johnson's deputy, George Croghan. Both men had the common goal of paving the way for Captain Thomas Stirling's expedition to the Illinois country, the latter noting that Fraser's role was *"to prepare the way for reception of troops coming up the Mississippi… by way of Fort Pitt & the Ohio."* Fraser's task was to ensure the inhabitants of the Illinois were fully informed on the terms of the Treaty of Paris and how it would affect them. Fraser and Croghan arrived at Fort Pitt 28 February 1765, but three weeks later, the zealous Fraser was impatient to be on his way. Croghan noted defensively in his journal: *"Lieut. Frazer informed Major Murray and me that the Generalls Instructions to him, was to be at the Illinois at all Events by the beginning of April, that as the Indians were not met here, he purposed to set off down the River in two or three days, as the service he was sent on, was of a different nature than mine."* Fraser departed 21 March 1765 with a sergeant and eight volunteer privates from the 42nd, a Frenchman, and three Indian interpreters/scouts. His reception in the Illinois was hostile to say the least and his entire party were made prisoner several times and roughed up. Only the firm intercession of the war chieftain Pontiac who was in the Illinois country at this time saved their lives, and Fraser soon had his men slip away to New Orleans and followed shortly thereafter. He returned with the 34th Foot in December 1765 to Fort de Chartres to complete his mission of issuing General Gage's proclamation. He then returned to New York with Thomas Stirling's 42nd company via New Orleans and Pensacola. As a reward for his singular efforts and hardships in the Illinois country, Fraser was taken off half-pay by Gage and gazetted a lieutenant 25 October 1766 in the 9th Foot, then stationed at St Augustine, Florida and the Bahamas. Eventually, the 9th Foot rotated back to Ireland, and Fraser was promoted to captain-lieutenant (20 May 1776), on the eve of the American Revolution. In a paper shuffle, he was transferred immediately to the 20th Foot, but then transferred again to the 34th Foot as a full Captain (11 November 1776). This was the same regiment he had traveled north with in 1765, up the Mississippi to occupy and garrison Fort de Chartres. Fraser's talents were quickly noticed on his arrival by Governor Guy Carleton who had soldiered previously with Fraser at Québec. He was detached from his regiment *"on command"* in 1776-77 to command Indians and light troops as Assistant Superintendent of Indian Affairs in Canada to Major John Campbell of Glendaruel, a former 42nd Foot officer (See 42nd Register). Carleton directed that every British regiment in Canada provide Fraser ten men to form an elite company of skirmishers and Fraser *carte blanche* to secure the army's most accurate weapons. Captain Alexander Fraser was made major in the Army in November 1776, then lieutenant-colonel, 1 March 1794. He transferred to the 45th Foot in 1795 then was stationed in the sickly West Indies, far removed from the Napoleonic wars in Europe. According to the 45th Regimental History *"in 1797 and 1798 no less than 13 officers died, namely, Lieut.-Colonel Frazer; Captains Morrison and Hutchinson..."* The Succession Book states he died 4 October 1797.

CBs; SBs; BALs; Hadden, *"Journal Kept in Canada and Upon Burgoyne's Campaign in 1776 and 1777,"* (Albany, 1884), 473-476; P.H. Dalbiac, *History of the 45th*, (Nottingham, 1902),18; *"Croghan's Journal," Gage Papers,* British Series, II, 3; Stewart, *Sketches,* II, 20-1.

John Macdonell [2], yr of Leek (1727-1813)
Lieut: 23 July 1757, 78th Foot; exchanged, (acting as ensign), 14 November 1763, 15th Foot; appointed QM, 14 November 1763, 15th Foot; 1770, ranked as lieutenant; resigned QM, 1 May 1775; transferred on pro-

motion; Capt: 27 August 1776, 1st/71st Foot; half-pay 4 June 1784; full pay, 3 June 1787, Berwick Invalid Company.

Second son of John Macdonell of Leek, a cadet branch of the Glengarry branch of Clan Donald. He is often confused with his father, John, who immigrated to Canada with his two brothers in 1773. John jnr first came to North America as a lieutenant with one of the three authorized Additional Companies in spring 1758; gazetted a lieutenant 23 July 1757; wounded during the siege of Louisbourg 1758; allowed to go home in fall of 1761 on account of his bad health. He returned to North America and exchanged into the 15th Foot, 14 November 1763. He returned to North America during the American Revolution as a captain in the 1st/71st Foot (Fraser's Highlanders). He married Elizabeth Duguid of Balquhain and, one of his sons, *"Red George"* Macdonell, was born 12 August 1780 in Newfoundland and went on to become famous during the War of 1812. He returned to England after the war and died a Captain of Invalids at Berwick-upon-Tweed in 1813.

CBs; SBs; BALs; MacDonald, "The Identity of *Red* George," *Clan Donald Magazine* [No.6], (1975); Stewart, *Sketches,* II, 20-1.

The Honorable Cosmo Gordon (c.1740-1760)
Ensign: 15 January 1756, 3rd Foot Guards;
Lieut: 24 July 1757, 78th Foot.

Came over to North America as a lieutenant with one of the three Additional Companies in spring 1758; fought at Louisbourg 1758; one of eight lieutenants stationed at Fort Stanwix during the winter 1758/59; and the Plains of Abraham, 1759; killed at Sillery 28 April 28, 1760; mentioned in Malcolm Fraser's Journal: *"Captain Donald MacDonald who commanded the volunteer company of the Army, and Lieutenant Cosmo Gordon who commanded the Light Infantry Company of our regiment, were both killed in the field..."*

CBs; SBs; BALs; Harper, *Fighting Frasers,* 103; Stewart, *Sketches,* II, 20-1.

David Baillie (c.1740-c.1785)
Lieut: 26 July 1757, 78th Foot; half-pay, 24 December 1763.

Came over to North America as a lieutenant with one of the three Additional Companies in spring 1758; fought at Louisbourg, 1758; the Plains of Abraham, 1759 and Sillery, 1760; the absent officers list shows *"Lieut. Bailey gone to England 12th Octbr. 1761 by General Amherst's leave,"* apparently *"to get rid of some difficulties in money matters";* retired on half-pay in 1763. Amherst refused to allow his purchase of John Macpherson's captaincy, ahead of the more senior John Nairn in the same year.

CBs; SBs; BALs; Amherst to Murray, 11 August 1761; *WO* 34/3: f. 105.

Evan Cameron, 13th Glennevis
Ensign: 2nd/ Halkett's, Dutch-Scots Brigade; resigned 18 April 1756; 5 January 1757, 78th Foot;
Lieut: 9 June 1758, 78th Foot; half-pay, 24 December 1763.

Son of Alexander Cameron, 12th Glennevis, and Mary Cameron of Dungallon. First cousin of Capt. Alexander Cameron of Dungallon, 78th Foot, and brother-in-law to Lt Alexander Grant, 77th Foot (see 77th Register); a Dutch-Scots officer gazetted an ensign on 5 January 1757; fought at Louisbourg, 1758; the Plains of Abraham, 1759 and Sillery, 1760; promoted to lieutenant 9 June 1758 after the Louisbourg landings; wounded 31 July 1759 in the ill-fated assault at Montmorency; on disbandment of the regiment, exchanged to half-pay in 1763.

CBs; SBs; BALs; "Evan Cameron," *WO 64/12;* Stewart, *Sketches,* II, 20-1; *DSB,* II, 421.

Allan [Stewart] Stuart (1735-c.1781)
Ensign: 7 January 1757, 78th Foot;
Lieut: 10 June 1758, 78th Foot, half-pay, 24 December 1763.

A former Jacobite captain in the Appin clan regiment, who, along with his brother, Captain Alexander Stewart of Invernahyle, was wounded at Culloden. The Duke of Argyll said he *"has a good interest & connections in Argyllshire."* Brother-in-law of Lieut. Duncan MacVicar, 55th Foot, and uncle of Anne McVicar Grant of Laggan, the famous author. Gazetted an ensign on 7 January 1757; fought at Louisbourg, 1758; the plains of Abraham, 1759 and Sillery, 1760; promoted to lieutenant 10 June 1758 *"in room of"* John Cuthbert killed at the Louisbourg landings; exchanged onto half-pay in 1763.

CBs; SBs; BALs; "Allan Stuart," *PRO WO 64-12; Muster Roll,*1745-46; *CU* 49/5; Stewart, *Sketches,* II, 20-1.

Simon Fraser [6]
Ensign: 9 January 1757, 78th Foot;
Lieut: 18 June 1758, 78th Foot.

Gazetted an ensign 9 January 1757; fought at Louisbourg, 1758; the Plains of Abraham, 1759 and Sillery, 1760; promoted to lieutenant in room of Simon "Tenykle" Fraser killed, 18 June 1758 during the siege of Louisbourg; died 4 October 1760 and was replaced by Alexander Gilchrist.

CBs; SBs; BALs; Stewart, *Sketches,* II, 20-1.

Archibald MacAllister (1741-1801)
Ensign: 13 January 1757, 78th Foot;
Lieut: 23 July 1758, 78th Foot; half-pay, 24 December 1763; full pay, 4 May 1767, 35th Foot; appointed QM, 14 November 1770, resigned QM, 25 July 1775 on promotion;
Capt: 25 July 1775, 35th Foot;
Major: *"in Army,"* 18 November 1790; 1 September 1795; 35th Foot;
Lt.-Col: *"in Army,"* 1 March 1794; 5 August 1799, 35th Foot;
Col: *"in Army,"* 1 January 1798.

Born in 1741, 2nd son of Charles MacAllister of Loup, Kintyre. Gazetted an ensign on 13 January 1757; fought at Louisbourg, 1758; the plains of Abraham, 1759; wounded at Sillery, 28 April 1760; a lieutenant in Capt. John Macdonell's company on disbandment, he exchanged to half-pay in December 1763. Returned to active duty in 1767 as a lieutenant in the 35th Foot, and three years later, was appointed the QM. He served for five years as QM before getting a company command. He officially became the battalion commander in 1799, but had been made a Lt. Col. *"in the Army"* five years previously. He died in 1801.

CBs; SBs; BALs; Stewart, *Sketches,* II, 20-1.

James Murray (c.1740-1784)
Lieut: 15 September 1758, 78th Foot; half-pay, 24 December 1763;
Capt: 21 March 1780; discharged dead, 1 December 1784.

Additional company officer gazetted a lieutenant 15 September 1758; fought at Louisbourg, 1758, the Plains of Abraham, 1759, and Sillery, 1760; a lieutenant in Captain Hugh Fraser's company on disbandment and exchanged to half-pay in 1763. He returned to active service in the new-raising 2nd Battalion of the 42nd during the American Revolution, his commission being free but granted with the stipulation he would receive no prospect of half-pay at the end of the war. He died 1 December 1784.

CBs; *SBs*; *BALs*; Stewart, *Sketches*, II, 20-1.

Alexander [William] Fraser [4], (c. 1735-1814)
Ensign: 15 January 1758, 78th Foot;
Lieut: 27 September 1758, 78th Foot; half-pay, 24 December 1763;

Second son of Thomas Fraser of Garthmore in Stratherrick; gazetted an ensign on 15 January 1757; promoted to lieutenant on 27 September 1758; fought at Louisbourg, 1758; the plains of Abraham, 1759, and was wounded at Sillery, 28 April 28, 1760; serving as a lieutenant in Capt. John Macdonell's company on disbandment; exchanged to half-pay 1763. The will of Capt. Thomas Fraser of Boleskine, Co. Inverness refers to his father as Capt. Alexander Fraser, *"late of Bunchgavy,"* who had *"served in North America under Wolfe."* Alexander died 2 May 1814.

CBs; *SBs*; *BALs*; Millar, 111.

John Campbell [3] (c.1740-1760)
Ensign: 27 September 1758, 78th Foot;
Lieut: 13 December 1758, 78th Foot.

Gazetted ensign 27 September 1758; an ensign among the officers who sailed for Louisbourg in 1758 for the siege and capture; promoted to lieutenant on 13 December 1758; Lt. Campbell and three private soldiers of the 78th with Murray's force of 2100 men sailing upriver to Montréal were killed by enemy artillery fire on 16 July 1760 passing the village of Deschambault. Parson Robert Macpherson noted that Murray's army navigated *"all the narrows and Passes to lake St Pierre within five and twenty Leagues of Montreal with the loss of only one – Lt John Campbell of our Regt."*

CBs; *SBs*; *BALs*; Knox, *Journals*, II, 469; Parson Robert Macpherson to William Macpherson, 4 Aug. 1760, Québec City, *JGP*.

Donald Cameron, yʳ of Fassifern (c. 1741-1817)
Lieut: 30 September 1758, 78th Foot; half-pay, 24 December 1763.

Son of John Cameron of Fassifern, and nephew of Lochiel; gazetted a lieutenant on September 30, 1758 in the 14th Additional Company; fought at the battle of the Plains of Abraham, 13 September 1759; wounded at Sillery on 28 April 1760; exchanged as a lieutenant of Captain Alexander MacLeod's company onto half-pay in 1763. Stewart of Garth states that he *"died a lieutenant on half-pay in 1817."*

CBs; *SBs*; *BALs*.

John Fraser, [3] of Errogie (1734-1810)
Ensign: 19 January 1757, 78th Foot;
Lieut: 22 April 1759, 78th Foot; half-pay, 24 December 1763.

Eldest son of Angus Fraser, 3rd of Errogie and his wife, Janet Fraser; gazetted an ensign 19 January 1757; listed among the officers who sailed for Louisbourg in 1758; promoted to lieutenant on April 22, 1759; retired on half-pay in 1763. Died 14 April 1810, at Errogie, aged 76. The Inverness *Journal* obituary described him as *"a most respectable and worthy character"* and noted he had *"served as a Light Infantry officer."* He was an accomplished Gaelic singer and collected fiddle tunes, as did his father, which were later published in his son's music collection *"The Airs and Melodies Peculiar to the Highlands of Scotland and the Isles"* by Captain Simon Fraser of Knockie, 42nd Foot.

CBs; *SBs*; *BALs*; 20 April 1810, Inverness *Journal*.

John Chisholm (c.1740-c.1807)
Ensign: 17 January 1757, 78th Foot;
Lieut: 4 September 1759, 78th Foot; half-pay, 24 December 1763.

Gazetted an ensign 17 January 1757; fought at all major battles and sieges of the regiment; promoted to lieutenant on 4 September 1759 *"in room of"* Simon Fraser; he was wounded at the battle of Sillery, 28 April 1760 and was the sole lieutenant serving in Major James Abercrombie's company on disbandment.

CBs; *SBs*; *BALs*.

Simon Fraser [7] (c.1740-1760)
Ensign: 21 January 1757, 78th Foot;
Lieut: 25 September 1759, 78th Foot.
Gazetted an ensign on 21 January 1757; promoted to lieutenant on 25 September 1759. He was wounded at

the battle of Sillery, 28 April 1760, and died several weeks later on 23 August 1760.

CBs; SBs; BALs; WO 34/94: f. 2; Knox, *Journals*, III, 140.

James MacKenzie, 4th Ardloch (c.1740-1781)
Ensign: 7 May 1757, 78th Foot;
Lieut: 25 September 1759, 78th Foot; half-pay, 24 December 1763; full pay, 27 December 1770, 12th Foot; transferred on promotion;
Capt: 19 December 1777, 1st/ 73rd Foot (MacLeod's Highlanders);
Major: 24 September 1778, 1st/73rd Foot.

James was eldest son of Alexander Mackenzie, 3rd Ardloch, Factor to the estate of Assynt for the Earl of Sutherland and, Margaret Sutherland, a daughter of Robert Sutherland of Langwell, sister to George, 12th of Forse. During the recruiting of officers for the two new-raising Highland battalions, the Mackenzies, Sutherlands and Sinclairs provided a high number of the officers to the 77th Foot. Captain John Sutherland, 13th of Forse, writing from Caithness to Lord Loudon, put in a good word for his Mackenzie cousin with his old regimental commander from the previous war: "*My Dear Lord - As many of my Friends believe that your Lordship honours me with some share of your Regard, I am often called upon for recommendatory letters to you: and tho' I'm not fond of being reckoned a troublesome Sollicitor, I now and then am forced to give your Lordship trouble this way, tho' not once in twenty times that I am dunned for such credentials - This will be delivered by a Cousine of mine, one James Mackenzie son to Ardloch, who is a very fine young Lad, at least he promised mighty well when I knew him 2 or 3 years ago in this Country. He is, I'm told, made Ensign some weeks ago in Colonell Montgomery's Battalion. If he behaves well I know your Lordship will give him your countenances and do him justice in point of promotion, which is all I have a right to expect for him ....*" Forse was brother-in-law to John Sinclair, senior captain in the 77th, and had intended that young James to join Montgomery's "MacKenzie-heavy" regiment. However, Forse's letter was incorrectly annotated by some staff officer with the words "*Capt. John Sutherland, Nottingham, May 7th 1758 [sic] recommends Ensign James Mackenzie of Ardloch in Col. Fraser's Regt.*" James was duly gazetted an ensign in the 78th Foot on 7 May 1757 and served at Louisbourg. He was wounded "*slightly*" at the battle of the Plains of Abraham, 13 September 1759. Parson Robert Macpherson wrote in 1761 that "*James McKenzie Ardlock our fourth [mess] member is an amiable sweet blooded genteel young fellow and an extream good member of Society.*" Ardloch exchanged to half-pay in December 1763 on the regiment's disbandment but returned to active service as a lieutenant with the 12th Foot in December 1770. He transferred on promotion to captain in the new-raising MacLeod's Highlanders in December 1777 and his regiment was initially assigned garrison duties in Jersey, largest of the Channel Islands off the coast of France. He was promoted the major before it was shipped out to Madras, India where it distinguished itself in fighting against the armies of Hyder Ali and the Tippo Sultan. He was killed in action at the Battle of Perambaucum, 28 August 1781.

CBs; SBs; BALs; *Loudon Papers*, Huntington Library, dated 7 May 1757; Parson Robert Macpherson to William Macpherson, 24 December 1761, Berthier, *JGP*.

Malcolm Fraser [1] (1733-1815)
Ensign: 18 July 1758, 78th Foot;
Lieut: 25 September 1759, 78th Foot; appointed adjutant 24 July 1760; resigned adjutant, 9 April 1763; half-pay, 24 December 1763;.
Capt: 24 June 1775, 84th Foot (RHE); [date] 60th Foot; resigned 1798.
Major: "*in the Army,*" 1797.

Born in 1733 in Scotland, son of Donald Fraser (c.1712-1746) who was killed fighting in the Fraser of Lovat regiment at the battle of Culloden, April 1746. Gazetted an ensign, 18 July 1757, a 24-year old Malcolm came to America with one of the three additional companies sent to America in spring 1758; wounded at battle of plains of Abraham 13 September 1759 and promoted to lieutenant, 25 September 1759; wounded again at Sillery, 28 April 1760; appointed adjutant 24 July 1760 and resigned appointment 9 April 1763. Exchanged to half-pay in 1763. Purchased the *seigneury* of Mount Murray from Brigadier-General James Murray. On the outbreak of the American Revolution, he helped recruit former Fraser Highlanders for the 1st Battalion, 84th Foot (RHE), in which he was gazetted a captain, 24 June 1775. In 1797, he was brevetted major "*in the Army*" and he died, 17 July 1815, aged 82.

CBs; SBs; BALs; 3 August 1798, *Military Papers* C931, 106-107; 8 October 8, 1798, *Military Papers*, C931, 109-109a.

Donald McNeil (c.1740-1762)
Ensign: 20 July 1757, 78th Foot;
Lieut: 17 October 1759, 78th Foot.

Gazetted an ensign, 20 July 1757, in one of the three Additional Companies; fought at Louisbourg 1758 and at the Plains of Abraham, 1759; promoted to lieutenant after the latter battle, 17 October 1759; wounded at the battle of Sillery near Ste-Foy, 28 April 1760. The absent officers list shows *"Lieutt. MacNeil gone to the Southern Colonies 20th Octbr. 1761 by leave of General Murray."* He died the following year, 16 October 1762.

CBs; SBs; BALs; WO 25/209: f. 231.

Henry Munro (c.1740-c.1800)
Ensign: 23 July 1757, 78th Foot;
Lieut: 12 December 1759, 78th Foot; half-pay, 24 December 1763; full pay, 26 August 1775, 42nd Foot; transferred on promotion;
Capt-Lt: 2 February 1779, 1st/71st Foot (Fraser's Highlanders);
Capt: 25 August 1779; 1st/71st Foot; retired 1 December 1781..

Gazetted an ensign in one of the three Additional Companies 23 July 1757; fought at Louisbourg, 1758 and at the Plains of Abraham, 1759; promoted to lieutenant after the latter battle, 12 December 1759; wounded at Sillery on 28 April 1760; exchanged to half-pay in 1763 on the regiment's disbandment. He returned to Scotland and returned to active service with the Black Watch in August 1775 and went to North America where he was captured at sea on the *Oxford* and held by the rebels for eight months. In February 1779, he was promoted and transferred to the 71st Foot (Fraser's Highlanders) to command the Colonel's company as captain-lieutenant and, by the end of the year, was a full captain. He retired 1 December 1781.

CBs; SBs; BALs.

Hugh Fraser [2] (1730-1814)
Adjutant: Appointed 12 January 1757, 78th Foot; resigned 24 July 1760
Ensign: 9 June 1758, 78th Foot;
Lieut: 29 April 1760, 78th Foot; half-pay, 24 December 1763.

Hugh Fraser was the original regimental adjutant, appointed 12 January 1757 and served in that capacity until 24 July 1760. Gazetted ensign, 9 June 1758, the day after the Louisbourg landings; promoted to lieutenant the day after the battle of Sillery, 29 April 1760; exchanged to half-pay in 1763. Hugh Fraser returned to

Scotland and married Elizabeth MacTavish, daughter of fellow officer, Lieut. John MacTavish of Garthbeg and brought her back to Albany, New York by September 1764. He also brought with him his younger brother-in-law, Simon McTavish (1750-1804) who would become the driving force behind the highly successful North West fur trading company and subsequently the richest man in Montréal. Fraser apparently had an agreement with Sir William Johnson to settle lands in the Mohawk Valley and brought with him an undisclosed number of settlers. By November 1780, disenchanted with the ongoing war, Fraser returned to Scotland with his family and settled on a farm called Brightmony, near Auldean, Nairnshire. He died at Perth aged 83, 21 January 1814.

CBs; SBs; BALs.

Alexander Gregorson, of Ardtornish (1730-1789)
Ensign: 10 June 1758, 78th Foot;
Lieut: 29 April 1760, 78th Foot; half-pay, 24 December 1763; full pay, 23 January 1788, Landguard Fort Invalid Company.

Born on the Isle of Mull, 1730, the eldest son of James MacGregor and Elizabeth Campbell of Airds. Initially a gentleman volunteer, he was gazetted an ensign 10 June 1758 after the death of Lieutenant John Cuthbert created a vacancy. Col Fraser had recommended him for the promotion before the regiment sailed for Halifax and Louisbourg in a 23 April 1758 letter to Lord Loudoun citing Gregorson as; *"very strongly recommended by Colonel Campbell, & to whose friends I am so much indebted that I should take his being provided for as a very great favor."* Gregorson, AKA Macgregor, fought at Louisbourg 1758 and the Plains of Abraham the following year. He was slightly wounded at the battle of Sillery near Ste-Foy, 23 April 1760, and was taken prisoner and almost killed by Indians; promoted to lieutenant 29 April 1760, *"in room of"* Cosmo Gordon killed. The absent officers list shows *"Lieutt. Grigerson gone to England 23rd Octbr. 1760 by General Amherst's leave."* He exchanged to half-pay in 1763 on the regiment's disbandment. He returned to active service in January 1788 as a 58 year old lieutenant in the Landguard Fort Invalid Company, and was discharged dead the following year.

CBs; SBs; BALs.

James Henderson (c.1740-1768)
Ensign: 23 July 1758, 78th Foot;
Lieut: 8 May 1760, 78th Foot; half-pay, 24 December 1763;

Gazetted an ensign 23 July 1758; promoted to lieutenant on May 8, 1760; exchanged to half-pay in 1763 on the regiment's disbandment. He died 20 September 1768.

CBs; SBs; BALs.

Lauchlan MacPherson, yr of Breakachy (c.1740-1766)
Ensign: 22 April 1759, 78th Foot;
Lieut: 9 July 1760, 78th Foot; half-pay, 24 December 1763; full pay, 2 August 1765, Lieutenant Captain Francis McMillans's African Independent Company; [later amalgamated in 1766 as Lieutenant O'Hara's Corps of Foot serving in Africa.]

Son of Donald Macpherson, the Laird of Breakachie, a devout Jacobite and a former captain in the Clan Chattan regiment married to Cluny's sister, Christian and was thus nephew of Major John Macpherson [see above]. Lauchlan served initially as a surgeon's mate to the 78th Foot but was gazetted an ensign on 22 April 1759, before the regiment departed New York to join Wolfe's army assembling at Louisbourg. He was promoted to lieutenant 9 July 1760, just before sailing upriver with General Murray's army to attack Montréal. Parson Robert Macpherson wrote a detailed character sketch and report to his best friend William Macpherson from Québec city, 4 August 1760: *"Lacky Breckachies son is up with Mr. Murray acting as Surgeon's Mate, his own merit, the quick preferment in the Corps and a small assistance from his friends here has already procured him a Lieutenantcy without having any obligation to his Father who is certainly the most unworthy of Mankind that would not advance 100 £'s to such a Son and upon such an Occasion- when his preferment, nay his Character was at Stake – Would you believe that the son of such a father would be one of the best principled, prettyest young fellows in the Army? I do declare I never knew a more promising boy nor any better liked- in the battle of the 28th when our whole Officers except three or four were killed or wounded & very few men indeed left in the field, he had the good fortune to carry off both our Colours out of Danger, and not to receive any hurt. In short he has very good skill and hands as a Surgeon and will do the Regt honour as an officer."* "Lacky" is listed as surgeon in the return of Major John Campbell's company when the regiment was disbanded in 1763 but there is no record of him in Peterkin and Johnston's

Commissioned Officers in the Medical Services of the British Army, an indication that he was never formally gazetted as a surgeon but was only *"acting"* and being paid in that capacity. With the disbandment of the regiment he exchanged onto half pay December 1763, but returned to active service 2 August 1765 as a lieutenant in Captain Francis Macmillan's new-raising African Independent Company. He died in Africa from disease the following year on 5 December 1766.

CBs; SBs; BALs; Parson Robert Macpherson to William Macpherson, 4 Aug. 1760, Québec City, *JGP.*

Charles Stewart (c.1730-1780)
Ensign: 1745, Stewart's Edinburgh Regiment; 25 September 1759, 78th Foot;
Lieut: 23 July 1760, 78th Foot; half-pay, 24 December 1763.

Son of John Roy Stewart, the colonel commandant of the Edinburgh Regiment at the battle of Culloden. Charles served as an ensign in his father's regiment and was wounded during the battle. He served initially as a gentleman volunteer in the 78th Foot and was gazetted an ensign 25 September 1759 after the battle of the plains of Abraham; wounded at Ste-Foy on April 28, 1760 and noted for his witty post-battle pronouncement *"From April Battles and Murray generals, Good Lord deliver me!"* a reference to his present circumstances and his wounding several years earlier under Lord George Murray at Culloden; promoted to lieutenant 23 July 1760; exchanged to half-pay, a lieutenant in Captain Ranald Macdonell's grenadier company on disbandment in December 1763.

CBs; SBs; BALs; Muster Roll, 1745-46;

Robert Menzies (c.1740-c.1809)
Ensign: 15 September 1758, 78th Foot;
Lieut: 23 August 1760, 78th Foot; half-pay, 24 December 1763.

A gentleman volunteer gazetted an ensign 15 September 1758; wounded at Ste-Foy on April 28, 1760; promoted to lieutenant on 28 August 1760; a lieutenant in Captain Hugh Cameron's company on disbandment; exchanged to half-pay in December 1763. Wallace mistakenly suggests that he was the major of the same name who served in the 84th Foot (RHE) who was subsequently killed at Boston in 1776, but the Commission and Succession books, as well as Menzies' continuous presence on the 78th Foot's half-pay ledgers and, in particular, the fact that he drew half pay as late as 1798, do not support such a claim.

CBs; SBs; BALs.

Alexander Gilchrist (c.1735-1780)

Ensign: 25 September 1759, 78th Foot;
Lieut: 4 October 1760, 78th Foot; half-pay, 24 December 1763;
Capt: 21 December 1777, 1st/73rd Foot (MacLeod's Highlanders).

A gentleman volunteer gazetted ensign after the battle of the Plains of Abraham effective 25 September 1759; promoted lieutenant on 4 October 1760 in room of Simon Fraser [6]; retired on half-pay in 1763. He returned to active service in 1777 as a captain in the new-raising 1st Battalion of the 73rd Foot with his old regimental colleague, James Mackenzie of Ardloch (see above), and was initially assigned garrison duties in Jersey, largest of the Channel Islands off the coast of France. Sent to India in 1779 under the command of Lord MacLeod, he fought in several major battles. Though sick with fever, Gilchrist fought at the disastrous battle of Conjevaram against the forces of Hyder Ali, 10 September 1780, but died on the retreat to Chingleput, 12 September 1780.

CBs; SBs; BALs; Stewart, *Sketches,* II, 87-91.

William Robertson (c.1740-c.1800)

Ensign: 17 October 1759, 78th Foot;
Lieut: 5 October 1760, 78th Foot; transferred on promotion;
Capt: 4 September 1762, IHC; half-pay, 31 January 1763; full pay, 25 December 1770, 36th Foot; exchanged, 11 January 1783, 104th Foot; half-pay, 16 April 1783; full pay, 20 October 1790;
Major: *"by brevet,"* 29 August 1777;
Lt-Col: *"by brevet,"* 19 February 1783.

A gentleman volunteer gazetted an ensign, 17 October 1759; wounded at the battle of Sillery near Ste-Foy, 28 April 1760; promoted to lieutenant 5 October 1760 in room of John Campbell [3] killed at Deschambault. The absent officers list shows *"Lieutt. Robertson gone to England 12th Octbr. 1760, wounded, by Governor Murray's leave."* He never returned to the regiment, instead raising his own Highland Independent Company and exchanging to half-pay in January 1763. He returned to active service as a captain in the 36th Foot in December

1770 and served with that regiment for the next 13 years. While serving during the 2nd Mysore War in India, he had had enough soldiering and exchanged into a junior regiment, the 104th Foot stationed in Ireland. On his return from India he immediately went on half-pay. He ended his career by returning to full pay as a captain of an Invalid Company in October 1790.

CBs; SBs; BALs.

George Fraser

Ensign: 23 June 1760, 60th Foot (Royal Americans); transferred on promotion;
Lieut: 24 April 1761, 78th Foot; half-pay, 24 December 1763.

Came from the Royal Americans on promotion to lieutenant, 24 April 1761. On disbandment, he was serving in Captain Hugh Fraser's company and exchanged to half-pay, December 1763.

CBs; SBs; BALs; PMG 4 Ledgers;

John Fraser [4] (c.1740-c.1785)

Ensign: 21 February 1757, 78th Foot.
Lieut: 2 January 1762, 78th Foot.

A nephew of William Fraser of Balloan and Donald Fraser in Easter Borlum, who applied to the Commissioners of Annexed Estates in 1769 for the lease of the farm of Bunchegavie. Probably a relative of Ensign Alexander Fraser (see above) whose son, Capt. Thomas Fraser of Boleskine, many years later described his father, Capt. Alexander Fraser, *"late of Bunchgavy."*

CBs; SBs; BALs; Millar, 130, 142-3;

Archibald Fraser, y^r of Culbokie (1736-1799)

Ensign: 7 April 1760, 78th Foot;
Lieut: 23 June 1762, 78th Foot; half-pay, 24 December 1763.
Capt: -
Major: c.1798, Glengarry Fencibles.
A gentleman volunteer gazetted an ensign 7 April 1760 *"in room of"* Malcolm Fraser who died of wounds after the battle of Sillery, 28 April 1760. He was described as brother of *"our quartermaster,"* viz. John Fraser of Culbokie (see above). He was made lieutenant vice Alexander Gregorson who retired on his pay in June 1762. Archie exchanged to half-pay on the regiment's disbandment in December 1763. He was later a major in

the Glengarry Fencibles, serving in Ireland during the rebellion of 1798, and died at Guisachen, Inverness-shire, unmarried in 1799.

CBs; SBs; BALs.

Alexander Fraser [5], (c.1740-1766)
Ensign: 13 December 1759, 78th Foot;
Lieut: 14 October 1762, 78th Foot; half-pay, 24 December 1763..
A gentleman volunteer gazetted an ensign on 13 December 1759; exchanged to half-pay in 1763. He died 1 June 1766.

CBs; SBs; BALs.

George Peacock (1748-1780)
Lieut: 2 March 1763, 78th Foot; half-pay, 24 December 1763; full pay, 7 January 1767, 7th Foot;
Capt: 18 January 1777, 7th Foot.

Born in Ireland, Peacock was commissioned a lieutenant 2 March 1763 vice William Robertson who was promoted in Scotland and given his own IHC. He served less than nine months with Fraser's Highlanders before exchanging to half-pay in December 1763. He returned to active service as a lieutenant in the 7th Foot and served with that regiment until his death, 19 October 1780.

CBs; SBs; BALs.

James Babbidge (c.1730-c.1791)
Sergeant: 15th Foot;
QM: appointed 21 December 1758, 15th Foot; resigned, 14 November 1763, 15th Foot;
Lieut: 14 September 1762, 15th Foot; exchanged with John Macdonell, 14 November 1763, into 78th Foot; half-pay, 24 December 1763; full pay, 30 December 1789, Plymouth Invalid Company; half-pay, 20 April 1791.

An English NCO and experienced QM of the 15th Foot who exchanged with John Macdonell of Leek (see above) so that the latter could serve in an older regiment and continue his military career. Babbidge went on half-pay with most other 78th officers the following month and returned to England. He returned briefly to full pay as a lieutenant in the Plymouth Invalid Company but would appear to have died in 1791.

CBs; SBs; BALs.

Ensigns

Lachlan McLachlan
Ensign: 11 January 1757, 78th Foot.

The Duke of Argyll called him *"brother to the Laird of McLachlan in Argyllshire"* and was gazetted ensign, 11 January 1757. He declined his commission and was replaced by James Mackenzie of Ardloch (see above).

CBs; SBs; BALs; CU 49/5; WO 64/12.

Malcolm Fraser [2]
Ensign: 18 June 1758, 78th Foot.
A gentleman volunteer gazetted an ensign on 18 June 1758 at Louisbourg; died of wounds received at Ste-Foy on April 28, 1760. He is mentioned in Ensign (later Lieutenant) Malcolm Fraser's Journal: *"Lieutenant Hector MacDonald and Ensign Malcolm Fraser died of their wounds, all very much regretted by every one who knew them."*

CBs; SBs; BALs; Harper, *Fraser Highlanders,* 103.

Malcolm MacPherson of Phoness (c.1700-c.1785)
Ensign: 4 September 1759, 78th Foot; retired, 19 May 1763.

Gentleman volunteer gazetted an ensign 4 September 1759, by which time he was well into his sixties. Born in Badenoch, Malcolm was one of Ewan of Cluny's six captains in the Jacobite Rising of 1745-6. He marched to Derby and back and was present at the skirmish at Clifton on 18 December 1745, and the Battle of Falkirk, 17 January 1746. He also took part in the Atholl Raid in March 1746. He went into hiding with his fellow officers until the amnesty allowed him to return home. Macpherson, like many other Highlanders of his time, was so exasperated with the faithless conduct of the French towards Prince Charlie, that he led twenty-five Badenoch men of his own family to serve under John Macpherson, Ewan of Cluny's brother, and Colonel Fraser's brother-in-law in the new raising 78th Foot. At the battle of the Plains of Abraham, *"Old Phoness"* as he was known, distinguished himself by hewing down so many Frenchmen that his conduct attracted the notice of General Townshend, who commanded the army on Wolfe's death. On *"observing Macpherson, when hostilities had ceased, regarding his handiwork with grim satisfaction, the General, after complimenting him upon his bravery, and congratulating him upon his marvellous escape, uninjured, remarked that the killing of so many Frenchmen appeared to afford him no little amount of pleasure."* Macpherson replied, *'I wish I could have cut down in the same way every one of the traitors* [in the '45]. *If the French had kept their promises to Prince Charlie, the Highlanders would never have lost Culloden!"* The absent officers list shows *"Ens. Malcolm MacPherson gone to England 18th Octbr· 1759 by General Monckton's leave."* In fact, General Townshend had been so taken with the old Highlander that he included him in a small retinue of officers that accompanied him back to England. Macpherson, on arrival in London, as reported in the papers of the day, was presented by General Townshend to George III. The King graciously extended his hand to the brave Highlander for the usual salute, but being unversed in Court etiquette, Macpherson placed his snuff-box in the King's hand and *"shook the royal palm with both hands with such ardour and emotion that the king was fain to cry out for quarter. Realising that anything but disrespect was meant, the King at once partook of a pinch from Macpherson's Badenoch mull, and was so much pleased with his chivalrous conduct and manly bearing that a handsome pension was there and then bestowed upon him, accompanied by a gracious intimation that he might either continue in the army or return to Badenoch and enjoy the pension during the remainder of his life."* Macpherson chose the latter, officially retiring 19 May 1763. While in London, Macpherson became something of a celebrity, being frequently pointed out with the remark, *"There goes the brave old Highlander with his famous sword."* Macpherson returned to Scotland in early 1760 for on 23 January 1760, Malcolm Macpherson of Phoness was made a free burgess and guild brother of the City of Edinburgh for good services, *"but particularly for the bravery for which he behaved at the Battle of Quebec."* Family tradition states that Malcolm always slept with his famous broadsword and that when he was dying, requested it be buried with him.

CBs; SBs; BALs; "The genealogy and descent of the Phoness Family," *The Old Church & Churchyard of Kingussie (St. Columba's)*, 10-15.

Duncan Cameron (1739-c.1798)

Ensign: 25 September 1759, 78th Foot; exchanged 8 July 1760, 15th Foot; exchanged 15 October 1761, 43rd Foot;
Lieut: 14 August 1762, 43rd Foot; appointed adjutant 6 September 1762; lieutenant's half-pay, 10 August 1763; full-pay 21 October 1763, 43rd Foot; resigned adjutancy on promotion 17 August 1773;
Capt: 17 August 1773, 43rd Foot;
Major: 19 February 1783, *"in the Army"*; 12 October 1787, 43rd Foot; transferred on promotion;

Lt-Col: 30 October 1793, 91st Foot; 1795, reduced on full pay.

A gentleman volunteer who *"carryed arms"* in the 78th Foot and fought at Louisbourg 1758 and on the plains of Abraham, 1759. Commissioned ensign after the latter battle and was wounded the following year at the battle of Sillery, 28 April 1760. Exchanged into the 15th Foot, summer 1760, then exchanged the following year into the 43rd Foot where he would spend the rest of his career. Promoted lieutenant at the siege of Havana and appointed adjutant in September 1762. He exchanged to lieutenant's half-pay but continued on in the regiment as its adjutant. He was back on full pay as a lieutenant two months later. Promoted captain August 1773 and served with the regiment in North America during the War of Independence. Brevetted a major *"in the Army"* February 1783, he was promoted major of the 43rd Regiment of Foot in October 1787. He was made Lt Colonel Commandant of Colonel John Fletcher Campbell's new raising 91st Foot which was sent to garrison the Cape of Good Hope and disbanded in 1795. He retired on full pay.

CBs; SBs; BALs.

James MacQueen

Ensign: 8 March 1750, Stewart's, Dutch-Scots Brigade; 29 April 1760, 78th Foot.

A Dutch-Scots Brigade veteran serving as a gentleman volunteer until a vacancy occurred. Gazetted an ensign on 29 April 1760, the day after the battle of Sillery, in which there were a high number of officer casualties. The absent officers list shows *Ensn. MacQueen gone to the Southern Colonies 20th Octbr. 1761 by leave of Governor Murray;* he had returned by the following year for he is shown on a *"Roster of the Officers of the Detachment of the 78th Regiment now lying at Quebec 1762"* in Captain John Nairne's Orderly Book; exchanged to half-pay in December 1763 as the ensign of Captain Hugh Cameron's company.

CBs; SBs; BALs; "Roster of the Officers," Nairne's OB, *MG 23*, G III 23, Vol. 4; *DSB*, II, 419.

Kenneth Stewart (c.1742-c.1800)

Ensign: 29 April 1760, 78th Foot; half-pay, 24 December 1763; full pay, 31 January 1771, 2nd Foot; retired 10 June 1772.

A gentleman volunteer gazetted an ensign, 29 April

1760, the day after the battle of Sillery, 28 April 1760; exchanged to half-pay in 1763 as the ensign of Captain Alexander MacLeod's company. He returned to active service eight years later as an ensign in the 2nd Foot but resigned the following year.

CBs; SBs; BALs.

Charles Burnett (c.1742-c.1815)
Ensign: 8 May 1760, 78th Foot.

A gentleman volunteer gazetted an ensign on 8 May 1760; exchanged to half-pay in December 1763, the ensign in Captain John Nairne's company.

CBs; SBs; BALs.

Malcolm Fraser [3] (c.1742-c.1785)
Ensign: 9 July 1760, 78th Foot; half-pay, 24 December 1763.

A gentleman volunteer gazetted an ensign, 9 July 1760; exchanged to half-pay as the ensign of the Colonel's Company in 1763. May have been the Ensign Malcolm Fraser who was a purchaser at the sale of the goods of the late Hugh Bain Fraser, tacksman of Tomvoit, in October 1763.

CBs; SBs; BALs; SRO, Wills of the Commissariat Court of Inverness, *CC* 11/1/6, 142-4.

Kenneth McCulloch
Ensign: 9 July 1760, 78th Foot; exchanged 15 December 1763, 2nd/60th Foot (Royal Americans); retired, 3 September 1766.

A gentleman volunteer gazetted an ensign 9 July 1760. He exchanged from the 78th Foot to the 2nd Battalion of the 60th Foot (Royal Americans) as an ensign with John Gregorson (see below) in December 1763. In July 1767, was allocated land at St Peters Bay and *"the carrying place to the Bay of Fortune,"* the site of present day St. Peters in King's County, PEI. He does not appear to have taken up this land grant as he reappears during the American Revolution listed as Captain Kenneth McCulloch of the Roman Catholic Volunteers, *"an advocate in Germantown, near Philadelphia"* as of 14 October 1777. McCulloch was killed at Hanging Rock, South Carolina on 6 August 1780 leading 150 men of the King's American Legion infantry in a charge against the American positions.

CBs; SBs; BALs; Tarleton, *History*, 95.

Charles Sinclair (1737-c.1793)
Ensign: 23 July 1760, 78th Foot; half-pay, 24 December 1763; full pay, 6 October 1779, Plymouth Invalid Company; transferred on promotion;
Lieut: 14 December 1779; 22nd Light Dragoons;
Capt-Lt: 25 March 1782, 22nd Light Dragoons;
Capt: 13 December 1782, 22nd Light Dragoons; half-pay, 11 June 1783.

A gentleman volunteer gazetted ensign 23 July 1760; exchanged to half pay on disbandment in December 1763. He returned to active service in October 1779 as an ensign in the Plymouth Invalid Company but transferred almost immediately on promotion to lieutenant of the new 22nd Light Dragoons, raised for home service. By March 1782, he was the captain-lieutenant commanding the Colonel's troop and by the end-year was a full captain commanding his own troop. He exchanged to half-pay on the regiment's disbandment in June 1783.

CBs; SBs; BALs.

Alexander Campbell
Ensign: 23 July 1760, 78th Foot; half-pay, 24 December 1763.

A gentleman volunteer gazetted ensign 23 July 1760; exchanged to half-pay in December 1763, the ensign of Captain Archie "Roy" Campbell's company.

CBs; SBs; BALs.

Norman MacLeod
Ensign: 24 July 1760, 78th Foot, half-pay, 24 December 1763.

A gentleman volunteer gazetted ensign 24 July 1760 vice Robert Menzies promoted; exchanged to half-pay in December 1763 as the ensign to Captain Ranald Macdonell's grenadier company.

CBs; SBs; BALs.

Alexander Fraser [6] (c.1743-1810)
Ensign: 4 October 1760, 78th Foot; half-pay, 24 December 1763.

A gentleman volunteer gazetted ensign 4 October 1760 *"in room of"* Alexander Gilchrist; exchanged to half-pay in 1763.

CBs; SBs; BALs.

John MacPherson [2] (1727-1815)
Sergeant: 78th Foot;
Ensign: 5 October 1760, 78th Foot.

Family legend has it that John Macpherson from Dail Einich in Badenoch served as an orderly sergeant to General Wolfe before becoming an officer, an event preserved in the oral history of the song entitled *After Quebec* and composed by a Macpherson bard of Badenoch circa 1764. Translated from the Gaelic it reads

> *O young John Macpherson whose family custom is to be in Dail Einich,*
> *Your conduct was valiant when you were needed*
> *You grasped the champion under your strapping arm*
> *When he received the wound that no doctor could heal. . . .*

Commissioned from the ranks as an ensign on 5 October 1760 *"in room of"* William Robertson. Parson Robert Macpherson said of him the following year in a letter to his friend, William Macpherson: *"Ensign John does very well and by no means is impudent or assuming upon his promotion and he is generally well liked."* He exchanged to half-pay as the ensign of Captain Alexander Campbell's company in December 1763. His gravestone in Laggan, Scotland reads *"Erected to the memory of Lieut- JOHN McPHERSON, of the 78th Regiment, who died at Blaragie, Laggan, on the 19th Septr. 1815, aged 88 years. Also his Relict, JANE McPHERSON, Daughter of JOHN McPHERSON of Invernahaven, who died 17th August 1828, aged 75."* The discrepancy between his half-pay regular rank and that on his gravestone could indicate he served in a local militia during subsequent wars.

CBs; SBs; BALs; Newton, *Indians,* 138-41; Reverend Robert Macpherson to William Macpherson, 24 Dec. 1761, Berthier, *JGP.*

Allan Cameron (c.1742-1767)
Ensign: 23 June 1762, 78th Foot; half-pay, 24 December 1763; full pay, 12 June 1766, 62nd Foot.

A gentleman volunteer gazetted ensign 23 June 1762; exchanged to half-pay December 1763 but returned to active service as an ensign with the 62nd Foot stationed in the West Indies. He died of disease the following year, 8 December 1767.

CBs; SBs; BALs.

John [Macgregor] Gregorson (c.1740-1783)
Ensign: 17 September 1760, 60th Foot, (Royal Americans); exchanged, 15 December 1763; 78th Foot; half-pay, 24 December 1763; full pay, 23 May 1777, Guernsey Invalid Company.

A kinsman of Lt. Alexander Gregorson (see above) and a last minute transfer before the regiment's disbandment, allowing Ensign Kenneth McCulloch, 78th Foot, to carry on with his career in an older regiment that was not being disbanded, in this case, the 60th Foot. Subsequently, Gregorson exchanged to half-pay nine days later with the other Fraser officers, but returned to active service during the American Revolution as an ensign in the Guernsey Invalid Company. He died 25 April 1783.

CBs; SBs; BALs.

Joseph Piper (c.1740-c.1791)

Ensign: 19 May 1763, 78th Foot; half-pay, 24 December 1763; full pay, 29 March 1764, 36th Foot; half- pay (Irish), 17 May 1766.

A gentleman volunteer commissioned ensign May 1763 *"in room of"* Malcolm Macpherson of Phoness retired. He exchanged to half-pay in December 1763 but returned to active service as an ensign in the 36th Foot in March 1764, then serving in the West Indies. He exchanged to Irish half-pay in May 1766.

CB; SB; BALs.

Chaplain

The Reverend Robert *"Caiphal Mhor"* Macpherson (1731-1791)
Appointed 12 January 1757; half-pay 24 December 1763. See Volume Two, Part Three – "An Unbounded Ascendancy."

Adjutants

Hugh Fraser [2] (see above)
Appointed 12 January 1757; resigned 24 July 1760.

Malcolm Fraser [1] (see above)
Appointed 24 July 1760; resigned 9 April 1763.

Charles Macpherson
Appointed 9 April 1763; half-pay, 24 December 1763.

Quartermasters

James Fraser [1] (see above)
Appointed 12 January 1757; resigned 27 September 1758.

John Fraser [1] (see above)
Appointed 27 September 1758; resigned 15 April 1760.

George Gordon
Appointed 15 April 1760; resigned 6 January 1763.

Simon Fraser [4] (see above)
Appointed 6 January 1763; resigned 14 March 1763.

John Fraser [4] (1745-c.1812)
Appointed 14 March 1763; until disbandment, 24 December 1763.

A letter of Major James Abercrombie, dated 3 January 1763, describes him as *"a young Gentleman of eighteen years old… strongly recommended to me by the officers of the Regiment. He is at present in Scotland. . . ."* He took over from the temporary QM, Simon Fraser on arrival in March 1763. He exchanged to half-pay in December 1763.

CBs; *SBs*; *BALs*; *PMG* 4 Ledgers; *WO* 34/94: f. 2.

Surgeons

John MacLean (c.1735-1779)
Appointed 12 January 1757; half-pay, 24 December 1763.

The absent officers list shows *"John MacLean, Surgeon, gone to England 20th Octbr. 1761 by leave of General Amherst"*; exchanged to half-pay in 1763. He died 2 May 1779.

CBs; *SBs*; *BALs*; *Roll of Army Medical Officers*.

Lachlan MacPherson (see above)

Was annotated *"Surgeon"* at disbandment of the regiment in 1763 but was only "acting" in MacLean's absence.

PART TWO

Dress, Weapons, Equipment,
&
Specialties

Highland Officer, c.1762. Painting of an officer of the 100th Foot (Campbell's Highlanders), who fought in Martinique alongside the "American Army's" regiments in 1762. All elements of a Highland officer's dress are present in this portrait such as the ram's horn-butt of his Highland pistol slung under his left armpit and the intricate basket hilt of his broadsword. Note the aiguillette on his right shoulder. (Courtesy, National Army Museum, Chelsea)

Highland Dress

Headdress

"With good blew bonnets on their heads"
Lt. Colonel William Cleland, *The Sword*, 1678.

"If I had a grup o yin or twa o the tam'd rascals, I sud let them ken what they're about," remarked an irate Highland officer on being pelted by apples from an anti-Scottish audience at Covent Garden theatre in December 1762. He had just returned from the successful siege of Havana and "The tam'd rascals" of course, were his men of the 42nd Foot.

The "tam" was the Highlander's distinctive headdress, the blue bonnet, worn by soldiers and civilians of the Highlands alike. Similar to the universal beret of today, it varied slightly in size and form from district to district but, in the Highland regiments, finally found a form that was standardized by sharp-eyed adjutants. The dark blue bonnet was larger than those of today and was pulled down towards the right ear. Knitted and felted, they were made of heavy blue wool with the flat edges of the top hanging down over the headband. Loose tufts of wool left in the center were twisted into tiny balls, but at a fairly early stage a decorative ball known as a "tourie" was added.

Some sources show a blue headband approximately one and half inches wide, although William Delacour's portrait of a 78th officer, entitled *The Pinch of Snuff*, clearly shows a red border as does an unattributed 1763 portrait of Captain John Campbell of Melfort of the 42nd Foot. As early as 1758, the 42nd were cocking their bonnets higher by not pulling the right side down so far so that the headbands were exposed as part of a new regimental pattern.

Above the left ear, the Highlanders wore a black ribbon cockade on the bonnet headband that served as an anchor for their black bearskins tufts, "not to be more than 5 inches in length" and termed "the Hair cockade." Just as the brightness of color in plaids and uniforms diminished over time, the bearskin fur tufts on the regimental bon-

nets faded from black to red. In 1761, the 42nd dress instructions noted that "as the hair cockades for the men's Bonnets are generally Roten or wore Rusty, the Cockades this year are intended to be of narrow black Rubban [ribbon]."

Officers initially wore bearskin tufts on their bonnets in the wilderness, as portrayed in *The Pinch of Snuff*. The custom of wearing black ostrich feathers to distinguish officers from the rank and file was officially introduced by the 42nd in May 1761, the officers of both battalions in Montréal being directed "to provide themselves with Black feathers for their Bonnets which for the future to be Regiment[l]. The none Commissioned Officers to wear Bearskin."

In July 1758, the officers of the 2nd Battalion of the 42nd being raised in Scotland were wearing black feathers, two years before Regimental Orders deemed them "Regiment[l]." Lieutenant John Grant fondly recalled the uniform he wore when he was seventeen, the headdress being "a Bonnet with a small black ostrich feather from the side cockade."

It seems that the 78th officers may also have adopted the fashion unofficially as early as 1760, for an engraving by Richard Short of a ruined Québec distinctly shows two Highland officers, each wearing two dark feathers on his bonnet. The bonnets in this engraving no longer appear to be as flat as a pancake as portrayed in the Delacour portrait, but are padded up and fuller-bodied. This trend may have been introduced with a view to providing greater protection from tomahawk blows or sword cuts or merely to make them warmer with the onset of the Canadian winter (see Winter Dress).

Incidentally, the British camp on the island of Montréal in 1760 constituted the only time when all three Highland regiments, the 42nd, the 77th and the 78th were encamped together on active service in North America. This has been commemorated in the name given to the modern-day race-track on the site of the open fields which once served as the campsite - *Blue Bonnets*.

Just as distinctive as the blue bonnet was the mitre cap made of fur that was worn by grenadiers, drummers and pioneers of the three

Highland regiments. A 1749 painting in the Queen's collection by Swiss artist David Morier shows a 42nd Regiment grenadier with a mitre-shaped cap some twelve inches high made of black bear fur. On the front was a red plate edged with white lace bearing the Crown over the George II cypher. On the back of the cap was a smaller red panel with the numerals 42 in white tape. The 1751 Clothing Warrant stated: "The Grenadiers of the Highland Regiment are allowed to wear Bearskin-Fur Caps, with the King's Cypher and Crown over it, on a Red ground in the Turn-up, or Flap." When created a Royal regiment in 1758, the 42nd would have switched to blue lace on its mitre caps and would be entitled to add a blue exploding grenade symbol on the rear panel of the cap.

The records of Cox & Co., the regimental army agents for the 42nd, reveal that from 1758 to 1761, the regiment purchased bearskin mitre caps for its "hachet men" or pioneers, drummers and grenadier officers. When the addition of the Second Battalion in 1758 necessitated the purchase of more grenadier officers' caps, a bill revealed that these cost 10 shillings and sixpence apiece.

Frasers' and Montgomery's' grenadiers, drummers and pioneers, styling themselves on the *Old Highland Regiment* livery , would have worn similar headdress, the differences being the color of tape used and the numbers displayed on the back panels.

Epigram from the satirical poem *The Sword* by Lieutenant-Colonel William Cleland of the Earl of Angus' Regiment written circa 1678, quoted in John Telfer Dunbar, *History of Highland Dress*, (London, 1962), 192; "Tam" quote from James Boswell, *London Journal, 1762-1763*, F.A. Pottle, ed., (New York, 1950), 71-2; 20 April 1761, 31 May 1761, *Stewart's Orderly Book*, [hereafter *SOB*], 38, 41; *Grant's Journal*, 25; Cloathing Warrant 1751, quoted in Dunbar, *Highland Dress*, 175; Rev. Percy Sumner, "Cox & Co., Army Agents: Uniform Items from their Ledgers," *JSAHR*, vol. XVII, (Spring 1938), 92-101, 135-57.

Hair

Highland officers did not commonly wear wigs as they were not compatible for wear with the blue bonnet. Instead they wore their hair powdered for

Above: Bonnets, c. 1760. A detail from a larger contemporary engraving by Richard Short showing the feathered bonnets of two 78th Regiment officers. Note the sword knot hanging on the basket hilt of one sword which denotes a field officer. (Courtesy, National Archives of Canada)

Below: Hairstyles. Front and back views of how Highland soldiers dressed their hair from a contemporary engraving in *Military Antiquities* by Francis Grose (1731-1791). (Courtesy, Fort Ticonderoga Muse-

reviews as the Stewart 42nd orderly book reveals: "The Reg^mt is to be reviewd on Friday morning next. The officers to be in Kelt. Plain regimentall, hair Albemarld, powdered, and buff coloured gloves. . . ."

The same book has several references to the men's hair being powdered for special parades as well. Encamped on Staten Island in 1761, Highlanders of the Black Watch were instructed to "curl their hair and put some powder in it the evening before they go to bed, which will make it dress more easily in the morning, when it is again to be powdered and qued taking care to week the powder off their ears and neck."

The Highland soldier wore his hair long, normally tallowed with wax or fats, then clubbed or "queued" at the back with black tape. That this practice was also followed by some officers is borne out by the fact that Colonel Simon Fraser's life was probably saved at the battle of Sillery outside Québec in 1760 by his clubbed hair! Lieutenant Malcolm Fraser noted that his colonel made a good target on his horse and "was touched at two different times – the second, got in the retreat striking against the cue of his hair, he receiv no other damage than a stiffness in his neck for some days."

A 42nd orderly book entry reveals that the Black Watch had its own barber who was expected to enforce a regimental standard: "The regimental barber is to cut the men's hair of an uniform length, allowing ten inches below the tying, eight inches of which to be Qued with ribbon and two inches at the end to be formed in a curl."

Orders for 78th Highlanders mounting guard in Québec City in 1762 noted: "The men for guard always to be well sheav'd have Clean shirts their hair ty'd behind & Clubb'd of it will admitt of it . . . every soldier whether he is on duty or not to have his face hands & knees wellwash'd – his hair well com'd cut short on the top of his head."

18 April 1759, New York, 9 September & 20 September 1761, Staten Island, *SOB*, 14; *Fraser's Journal*, 165; Regimental Orders [R.O.s] Québec, 11 May 1762, *Nairn's Orderly Book, 1761-62*, [hereafter *NOB*].

Jackets and Waistcoats

Jackets or coats of Highland regiments resembled those of their countrymen and remained short throughout the Seven Years' War. They were single-breasted initially with small cuffs and cropped skirts known as a "jacket" (later, a "coatee"), a pattern common throughout Scotland and not confined to the Highlands. Field Officers [majors and above] wore lapels on their jackets displaying the regimental facing as early as the 1740's. Company officers (captains, lieutenants, and ensigns) according to 42nd orderly books did not adopt lapels until February 1760. Delacour's painting of a company officer of Fraser's Highlanders, thought to be from 1760, shows him with a white-buff collar tag and no lapels.

An order of dress in the Royal Highlanders of January 1760, reads: "The officers of both battalions (it is agreed) are to be uniform in their regimental frocks, which are to be made with a lapel, a collar and a slash cuff, the buttons to be the same as those sent from England for their new Lac'd Regimentalls."

One could tell the difference between a Highland officer and an enlisted man at a distance by the color of their coats. The former, as well as sergeants, wore scarlet coats while lower ranks wore a brick red jacket. In addition, other badges of rank were added to the coat or worn over it to distinguish officers and sergeants from the men.

These included a crimson sash of netted silk worn over the left shoulder by officers and a red worsted wool sash with a stripe of the facing color down the center, worn in the same fashion by sergeants. There were quantities of gold and silver lace around bastion-shaped buttonholes (sergeants wore a narrower lace, much like piping), cuffs, collars, lapels and waistcoats, as well as gold and silver shoulder knots for NCOs or aiguillettes which hung off the right shoulder for officers. In addition, officers wore a silver or brass gorget about their neck – the last vestige of medieval armor now reduced to small engraved crescent bearing the King's royal cypher and the regimental number. The gorget was suspended below the throat with a ribbon of the regimental color.

"Regimental Frocks." A portrait of John Campbell, Earl of Loudoun, commander in chief in North America from 1756 to 1758, which illustrates an Highland officer's dress, c. 1756-60. His jacket has full lapels which were worn only by field officers in the Highland regiments until 1760. Thereafter, all officers' coats had them. (Courtesy, Library of Congress)

Corporals were only distinguished by a right shoulder-knot of white or regimental facing color.

One could also tell to which regiment an officer belonged by his lapel, collar and cuffs facings. If the facing was blue, he was a Royal Highlander; green, a Montgomery Highlander; off-white, a Fraser Highlander.

Initially, the 42nd officers in North America had buff facings, but when King George II granted them the honor of being a Royal Regiment in July 1758, it entitled them to change the facings on their uniforms, and the backing of their regimental color to royal blue. The officers of the Second Bat-

talion of the Royal Highland Regiment raised in Scotland during 1758 therefore arrived in North America wearing their new laced regimentals. "Our dress was a red coat turned up with blue," recalled Lieutenant John Grant, "laced button-holes – blue waistcoats. . . ."

Officers and Sergeants had two coats, referred to in orders as "Plain Regimentalls" and "Lac'd Regimentalls." The principal difference was that the former coat was stripped of all fancy adornment for campaigning, making its owner less of a target, while the more ornate jacket was reserved for dress reviews and social events such as balls and formal dinners.

As early as 1758, experienced officers, used to campaigning in the wilderness and ever-conscious of Indian and Canadien marksmen, took measures to ensure they more closely resembled their men by discarding their sashes and gorgets, carrying fuzees and wearing their older, unlaced regimental coats without lapels. Lieutenant John Grant remembered that the men of the 42nd were experienced veterans by the time they reached the siege of Havana in 1762, and freely admitted that "we were equipped in jackets without lace made to resemble soldiers."

Adaptations to dress had to be made for campaigning in the tropics These were highlighted in an order issued before the attack on Martinique to all twenty-three battalions, including both battalions of the 42nd and the 77th Foot, assembled at Bridgetown, Barbados: "The Commanding Officers of the Corps will order the linings to be ript out of the men's coats, the lapels taken off, and the skirts cut shorter. The General recommends to them, providing their men with something that is thin, to make sleeves for their waistcoats, as the troops may be ordered to land in them."

This command already echoed one made four years earlier to standardize jackets and waistcoats worn by the light infantry of the army. It directed that

> the sleeves of the coat are put on the waistcoat and, instead of coat-sleeves, he has two wings like the grenadiers, but fuller; and a round slope [tailor's term for large opening under the armpit]

reaching about halfway down his arm; which makes his coat of no encumbrance to him, but can be slipt off with pleasure; he has no lace, but the lapels remain: besides the usual pockets, he has two, not quite so high as his breast, made of leather, for balls and flints; and a flap of red cloth on the inside, which secures the ball from rolling out, if he should fall.

Men's coats were issued on a scale of one new coat per year, the older, faded coat usually being converted into a red waistcoat, the newer coats being reserved for reviews or guard mountings. Numerous orderly book entries directed that only old coats were to be worn on fatigue parties out of camp or on campaign.

Every spring, each Highland regiment went through the necessary process of rotating worn-out coats and plaids and replacing them with new, a process that demanded trained tailors being assigned to every company. For example, the 42nd took advantage of the winter months of 1760 to re-outfit, an instruction dated 2 January 1760 stating that "before the new coats are delivered out to be fitted it will be necessary that a tailor of each company measure the length of each coat also the breadth between the shoulders and to fit every man as near as possible according to his size. If any of the coats are found to be tight under the arm-pit a gore may be put in which every tailor will understand."

31 January 1760, *SOB*, 30-1; John Grant, *Journal of John Grant, 2nd Battalion 42nd Regiment, covering service from 1758 to 1761*, [hereafter Grant's *Journal*], Register House Series 4/77, Microfilm, 25, 82; *NOB Nairn's Orderly Book, 1761-62* ; *National Archives of Canada (NAS)*, MG 23, Series K34.

Shirts

The Highlander's loose-fitting white linen shirt was his principal undergarment, required in order to wear the belted plaid. The standard issue for a soldier was four shirts with attached collars and these were usually worn with a white neck cloth or stock. Shirts were bought locally by the regiments while serving in North America and by 1761, the 42nd had added checkered shirts to the soldier's

Camisade. Detail from a painting depicting Private Robert Kirkwood of the 77th Montgomery Highlanders being captured at Fort Duquesne in September 1758. During the night prior to the attack, he remembered: "Every one had a white shirt over his coat [so that] we might the better distinguish our own people." This precaution of wearing white shirts over coats or waistcoats was to prevent incidents of friendly fire in the darkness and was known as a "camisade." (Courtesy, Robert Griffing and Paramount Press)

inventory. On 28 February 1759 the "Commanding Officers of Companys to provide their men furth with with cheque shirts to the number returned wanting in each company."

Besides their principal purpose, shirts were sometimes used as recognition symbols or distinguishing marks for soldiers conducting a night attack called a camisade. Private Robert Kirkwood of the 77th Montgomery Highlanders, who had survived Major James Grant's botched raid against Fort Duquesne in September 1758, recalled that before the attack "every one had a white shirt over his coat we might the better distinguish our own people." This precaution of wearing white shirts over coats to prevent incidents of friendly fire in the darkness was corroborated by Lieutenant Alexander Robertson, 77th Foot, in a letter home: "We were ordered to put a shirt on above our clothes in order to distinguish our men from the enemy."

---

28 February 1759, 2 January 1760, *SOB*, 2, 30; Robert Kirk[wood], *The Memoirs and Adventures of Robert Kirk, Late of the Royal Highland Regiment*, (Limerick, c.1775), 6; Lt. A. Robertson to Sir Henry Munro, dated January 1759, in the *Ballindalloch Papers*, Ballindalloch Castle Library.

The Belted Plaid

Siud b'èideadh nan diunlach,
fèileadh-beag
's breacan-guaille,

This is the uniform of heroes: the kilt
And the shoulder plaid
folded thickly . . .

Unknown, *After Quebec*, c. 1764

All of the Highland regiments that served in North America wore the belted plaid or the *feileadh mór* [literally "big wrap"] that consisted of 12 yards of 5 foot wide woolen tartan cloth. The plaid was always worn over other clothes. At the very least, a long shirt, tied between the legs and serving as underwear, would be worn under the plaid. Other items of clothing might include hose, shoes and jacket, or, in the case of North America, leggings. The plaid was usually discarded before any physical exertion as it was bulky, especially when wet, and would easily become entangled in the undergrowth. In order for a soldier to put on his plaid he would stretch it out flat on the ground and pleat or "kelt" it. He would then lie down with the top edge of the plaid just above his head, and the bottom level with a line just above his knee. Sliding a belt under the plaid at his waist, he would wrap the plaid about his lower half and fasten the belt.

When he stood, the half below the belt formed the kilt proper, and the extra material of the plaid hanging down to his ankles was gathered behind and fastened by a shoulder button at his left shoulder, leaving his right arm free to wield a sword.

The plaid quickly became a multi-purpose piece of kit for Highland soldiers in North America: a blanket at night, a cloak for inclement weather to protect both the soldier and his weapon, a stretcher for carrying the wounded, a knapsack or blanket roll for carrying provisions on long wilderness marches and sometimes a sail.

In 1759, on General Amherst's expedition against Fort Ticonderoga and Crown Point, both battalions of the 42nd were ordered "to embark in their leggings" with their "plaids well packed except such as are intended for sails." In November of 1759, Lieutenant John Grant of the 2nd /42nd recounted in his Journal that they were using a plaid for a sail to cross Lake Oneida from west to east, when a sudden squall threatened to capsize the boat and he was forced to slash the plaid with his dirk to save the boat and crew!

A 42nd orderly book entry two years later stated that the men of the 42nd were to be "in little kilt" for their bateau trip from Ile aux Noix up Lake Champlain to Crown Point in June 1761, but all were to have their plaids readily available in case of rain, the first mention in regimental records that the two items were now considered two separate items of dress. Regimental orders of the 78th Foot dated 11 May 1762, instructed that "the *filibeg* or little kilt to be always worn in summer or harvest except upon duty or when the Detachment are under arms."

The usual rule of thumb in the Highland regiments was to convert plaids into kilts or *philabegs* (in Gaelic, *feileadh beag* meaning "little wrap") after one year of wear, the wearing of the bulkier belted plaid usually reserved for dress parades and reviews only. On ceremonial occasions, such as the 42nd being drawn up in three ranks in Montréal in 1761, the older faded plaids and waistcoats of the soldiers were given to the center rank men to wear, while the newer and brighter plaids were worn by the front and rear ranks so "that the battalion may appear to the best advantage."

Belted Plaid. Soldiers in the Highland regiments wore the belted plaid or the *feileadh mór* [literally "big wrap"]. In order to put on his plaid, a man would stretch it out flat and pleat or "kelt" it. He would lie down on it with the top edge just above his head, and the bottom just above his knee. Sliding a belt under the plaid at his waist, he would wrap the plaid about his lower half and fasten the belt. When he stood, the half below the belt formed the kilt proper. The extra material of the plaid was gathered and fastened by a button at his left shoulder, leaving his right arm free to wield a sword. Illustration by Gerry Embleton from "*Men-at-Arms 118: The Jacobite Rebellions 1689-1745*" by Michael Barthrop. (Courtesy, Osprey Publishing, UK)

After two years, the plaid became the soldier's personal property but the commanding officer still exercised some control over its disposal. The price, if retained for regimental use, was settled on by the soldiers themselves, through a vote supervised by the sergeants.

Abraham in his plaid, *Memoirs of the Life and Gallant Exploits of the Old Highlander, Serjeant Donald Macleod…*(London, 1791); Lt. John Grant claimed that in the Caribbean campaign, their spare shirts and other gear wear rolled in their plaids, then slung like bandoliers around their bodies, Grant's *Journal*.

Song – Newton, *Indians*, 39; 11 October 1759, 4 June 1761, *SOB*, 25; 11 May 1762, *NOB*; On the use of plaids for carrying wounded, Sgt Donald McLeod of the 78th claimed that General Wolfe's corpse was carried down from the heights of

The Little Kilt or *Philabeg*

One of the enduring myths about the little kilt is that it was invented in 1725 by an Englishman,

Thomas Rawlinson, owner of an iron works in Glengarry and Lochaber. This gentleman had a number of Highlanders in his employ and personally adopted their Highland dress. However, the machinery and fires of the iron works posed a danger to Highlanders' wearing voluminous plaids so Rawlinson modified them by cutting off all material above the waist and tailoring the remainder to resemble the well-known kilt of today.

To the great delight of Highlanders everywhere, recent research disproves that a Sassenach "invented" the *feileadh beag*. The Armorial Bearings of the Chief of the Skenes (1692) clearly shows a man wearing a *philabeg* and other depictions have also been mustered to show that the practice of wearing the *philabeg* predates the safety-conscious foundry owner's kilt. Peter MacDonald, textile and costume adviser to the National Trust for Scotland and the Royal Scottish Museum noted recently, " the *feileadh mor* [belted plaid] was formed from two pieces of cloth joined length ways. It is therefore not beyond the wit of man not to join them and this seems to have come into fashion in the latter part of the 17th century as socio-agricultural practices, and perhaps also the nature of warfare, changed."

Certainly, the wearing of *philabegs* by Highland regiments did not start in North America, as some believe. The 1756 painting, now at the Black Watch Museum in Perth, of the 42nd Foot on Glasgow Green prior to its departure for North America, clearly shows two drummers in *philabegs* standing next to their mounted commanding officer while he puts his companies, dressed in belted-plaids, through their firing drills.

The gradual adoption by the Highland regiments in North America of the *philabeg* or kilt in place of the belted plaid as everyday work dress is recorded as early as 1758 in letters and orderly books of the day. One staunch advocate of the *philabeg* in the North American theater was Lord George Augustus Howe who was the senior brigadier on General Abercromby's 1758 expedition against Fort Ticonderoga. In a letter from Albany dated 29 May 1759, Dr Richard Huck informed John Campbell, Earl of Loudoun, that the Highlanders had finally been prevailed upon

Philabeg. Usually Highland regiments converted plaids into kilts or *philabegs* (*feileadh beag* meaning "little wrap") after one year of wear. In North America, the wearing of the bulkier belted plaid was reserved for dress parades and reviews. Detail from a painting by Mike Chapell in *Men-at-Arms 261: 18th Century Highlanders* by Stuart Reid. (Courtesy, Osprey Publishing, UK)

"to put on Breeches and Lord How's Filabegs," for the upcoming campaign.

At first, the little kilt was made from worn-out plaids, three to three and a half yards being sufficient for that purpose. By 1759 little kilts were the accepted basic dress for camp duty, fatigues and batteaux work, although most men had acquired breeches over the winter in upstate New York (see Winter Dress). For example, by April 1759, the 42nd Foot was ordered "under arms with their Linen britches and leggans and packs tied up properly with their tomplines " for the march northward, with "the officers to be in their leggans also." At Albany later in the year, it seems some soldiers had preferred breeches and leggings to the kilt causing the following order: "The Non Commissioned Officers and men are at all times in Camp to wear their kelts except when otherwise ordered."

Dr Richard Huck to Lord Loudoun, 29 May 1758, *Huntington Library,* Loudoun Papers: American Series (hereafter *LO 5837*). Materials from the Loudoun Papers, Huntingdon Library are hereafter cited as *LO xxxx; SOB.*

Fraser Tartan. A detail from an engraving of the painting *The Death of General James Wolfe* completed by Benjamin West in 1770 which shows Colonel Simon Fraser of the 78th Highlanders wearing a full belted plaid. In the painting, the plaid appears to be a brownish-red sett with broad green, double-red and black stripes. In fact, Fraser was neither at the battle nor present at Wolfe's death. (Courtesy, Library of Congress)

Tartans and Setts

Tartan (from the Gaelic "*tarsuin*") is the characteristic woolen cloth of Scotland, woven in stripes and dating from pre-historic times. Today, the word "tartan" is universally misapplied, used to mean the "setts" or patterns of square color (in Gaelic, "*breacan*" meaning checkered) woven into the cloth. The Highlander's historical preference for checkered cloth was not just vanity but a practical recognition that a disrupted pattern on one's clothing acted as excellent camouflage. George Buchanan, a Stirlingshire historian who published *Rerum Scoticarum Historia* in 1581, noted that all Highlanders

> delight in variegated garments, especially stripes, and their favourite colours are purple and blue. Their ancestors wore plaids of many colours, and

numbers still retain this custom, but the majority now in their dress prefer a dark brown, imitating nearly the leaves of the heather, that when lying upon the heath in the day, they may not be discovered by the appearance of their clothes; in these wrapped rather than covered, they brave the severest storms in the open air, and sometimes lay themselves down to sleep even in the midst of snow.

Echoing Buchanan, although about different terrain and people, Robert Kirkwood of Montgomery's Highlanders noted "that trees and the Indians were of the same color, and this circumstance, trifling as it may appear, ought always to be consider'd, by forces who mean to operate with success against them, as at that season they have a full view of you, but you can't have the least idea of them."

Highland dress authorities and experts now generally agree that clan setts did not exist before the '45 though regional and district patterns had been in existence for some centuries. What is known as the Black Watch sett today, was known in the 18th century as the "Government Sett." It is a dark pattern of blue and green which has formed the basis of many British regimental setts down to the present day, the differentiation achieved with white, yellow, or red overstripes. The "Government Sett" was worn by the 42nd, 77th and 78th Foot during the Seven Years' War. Nevertheless, there is a growing body of evidence that the Fraser officers, at least, appear to have wore their own pattern sett, a reddish-brown background with varied patterns of black, blue and green lines.

The debate over what Fraser's Highlanders' actually wore has been under discussion for some fifty years. A snippet of the plaid, worn by Captain Thomas Fraser of Struy of the 78th Foot (see Part One) and passed down through his family, is now in possession of the David M. Stewart Museum in Montréal. It is a faded reddish brown color and has lost much of its original vibrancy through exposure to the elements and the passage of time. At least three contemporary paintings show the the 78th Foot wearing a red-based sett with brown, blue and green stripes *The Pinch of Snuff* by William Delacour, executed around 1760, shows a company officer on campaign in North America wearing a reddish-brown sett with black or green overstripes. *The Death of Wolfe* completed by Benjamin West in 1770 shows the red-haired Colonel Simon Fraser wearing a belted plaid, a sett of brickish-red background with broad green stripes and double-red overstripes. A recently-discovered portrait of Colonel William Amherst at the foot of Flagstaff Hill (Signal Hill) at St John's Newfoundland, 1762, shows a crouching Fraser Highlander wearing a red-brown tartan with green stripes. The figure might be Captain Charles Macdonell of Glengarry, who was mortally wounded in the subsequent assault.

American-born Benjamin West was working in New York in 1757 and probably saw the 78th pass through the city on its way to winter quarters in Connecticut. West prided himself on the detail in his paintings and collected actual equipment and weapons used in the Plains of Abraham battle including Wolfe's fuzee, and a grenadier's cap. When he painted a figure which resembled Robert Rogers, he gathered some of Rogers' equipment to be used in the portrait. Given West's attention to detail, one may assume that his portrayal of Simon Fraser's plaid is correct.

The late Ralph Harper, a scholar of Fraser regimental history and founder of the recreated Old 78th Fraser Highlanders in Montréal, made a most convincing argument as to the reddish sett. *The Death of General Wolfe* was painted in 1770, seven years after the disbanding of Frasers' Highlanders. The original was offered to King George III who declined to purchase it as the figures were in modern dress After the inaugural exhibition, the painting was purchased by Lord Grosvenor. King George III then changed his mind and ordered a copy for the Royal Collection. Harper saw this as a seal of Royal approval as he believed that the King, who was ultimately responsible for the approval and issuing of clothing warrants for the British Army, to be stickler for detail. "The King would have questioned the red-based plaid" if it had not been correct, he stated, "and would certainly not have purchased a work of art containing errors of that sort while the Proscription Act was still in force."

For best collection of twentieth-century scholarship on the existence of clan tartans before the '45 see Dunbar, *Highland Dress*, 51-81, 29; Kirkwood, *TSMD*, 5; For the best collection of the prevailing 20th century opinions on the color of the Fraser Highlanders' sett, see Colonel J. Ralph Harper, *The Fighting Frasers*, (Montréal, 1979), 30-36, 43. In 1964, Colonel Harper, OBE, was the driving force behind the raising of the recreated Old 78th Highlanders at the David M. Stewart Military and Maritime Museum of Montréal; For an excellent color plate of "*The Pinch of Snuff*" see Plate 49 in Lady Christian Hesketh, *Tartans*, (London, 1961), 41; In Benjamin West's *Death of Wolfe* (of which three original ± 5 ' x 8' copies exist in North America, one at the National Gallery of Canada, one at the University of Toronto, and the other at the William C. Clements Library in Ann Arbor, Michigan) included several grieving officers in his group scene around the dying Wolfe, including Simon Fraser who had been wounded in the leg two months previously and who, along with some of the other "grievers," was not even on the battlefield.

Sporrans

The *sporran* or *sporran molash* (Gaelic for "hairy purse") was a personal item of kit for both officers and men. They were a field item only and not worn on guard or parades and they were not standard issue and therefore not uniform in appearance.

Essentially it was a hanging frontal pouch for storing money, pipes, tobacco or other small personal items. According to Grenadier Sergeant Thompson, in Scotland, badger skin or otter skin was used to make the purses initially and later in Canada, some soldiers acquired beaver head purses.

Surviving officers' sporrans indicate to us that, like dirks, sporrans were a matter of personal taste and design. While a private soldier's sporran was commonly made from goat or doe skin closed with a frontal lap of the same material and three decorative tassels hanging below, officers' sporrans had hinged semi-circular metal clasps for the tops of their sporrans ranging from simple brass to highly decorated silver.

One 18th century example in a Scottish museum has the words "Open my mouth, cut not my skin, and then you'll see what is therein" engraved on its silver margins while others sport depictions of thistles, roses and Celtic designs.

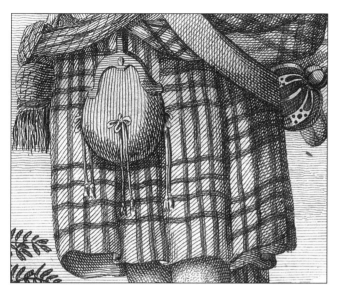

Left: Sporran. Detail from a contemporary print which appears in *Military Antiquities* by Francis Grose (1731-1791). Although not Government issue, the sporran was universally used to hold money, cards, dice, food, or tobacco and was made of leather or fur. Officers' sporrans were often more elaborate purses with clasp openings made of silver or gilded metal. (Courtesy, Fort Ticonderoga Museum) Right: Wilderness leg and footwear. A Highland light infantryman sports Indian moccasins and Indian *mitasses* or leggings to protect his legs from brambles and poison ivy. A detail from painting by Mike Chapell in *Men-at-Arms 261: 18th Century Highlanders* by Stuart Reid and illustrated by Mike Chapell (Courtesy, Osprey Publishing, UK)

Elgin Museum, Scotland; Harper *The Fighting Frasers*, 25. See also Dunbar, *Highland Dress*, 217-8.

Hose and Leggings

Hose (in Gaelic, "*caddis*" meaning "striped") were the woolen stockings worn by the Highlander and usually woven with a standardized pattern of diagonal stripes, the most common being red crossing and mingling with white. The 42nd on occasion however used the Government Sett cloth to make hose, and the Frasers' at Québec 1759-60 were forced to cut up captured French blankets to replace worn-out hose when their new clothing did not arrive before the onset of winter. Although he was from Ayrshire in the Lowlands, Colonel Archibald Montgomery was very attentive to his Highland soldiers' needs. He wrote to General John Forbes from Charleston in spring 1758 noting that Sir Allan Maclean of the Additional Companies arriving at New York had

> brought out two large bales of caddis for the Battalion. I must beg the favour of you to order it to be sent from New York to Philadelphia by the

surest conveyance, let the expence be what it will, for the Battalion cannot march without it, unless the men wear stockings, for their hose are quite wore out, and that alternative will not answer quite so well for a Highland Regiment.

Hose was held up at the top with garters of red tape tied on the outside. As tape and hose wore out quickly, and re-supply from Scotland was problematic, most battalions resorted to local purchase. For example, by 1761, the Fraser Highlanders had contracted with the Ursuline Nuns of Québec city to supply their red and white hose requirements, no doubt a reflection of the close bonds developed between the religious order and the Highlanders during their first winter in the captured city. According to the British Army historian, J. W. Fortescue, the Ursuline's also made woolen vests and leggings for the Highlanders.

Hose was not worn in the field or for batteaux work as the men were usually ordered into "leggans" or buskins. Major George Scott claimed were better than trousers as one pair of Buskins would keep a soldier "from the Snow and cold in

Winter and Flies in Summer." Other names for buskins were "Indian leggings" or *"mitasses"* which John Knox described.

> Leggers, leggins or Indian spatterdashes are usually made of frize or other coarse woolen cloth . . . at least three quarters of a yard in length; each leggin about three quarters wide...then double it and sew it together from end to end . . . fitting this long narrow bag to the shape of the leg . . . tied round under the knee and above the ankle with garters of the same colour; by which the legs are preserved from many fatal accidents, that may happen by briars, stumps of trees, or underwood, etc. in marching through a close, woody country.

Montgomery to Forbes, Charles Town, 27 April 1758, *NAS* GD 45/2/87: f.3. Knox's *Journal*, II, 272, 309; J.W. Fortescue, *A History of the British Army*, Vol. II, (London, 1910), 395.

Footwear

Highlanders wore standard regulation army shoes of black leather made to a common pattern and fastened with a brass buckle. When issued, they were not form-fitted to either foot. Soldiers were commonly ordered to change their shoes around every other day in order to prevent them from "running crooked" and thus wearing out sooner. Grenadier Sergeant Thompson of the Fraser's Highlanders remembered that the 42nd Foot with its older private soldiers, many from well-bred families, was better shod than the two junior Highland regiments, "the officers as well as the private men had silver shoe buckles, all of the same pattern" while "our men wore only leather thongs in their shoes." Only officers would have worn riding boots with breeches.

Many of the Highland soldiers, especially those of the light infantry companies, adopted the Indian moccasin for wear while in North America. The moccasin closely resembled the Highland pump, or laced heel-less shoe known as a *cuaran*, that was worn back in Scotland. This footwear was made of untanned deerskin or cowhide, worn with the hairy side out and fastened by thongs which criss-crossed over the instep and ankles.

This lightweight shoe was ideal for moving swiftly over the hills and countryside but wore out quickly as did North American moccasins. Moccasins were described by one Ulster Scot as "slippers" generally

> made of the skin of a beaver, elk, calf, sheep, or other pliant leather, half-dressed: each moggosan is of one intire piece . . . they have no additional sole or heel-piece and must be used with three or four frize socks, or folds of thick flannel wrapt round the foot; they are exceedingly warm, and much fitter for the winters of this country than our European shoe, as a person may walk over sheets of ice without the least danger of falling.

Thompson's *Memoirs*; Knox's *Journal*, II, 309.

Winter Dress

One of the two Highland regiments newly raised for service in North America was ordered to adopt the normal dress of an English line regiment on its arrival there. Stewart of Garth wrote that "the cold climate it was feared, would prove too severe to the Frasers, who wore the kilt, and an attempt, kindly conceived no doubt, was made to change the garb of old Gaul for the trews. The proposal aroused strenuous opposition, officers and men opposed the change and finally, through pleas from Colonel Fraser were successful."

Grenadier Sergeant James Thompson remembered that "Colonel Fraser, with great determination, succeeded in getting the order canceled and the Regiment continued to wear full Highland dress, similar to that of the Old Highland regiment, during the whole of their service – and in the course of six winters we showed that the doctors did not understand our constitutions for, in the coldest weather, our men were more healthy than those in the regiments that wore breeches."

To compensate for cold weather, leggings were allowed to be worn with the full-belted plaid in the 42nd Foot. A 6th November 1759 orderly book entry at Crown Point reveals: "The Non-Commissioned Officers & men will be allowed until further orders to do duty in there Kilt over their leg-

Wood Detail, Quebec, 1760. Collecting wood was a dangerous task for troops of any fort or camp during the North American winter and here Highlanders of the 78th Foot provide a daily protection party for the wood cutters' sleighs. Woodcutters and their guardians were paid five shillings per cord and usually returned frost-bitten for their troubles. Fraser's did not wear feather bonnets as this artist has fancifully depicted, but wore flat blue bonnets, probably pulled down over their ears and secured with scarves. (Private Collection)

gans." However "no man" was permitted "to go to work with his plaid" and with the onset of winter, company commanders were ordered "to review the state of the men's britches and the new britches to be immediately made up taking care that those who are the most needful be first provided."

When both battalions of the 42nd went into "Winter Qt^rs," one of the first priorities was to ensure that "the new clothing is to be fitted and the waistcoats made as fast as possible that the men may be warmly clad during the severity of the Winter, and it is recommended to the Commanding Officers that every man has a warm cloth cap made."

The 78th Frasers' Highlanders, facing the sub-zero Canadian weather on garrison duty in the roofless city of Québec, found themselves "in a pityfull situation having no breeches, Philabeg not at all calculated for this terrible climate," wrote

Lieutenant Malcolm Fraser in December 1759. "Colonel Fraser is doing all in his power to provide trousers for and we hope to soon to be on a footing with the other regiments." By January 1760, the Frasers were indistinguishable from all the other regiments, "the weather such that are obliged to have all covered but [our] eyes, and nothing but the last necessity obliged any man to go out of doors." Captured French blankets from the city stores were issued to all regiments and cut up to provide woolen socks and mittens for the men.

Lieutenant John Knox, an Ulster Scot, declared the assorted dress of the sentries and wood gathering parties in December 1759 resembled "a masquerade rather than a body of regular troops. Our guards on the grand parade, make a grotesque appearance in their different dresses; and our inventions to guard us against the extreme rigour of this climate are various beyond imagination; the uniformity, as well as the nicety, of the clean, methodical soldier, is buried in the rough fur-wrought garb of the frozen Laplander." With temperatures consistently registering at -20° F., without wind-chill factored in, officers and men cared little about their personal appearances.

A year and a half later, the Fraser Highlanders stationed at Québec in the summer of 1761, received their "share of the Grey Cloth which the Quakers of England hearing that the Highlanders were gone to serve in America, and likely to suffer from the severity of the climate, had subscribed for, and sent out to us at Québec at their own expense, calculated at a Great Coat and a pair of leggings each for 1400 men," noted Grenadier Sergeant, James Thompson.

The Quakers had "thought they were called upon to do something or other to show their Loyalty and accordingly, decided upon clothing the naked limbs of the Highlander." Most Highlanders, however, were now veterans of four North American winters, and sold the cloth or gave it away to the Canadien families at whose farms they were billeted.

The Quakers of England were not the first to attempt to clothe the naked Highland savage. The Ursuline Nuns became good friends of the soldiers of Fraser's Highlanders during their first winter at Québec, many of the rank and file chopping firewood and shoveling snow for the Sisters in addition to their regular military duties. In gratitude, the Sisters supplied their bare-legged benefactors with "a supply of long woolen hose knitted for them," according to the British Army's historian, J.W. Fortescue, who added "perhaps as much for decency's as for charity's sake."

SOB, Knox's *Journal*.

Highland Weapons

The Highland Dirk

No less suited to thee is a dirk,
as good as cometh out of the forge,
with much twined interlacing
on its ridged, rugged handle;
tis finely wrought, shining,
straight, thin and well-polished . . .

Duncan Ban McIntyre,
"Song to Captain Duncan Campbell"

One of the deadliest weapons in a Highlander's arsenal was his dirk, a dagger that had evolved purely and simply for fighting and killing with deadly efficiency. Combining elements of stabbing knives such as the ballock knives, *poignards* and *quillon* daggers used by medieval knights on the field of battle, the first known reference to a Highland dirk specifically by name occurred in 1617. Richard James wrote in his *Description of Shetland, Orkney and the Highlands of Scotland*: "The weapons which they use are a longe basket hilt swoarde and, longe kind of dagger broade in the backe and sharpe at the pointe which they call a durcke."

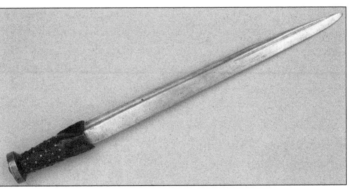

Highland Dirk. Used by Ensign Peter Grant, 42nd Foot, at the Battle of Ticonderoga, 1758. The 78th Fraser light infantry used them with deadly effect against French grenadiers in the bloody battle for Dumont's Mill near Québec, 28 April 1760. (Courtesy, National Army Museum, Chelsea)

The 18th century Highland dirk was a personal weapon and thus reflected the owner's tastes as well as his means. Worn on the right hip to counterbalance the broadsword on the left, a Highlander would draw the dirk with his left hand after he had drawn his broadsword with the right.

On average, dirk blades were from 10 to 18 inches the long (the latter's length usually a good indication that the weapon had been made from a cut-down sword). Grenadier Sergeant James Thompson while in winter quarters at Stratford, Connecticut in 1757, confessed that he

was sadly off for want of a Dirk, and coaxed our regimental armourer to make a blade of one out of a sword blade I had got. . . . He said he would try his hand at it, and accordingly set to work – he found great difficulty in shaping it on account of the hardness of the steel, but at length he continued to finish it tolerably well. I myself carved the handle and got a silversmith to mount it from a pattern which I got for him.

There were no standard issue dirks during the Seven Years' War. Regulation dirks for pipers, bandsmen and sergeants came much later in the 19th century. If they chose to carry them, privates had to supply their own dirks and these were usually mounted in brass and were not as ornate as the officers' dirks. The latter, in many cases, were expensively handcrafted works of art. Their hilts, made of rare hardwoods such as bog-oak, boxwood, or ivy, were intricately carved with interlacing Celtic patterns while the pommels and handles were worked in silver and brass. For example, the dirk carried by Captain Charles Macdonell of Glengarry of the 78th, who was mortally wounded at the storming of Signal Hill in St John's, Newfoundland, 1762, has all the classic features of an 18th century Highland gentleman's dirk. It is of superior quality, its mounts engraved silver and the hilt studded with silver nails and tipped with an engraved silver pommel. The flat silver mouth of the scabbard or *crampit* is engraved with a single word *Glengarry* in a fine script. Along the scabbard are two smaller sheaths or pockets for a knife and fork.

To a Highlander, to swear on one's dirk was a most serious oath "having all the solemnity of the Crusader's kiss on his sword" according to Scottish authority, John Dunbar. For example, General Wade found out early in his campaign to wipe out the widespread practice of outlaw clans demanding protection money or "blackmail" from weaker clans, that persons willing to testify, or offer up names, were few and far between. One of the most notorious, cattle-thieving outlaw clans, the Camerons, maintained an oath of silence when any of their members were taken by the Government troops. "This oath they take upon a drawn dagger," observed Wade," which they kiss in a solemn manner, and the penalty declared to be due to the breach of the said oath is to be stabbed with the same dagger; this manner of swearing is much in practice on all other occasions to bind themselves to one another."

All officers and sergeants, at least in the 78th Foot, were required to wear dirks on duty, as Grenadier Sergeant Thompson tells us: "Serjeant Fraser of our Regiment, having lent his dirk to one of the Officers of his Company and having occasion to go somewhere or other, on duty, he borrowed mine. . . ."

Dirks were best suited for close-quarter fighting and it became a favorite weapon of the Highland troops. For example, on 28 April 1760, the light infantrymen of the 78th, led by Lieutenant Cosmo Gordon, fought a vicious hand-to-hand, inch-by-inch battle with the grenadiers of the French army for Dumont's Mill at the Battle of Sillery. A Scot who was in the French service wrote that the mill complex

> was alternately attacked and defended by the Scottish Highlanders and the French Grenadiers, each of them taking it and losing it by turns. Worthy antagonists! – the Grenadiers with their bayonets in their hands forced the Highlanders to get out of it by the windows and the Highlanders with their daggers getting into it again by the door immediately obliged the Grenadiers to exit it by the same means. Both of them lost and retook the buildings several times and the contest would have continued whilst there remained a Highlander and a Grenadier alive, if both generals had

not made them retire, leaving the buildings neuter ground.

Translation of *"Song to Duncan Campbell, Edinburgh Town Guard,"* in *Songs of Duncan Ban McIntyre*, Scottish Gaelic Texts Society, 1952; Richard James, quoted in James D. Forman, *The Scottish Dirk* (Bloomfield: 1991), 8. This is a fine synthesis of a number of scholars and arms experts' opinions and observations on the Highlander's fighting dirk. Also see Charles E. Whitelaw "The Origin and Development of the Highland Dirk," *The Transactions of the Glasgow Archaeological Society*, New Series, Vol.V., 1908, 32-42; Thompson's *Memoirs*; Darling, *Highland Weapons*, 13; General Wade, quoted in Dunbar, *Highland Dress*, xx; , James Johnstone, *The Campaign of 1760 in Canada. A Narrative attributed to Chevalier Johnstone*, (Literary & Historical Society of Québec: 1868), 11.

The Highland Broadsword

Men of élan and mettle with blue blade in pommel...
Duncan Ban McIntyre

There were two types of Highland broadswords used by the Highland regiments. The most common was the enlisted man's sword, the design of which was used as early as 1745. Supplied by the colonels of the regiment for their soldiers, and deducted in off-reckonings from their pay, these poor quality weapons cost about eight shillings and sixpence each. Sword experts agree that the blades were mass produced in Birmingham, as were the sheet metal basket hilt guards which were painted with a black anti-rust preservative. According to a Highland weapons expert, Tony Darling, "relatively few of these enlisted men's swords have survived and a miniscule number have their original grips; most often their appearance is that of having been through a fire."

The second type of sword was not issued by the regiment. These were owned by officers, NCOs and privates from well-to-do families and were masterpieces of the sword maker's art. They had two-edged blades, varying in lengths from 28 to 38 inches, usually imported from the steelmakers of Solingen in Germany, although some came from French forges. The basket hilts were crafted in Glasgow and Stirling by the Hammerman Guilds, each of which had its own distinctive marks, patterns and decorative flourishes.

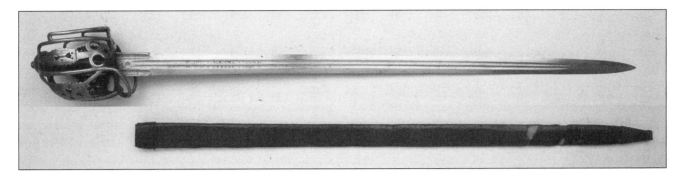

Highland Broadsword, c.1758. A fine example of an officer's broadsword used by Ensign Peter Grant, 42nd Foot, at the Battle of Ticonderoga, 1758. (Courtesy, National Army Museum, Chelsea)

There is strong evidence that the 77th, with the exception of the officers, discarded their regimental issue swords for the 1758 campaign against Fort Duquesne. Lieutenant Colonel Montgomery wrote a letter to General John Forbes from South Carolina requesting permission to stow his men's swords in Philadelphia prior to marching to the Pennsylvanian frontiers. "Our men are young and the less they are loaded the better," he reasoned. "If you can give us a little help in carrying their baggage, they'l march like so many Grey-Hounds."

Lieutenant Colonel Graham of the 42nd reported that his "Highlanders on several occasions declined using Broad-Swords in America; that they all prefer'd Bayonets; and that Swords for the Battalion Men, 'tho part of their Dress and Establishment are Encumbrances."

In contrast, there are many accounts of the 78th using its swords in action, including one contemporary print showing two officers surveying the ruins of Québec, each wearing a basket-hilted broadsword. A sword knot hangs from the pommel of one sword, denoting the owner as a field officer, either a major or lieutenant colonel. On Staten Island in July 1761, as they prepared for the pending Caribbean campaign, company commanders of the 42nd were ordered "to compleat their men immediately the best and lightest swords."

Two good articles dealing with the swords of the 78th are: Anthony D. Darling, "A Relic of the First Raising (1757-1763) of Fraser's Highlanders?" *Arms Collecting*, Vol.24, No.4, (November 1986), 127-29, and, Patrick C. Donelly, "A Sword of the Second Battalion, (Fraser's Highlanders) With a Signed

Basket Hilt," *Arms Collecting*, Vol. 28, No.4, (November 1990), 123-25; Excerpt from *Songs of Duncan Ban McIntyre*, Scottish Gaelic Texts Society, 1952; Darling, *Weapons*, 16; Montgomery to Forbes, Charles Town, South Carolina, 27 April 1757, *GD 45/2/87/3*; 28 July 1761, Staten Island, *SOB*, 44; *WO 27/35*.

Tomahawks

Elite soldiers of the Highland regiments were issued with tomahawks and powder horns, 1760 regimental orders of the 42nd Foot stating "Tomihauks and Powder Horns and Shot Bags belonging to the Light Infantry company to be delivered into the Store." Major George Scott, one of the first British officers to extol the utility of the tomahawk over swords claimed that "a blow from an Ax is infinitely more dangerous to him that receives it, than two or three from a broad-Sword would be, and besides this, the Scalping-Ax will be found of great use in marching through woods and Encamping."

Tomahawk, c.1758. A tomahawk head found during excavations at Ticonderoga. (Courtesy, Fort Ticonderoga Museum)

A soldier who served at Québec 1759 illustrates how the tomahawk was an important back-up to the musket and dirk in close-quarter fighting, but only if one was well-skilled in its use. In "an Engagement between our Scouting Parties and the Indians," Sergeant John Johnson recorded how his friend "saw an Indian who fir'd at him, but missed him . . . he levelled his Piece and fir'd at the Indian and miss'd him likewise; upon which the Indian immediately threw his Tommahawk at him and miss'd him; whereupon the Soldier catching up the Tommahawk, threw it at the Indian and levell'd him, and then went to scalp him; but 2 other Indians came behind him, and one stuck a Tommahawk in his Back; but did not wound him so much as to prevent his Escape from them."

John Johnson, "Memoirs of the Quarter-Mas'r Sergeant" [hereafter *QM Memoirs*], in *The Siege of Quebec and the Battle of the Plains of Abraham*, A.G. Doughty & G.W. Parmalee, eds., Vol. V, (Québec, 1901) 115.

Powder Horns

I powder with
My Brother Ball a Hero like
Do conker All. O love
If a Fin Flower Sun
Will deca[y] and Fead
A way.

Powder Horn inscription, Jonathan Webb,
Lake George, 1758.

Powder horns, in some cases, became personal pieces of kit and were decorated in scrimshaw by some of the more artistically-inclined men. Many were adorned with maps and the names of their owners. Easily ready to hand and slung off the left shoulder and under the right armpit, they contained "pistol powder" with its finer and more combustible grain so the horn was a quicker and more convenient way of priming one's musket.

According to Major George Scott, the utility of a powder horn was that it prevented the most common "fault which Men are subject to in time of Action . . . Viz., that of spilling one half of their Cartridge of powder and sometimes more in priming and shutting their Pans." The result of such nervousness or sloppiness on the part of a soldier in a firefight meant "the Ball is not sent with half the force it is intended or anything near the distance it aught to go."

Dunbar, *Highland Dress*, 216-6; 19 April 1761, Montréal, *SOB*, 38.

Muskets and Rifles

Bhur musgaidean croma 'cur faileas
le'n loinnear
'S bu bhòidheach an sealladh nuair
Dh'èight am paràd.

Your angular muskets reflect light with
their shininess

Powderhorn, c.1757. A carved light infantryman's powder horn which was usually slung from the left shoulder across the body and under the right armpit. Horns provided a more efficient way to prime a musket in the midst of a firefight. (Courtesy, Fort Ticonderoga Museum)

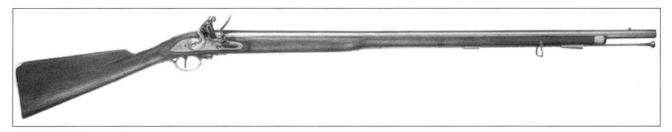

Cut-down Brown Bess. A cut-down musket similar to those used by Highlanders in North America during the Seven Years' War. The shortened barrels made the weapons lighter and less cumbersome for the bush-fighting that marked wilderness warfare. (Private Collection)

> When the parade was assembled the
> sight was marvelous.
>
> Unknown, *After Quebec*, c.1764.

The 42nd Foot began the war equipped with regulation King's Pattern 1742 Long Land muskets, known familiarly throughout the British Army as the "Brown Bess." These weapons were equipped with a double-bridle lock, walnut stock, a 46-inch long, .75 caliber round barrel and a wooden rammer.

By 1758, the 42nd Highlanders had cut their musket barrels down to 42 inches in length to make them lighter and easier to carry through the woods. Payments to blacksmiths "for cutting short the arms of the 42nd Regiment" dated 14 March 1758 and 24 November 1759, and archaeological evidence from digs on Rogers' Island gives proof of these modifications. After excavating a site near Fort Edward in 1969, Earl Stott wrote that "perhaps the most interesting items taken from . . . smith's site were the cut ends of musket barrels ranging from 4, 6 to 8 inches in length."

By contrast, the 77th (Montgomery's) and 78th (Fraser's) arrived in North America in 1757 equipped with 37-inch carbines with iron ramrods. Lieutenant Colonel Simon Fraser informed Lord Loudoun in April 1758 that his regimental arms were "the Carabines the horse had before they were reduced to Dragoons, and are excellent Arms in every respect, but that they are rather slight for hard use. . . ."

These smoothbore carbines were similar to those issued to the artillery and various orders of the day indicate that those same carbines were re-issued to the various regimental light infantry companies. For example, before the 1758 Louisbourg campaign began, the men of the three yet-untrained 78th Additional Companies which were to be left behind in Halifax were ordered to exchange their carbines for Brown Bess muskets, one-for-one, with the light infantry of Major George Scott's Provisional Battalion.

Rifles were limited-issue firearms. The 42nd received 10 rifles for its best marksmen, as did seven other regiments, just prior to the battle of Ticonderoga, 8 July 1758. These 80 rifles came from a batch of 300 rifled carbines, each fitted with bayonets and steel rammers, that were brought to North America by Colonel James Prevost of the Royal Americans.

An 1758 orderly book tells us that while at the Lake George camp in June, the Highlanders and other Light Infantry marksmen "who have the rifled barrel pieces" were "to fire three rounds each" before embarking on the boats. Eighty men firing three rounds apiece does not sound like a very comprehensive target practice, nor was it intended to be. It was the men zeroing in their new rifles, as each piece was handcrafted and each weapon had to be adjusted to its user. By adjusting the rear sight at given ranges, a rifleman could determine his line of sight and whether his personal firelock aimed high or low.

Musketry and target practice, commonly referred to as "firing at Marks" [hence marksmen] became a top training priority for British troops during the war in the Americas. By the spring of 1761, when the battalions of his "American Army" were preparing for service in the Caribbean, General Amherst could observe with satisfaction that "in general all the men are so good marksmen, that it requires only a little practice to keep their hands in."

Earl Stott, *Exploring Rogers' Island*, (Rogers Island Historical Association, 1969); Colonel Simon Fraser to Lord Loudoun, *"from on board the Halifax, off Nantasket Lighthouse,"* April 23rd, 1758, *LO* 5447; Iron ramrods, 77th/78th Regiments – WO 4 Vol. 53 (Selections) NAC microfilm C12585; for a thorough discussion of British military firearms during the Seven Years' War see the following works by De Witt Bailey: *Pattern Dates for British Ordnance Small Arms 1718-1783* (Gettysburg, 1997); *British Military Flintlock Rifles 1740-1840*, (Lincoln, 2002); and "British Military Small Arms in North America, 1755-1783," American Society of Arms Collectors, *Bulletin*, No. 71, (October 1994), 3-14. *AJ*

Bayonets

"Highlanders on several occasions
declined using Broad-Swords
in America . . . they all prefer'd Bayonets. . . ."

Lt. Col. Gordon Graham, CO, 42nd Foot.

In standard use with the Long Land musket during the Seven Years' War was a 17-inch long socket bayonet with a triangular blade. This weapon left a triangular wound. The socket of the bayonet fitted onto the musket over the barrel and when pushed down and twisted, it locked onto a barrel lug which resembled a foresight. Muskets and carbine rifles could be both fired with their bayonets attached.

The Highland Pistol

Lord Loudoun's Highlanders and the 42nd Foot in the mid-18th century were issued with all-metal Highland pattern pistols. This "issue" or regulation pistols were all-steel or iron, barrels unblued, with rams horn or scroll butts and steel ramrods. Examples in the National Scottish Museum have "R.H.R." (Royal Highland Regiment) engraved on top of the barrels.

Only one pistol, usually 12-inches in length, was issued to each man. These Highland pistols were usually 12 inches in length. They had no trigger guards; the triggers were tipped with a spherical ball approximately the size of a pea; the pricker used to clean the weapon was stowed or screwed into the end of the butt; and there was a belt-hook or slide affixed to the reverse side. The pistol was carried on a narrow strap slung from the right shoulder, so that the weapon hung under the left armpit. This is clearly seen in the prints of early Black Watch uniforms published by Bowles in 1743 and 1746.

At first pistols were purchased for the soldiers by the colonel of the regiment out of his clothing allowance, but when the 77th and 78th regiments were raised, pistols were issued by the government. The records show that each of the new Highland Battalions received 1080 "side pistols." The 60 pistols above the total for the other ranks were to be distributed to the sergeants and corporals if they so wished. These mass-produced factory pistols were of poor quality and vastly inferior to those made for private use. Many of the men, and all of the officers carried their own personal pistols, handcrafted and sometimes inlaid with silver and gold. The non-issue Highland pistols varied in length from eight inches to as much as just over sixteen inches.

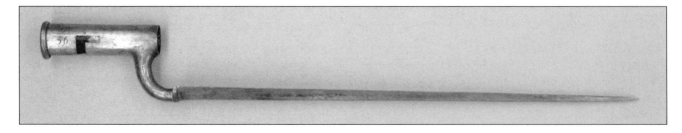

Bayonet, c.1757. The 17-inch long socket bayonet with a triangular blade was in standard use during the Seven Years' War. It fitted over the musket barrel and locked onto a barrel lug when pushed down and twisted, and permitted the soldier to fire his musket with the bayonet fixed. Soldiers without dirks preferred the bayonet to the sword when it came to hand-to-hand fighting. (Courtesy, Fort Ticonderoga Museum)

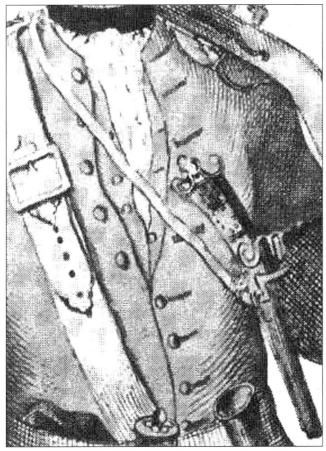

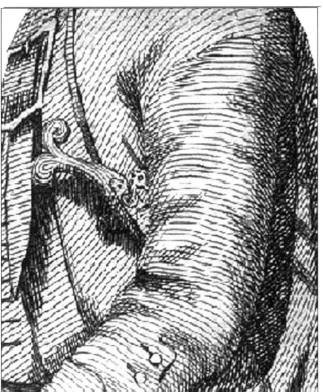

When the Additional Companies of the 77th arrived in Pennsylvania from Scotland, in the spring of 1758, Colonel Henry Bouquet informed General Forbes that the Highland recruits were equipped with "300 bad pistols" which, given Colonel Montgomery's agreement, he could give away as presents "as they would suit the Indians very Well."

Bouquet to Forbes, 22 May 1758, *BL,* Add. MSS. 21652: f.10; Fraser to Loudoun, 23 April 1758, *LO* 5447; for further information see Major Ian H. Mackay Scobie's excellent article "The Regimental Highland Pistol," *JSAHR*, Vol. VII, (Spring 1928), 52- 57.

Halberds/Spontoons

Pic de'n iubhar dhonn chaol
'Na sheasamh ri d' thaobh
Gu barr a dheis fo fhaobhar . . .

A pike made of slender, reddish yew
Standing at your side,
A double-edged blade to the tip . . .

Calum Mac an Fhleisdeir,
A Song to Allan Maclean of Coll, 1757

Typically carried by sergeants and officers respectively as a badge of their office in Europe, halberds and spontoons were archaic holdovers from the days when pikemen formed phalanxes to protect vulnerable infantry from cavalry charges.

The painting, *Glasgow Green,* at the Black Watch Museum in Perth, Scotland shows Highland NCOs carrying their halberds on parade, but these were more useful as an instrument for ensur-

Highland Pistol. Highland soldiers were each issued an all-metal Highland pattern pistol. This weapon was about 12-inches in length and had either a ram's horn butt or scroll butt. It was loaded using a steel ramrod. It was carried on a narrow strap slung from the right shoulder and hung snugly under the left armpit as shown in these front and side views taken from contemporary engravings. (Courtesy, Fort Ticonderoga Museum and Trustees of the Black Watch Museum, Perth)

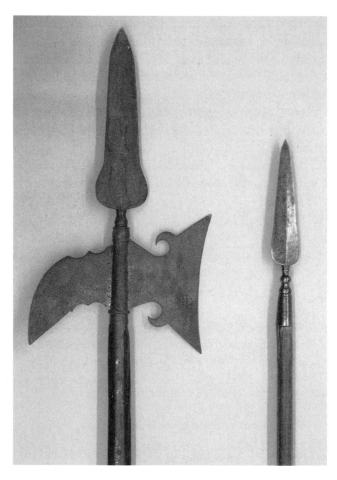

Polearms, c. 1758. The halberd was carried by sergeants as a badge of office. It had a pike-pointed steel head with a 7-inch spike and a six inch axe blade, the pole *"not to exceed seven feet in length."* **Officers were quick to discard their spontoons which were styled after boar-hunting spears and similar in length to the halberd.** (Courtesy, Fort Ticonderoga Museum)

ing the ranks of young recruits were straight than a serious weapon intended for use in North America. When on recruiting detail, sergeants used halberds to measure the heights of men as depicted in William Hogarth's famous print *The Invasion, England Plate 2*, which was published in March of 1756 and which is accompanied by David Garrick's poem which begins, *"See John the Soldier, Jack the Tar. . . ."* The halberd had a pike-pointed steel head with a six inch axe blade and hook opposite the axe, the pole "not to exceed seven feet in length." and the pointed pike was often 7 or more inches long. The 77th and 78th were each issued with 40 "Halberts."

The spontoon was styled after a boar-hunting spear and similar in length to the halberd. On landing in North America, most officers were quick to discard their spontoons. Instead, officers adopted instead a light musket or fusil and retained their pistols, dirks and swords. Somewhat incredulously, Lieutenant John Grant of the 2nd/42nd recorded at Martinique in 1762 that, while his men were in their faded soldiers' tunics, with blanket rolls slung across their chests, and tomahawks on their hips, the 76th Foot "who had lately arrived from the taking of Bellisle, landed in White Spatterdashes, Gorgets, & spontoons and sashes. . . ."

NCOs seem to have been more reluctant to discard their distinctive badges of office. Stewart's orderly book reveals the 42nd was ordered to take "firelocks" to the field instead of "Halberts" for the 1758 and 1759 campaigns.

Poem - Newton, *Indians*, 49; Halberds – WO 4 Vol. 53 (Selections) NAC microfilm C12585; Grant's *Journal*; 31 May 1759, *SOB*, 31.

Bagpipes

The instruments with which they make their mirth are great lowd bagpipes upon which they plaie and tune battails and combats and other such songes as they have.

Richard James, *Description of Shetland, Orkney and the Highlands of Scotland*, 1620

After the '45 rebellion, bagpipes were considered "instruments of war." It was recognized from the outset that the piper's role was essentially a martial one, as he marched into battle alongside his comrades and encouraged them to deeds of valor with the rant of his pipes. Court records after the '45 noted that a Highland unit "never marched without its piper" and therefore the player and his pipes were an intrinsic part of a regiment's fighting ability.

Bagpipes were not army issue. They were the personal property of the pipers that the Highland regiments brought to North America with them. The earlier pipes had two drones and a chanter.

The three-droned Great Highland bagpipes, with the addition of a bass drone, had made an appearance by the time of the '45. For example, a stand of pipes, believed to be used by one of the Mackay independent companies of 1745-47, survives in the Scottish National Army Museum (formerly the Scottish United Services Museum). It is three-droned, of indigenous wood, horn-mounted and has pear-shaped terminals. While it is smaller than the modern three-droned bagpipe of modern times, it takes the same-sized reeds and has a fine resonant tone. Early 18th century chanters and drones were made from local, close-grained woods such as boxwood, laburnum, holly, and fruit woods such as plum and apple. The mountings were made out of horn, lead and pewter. After about 1780, the woods used were African blackwood, ebony and cocus, and the mounts were to be found in ivory and silver.

Quoted in I.H. Mackay Scobie, "The Independent Highland Companies of 1745-47," *JSAHR*, Vol. XX, (1941), 29n.

Instrument of War, c.1745. Bagpipes were not Government issue but were the personal property of the pipers of the Highland regiments. They were of two kinds: the most common, the two-droned bagpipe (as shown in this contemporary engraving), and the three-droned Great Highland bagpipe. (Courtesy, Fort Ticonderoga Museum)

Equipment: Officers & Men

Belts, Cartouche Boxes & Canteens

The belts worn by Highlanders were made from black leather. The waist belts had to be sturdy enough to hold the kilt in place, as well as to suspend bayonets, tomahawks and frogs (holders) which were worn on the left hip. If a man had a dirk, it was worn to the right.

The cartouche boxes containing gunpowder cartridges were usually worn centered on front of the waist belt so that a man's ammunition was easily accessible. These oblong wooden boxes were covered in black leather, the leather flap coming over the top with the front usually decorated with a brass GR royal cypher (as the 42nd had), or with a stamped, embossed or painted rendition of the GR. Light infantry usually carried shot pouches instead of cartridge boxes, or carried ball and cartridge in leather pockets sewn onto the upper chest of their waistcoats so they could load lying down.

A black leather sword belt was worn over the right shoulder to hold the broadsword. A metal canteen covered with colored baize material to prevent glare and clinking on other equipment was suspended on a separate cord from the left shoulder, as was the powder horn for the light infantry.

Weapon Cleaning Kit

The Regimental Orders for the 78th Foot of 11 May 1762, stated "Every soldier to be provided with a brush weir [wire,] worm stopper, turn key screw & a rag for his arms." Another entry from a 42nd Highlander orderly book reveals that in addition for every man being responsible for keeping his weapon well-oiled and free of rust, he was obliged to plug his muzzle to keep his barrel free of unwanted dust and dirt. "It being a general complaint the locks are stiff for want of oyl, the Commanding Officers are to cause their men to provide oyl for them if possible to be had. The firelocks to be made thoroughly clean in the inside, after

Accoutrements. A detail from an engraving of Private Farquhar Shaw which, as in the engraving of Corporal Macpherson, shows how cartouche boxes, dirks, bayonets and sporrans were worn off the belt that also served to secure the plaid. The sword was suspended on a separate buff-colored belt slung from the right shoulder. (Courtesy, Trustees of the Black Watch Museum, Perth)

which every man (except those on duty) to have their stoppers constantly in their pieces."

Before going on campaign, all officers were reminded to check that their men's arms were in "perfect repair and to be complete in stoppers, pickers, brushes and hammer caps." Caps or capes, also known as flint capes, protected the firing mechanism [hammer, flint and frizzen] and kept them dry and clean.

30 September 1759, Crown Point Camp, 30 January 1760, Fort Edward, *SOB*, 23, 31; 11 March 1762, *NOB*.

Highland Colors (Flags)

Every Highland regiment had two Colors or flags the designs for which had been standardized in the British Army since 1751. The painting *Glasgow Green* shows the two 42nd colors on parade. On the right was the King's Color, a Union flag, six feet on the pole by six feet six inches in the fly and made of silk. On the left was the Regimental Color, made of the same material and size, which had as

Left: The Colours. Every Highland regiment had two Colours or flags. This detail from the painting *Glasgow Green* **shows the two 42nd Colours on parade. On the right is the Union flag, six foot by six foot six inches, made of silk and known as the King's Colour. On the left is the Regimental Colour of the same material and size, but buff which was the color of the regimental facings. In the center of each Colour was a wreath of roses and thistles surrounding the regimental "rank" or number in Roman numerals. (Courtesy, Trustees of the Black Watch Museum, Perth) Right: Haversack. A small square bag of canvas, used to carry personal gear including food and spare clothing. Often suspended from the left shoulder, it could also be worn as a back-pack. This detail is from a painting entitled** *"Warriors"* **by Robert Griffing.** (Courtesy, Robert Griffing & Paramount Press)

a background color that of the regimental facings. Superimposed in the center of each Color was a central wreath of roses and thistles surrounding the regimental "rank" or number, usually depicted in a roman numeral. When the 42nd was made a Royal regiment, the background of its Regimental Color changed from buff to royal blue. The 77th Regimental Color had a background of gosling green, The Regimental Color of the 78th was off-white: it would not have done for a Highland regiment to bear the cross of St George, as in the naval White Ensign. As the most junior officers [Ensigns] carried the colors on parade or into battle, a newly-joined one was often said to have "purchased his colors."

Thompson's *Memoirs*; 21 November 1759, *SOB*, 29; Malcolm Fraser, *"The Capture of Quebec. A Manuscript Journal Relating to*

the Operations Before Quebec From 8th May, 1759, to 17th May, 1760. Kept by Colonel Malcolm Fraser. Then Lieutenant in the 78th Foot (Fraser's Highlanders)," JSAHR, XVIII, (1939),[hereafter Fraser's *Journal*], 161; Knox's *Journal*, II, 272, 309; Fortescue, *History of the British Army*, II, 395.

Haversacks

A small square bag, made of canvas and called the haversack, was suspended from the left shoulder and was used to carry all sorts of personal gear including food and spare clothing. The Highlanders also carried a backpack which was centered high on the back, Indian-style, with under arm straps, which was used to carry food, extra clothing and extra ammo. When the 42nd prepared to leave New York, R.O.s for 30 April 1759 read: "The Regimt to be under arms on Wednesday morning with their Linen britches and leggans, and packs tied up properly with their toplines [tumplines]."

30 April 1759, New York, *SOB*, 14.

Snowshoes

In order to patrol, forage or skirmish in the winter, Highland soldiers in garrison at isolated posts such as Fort Stanwix in the Mohawk Valley or Ancienne Lorette outside Québec City, needed to have the same mobility over snow that their enemies possessed. All had to learn the art of snow-shoeing, a skill taught to them by their ranger or Indian auxiliaries. John Knox described how soldiers at Québec became very proficient on snow-shoes made from "hoops of hickory, or other tough wood, bended to a particular form, round before; and the other two extremities of the hoop terminate in a point behind, secured together with strong twine; the inward space is worked like close netting, with catgut or the dried entrails of other animals....They must be used under mog-gosans, as well for the sake of the wearer's feet, to keep them warm and preserve them from the snow." Hard-sole shoes, Knox added, could be used in a pinch but "they will not bind on so well" and would wear out the snowshoe sooner.

Knox's *Journal*, II, 309.

Tents

According to Highlander orderly books, companies were organized "into Messes allowing six men to a tent" and "the camp necessaries ...given out accordingly." A 42nd Foot orderly book entry in New York in 1759, advised that all officers were "to provide themselves forthwith in tents according to the patern tent which is to be seen at the tentmakers....No more than one tent will be allowd for two subalterns, they are therefore to divide themselves and bespeak their tents accordingly as none is to be bespoke for them."

Captains, field officers and general officers were entitled to their own tents. Orders also reveal that new tents were "first to be dipped in salt

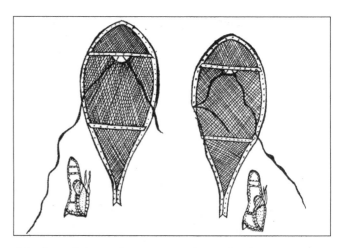

"Rackets." In order to travel in the heavy winter snows of North America, Highlanders used snow-shoes, or racquettes [rackets]. This early drawing by French explorer Charles de Granville, circa 1701, shows how little they have changed over the years. (Private Collection)

water, to prevent their being mildewed." Old worn out tents were recycled, "cut down, washed and made into short drawers [breeches]."

22 February 1759, New York, 2; 31 January 1760, Fort Edward, 32; 4 October 1760, Staten Island, *SOB*, 31-2, 49.

Below: Tents, c. 1762. The tent lines of a regiment encamped outside the captured French fortress of Fort Royal on the island of Martinique illustrate the various tents used. On the left are soldiers' tents which could sleep 4-6 men, and on the right are the larger tents used by the officers, or to store firearms. A contemporary engraving by Sub Engineer and Lieutenant of Foot Archibald Campbell. (Courtesy, William L. Clements Library)

Specialist Officers

Chaplains

See "An Unbounded Ascendancy" in Part Three.

Surgeons

The regimental surgeon was a commissioned officer. Several were graduates of universities while others achieved status as surgeons through apprenticeships and long service. The regimental surgeon was assisted by a warranted surgeon's mate, regimental orderlies and those regimental women who acted as nurses.

Each regiment would establish its own "hospital" in a dwelling or a tent when encamped, which was then run by the Mate and his orderlies. Each morning, sick or injured soldiers would attend the daily "sick parade" with only medical cases beyond the Mate's scope and expertise being referred to the surgeon.

Field hospitals, with additional specialist officers attached to them, were established in time of war to take over the sick and wounded overflow from the regimental hospitals. There was a General Hospital established at Albany early on in the Seven Years' War and the French hospitals captured at Québec were put into good use at Québec in 1759.

Barracks in New York, Elizabethtown and Amboy were converted into hospitals in 1762 in an attempt to treat the huge numbers of fever-ridden men coming back from the Caribbean operations. When these became full and hospital beds were at a premium, some sick and wounded Highlanders found themselves billeted with the inhabitants of the colony in which their regiment was campaigning.

The directors of the hospitals were responsible for maintaining quality control on surgeons and their equipment. A 42nd R.O. for 22 March 1759 reads: "The Surgeons of the severall regim^ts will prepair their medicine chests with every thing that may be necessary for the use of the Regimts during the Campaigns and all the chests are to be inspected by Mr. [Napier] the Director, or a proper person appointed by him."

A surgeon treating a gunshot wound in the field would typically stuff it with bandages moistened with wine or brandy, and, if infection and suppuration threatened, antiseptics such as tincture of myrrh, hot turpentine, balsam of Peru or camphor would be applied.

Trephining was a routine procedure used for head injuries; cauterization of blood vessels after amputation was a routine procedure. One British account of the standard battle wounds that could be expected in the mid-18th century, as well as their treatment, stated:

> It's impossible to describe the variety of wounds from cannon shot, small arms, swords and bayonets. My first intention in dressing wounds was to stop bleeding, which I did by stitching the vessels, dry dressings, bandage etc. Having no assistant, I avoided amputations as much as possible, the necessity obliged me in some cases. . . . Slight wounds were dressed with Balsalm Traumatic . . . Contusions from cannonballs seldom recover . . . soon spread upwards and downwards commonly attended with large emphysema over the whole body. . . Drought (dehydration) is the most universal complaint from all the wounded and surgeons would do better in filling their medicine chests with proper liquors for this purpose, than stuffing them with apothecaries drugs.

22 March 1759, *SOB*, 8; see also Sir Neil Cantlie, *A History of the Army Medical Department, 2 Volumes* (London 1974); John Laffin, *Surgeons in the Field,* (London 1970); and my article "Battlefield Medicine in the 18th Century," *Osprey Military Journal*, Vol. 4, Issue 4.

Adjutant

A battalion staff officer, the adjutant was responsible for the commanding officer's paperwork in garrison, compiling the endless number of monthly returns, as well as the issue of the daily regimental orders. His position was a paid appointment as well as a rank and it was possible for officers already holding commissions as ensigns, lieutenants and, sometimes but rarely, captains lieutenant and captains, to serve as adjutants. Working closely with the major and the Sergeant Major, the

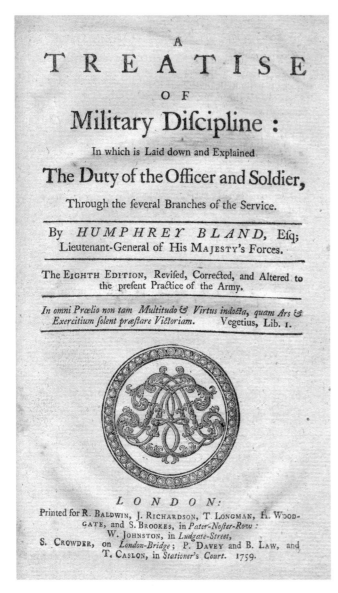

church). For example, R.O.s would periodically instruct new officers who had never attended a battalion review, parade or exercise to drill with the men in order not to embarrass themselves. A May 1761 entry for the 42nd in garrison at Montréal reads: "Such officers that never stood a review with the battalion to be out with their Feuzees [fusils] to morrow at 10 o'clock."

1 May 1761, Montréal, *SOB*, 39.

Quartermaster

The battalion quartermaster, or simply, the QM, took charge of the regiment's equipment and stores, the re-supply of food and ammunition as well as the forage for the battalion horses. He and his assistants, the camp-color men and QM personnel assigned to assist from each company, were responsible for helping set up and lay out the regimental lines when encamping outside a town or on the march. In short, they ensured the officers' and men's billets, whether they were tent or house, were properly organized.

The ideal QM was "an honest, careful officer, exact of his pen and a steady accomptant very well skilled in the detail of the battalion and perfectly well-acquainted with every individual circumstance of its duty and finances." During the Seven Years' War, a practice of raising senior sergeants to commissioned rank as Quarter Masters evolved in the British army. For example, we find in the Regimental Orders of the 1st/42nd, dated 15 October 1761, that "His Excellency Sir Jeffery Amherst has been pleased to promote Colin MacPherson, late Serjt. Major to be Qr. Mr. in room of Lt Graham preferred, Serjt. William Munro of Capt MacNeill's Coy. Is app. Serjt-Major." Colin Macpherson would die of fever aboard a hospital ship off of Havana, 9 September 1762. William Munro, formerly sergeant major of the 1st/42nd, was also commissioned to this important post for the Caribbean campaign of 1762 against Martinique and Havana. Not only were these men well-acquainted with the inner workings of the battalion and usually adept at performing the job, the post served later in the century as a means of

Bland's Military Discipline. Frontispiece from Major General Humphrey Bland's mid-18th century treatise on drill, administration and tactics of the Georgian infantry. (Courtesy, Fort Ticonderoga Museum)

adjutant looked primarily after personnel, both officers and men, and thus concerned himself with enlistments, discharges, punishments, drill and the drawing up of duty rosters. He was also responsible, to a degree, for the discipline of the junior officers and their military training, especially ensigns and lieutenants. Besides the example below, there are several other admonishments in the Regimental Orders with regard to junior officers training, dress and behavior (not attending rewarding experienced and meritorious NCOs with a modest half-pay on disbandment.

Simes, *A Military Course for the Government and Conduct of a Battalion*, (London, 1777), 228; *Oeconomy and Discipline: Officership and Administration in the British Army 1714-63*, (Manchester, 1985), 14-15; 15 October, Staten Island, *SOB*, 49.

Specialist Soldiers

Sergeant Major

The Sergeant Major was the most senior non-commissioned officer (NCO) of the regiment and the commanding officer's principal and trusted link to the enlisted men. In the Highland regiments, he was usually of the same social standing and class as most of the officers. Some sergeants and several sergeants-major were commissioned as officers during the Seven Years' War.

The sergeant major's principal duties were to maintain high standards of drill, dress and discipline in the regiment and oversee the regimental duty rosters and guard mountings. He was a key player in the daily workings of the battalion and cooperated closely with the major and adjutant, the other two principal officers responsible for administration.

15 October, Staten Island, *SOB*, 49; *SBs*; *Cbs*. Anthony Bruce, *The Purchase System in the British Army, 1660-1871*, (London, 1980).

Pipers

Mo dith, Mo dith, 's mi gun Tri Lamhan,
Da Lamh 'sa Phiob is Lamh 'sa Chlaidheamh!

My Loss, My Loss, without Three Hands,
Two for the Pipes and one for the Sword!

Clan MacDougall's Incitement to Battle, c.1299

So a piper lamented his inability to fight the enemies of his clan and play his pipes at the same time. "In room of Drum," an English clergyman observed of clansmen going to war at the turn of the 17th century, they "make use of a Bag-pipe," a comment that underlines the significance of this particular type of specialist soldier.

Akin to a drummer who could sound various calls in camp, on the march or on the battlefield, a Highland piper was the eighteenth-century equivalent of a modern-day signaler. Pipers were not on the regimental establishment. The 1758 Royal Warrant authorizing the creation of a Second Battalion for the 42nd Foot and making it a "Royal Regiment" designated one piper to each grenadier company, for a grand total of two on establishment during the war. Pipers could also be accounted for under contingent men.

Additional pipers were certainly taken on strength as drummers and it is interesting to speculate that the early "quick marches" of the Highland regiments of the late 18th century may have evolved from this blending of the piper and drummer function in one musician.

A 42nd orderly book reveals that on 10 April 1759, "Peter McIntyre pipper in Capt. MacNeill's company is for the future to be on the footing of a Drum and to be subsisted accordingly." The same

Sergeant Major. A detail of a senior non-commissioned officer by Francis Grose. The sergeant major was the senior and most experienced NCO in a regiment. A key player in the daily workings of the battalion, his principal duties were to maintain high standards of drill, dress and discipline and to oversee the regimental duty rosters and guard mountings. (Courtesy, Fort Ticonderoga Museum)

Ticonderoga. Sheet music for a modern-day pipe tune commemorating the gallantry of the Black Watch at the battle of Ticonderoga, 8 July 1758 by Pipe Major Hugh Macpherson. (Courtesy, CWO (ret'd) Hugh Macpherson)

entry also announced that "Owen McIntyre pipper in the Grenadier Company is appointed pipper-major and is this day to receive the clothing accordingly."

But the piper was expected to do more than just relay the daily orders of his officers. Pipers were gifted musicians, many from traditional piping families such as the MacCrimmons, MacArthurs or MacIntyres where compositions and playing techniques were passed down from generation to generation.

Clan pipers were men of high musical attainments and accorded near deity status. The long courses of training they underwent at such piping schools as those of the MacCrimmons and MacArthurs turned out finished performers. According to an old Gaelic saying , "Into the making of a piper go seven years of his own learning and seven generations before."

The piper was responsible for playing tunes before and during the battle to inspire the men to greater deeds. After the battle he was also expected to compose laments to honor the fallen, or in happier circumstances, to commemorate the brave exploits of the clan or of a particular warrior. Thus the piper played an important role in regulating clan regiments and later the Highland regiments embodied in the British army. Pipe tunes are still used today by all surviving Highland regiments to announce the various duties, whether in camp or on the line of march, though on a modified, more symbolic level.

The senior and most experienced piper was called the pipe major and he was responsible for teaching as well as maintaining the duty roster for the other pipers. For a detailed essay on some of more famous pipe majors and pipers of the 42nd, 77th and 78th Highlanders during the Seven Years' War, see Dr William Forbes' excellent article in Part Three.

Rev. James Brome, *Travels over England, Scotland and Wales*, (London, [2nd edition] 1707). The author, while serving as the Commanding Officer of the Black Watch (Royal Highland Regiment) of Canada, remembers the "Orders Parade" call where delinquent soldiers were marched in for judgment to the tune of "A Man's a Man for a' that." Other duty calls were the Reveille "Johnnie Cope"; 1st Duty Call, "Up Early in the

Morning"; Commanding Officer's Call – "The Blue Bonnets"; and Lunch Call -"Brose and Butter." For a detailed list of various duty calls used in the British Army see Major I.H. Mackay Scobie's excellent *Pipers and Pipe Music in a Highland Regiment*, (Dingwall, 1924), 5-6; 10 April 1759, New York, *SOB*, 13.

Drummers

Before the bugle was introduced during Napoleonic times, the 18th century British Army was regulated by the beat of a drum. All troop movements and maneuvers on the battlefield were relayed through the din of battle by the drummers, so the Highland regiments, in order to function alongside their Sassenach counterparts in battle, had to maintain drummers.

Drummers. Detail from the painting *Glasgow Green*, c.1756, showing two 42nd drummers wearing *philabegs* to provide greater freedom for beating the drum. Drummers wore jackets of 'reversed colors' so they are wearing buff tunics edged with red cuffs, collars, and lace. The drum belts worn in the painting *Glasgow Green* are also red. (Courtesy, Trustees of the Black Watch Museum, Perth)

A 42nd orderly book entry gives us a basic idea of how the system worked in a brigade: "The drums of the regiment repeat the beats of the signal drum once, and the regiments make their movements from their own drums."

The painting entitled *Glasgow Green* depicts the 42nd drilling on the common and shows two orderly drummers dressed in *philabegs,* set to relay the commands of the mounted field officer. They are wearing *philabegs,* as full plaids would have interfered with the freedom required by drummers to enable them to beat their already heavy drums. Their drums were made from a round wooden shell, two feet long and the same in diameter, with calf-skin drumheads which were tightened by ropes and leather lugs. Usually the Royal cypher and the roman numeral of the regiment were emblazoned on the front of the drums, the backing color matching the facing of the regiment. The hoops or rims of the drums were also painted the facing color. Thus a 77th drum's rims and front would have been painted gosling green while the Fraser's drum ciphers would be backed with off-white. The drums of the 42nd would have been buff-colored, until they switched to royal blue in 1758.

Contrary to popular belief that drummers had a relatively simple and non-combative job that could be done by mere boys, most drummers were men. The number and complexity of drum beatings, as well as the need to interact with officers, demanded a highly-qualified and well-trained soldier who could remain calm in the thick of battle. Drummers were considered important enough to be classed as non-commissioned offices and paid four pence more a day than the private soldiers.

As a mark of their uniqueness, drummers wore reversed colors, that is, jackets of the color of the facing of the regiment (buff, green or white) trimmed with red cuffs, collars and lace. Not following this custom, the Royal Regiments' drummers wore red coats with blue facings. The drum belts worn over the buff drummer jackets depicted in the painting *Glasgow Green* are scarlet. To top off their sartorial splendor, drummers in the Highland regiments usually wore the grenadier's coveted fur mitre-cap and grenadier wings.

The Drum Major was the most senior drummer and helped to maintain the duty rosters for the regimental guard mountings. R.O.s from Fort Ontario in July 1760, give us an insight into some of his specific responsibilities: "The Drum Major to sett the drums of the regimt in repair immediately and he is to be out with them to practice till further orders from Trap beating to 10 o'clock and from 4 in the afternoon to 6 o'clock. He is to be answerable that the drums are properly dressed every morning before Trap beating."

Aspiring drummers were also expected to pay the Drum Major for his patient tutelage. An entry from the 42nd orderly book for 25 April 1759, reveals: "The young drummers entertained since the regiment came to this country to pay the Drum-Major for teaching them…" A month later we learn that only one "Drum" per company was allowed on campaign, "the rest put in the ranks."

While in garrison at Charleston during their first winter (1757-8), Montgomery's Highlanders had no drummers. "There is one thing I'm in great want of," wrote their Colonel to General John Forbes on 22 March 1758. "If you can assist me, I should be greatly obliged to you. It is a Drum Major. We have not one drum in the Regiment, and without a proper person to teach them now. I would gladly pay money . . . but any will do better than want. "

One unpleasant task assigned to the drummers was administration of the floggings in a regiment. In the Highland regiments, this was such a rare occurrence that the drummers were well-liked, whereas in other regiments, they were sometimes shunned and ostracized as creatures of the disciplinary establishment.

A good source for additional background on military drums and drumming is Hugh Barty-King, *The Drum*, (London, The Royal Tournament, 1988); 25 April 1759, New York, 31 May 1759, Halfway Brook, 21 July 1759, Fort Ontario, *SOB*, 14, 31, 35; Montgomery to Forbes, Charlestown, 22 March 1758, GD 45/2/87; f.1.

Grenadiers

The grenadiers were the tallest and strongest men of the regiment, the elite shock troops who led the

GRENADIER, 42ᵗ REGᵗ 1751.
(From a painting at Windsor Castle.)

Elite Soldier. A Grenadier of the 42nd Royal Highland Regiment of Foot, wearing a bearskin mitre cap which distinguished him from other men in the "bonnet" companies. From 1758 on grenadiers were often brigaded to be used as "shock troops" or for other special tasks because of their size and strength. (Courtesy, Fort Ticonderoga Museum)

charge. Their uniforms were designed to make them appear even more imposing, with grenadier wings on their shoulders to make them look wider and 12-inch tall bearskin fur mitre caps to make them look taller.

Their name derived from the function they had performed in the 17th century of lobbing hand grenades over enemy walls and into entrenchments prior to the final assault. Despite this practice dying out at the beginning of the 18th century,

the match cases which used to contain the smoldering cord or "slow match" for lighting their explosive devices, were still retained and attached prominently to their sword shoulder belts as a mark of distinction. The records of Cox & Company, regimental army agents for the 42nd, reveal that from 1758 to 1761 the regiment made several purchases of match cases for its battalion grenadier companies.

Army commanders would customarily brigade the regimental grenadier companies into a special grenadier battalion which they could use to spearhead attacks on critical points. While this practice deprived the regiments of their best and biggest soldiers, commanding officers recognized that it was for the common good of the army.

Sumner, "Cox & Co., Army Agents: Uniform Items from their Ledgers," *JSAHR*, vol. XVII, (Spring 1938), 92-101, 135-57.

Light Infantry

The year 1757 in North America saw British commanders introduce an experimental, temporary Corps called "light troops" or "light infantry." This elite *ad hoc* Corps was designed to better meet the problems presented by the terrain as well as by the tactics of an elusive and savage foe. The men chosen were from among the better marksmen and the shorter, more agile men of the regiments. A light infantry soldier was "a chosen man," the most "active marcher," an "alert, spirited soldier able to endure fatigue," an "artificial savage'" and "expert at firing ball" to quote some contemporary descriptions of the day. He was proficient at scouting and skirmishing and could scrap with the best the French and their Indian allies could muster. He was at ease in canoes, whaleboats, and bateaux, shooting rapids or on portage, but as equally comfortable leading the way on major amphibious assaults in conjunction with the Royal Navy. He was extremely fit and agile, could use snowshoes, scale crags in the face of furious fire using the terrain or traverse swamps and jungle terrain by day or night.

In essence, the light infantryman was the most resilient and motivated redcoat of Britain's

"American Army" during the Seven Years' War, and by the end of that conflict had surpassed the grenadier as the elite soldier of choice and led the landins and/or attacks at Louisbourg, Ticonderoga, Québec, Havana and Signal Hill.

For a detailed study on light infantry see Warrior #88 in the Osprey series by the author entitled *British Light Infantryman of the Seven Years' War, North America 1756-63*, (Oxford, 2004).

Below: Light Infantry Ambush.
Two light infantry soldiers from the 42nd Foot, circa 1758, form part of an ambush. Both wear philabegs and have replaced their swords with tomahawks. A detail from a painting by Steven Noon in Ian McCulloch's and Timothy Todish's *British Light Infantryman in the Seven Years' War, North America, 1756-1763.* **(Courtesy, Osprey Publishing, UK)**

Hatchet Men (Pioneers)

"The Hatchet men are at all times the Regim[t] is under arms to parade
with their caps and pioneer tools and form on the Right of the Reg[t]."

So reads an entry of 42nd R.O.s for July 1759 at Lake George camp. These were the artificers of the regiment, men adept with axes, saws and hammers who, later in the British Army infantry regiments, were formally known as the Pioneers. They were skilled carpenters, masons, and wheelwrights who received extra pay for their work and took a leading role in erecting field defenses, siege works and supervising the construction of fortifications such as Fort Ontario at Oswego or Crown Point on Lake Champlain.

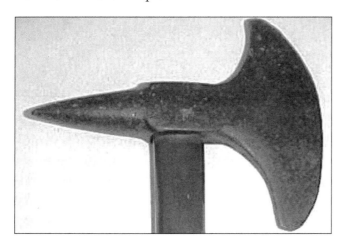

Broadaxe. A British Army issue broadaxe carried by the pioneers or "hatchet men" of the Highland regiments. (Private Collection)

They were the first infantry soldiers that the Engineers employed as overseers. They were allowed to wear the same mitre caps as the grenadiers and drummers because of their elite status and special duties. They were, in effect, the regiment's own personal corps of engineers.

13 July 1759, Lake George Camp, *SOB*, 21.

Women

While they were not soldiers, women campaigned alongside their men-folk in the Highland regiments, a total of six normally permitted in each company of 100 men. These women were on the regiment's establishment and therefore entitled to rations. Simply referred to in the orderly books as the *"Women,"* they tended to be attached to the more senior enlisted men such as sergeants and corporals and were expected to perform a myriad of chores ranging from cooking and sewing to nursing and laundering in exchange for their government rations. Widows of slain soldiers would attempt to find new partners within the regiment to maintain their ration status for themselves and their children.

In December 1758, as the 42nd Foot recuperated from the bloody battle of Ticonderoga in New York city, we find two marriages recorded in the 1st and 2nd Presbyterian Churches of New York:

> December 11, 1758: Donald Blake, Soldier in the 42nd Regiment, and Janet Macdonald, Widow
> December 27, 1758: John Smith, Soldier in the 42nd Regiment, and Hannah Murray, Widow.

The 42nd Foot orderly books for the 1758 and 1759 Ticonderoga expeditions reveal that women were not permitted to follow the army on campaign. Instead, they were instructed to report for service as nurses at the General Hospital in Albany. Orders on 15 May 1758 stated that all regimental commanding officers were " to give in the womans names they intend should receve the allowance for provision this campaign and are to recommend - The first that came with the Reg[t] from Europ if they are willing to be nurses to the Gen. Hosp[tl] when required. They are not to exceed 4 per company."

An entry from Crown Point in the 42nd Orderly books dated June 1761, indicates that *supernumerary* women, that is, extra women carried over and above those on regimental establishments, were only tolerated to accompany their husbands on the clear understanding they did **not** draw rations. Subsequent orders implied that too many unruly women and their families were at Crown Point and things were getting out of hand. The women were ordered "to go down the country" and "to be ready to depart early on Saturday morning with their children and baggage, they will have Batoes to carry them to Ticanteroga and must embrace the first opportunity of going across Lake George. If any of them presume to remain after this order, or to return to Crown Point; may depend on being drummed out of the regiment."

These orders obviously did not have the desired effect, as it seems many women and children took to the woods rather than leave their men. A day later, orders took on a more strident tone. "The women who have absconded this morning and have not obeyed the order of yesterday must depart tomorrow morning at Sun rising with their baggage, their husbands to be acquainted that if they disobey, that their names will be put in orders discharging them forever from the regiment." There was no further mention of the incident, indicating that compliance was swift.

Women also accompanied sutlers as did camp followers who were prostitutes. The latter were to be found in the many towns and cities of North America, wherever armies and fleets gathered. Some followed the regiments as they moved from garrison to garrison.

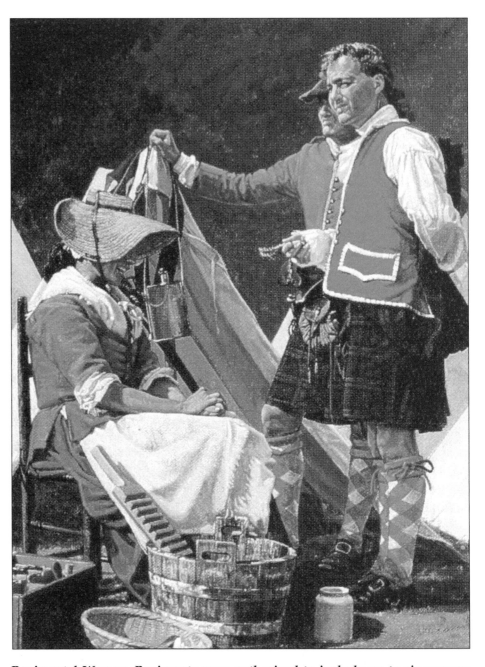

Regimental Women. Regiments were authorized to include up to six women and their children per company, depending on company size. Women performed a range of house-keeping chores as well as acting as nurses. This camp laundress, c.1758, is a detail from the painting *"Passing the Time of Day,"* (Courtesy, John Buxton and Paramount Press)

One provincial soldier at the Lake George Camp in October 1758 recorded with some disgust in his diary: "this afternoon their [sic] was a Lobster Corporal married to a Road Island whore."

Some of the women who acted as sutlers were

often enterprising soldiers' wives who wished to make extra money. They acted as money-changers or sold small luxury items not provided by the army such as: "rolled tobacco, tobacco leaf, Scots snuff, hard soap, lump sugar, ordinary smoking pipes, Dutch pipes, threads, needles, pins, tapes, flannels, coarse woolen cloths, nails, bolts, locks hasps, garden tools and stationary supplies." Fiercely independent and aggressive, they sometimes incurred the wrath of commanders by selling too much liquor or flouting camp discipline. The 42nd Highlanders' orders for 17 May 1759 in Albany stated that "all the petit Sutlers tents in the rear or any other whereabout the Reg^t" were to be "struck immediately and if any woman whatsoever pretends to pitch tent about after this, near the regt, the Qr. Mr. is to order it to be struck and burnt directly."

When the sale of rum at the siege of Louisbourg was eroding the discipline of the troops, Admiral Edward Boscawen suggested an immediate ban to General Amherst, noting that "the women of the Highlanders [78th Foot] & the Royals to be notorious sutlers."

These same women also incurred the ire of Major James Clephane who was in command of four companies of Fraser's at Fort Stanwix during the winter of 1758-59. On 11 November 1758, he warned the "married Women" of the garrison that should any of them be discovered selling rum, he would not only "turn them out of their Hutts; But will Cut them of the King's Provision & chase them Shamefully away." The same threat of losing provisions was again used four months later when Major Clephane felt the women were charging extortionate prices for doing the men's washing. He ordered that "no Woman Presume to take more than One Penny for a shirt, and one Penny for Each Waistcoat." Woman daring to charge higher rates he declared would be cut off the "List of His Majesty's Provisions."

"Major Clephane's Orderly Book," Fort Stanwix, 1 February to 9 April 1759, *GD* 125/34/4: f.14; *SOB.*

PART THREE

Essays

Final Comfort. An unidentified chaplain comforts a dying Highlander at the battle of Fontenoy, 1745. A painting by W. Skeoch Cumming (1897). (Courtesy, Trustees of the Black Watch Museum, Perth)

Essay One

"The Apparent Blue-Green Sheen of a Crow Flying Against the Sun": Two Oral Histories of Captain *"Donull Gorm"* Macdonell, 78th Foot (Fraser's Highlanders)

By Ian McCulloch

Donull Gorm Macdonell, of Benbecula (c.1728-1760) was the second and natural son of Ranald Macdonell, 17th "Old" Clanranald, and a half-brother to the 18th "Young" Clanranald. His younger half-brother, William, also served in the 78th Foot. *Donull Gorm* had joined the French Army before the Jacobite rebellion in 1745 and had fought at Stirling where he was wounded and subsequently went into hiding on Uist.

When he heard of the surrender of his regiment after Culloden, he acted swiftly to ensure he was treated as a French officer vice a rebel as Britain had a cartel with France and Spain for the exchange of prisoners of war.

After giving himself up, he wrote from his cell in Edinburgh Castle, 15 December 1746: "I went to France in year 1742 and served as Cadet in Booth's Reg^mt. till I got a Company in Drummond's Reg^mt. [*Royal Ecossais*] the year 44 and came along with it to Scotland in Novr. 45, and being wounded before Sterling, I returned to my father's country, where I remained till hearing that all my Reg^mt. surrender'd themselves prisoners of War at Inverness, after the Battle of Culloden, I was desirous of doing the same, and I surrendered myself to Capt. John Mackdonald [yr of Glenlyon, 43rd Foot, and brother of "Archie Ruadh (Roy)" MacDonald, who also served in the 78th Foot] as soon as he came to the Country I was in, in July last. . . ."

In 1756, the Duke of Argyll said of him: "brother to Clanranald was sent into the French Service when a boy, & had a Company several years, which he quitted some months ago upon the late Act of Parliament & took the Oaths to the Government; for these facts, as well as for his Character, he appeals to My Lord Holderness & undertakes on this occasion to raise 100 men."

Captain Macdonell was accepted as one of the original company commanders of the newly-raised 78th Foot and raised his company quickly by draconian methods on the outer isles of Skye (Macdonells, MacLeods), Uist (Clanranald Macdonells) and Barra (MacNeils) [see poem *I am not Well* in Volume One, Chapter Two].

He replaced Charles Baillie as Captain of Grenadiers, the latter killed at Louisbourg, 8 June 1758, and was wounded himself six weeks later, on the night of 21 July 1760 in the approach trenches. He was killed at the Battle of Sillery outside the walls of Québec on April 28, 1760.

Donull Gorm was not well-liked by the Highlander rank-and-file, according to Grenadier Sergeant James Thompson who unabashedly styled him "a surly cross dog," and in his *Memoirs* hinted that MacDonnell was intentionally wounded or "fragged" by his own men at the siege of Louisbourg on 21 July 1758: "Our Captain had a ball passed through his left wrist and nobody could tell how it came and afaith he immediately shifted his position to the other end of the ground."

Thompson was rebuked on several occasions by *Donull Gorm* for being too familiar with the men and finally during the winter of 1760-61 they had a face-to-face meeting.

> After we had taken Quebec, he one day sent for me to his Quarters in the lane leading to the Esplanade, I accordingly went and found him sitting at a table with another officer.
>
> "Jim, you have all along thought that I was hard upon you."
>
> "Aye Sir," I replied, "I did indeed think that you were harsh to me when there was not a great necessity for it."

"I treated you," says the Captain, "in that manner because you were too familiar with the private men."

"Sir," I replied again, "how came you to think that to be wrong in me, when you yourself know that it is impossible to act otherwise? Our men, you know, are not like those of other Regiments – they were all acquaintances before they became soldiers, and many of the private men are from as good families as the officers themselves.

Captain Macdonell offered Thompson a drink, which he accepted and the grenadier sergeant soon learned that he had been summoned because his company commander had "found that I had a friend somewhere, who had got wind of his harsh treatment of me, and he wished by all means to wipe off the scores" with him.

Donull Gorm offered him a second drink which Thompson took but he departed with "no better opinion of his friendship after all." Thompson was a highly respected Freemason in the garrison, as was his Colonel, Simon Fraser, who was elected a grandmaster of the first Grand Lodge of Québec. No doubt, Thompson's "friend" was the *Mac Shimi* himself.

Markedly, at the battle of Sillery, 28 April 1760, none of Macdonell's volunteers were drawn from the 78th Foot. Oral tradition in the Highlands of Cape Breton, where several Fraser soldiers returned to settle on the eastern Bras d'Or Lakes of Cape Breton (Barra MacNeils, MacEacherns, and Clanranald Macdonells) maintains that it was at this 1760 battle that "the de'il finally got him," and that the cursed Captain finally got his due reward by succumbing to one of the oldest Gaelic curses, "May you die amongst strangers."

Harper, in his book *The Fraser Highlanders*, did not include Thompson's somewhat satisfied description of his nemesis' gory end - "a stronger body of French overpowered and completely butchered his whole party, and he himself was found cut and hack'd to pieces in a most shocking manner. There was an end of him!"

According to Thompson, *Donull Gorm* was a marked man by the Indians and *Canadien* militia who had been harried ruthlessly all winter long.

Many French-Canadians had watched helplessly as he indiscriminately burnt several of their farms during winter raids and sorties against the outlying countryside of Québec, leaving the occupants to freeze and starve. Retribution was final and ghastly, and to the Gaelic mind, necessary for the restoration of the balance of nature.

Here then are two versions that evolved in the Gaelic oral tradition: one in the Highlands of Cape Breton along the shores of the finger lochs of Bras d'Or, a vast inland sea abounding with shellfish, waterfowl and forest; the other, by the hearths of cottars in the sea-girt isle of South Uist, who helplessly watched their young men pressed into *Donull Gorm's* company.

Note the more fanciful and superstitious rendition that lingered in the Outer Isles of Scotland, his legacy not one of honor, but of infamy. He became the bogeyman, the evil one of Gaelic story telling tradition, the embodiment of everything that was not proper, right or just. In essence, he was the antithesis of what a Highland war chieftain should be.

Sources CBs; SBs; BALs; Stewart, *Sketches*, II, 20-1; "Donald McDonald" *PRO*, WO64-12; *CU* 49/5; William Amherst's Journal, 29; *GD* 201/4/81; *Muster Roll of Prince Charles Edward Stuart's Army 1745-46*; Harper, *Fighting Frasers*, 101-2, Thompson's *Memoirs*.

Cape Breton Version
(as told by J. J. MacEachern)

"In Gaelic, I am called *Iain Macdhomhnuill 'ic seon aidh Dhomhnuill Oig*," states J.J. MacEachern, a noted local historian & genealogist, sitting in the *An Drochaid* ("The Bridge" Museum of Mabou, Nova Scotia, also home to the *Mabhu* Gaelic & Historical Society. "In English that would be: John MacEachern, son of Donald, son of John, son of younger Donald and this is my *sloinneadh* (family tree)":

My traditions came to me from my grandmother, Mary Ann MacVarich, her male line coming from the Morar-Arisaig district of western Inverness in Scotland. Her mother was a Campbell from South Uist and her mother a Macdonell from the same island. Mary

Ann MacVarich married John MacEachern whose male line also came from Arisaig and before that South Uist. His mother's people also came from the island, thus most of my paternal forbears were of Uist stock.

Our family tradition is that MacEacherns and others fought at Louisbourg with Captain Donull Gorm Macdonell in Colonel Fraser's regiment. On a patrol between the East Bay arm of the Bras d'Or Lake and Louisbourg, my ancestors saw the land they hoped to get after war's end. Donull Gorm, for so he is usually called, is remembered in my grandfather's time (1890's to 1980's) as a cruel man, caring little for his men. Nevertheless, he did bring his men to this land, my grandmother would say.

The Gaelic word "ghuirm" or "gorm" as applied to Donull Gorm Macdonell is a strange one. Literally, it means blue-green, but it may also mean the apparent green sheen on a crow flying against the sun. Others say it is the colour of the sea in twilight. Whatever the word may mean, the connotation is not good. For Donull Gorm, it meant swarthy and diabolical, a man of violence and one not to be crossed.

Donull Gorm's recruiting was done in the area of Uist, Benbecula and Barra and his pressing of men by force or enticement was the core of many a fireside tale. In Gaelic tradition a curse is put upon one when he takes a widow's son, and the fulfilment of the curse restores the balance of nature.

Now it was some years before Cape Breton was open to settlement. The men of Louisbourg did not see their new lands in their own times* but their descendants did. It is not clearly known if the descendants who came were children, grandchildren or nephews. According to tradition the lands granted in the 1790's were on the basis of military service. Whatever the story, Donald MacEachern's sons, Angus, Allan and John took land along East Bay in the very area travelled by Donull Gorm's soldiers

---

Author's Note: Four MacEacherns appear on the disbandment rolls of the 78th Fraser Highlanders dated December 1763 in Québec; all four soldiers shown as returning home to Scotland to be mustered out. Their names, interestingly enough, were Angus, Angus, Allan and John.

It is therefore not impossible that these discharged Fraser soldiers did return in the 1790's when the Highland Clearances were in full swing, for they would have only been in their fifties (given that the average age of most young recruits

of joining the 78th Foot in 1757 was eighteen). They may have come via Prince Edward Island [PEI], for Allan Macdonell, the Laird of Glenaladale, sold his estate on Uist in 1772 and brought over 250 Catholic Highlanders to settle on the island. Many of these men then joined the Royal Highland Emigrants for the duration of the American Revolution, some of their officers former Fraser, Montgomery and Royal Highland officers who had remained in North America. Many were given land grants in Nova Scotia in recognition of their services, in addition to the land they already had farmed in PEI.

The Barra MacNeils of Iona, Cape Breton, claim that four MacNeil soldiers of *Donull Gorm*'s initial company went home to Scotland on disbandment of the regiment, gathered their families and kinsmen and returned to the Bras d'Or lakes after the French and Indian War and settled at Iona.

South Uist Version
(as told by Major R. Gillis)

Among Simon Fraser's officers was one Donald McDonald, generally referred to as Donull Gorm having a peculiarly swarthy countenance with a bluish cast. He was cruel and heartless, but brave and clever as a soldier. In his younger days, he was head of a press gang whose duties were to go through the Highland districts impressing all eligible young men for service in the army, paying no heed to the conditions of the families of those men, whether they were the sole support of aged and infirm parents or not. Great hardships and cruelties were inflicted on poor people in this way, but Donald seemed to have no heart for their afflictions nor paid any heed to their wailings.

On one occasion he visited the shealing of a poor widow with an only son as her sole support. The son was at once seized and despite the pleadings and wailings of the woman the young man was taken away. (in Volume One, Chapter Two - see the Gaelic song "I am Not Well" originating in South Uist sung by a widow who lost four sons to *Donull Gorm*).

The mother at first pleaded, but when she found that was of no avail she poured the most terrible curses on Donald, ending with the prophecy that he would never die a natural death, but would be taken away body and soul into the infernal regions.

Many years passed and Donald went through all the hardships and dangers of battles and engagements of all kinds, but escaped without a wound.

After the wars were over and peace restored, Fraser's men were at Quebec waiting for a transport to carry them back to their homes. One evening just about dusk a group of officers were resting in front of their quarters enjoying the beautiful spring weather, when a man was seen coming up the steep hill on which they were lounging. Just as the man came near enough for them to see all above his waist over the skyline he halted and hailed the group of officers, asking if Donald Gorm was present.

Donald replied in the affirmative, asking him what did he want of him. The stranger said he wanted a private interview which would have to be at the foot of the hill. The other officers advised Donald to have nothing to do with the stranger but his reply was that he never *feared man or devil and would meet the stranger as requested, and he immediately got up and went towards him, when both of them walked down the hill apparently in deep controversy of some kind.*

Hours passed and Donald did not return, when searching parties were sent in all directions, but no trace could be found, dead or alive, and to this day the Highlanders firmly believe that the prophecy of the widow was literally fulfilled and Donald Gorm was carried off by the evil one into the infernal regions.

Source: Major R. Gillis, *Stray Leaves from Highland History*, (Sydney, NS, 1918), 22-3.

Essay Two

"An Unbounded Ascendancy": Highland Chaplaincy in the French and Indian War, 1756-1767.

by Ian McCulloch

Captain Francis Grose's satiric *Advice to the Officers of the British Army*, first published in 1783, was a sarcastic account of the failings and weaknesses of officers in the British army, including NCOs and enlisted soldiers. According to Scottish poet Robert Burns, Grose "had been thrown into the Army from the Nursery" and had retired as a captain on half pay, as well as doing a unfortunate stint as paymaster and adjutant of the Surrey Militia in which he lost most of his personal fortune.

In spite of his less-than-illustrious military career, Grose echoed the prevailing views of the 18th century British army regarding religion in the ranks. Tongue-in-cheek, but with an eye to reality, he cautioned the would-be-chaplain:

> The chaplain is a character of small importance in a regiment, though many gentlemen of the army think otherwise. . . . If you are ambitious of being thought a good preacher by your scarlet flock, you must take care to keep your sermons short.... Never preach any practical morality to the regiment. You would only be throwing away your time. . . . You may indulge yourself in swearing or talking as much as you please; this will only show you are not a stiff high priest. Moreover, example being more effectual than precept, it will point out to the young officers the ugly and ungentlemanly appearance of the practice and thereby deter them.[1]

Grose's view was based upon practice. In 1760, General Jeffery Amherst, the Commander in Chief of British Forces in North America wrote from Montréal to Dr. Philip Hughes, Chaplain of the 44th Foot who was in New York, about the laxity with which regimental chaplains performed their duties. The general was somewhat annoyed:

> The bad Choice that has been Made of Persons to Officiate for the Chaplains of the Army, Which has made it necessary to Discharge one lately for imbibing Seditious principles into the Soldiery, & the Other Your Deputy having Seldom Appeared during the Campaign, added to the few Chaplains that have come out to Attend their Duty: rendering it of Absolute Necessity, in Order to Convince His Majesty's new Acquired Subjects, that their Brethren have a Sense of the Duty they owe to God; that all those Who are Appointed to have the Care of their Souls Should Attend to Discharge that trust; And the Regimt. to Which You belong being to Winter in these Parts.
>
> I can no longer Admit of Your Absence from the Same; You will therefore immediately upon the receipt hereof. Set out for, and with all possible Diligence, repair to this place, in Order to remain with them & duly to Discharge the Office, You have taken upon You by the Acceptance of the Commission You Enjoy.
>
> Doctor [John] Ogilvie [60th Foot, Royal Americans] is likewise to remain here, and is gone to fetch his Family; And in case You Should Chuse to bring Yours likewise, I here add a pass to procure to You and them, all the facilities You May Stand in need of, on the Road. . . .[2]

Whatever the actualities in regiments of the line, things seemed to be different in the Highland regiments that came to North America during the Seven Years' War 1755-1763. In all three Highland regiments, the chaplain was the acknowledged keeper of the regiment's morality and the fount of spiritual comfort.

There is also strong evidence to suggest that he represented an intellectual focus for the oral traditions of the Highlands and actively encouraged original compositions in song and poetry that tended to reinforce the warrior ethic so crucial to good morale. The importance of what was proper (*còir*), what was right and just (*ceart*), what was necessary or obligatory (*dligheach*) and the need for strict loyalty (*dìleas*) were all key elements of a preaching military chaplain's ministry and canny clergymen of the day were not averse to using the current Gaelic poetry and songs of the day to underline his message.[3]

The Black Watch had sterling ministers from the day of its raising, and as such, set a high standard for all Highland regiments that followed: standards which contemporary Sassenach line regiments could not seem to match. The 1745 issue of the Articles of War included mandatory attendance at "Divine Service and Sermon," and the Duke of Cumberland included particular instructions for all battalions employed in Scotland to ensure "Divine service" was "to be regularly performed in Camp which the Officers and Soldiers are to attend to."

A pamphlet entitled *A System of Camp Discipline* published ten years later emphasized that an army on campaign should have Prayers "read every morning at the head of each brigade at nine; the Chaplains of each Brigade to take it in turns, beginning with the Eldest [i.e., the most senior]."[4]

Stewart of Garth cites early Black Watch orderly book entries to show that such encouragement was not necessary in the early Highland regiments. "Great regularity was observed in the duties of public worship," he wrote, and "the greatest respect was observed towards the ministers of religion."

As example, he identified Dr Adam Ferguson who, fresh out of Divinity school, and directly ordained to serve in the 42nd as probationary chaplain, was beloved by his men. They said of him that he never shied away from his flock whether in the thick of battle or billeted in peacetime garrisons, and that his behavior alongside them during a particular battle earned him their undying respect:[5]

> When the regiment was taking its ground on the morning of battle, Sir Robert Munro perceived the chaplain in the ranks, and, with a friendly caution, told him there was no necessity to expose himself to unnecessary danger, and that he should be out of the line of fire. Mr. Ferguson

thanked Sir Robert for his friendly advice, but added, on this occasion he had a duty which he was imperiously called upon to perform.

> Accordingly he continued with the regiment during the whole of the action, in the hottest of the fire, praying with the dying, attending to the wounded, and directing them to be carried to a place of safety. By his fearless zeal, his intrepidity, and his friendship towards the soldiers (several of whom had been his schoolfellows at Dunkeld), his amiable and cheerful manners, checking with severity when necessary, mixing among them with ease and familiarity, and being as ready of any of them with a poem or heroic tale, he acquired an unbounded ascendancy over them.[6]

Stewart fancifully claims that this battle was Fontenoy, but records clearly show that Ferguson was still at school on the actual date the battle was fought and that the young student was only examined and ordained in Dunkeld on 2 July 1745, six months **after** Fontenoy. The battle described must be a later engagement, or rear-guard action, fought later in the year or a following year. Ferguson himself wrote to a friend from Vilvoorden Camp in Flanders saying that he did not take up his post as assistant minister with the regiment until September 1745.[7]

On 30 April 1746, Ferguson officially replaced the Hon. Gideon Murray as the principal chaplain, the latter the brother of Lieutenant Colonel James Murray of the 15th Regiment of Foot, who later distinguished himself as one of Wolfe's brigadiers at Quebec in 1759.[8]

Ferguson remained as 42nd chaplain for the next ten years but, on the announcement that the regiment was ordered on North American service, he retired on 20 December 1757. His replacement was a younger man, James Stewart, who went out to the Americas in 1758 with the Second Battalion of the newly-honored "Royal Highland Regiment." In August 1759, Stewart would resign and return home to Scotland and take up duties as Minister of Dull. He was replaced by an old schoolmate, Lachlan Johnston, who would minister to both battalions of the regiment for the next three years.[9]

There was some talk in 1761 that Johnston, a married man, might return to Scotland allowing Presbyterian parson and bachelor, Robert Macpherson, the *Caipal Mhor* ["Big Chaplain"] of the Fraser's Highlanders to exchange into the Royal Highland Regiment. But the drums did beat and the war went on, and Johnston was obliged to go to the Caribbean and do double-duty for the two battalions at Martinique, and again at the even more grueling siege of Havana. He would witness firsthand over 500 of his flock die from disease and wounds and in early August 1762, succumb himself to the "yellow jack." By the time Macpherson heard of the death vacancy, it was too late, and he had already decided to return to Badenoch to become a gentleman farmer.

As the Seven Years' War was winding down the following year, the veteran chaplain, Dr. Ferguson, now a professor at Edinburgh University, returned as a stopgap chaplain according to the British Army Lists, but there is no record however that the good doctor actually crossed the Atlantic to join his flock in the middle of Pennsylvania's forests. With most of Scottish society talking excitedly of the prospect of the three Highland regiments returning home after six years abroad and he probably felt he could join his flock when it arrived back on Scottish soil.

When it became apparent however that the regiment was not returning home immediately because of the western Indian uprisings in the spring of 1763, the professor's primary job was to find a new young chaplain to go out to the Ohio on behalf of Lord John Murray.

In 1764, at a Chapel of Ease in Amulree, Ferguson finally found an ideal candidate who was possessed of the "Irish tongue" and whose mind held a wealth of poems and heroic tales. James Maclagan, son of Dr. Maclagan of Little Dunkeld, one of the principal clergymen of the Presbytery of Dunkeld who had ordained Fergusson back in 1746, was dispatched to America and took up his post at Fort Pitt at the Ohio Forks.

Educated at St Andrew's University (1750-51), Maclagan was a 34-year old Gaelic scholar and accomplished poet. Eight years earlier, whilst a divinity student in 1756, Maclagan had composed

a Gaelic song - *To the Highlanders Upon Departing for America*- in honor of the 42nd Highlanders. Although written well before he himself would serve in the regiment, Maclagan was inspired to record the historic event in the time-honored tradition of the Gaelic bards, as he had family and friends serving in the regiment. An older brother, Alexander, had served the British Crown as a lieutenant in Lord Loudoun's Highlanders (1745-48).[10]

There is also some evidence in the lyrics of later verses of this song (attributed to 1756) that Maclagan added onto it whilst serving with the regiment in North America from 1764-1767.[11]

Maclagan's departure song reflected all the traditional bardic devices commonly used to inspire the Highland soldier to martial action: an appeal to their hereditary prowess as gallant warriors fighting for their families and clans; veiled promises of material wealth and young ladies' favors; and the widely held belief that traditional weapons and kilts, as well as highland honor and old homelands, would be restored to all Scots for their current loyalty and service.

It was a mixture of religious and pagan tradition: a fiery cross of rhetoric on one hand, exulting in how "the hardy band of Lord John...will make enemies mourn and allies rejoice" when "Scots go hunting after treacherous Frenchmen and Forest-folk." On the other, it was a sermon exhorting the best behavior and conduct possible on the part of the Highlandmen. Maclagan reminded his flock that they would be conspicuous in their red coats and dark tartan and thus scrutinized by "Britain and Ireland and all of Europe." As a final benediction, he promised

> Your land, and myself like a kindly mother,
> Will pray to Heaven that you will succeed
> Rejoicing or lamenting according to
>   your fortunes.
> Always keep the Lord God in your minds.
> Now, take blessings with you, full of
>   happiness and success.[12]

The two younger Highland regiments raised for service in North America, the 77th and 78th, were both blessed with outstanding chaplains who served with them for the entirety of war thus providing continuity and stability for those regiments until they were disbanded.

Henry Munro was commissioned chaplain in the 77th Foot, 12 January 1757, and accompanied his regiment to Charles Town, South Carolina that same year. Born 1730 in Inverness, Scotland, Harry studied divinity at Edinburgh University, was ordained in 1757 and appointed chaplain to the 77th Highlanders at the age of 27, no doubt through his mother's connections, the daughter of John Munro, 4th Laird of Teanourd.

Harry accompanied the regiment on General Forbes's expedition to Fort Duquesne, (site of present day Pittsburgh) as well as participating in the capture of Ticonderoga and Crown Point in 1759, and Montréal in 1760. He preached a thanksgiving sermon to the victorious armies of Amherst, Haviland and Murray at the foot of Mont Royal, September 1760.

He subsequently served in the West Indies with nine companies of his regiment and returned with it in 1762 to New York having witnessed hundreds of his flock succumb to the ravages of yellow fever at the successful but costly Siege of Havana.

His decision to remain in North America after the disbandment of his regiment in 1763 was an easy one for he had married a New Jersey beauty in 1762, one Miss Stockton of Princeton. During the American Revolution he was imprisoned as a Loyalist but escaped to join the Royal New York Regiment in Montréal where he served briefly as their chaplain. He returned to Britain in 1778 to study, intending to return after a British victory which was not to be. He finished his days in his native Scotland, dying in Edinburgh in 1801.[13]

The 26-year old chaplain of the 78th Fraser Highlanders was The Reverend Robert Macpherson, known affectionately to his men as the *Caipal Mhor* because of his towering physique. Macpherson was not shy soldiering alongside his men like the redoubtable Ferguson of the Black Watch and he ensured that "their religious discipline was strictly attended to…and was indefatigable in the discharge of his clerical duties," so much so, that "the men of the regiment were always anxious to conceal their misdemeanors from the *Caipal Mhor*. . . ."[14]

After the conquest of New France in 1760, Macpherson, a Freemason, served as chaplain to the Québec Select Lodge composed of officers serving in the various regiments then in garrison. Sergeant James Thompson, himself a Free Mason and Senior Warden of Canada Lodge No.6 in the 78th, recorded that on St. John's Day in the winter of 1761, the members of his lodge "Walked in procession in due form at one o'clock attended by the Reverend Brother Robert Macpherson, Member of the Select Lodge at Québec from whom we had a sermon on the Occasion in the Church of St Valier."

On disbandment of Fraser's Highlanders, Robert Macpherson exchanged to half-pay like many of the 78th officers and returned to Badenoch where he petitioned the Factor of the forfeited estates at Aberarder in 1766 stating he had *"served in America for seven years, on reduction put on half-pay. Being a half-pay chaplain, he is prevented by an act of Parliament from holding an ecclesiastical position. He therefore wants to try farming. Seen methods while traveling home and abroad which he thinks will enable him to carry on better than most. Therefore requests Aberarder and Tullochrom comprehending Strachronnachan as possessed by Ronald and Alexander Macdonell."*

He took up residence at Aberarder by 1770 where he was known for many years by his neighbors as *"Parson Robert."* He married Louisa Campbell, daughter of Duncan Campbell of Achlyne in 1775, and of his five sons, three entered the army, Duncan attaining the rank of Lieutenant-General. His eldest son, John Macpherson of Ness Bank, was Factor to both Lord Macdonald in Skye and to the Lovat estates at Inverness. The *Caipal Mhor* died in March 1791 and is buried in Perth.[15]

Unlike so many of the chaplains of the day in other line regiments of the British Army, the Highland regimental chaplain by comparison was the foundation for the regiment's moral and spiritual character as well as an active promoter and guardian of the Highland oral tradition. By placing high value on poetry, music and heroic tales as part of their ministry, chaplains, through their conduct before, during and after battle, reinforced the Highlander's warrior code.

They were, without a doubt, key players in maintaining the morale and *esprit de corps* of their units with powers and influence sometimes surpassing that of the colonel commandant.

In many respects, although some of them would have recoiled at the analogy, they were 18th century equivalent of the ancient druid-bards who had special place in the Celtic tribal structure, with *dìleas* their battle-cry.

---

1. Francis Grose, *Advice to the Officers of the British Army: With the Addition of Some Hints to the Drummer and Private Soldier,* (London, 1783), x; also see Francis Grose & D. J. Cragg, *The Mirror's Image: Advice to the Officers of the British Army. With a Biographical Sketch of the Life and a Bibliography of the Works of Captain Francis Grose, F.S.A.,* (Philadelphia, 1978). Francis Grose (1731-1791), once referred to as *"the greatest antiquary, joker and porter drinker of his day,"* was the eldest son of Francis Grose, the Swiss jeweler that fashioned George II's coronation crown. Francis, junior, retired from the British Army with the rank of captain to study art and was, at one time, the Richmond Herald in the College of Arms. He served as Paymaster and Adjutant of the Surrey Militia, a position he was highly unsuited for, since he kept no books and gave no receipts. The private fortune he inherited from his father was quickly drained to make up for his huge deficiencies. He published his *Antiquities of England and Wales* in 6 volumes between 1773 — 87 and *The Antiquities of Scotland* in 2 volumes, in 1789 and 1791. Scotland's immortal bard, Rabbie Burns, met Grose while he was in Scotland collecting material for his Scottish volumes and, becoming fast friends, agreed to write his greatest narrative work, *"Tam o' Shanter"* for Grose's pending volumes. Writing to a Mrs. Dunlop from Ellisland on 17th July 1789, Burns told her: *'Captain Grose, the well known* [author] *has been through Annandale, Nithsdale and Galloway, in the view of commencing another publication, The Antiquities of Scotland. . . . I have never seen a man of more original observation, anecdote and remark…. His delight is to steal thro' the country almost unknown, both as most favorable to his humor and his business… if you discover a cheerful looking grig of an old, fat fellow, the precise figure of Dr. Slop, wheeling about your avenue in his own carriage with a pencil and paper in his hand, you may conclude: "Thou art the man!"*

2. Major General Jeffery Amherst to Dr. Phillip Hughes, 44th Foot, 20 September 1760, WO 34/85: f. 123.

3. For an excellent study on how Gaelic poetry was an integral part of maintaining the Highlander's warrior code and how it provides an authentic window through which one can view and understand the Highlanders' feelings, perceptions and opinions of the time, see Michael Newton's pioneering study on the Highlander oral tradition and its meaning in North American history, *We're Indians Sure Enough: The Legacy of the Scottish Highlanders in the United States,* (Richmond: 2001) [hereafter *Indians*]. Also his recent article "Jacobite Past, Loyalist Present" in the online magazine, *eKeltoi, Journal of Interdisciplinary Celtic Studies,* Vol.5, "Warfare."

4. *Rules and Orders for the better Government of His Majesty's Forces Employed in Foreign Parts* (1747); *Orders for the Troops in Scotland, 1753-57,* Military Library, Edinburgh Castle; *A System of Camp Discipline,* Part II (1757), 11.

5. Adam Ferguson was commissioned Chaplain to the 42nd, 30 April 1746, just a few days after the Battle of Culloden. He was the ninth child of Adam Ferguson (1672-1754) of Logierait and Mary Gordon of Hallhead. Ferguson had a large portion of his college courses waived in order that he might join his regiment promptly as the regiment was told off for duty in Flanders. Lord John Murray, the Colonel of the 42nd made representations to the 1745 General Assembly of Dunkeld that he and his regiment were inclined "to have a chaplain of the communion of this church, having the Irish language, who must be soon ordained to that office; and that Adam Ferguson, student in Divinity, son to the minister of Logierat, in the Presbytery of Dunkeld, is pitched upon for that purpose." Quoted in, Nathaniel Morren, *Annals of the General Assembly of the Church of Scotland,* (1840), Vol. I, 73f; Dr. Ferguson, on resigning from the Regiment 20 December 1757, became a tutor for two years before accepting a Chair as Professor of Natural Philosophy at the University of Edinburgh. He later surrendered this Chair for that of Moral Philosophy and is now acknowledged as one of Scotland's leading men during the Enlightenment and "The Father of Modern Sociology." It was at Ferguson's house, that Robert Burns and Walter Scott met for the first and only time. On retirement from university life, Ferguson moved back to St. Andrews (his house, with sundial over the door, can still be seen on South Street), and is buried in the Cathedral grounds. The epitaph on his memorial is by Sir Walter Scott. Newton, *Indians,* 120-1; James Ferguson and Robert Menzies Fergusson, *Records of the Clan and Name of Fergusson, Ferguson and Fergus,* (Edinburgh, 1895).

6. David M. Stewart, *Sketches of the Character, Manners and present State of the Highlanders of Scotland…,* Vol. II, (Edinburgh: [reprint 1822 edition] 1977), Appendix KK, lvii. [hereafter *Sketches*] There is an 1897 water colours by W. S. Cumming, allegedly of Reverend Adam Ferguson kneeling beside a wounded soldier, a Highland broadsword at his waist, in the Black Watch Museum at Balhousie Castle in Perth. A black and white reproduction appears in Eric and Andros Linklater's *The Black Watch: The History of the Royal Highland Regiment,* (London: 1977), 26.

7. Records of the Presbytery of Dunkeld, 1745, NLS; Jane B. Fagg, *The Ministry of Adam Ferguson,* University of North Carolina PhD thesis, (1968), 3; Stewart, *Sketches,* I, 292-93n.

8 Gideon Murray (1710-1778), third son of Lord Elibank and Elizabeth "Bare Betty" Stirling. Educated at Musselburgh school, he matriculated at Balliol College, Oxford, on 24 January 1728. Intended originally for the army, he turned towards the Church and entered Holy Orders from Oxford, 28 December 1733, becoming MA, 6 June 1735. He served as Chaplain

to the Earl of Stair during operations in Germany in 1743 and was present at the battle of Dettingen in June of that year. He was commissioned Chaplain to the 42nd in 1739 and served in that capacity until 1745. Clerical appointments included Vicar of Gainsborough, Lincoln; Prebendary of Corringham and Stow in Lincoln Cathedral; and Prebendary of the Third Stall in Durham Cathedral 20 August 1761 at which time he was made a Doctor of Divinity. Tradition has it that the Jacobite leanings of his brothers Patrick and Alexander spoiled any chances he had of obtaining a bishopric. Col. Arthur C. Murray, *The Five Sons of "Bare Betty,"* (London: 1936), 85-6; an oil portrait of Gideon Murray is reproduced on page facing 86 in aforesaid book.

9. Robert Macpherson to William Macpherson, 21 December 1761, Berthier, Québec, *JGP*; *British Army Lists* [hereafter *BAL*].

10. A younger brother, Ensign George Maclagan, was commissioned in the 42nd on 27 Jan 1756 and resigned under a cloud in 16 May 1757. Ensign Maclagan appears to have been a quarrelsome drunk and other junior officers eventually refused to do duty with him. John Campbell, Lord Loudon, personally noted in a list of commissions sent to the Duke of Cumberland 3 June 1757 that Maclagan "had suffered himself to ill use," that "the Regt refused to do duty with him" and he subsequently, "Resigned his Commission." Loudon noted that volunteer Peter Grant had been given the vacancy upon paying 50 pounds "to cary Ensign Maclagon home." Quoted in Stanley Pargellis, ed., *Military Affairs in North America 1758-1763: Selected Documents from the Cumberland Papers in Windsor Castle*, (London & New York: 1936), 362.

11. In 1756, the Black Watch's knowledge of North American geography was limited. The men merely knew they would be fighting the French and hence Maclagan's mention of "routing and extirpating every Monsieur who leaps over the St Lawrence River" in an early verse of the song. However by verse 14, the subject matter of the song has drastically changed and talks about returning home to Scotland after many years away, a very good indication that this song is a composite to which later verses were added to provide a chronological and oral record of the regiment's service. When Maclagan took up his post at the Ohio Forks in 1764, his homesick flock had been in North America for eight years and would remain for another three. The verse's lines are crafted to reassure the Highland soldiers of the 42nd that they will not be forgotten in the wilderness and their duty is almost at an end. "After leaving them with peace and all/the goodness that comes with it/ . . . about the lovely Ohio of many bends/You will return to your residences/Going across the ocean with rhythmic pipe music/with merry rejoicing. . . ." There was no way Maclagan would have known the regiment would be stationed on the Ohio in his 1756 composition. This habit of adding new verses to an existing song is seen more clearly in the Gaelic song "*At the Siege of Quebec, 1759*" which chronicles the exploits of the 78th Foot (Frasers' Highlanders). Newton, *Indians*, 124-7, 131-36. Maclagan is listed as one of the participant in peace talks with Shawnee, Delaware and Iroquois Indians at Fort Pitt, 9-10 June 1766. See Croghan to

Gage, 15 June 1766, Clements Library, *Gage Papers*, American Series, Vol.52; Reel 10; *BL*, Add. MSS. 21634: f.178c.

12. Newton, *Indians*, 127.

13. Reverend Harry (Henry) Munro was born 1730 in Dingwall, Scotland, son of Dr. Robert Munro of Dingwall and Anne Munro (1718-1748). Harry Munro married three times. His first wife, the widow of a regimental officer of the 77th Foot, died in 1760 leaving him with an infant daughter, Elizabeth. In 1762, on his return from the West Indies, he married a "Miss Stockton" from Princeton, New Jersey and built a house there. She died bearing him a son a year later. During the 1760s, Munro's religious beliefs had evolved to a point where he went to England to pursue Anglican Holy Orders. Munro was ordained in the Church of England in 1765 and returned to America where he conducted a mission on Philipsburgh Manor in Westchester County. In 1766, he met and married his third wife, 38-year-old Eva Jay - the sister of the American lawyer (and later Revolutionary War patriot) John Jay. In 1768 he became rector of St. Peter's Church, Albany, and, at Sir William Johnson's request, acted as missionary to the Mohawk Indians at Fort Hunter. In 1770, he was appointed chaplain at Albany with an annual salary of fifty pounds and received an honorary M.A. degree from Kings College in 1772. During that time, he sought to develop his wartime bounty land - 2,000 acres "between the Hudson River and Lake Champlain" called "Munrosfield." He built a large cabin there (later the town of Hebron) and held summertime services for the many ex-soldiers of the 77th and other regiments that had settled there on disbandment. However, his subdivision of the tract into smaller farms in 1774 found few takers. His son later sold the patent. As the situation between Crown and colonists deteriorated, Munro found himself more at home at the Fort Hunter Mohawk mission than at Albany. St. Peter's Church ceased operations in 1776 with his arrest and other prominent Tories. In October 1777, Munro and others escaped the Albany jail and fled north to join the British army in Montréal. After serving briefly as a military chaplain to the King's Royal New Yorkers, Munro sailed for England in 1778 leaving his wife and only son behind. He preached in London and studied languages, intending to return to America when the war was finished but the success of American arms discouraged him. When his wife declined to join him and remained with the Jay family in Westchester, Munro decided to retire in Scotland. Suffering a stroke in 1791 that partially paralyzed him, he moved from the countryside to Edinburgh where he died in 1801. Edward F. De Lancey, "Memoir of the Reverend Dr. Harry Munro, The Last Rector of St. Peter's Church, Albany, under the English Crown," *New York Genealogical and Biographical Society*, 4:113-24.

14. Born 19 December 1731, Robert Macpherson, y^r of Banchor, was the third of six sons of John Macpherson of Bancho, and the first son of the second marriage to Christian Macpherson.

15. Robert MacFarlane, "The Macdonells of Arerarder," *Clan Donald Magazine*, No. 12 (1991); *Sketches of the Old Seats of Families and Distinguished Soldiers, Etc.*, 335-36.

"War Dance" – This painting shows a Highland soldier performing a sword dance. Dancers were not to touch the blades of the sword while performing the intricate footwork of the dance. (Courtesy, Robert Griffing & Paramount Press)

Essay Three

"An Instrument of War":
Pipers of the Highland Regiments in Colonial North America, 1756-1767

by Dr. William M. Forbes, PhD Ed.

In the aftermath of the failed Jacobite rebellion of 1745-1746, trials were held to pass sentence on captured Rebels. Such a trial was held in York in September of 1746, during which, one James Reid was tried for being a piper in Ogilvy's Regiment, raised and rallied in Angus for the Stewart cause. Though witnesses for the Crown clearly testified that Reid had never borne arms against the Government, and the jury subsequently made a recommendation to the court that he be acquitted, the court surprisingly rejected the recommendation and rendered the following verdict:

> every person who joined any Set of People engaged in an open Rebellion, tho' they did not bear Arms, they were guilty of High Treason; that no regiments ever marched without Musical instruments, as Drums, Trumpets of the like; and that in a Highland Regiment there was no moving without a Piper, and therefore his Bagpipe, in the Eye of the Law, was an Instrument of War.

The court then found Reid guilty of high treason, as charged, and he was executed 15 November 1746, thus establishing a precedent for evermore that, the pipes were an integral part of Highland regiments and were to be regarded henceforth as instruments of war, rather than as entertainment. Officially on establishment or not, pipers had always been part of Scottish regiments. Sir James Turner, who served in the 3rd Foot Guards (now Scot's Guards), recorded in his 1671 book, *Pallas Armata*, that "any Captain may keep a piper in his company, and maintain him too, for no pay is allowed him, perhaps just as much as He deserveth." He added that "the bagpipe is good enough music for them that love it, but sure not so good as the Almain whistle."

Pictorial evidence is also provided from this period in the painting *Destruction of the Mole at Tangier 1684* in which four pipers of the 1st Foot or the Royal Regiment (later the Royal Scots) are clearly depicted playing during the action.

Certainly Lord Loudoun, who was to become the Commander-in-Chief in North America, was entirely familiar with pipers. During the Jacobite Rebellion in 1745-46 he was Colonel of the 64th Foot (Loudoun's Highlanders) and as a general officer was instrumental in the raising of several of the eighteen Independent Highland companies raised to counter the rebellion, as well as the three Additional Companies of the 42nd Foot. There were numerous pipers recorded as serving in his regiment, the Independents and the Additionals.

Indeed, Donald Ban MacCrimmon of Skye, hereditary piper to the McLeods of Dunvagen, known to his contemporaries as *"The King of Pipers,"* served in Captain John MacLeod's company of Loudoun's Highlanders and was killed at the Rout of Moy on the night of 16/17 February 1746. Legend holds that MacCrimmon foresaw his own death and composed the haunting tune *Cha Till Mi Tuille* (I'll Return No More) prior to his departure on campaign.

It's not improbable that some of the pipers who served in Loudoun's regiment and the Independents also ended up in North America, but with the great similarity of names on the regimental rolls, is almost impossible to decipher with any certainty. Certainly some tantalizing glimpses of the 42nd Foot's pipers after their arrival in North America may be gleaned from provincial soldiers' diaries.

Captain Edmund Wells of the 4th Connecticut Regiment writing from Fort Edward in September 1756 was moved to record that the Highland regiment arrived with "Drum, trumpets and bagpipes going, sounding sweetly." In the same month, the 42nd musicians accompanied Lord Loudoun northwards to Fort William Henry, where they entered with "drums beating and music playing, the Highlanders in front."

One of the main duties of pipers, before the regiments deployed to North America, was to go on recruiting parties to help raise fighting men for the regiments. Given that bagpipe music was banned in the Highlands (except for those pipers in the King's service), an officer with a few dancers and a good piper in attendance, could draw large crowds of potential recruits. Lieutenant John Grant found this method to work splendidly in 1758 when recruiting for the 2nd/42nd Foot, easily filling his quota along Speyside in the northeast of Scotland.

Pipers did not lead from the front in battle, as popular paintings would have us believe, but played in the rear, urging the men forward by playing tunes which stirred their blood. The carefully selected tunes reminded the men of their homes, ancestors and past glories, encouraging them with a *Brosnachadh Catha*, an incitement to battle, or *Mir Cath*, the joyous frenzy of battle. The music of this period was primarily *Ceol Mhor*, today more generally known as *Piobaireachd*, the classical music of the bagpipe. Each clan had its own music made up primarily of Gatherings, Salutes and Laments, and the men of the clan would respond energetically and emotionally to their music whenever it was played.

Some of the tunes which would have been well known in all three regiments, given the strong influence and presence of Campbell and Macdonald men, were such tunes as: *Bodaich nam Briogas* (The Carles wi' the Breeks); *Cogadh no Sith* (War or Peace); *Cill Chriosd* (Glengarry's March); and *Piobaireachd Dhomhnuill Dubh* (Black Donald's March). The men of the 78th were no doubt familiar with *Cumha Mic Shimidh* (Lord Lovat's Lament), a more contemporary piece composed by David Fraser in 1747. However, the actual tunes that were first played in North America must remain speculative at best, though there is a strong (but undocumented) tradition that the *An Cath*

Gailbheach (The Desperate Battle) was played at Ticonderoga in 1758 by 42nd pipers.

Certainly a vast knowledge and repertoire of Highland music was represented collectively by the three Highland regiments that came to North America, each with representatives of the great piping schools of the MacCrimmons, MacArthurs, MacIntyres, MacKays, MacGregors and Rankins present in their ranks. While tracing and identifying these pipers is made problematic by the fact that many were listed on the rolls as drummers or private soldiers in order that they could be paid and fed, there are enough references and documentation of the better known pipers that we can actually identify some by name in the respective regiments.

42nd Foot (Lord John Murray's)
The Royal Highland Regiment

Although pipers were not officially recognized by the War Office in the mid-18th century, there were certainly pipers in the 42nd Foot prior to their leaving for North America in 1756. Their Colonel, Lord John Murray, outfitted them and paid their salaries out of his own purse and we find pipers listed in his company, the Colonel's, as well as the Lieutenant-Colonel's company and the Major's company. He also instructed that two pipers be sent with the recruiting parties to Scotland in January 1756 when the regiment was told off for overseas service.

Murray took great pride and interest in his pipers, and as he footed the bill, he could dress them as he pleased. In June of 1757, he sent the regiment four piper's coats, four piper's caps with red feathers and four piper's knots. This would seem to indicate that at this time he had increased his "official" establishment by one piper, perhaps adding a Pipe-Major to the three already existing company pipers. It is also interesting to note the use of the red feathers in the regiment long before the red hackle was allegedly introduced as a regimental distinction in 1795.

Later, when the 2nd Battalion was raised in 1758 and one piper was officially allowed by royal warrant to each of the battalion's grenadier companies, Murray indicated that he intended to continue two pipers on soldier's pay in each battalion in addition to the Piper Majors. He also informed Francis Grant, the commanding officer, that he wished to provide each of his regimental pipers with a distinctive embroidered silver cap and was sending over a pipe banner for each battalion of the Regiment as well.

The following list of regimental pipers is made up of men who can be definitely identified as pipers in the Regiment during the French & Indian War in North America:

John (Iain) Macdonell – The piper of Lord John Murray's Company and born in the parish of Dowally, near Dunkeld in Perthshire. He joined the regiment in 1745 and was present with the regiment at Ticonderoga in 1758. In 1801, at a very advanced age, he competed in the Highland Society of London's Competition and was noted, at that time, as being the Piper to Glengarry for some generations. Since he was the piper in the senior company of the regiment- the Colonel's - it may be safely assumed he was the Pipe Major of the regiment, and subsequently, the 1st Battalion.

David Noble – The piper of Lieutenant-Colonel's Company who hailed from Inverness. He joined the regiment in 1746 and was discharged from the regiment in 1762 after the siege of Havana, being noted as consumptive and no longer able to serve.

Hugh Ross – The piper to the Major's Company and a native of Tain in Ross-shire. While serving at Breda in Flanders in 1748, he was found guilty of being drunk and abusing the sentries at Lord Albemarle's door, and was subsequently awarded 250 lashes. His retention in a regiment which prided itself on high moral standards was probably a testament to his musical skills, for if one believes everything Stewart of Garth has ever written at face value, Ross should have been immediately discharged for disgracing the regiment.

Evan (Owen/Ewan) McIntyre – A piper from Skye who joined the regiment in 1752 and was posted to the Grenadier company. Most probably the "Owen" McIntyre referred to in Regimental Orders, 10 April 1759, at New York and appointed "Pipper-Major" of the 2nd Battalion "and is this day to receive the cloathing [sic] accordingly." He died of fever at Havana, 6 August 1762. It is also quite possible that he is the Ewan McIn-

tyre who hailed from Trotternish in Skye and was listed as one of the pipers in the Macdonald Independent Highland Companies raised to help in the suppression of the Jacobite Rebellion.

Peter (Patrick) McIntyre – A piper from Uist serving in Captain John MacNeil's company. When Evan McIntyre was made Pipe-Major to the 2nd Battalion, Peter was placed on the footing of a "Drum" and "subsisted accordingly." He later replaced Evan McIntyre as "Pipper-major" to the 2nd Battalion at the siege of Havana, 1762, and was mustered out of the regiment in 1763, his discharge noting him to be worn out and no longer fit for service.

Roderick McDonald – Born at Dingwall and apparently joined as a piper when the regiment was recruiting for North America in 1756. He served with the regiment through all its campaigns and was sent home to Scotland in 1766 with an advance recruiting party. When the regiment returned to Ireland in 1767 he was mustered out, noted as being very ill and no longer fit for service.

Donald Fraser - Noted in 42nd Rolls as being a piper and being amongst the Invalids at Albany, New York in August 1763, but "fit for Service." He stayed in the regiment when it was downsized to peace establishment in October 1763 and he was posted to Captain William Murray's company in garrison at Fort Pitt. He was still there in 1767 when the main part of the regiment had left from Philadelphia for Ireland, and his company was awaiting their relief by the 18th Foot.

77th Foot (Montgomery's Highlanders)

Robert Griffing's fine painting "Major Grant's Piper" (which adorns the cover of this book) is perhaps the most striking representation of a piper of Montgomery's Highlanders. It depicts Major James Grant's piper playing a rant on the summit of a hill with Fort Duquesne in the background, urging the men to stand firm on the morning of 14 September 1758.

Grant's force of Highlanders and provincials were surrounded in short order by a larger force of Indians and Frenchmen and defeated in detail. It is interesting to note that the artist chose to show a two-drone set of pipes. The three-drone bagpipe had been introduced sometime in the beginning of the 18th century with the addition of a third bass drone, but it is possible some of the pipers in North America were still using the older pipes with just two tenor drones.

The playing of the drums and pipes at Grant's defeat are the only mention of bagpipes being used in action by the 77th Foot. Very few named pipers can be identified as documentation is scarce for this short-lived regiment which existed for only seven years. However we do know that the initial ten companies that went over to North America each had a piper, for clothing records show that ten plaids and bonnets of the same quality as those worn by sergeants were ordered and received in the regiment in April 1757 for their exclusive use. Some pipers can be positively identified from other sources external to the regiment and are as follows:

Neil MacArthur – Born on the Isle of Skye into the famous MacArthur family, hereditary pipers to the MacDonalds, Lords of the Isles, and renowned for their piping college. Neil's son, John, later moved to Edinburgh and became known as "Professor" John MacArthur, piper to the Highland Society of Scotland. Little is known of Neil's military life, and perhaps he was loaned to the regiment, for the 77th's Colonel, Archibald Montgomery, was married to one of the sisters of Alexander MacDonald of Sleat. MacArthur unfortunately died at the siege of Havana in 1762 like so many other of his fellow Highlanders. His will was filed in the Edinburgh Commissary Court in 1767 and among his effects delivered by Capt. Alexander MacKenzie to Capt.-Lt. James Grant at Cuba on 13 August 1762, was the sum of 364 pounds, ten shillings, Scots, a considerable amount for a soldier in those days. This information might indicate that he was Capt. MacKenzie's company piper, and, given his status in the piping world, it would be also reasonable to assume that MacArthur was the Pipe Major of the regiment mentioned by Piper William Munro in a 1757 letter quoted below in his entry.

Neil McLeod – Born near Inverness circa 1707. He was disabled in the right foot at the end of the war and admitted to Chelsea Hospital, 10 May 1764, after serving a full seven years in the regiment.

John McKenzie – Born at Caithness c. 1734, and was severely wounded while serving in North America. He was admitted with fellow piper, Neil McLeod, on the same day into Chelsea Hospital, 10 May 1764.

William McMurchy – A piper and bard from Kintyre who is said to have been a piper in Montgomery's. In *The History of Kintyre* by Peter MacIntosh (1786-1876) published in 1861, several vague references are made concerning a musician and poet called William McMurchy, stating he was one of the pipers to MacDonald of Largie in 1745. It may be significant that Alexander Campbell, appointed Chamberlain and Baillie of North and South Kintyre by the Duke of Argyle on 11 November 1767, knew McMurchy well, and collected several ancient Gaelic poems and songs from the former piper for the Highland Society. Campbell had been a lieutenant in the 77th Foot (Montgomery's) commissioned an ensign in an Additional company of Montgomery's Highlanders in 1759 and had reached a position as adjutant by August 1763 (see 77th Register, Part One).

William Munro – A deeply religious young soldier who was not a piper when he entered the 77th Foot in 1757. In a letter written to his father from Cork dated 9 June 1757 however, he cheerfully announced: *"The Colonel paid Two Guineas to the Pipe Major for learning me. Captain Munro has no piper, and Lieutenant* [Archibald] *Robertson, the Colonel and Captain Munro all promised that I would be in their company how soon I am learned."* The fate of this novice bagpiper is unknown. Captain George Munro was killed by Indians at Fort Duquesne the following year and Lt. Robertson was wounded but escaped with some of the Highlanders and made it back to the safety of the regiment.

78th Foot (Fraser's Highlanders)

In 1816, Simon Fraser of Knockie, the son of John Fraser of Errogie, a former 78th officer who was renowned for his singing and knowledge of ancient Gaelic tunes and airs, published many of his father's and friend's tunes in a collection called *The Airs and Melodies Peculiar to the Highlands of Scotland and the Isles.*

A key contributor, besides Knockie's father, was Captain Alexander Fraser of Culduthel, who was a collector himself and an accomplished singer (see 78th Register in Part One for John and Alexander). Contained within his collection were several pipe reels and airs that might have been played by the pipers or fiddlers of Fraser's Highlanders off-duty in their barracks or encampments.

According to the notes which accompany the tunes, many of them had North American connections to the various French & Indian campaigns of the 78th Foot. For example, one of the tunes, No. 95, *An t-aiseadh do dh'Eiran* (Crossing to Ireland) has the following note: "The editor discovered this air in an ancient manuscript in the possession of his father, of some of the band music of the 78th Regiment to which he belonged." The same note indicates that a MacArthur was master of the band, perhaps signifying that this was the name of the pipe-major but there were quite a few MacArthurs in the regiment according to rolls and no definitive indications that any of them were actually pipers.

The use of the word "band" raises an interesting point since there were no official Highland pipe bands until the time of the Crimean War in 1874. But here, we have a reference to a band in the 78th, and we also have documentation that the 42nd played with "Drum, trumpets and bagpipes going, sounding sweetly" on their arrival at Fort Edward in 1756. And while pipers considered themselves purely musicians, the merging of pipe reels and tunes with drum-beatings and the development of quick marches separately from the *Ceol Mhor*, might be directly attributable to the fact that many of the pipers during the Seven Years War had to be carried on the regimental rolls as drummers and were required to fulfil that function **in addition** [author's emphasis] to their piping duties.

Of all the Highland regiments during this period, the pipers of Fraser's Highlanders are the most elusive. During the Jacobite Uprising of 1745-46, there were two pipers in the Fraser of Lovat regiment, nominally led by Simon, Master of Lovat, but wisely absent at the battle of Culloden. They were David and William Fraser.
David, born in 1716, was Lord Lovat's personal piper. He had signed an indenture in 1743 binding himself for seven years to Lord Lovat who, in return, sent by him for seven years tutelage at the MacCrimmon school in Skye. It was David Fraser who composed the lament *Cumha Mhic Shimidh* on the execution of Lord Lovat in 1747.

It is also quite possible that David Fraser accompanied Simon Fraser to North America and could easily be another candidate (in addition to MacArthur previously mentioned) for pipe major of the regiment. However, there is no definitive documentary evidence of his presence in the regiment, nor of William Fraser, though many David and William Frasers feature in the muster rolls.

Another possible piper recruited for the 78th was the Private Donald MacCrimmon of the Colonel's company who appears on *"A Return of the Sick men of the First Highland Battalion left in the Hospital at Corke"* in May 1757. His service was short, for weakened by dysentery and fever, Dr. Allen Stuart, the regimental surgeon discharged him from the Regiment.

There are two 78th pipers however, who can be positively identified:

Alexander McIntyre - Returns from Stratford dated 14 December 1757 show that Sergeant Thompson's grenadier company, consisting of "1 Captain, 2 Lieutenants, 4 sergeants, 2 drummers, 97 men, 7 women victuallers, Lieutenant Cuthbert's servant, Alexander McErtar [McIntyre] musician" shared the town with Colonel Fraser's own company numbering "1 Captain, 1 Lieutenant, 1 Ensign, 4 Sergeants, 3 drummers, 104 men, 6 women victuallers."
The afore-mentioned Alexander McIntyre, musician, was, of course, the grenadier company's piper, an important man in the regiment. The McIntyres, hereditary pipers of Clan Menzies, were almost as legendary as the MacCrimmons of Skye, and other kinsmen of Alexander of the 78th —Ewen and Peter McIntyre of the 42nd Foot (see above)—were also serving as pipers in North America.

Archibald MacDonald - Born near Inverness, Piper MacDonald was wounded in the right arm and eventually admitted to Chelsea Hospital, 8 September 1761. He later served as a piper in one of the Invalid Companies. If the *Memoirs* of the Grenadier Sergeant James Thompson are to be taken at face value, the regiment had only one piper by 1759 which may explain the difficulty in identifying any more pipers. At the battle of the Plains of Abraham at Québec in September 1759, Thompson confirms the presence of at least one piper in the regiment, claiming that the unnamed musician shamed himself at the battle, but entirely vindicated himself the following year by his conduct at the battle of Sillery (Ste Foy) in April 1760. (see Volume One,

Chapter Ten). Thompson remembered for the first battle

> we had but one Piper and because he was not provided with arms and the usual means of defence like the rest of the men, was made to keep aloof for safety – When our lines advanced to the charge . . . General [James Murray] observing that the Piper was missing and he knowing full well the value of one on such occasions, he sent in all directions for him and he was heard to say aloud: "Where's the Highland Piper?" and "Five pounds for a piper," but de'il did the piper come forward the sooner. However, the charge by good chanse [sic] was pretty well effected without him. For this business the Piper was disgraced by the whole of the Regiment, and the men would not speak to him, neither would they suffer his rations to be drawn with theirs, but had them served out separately by the Commissary, and he was obliged to shift for himself as well he could.

Ostracized for a half year, the piper made sure he marched out to do battle on a cold grey April morning in 1760, as General Murray's army, including 400 very sickly Highlanders, formed up to meet an approaching French army. Legend has it that the impetuous Murray had forbidden the use of pipes at this battle where the general's personal ambition and recklessness caused him to forsake good defensive ground and move too far forward.

When the British army's flanks were overwhelmed, James Thompson says the young Highlanders *"got into a great disorder"* during the British retreat and became *"more like a mob than regular soldiers."* But *"as soon as the Piper discovered that his men [were] scatter'd and . . . in disorder . . . he luckily bethought himself to give them a blast of his pipes,"* recalled Thompson. *"This had the effect of stopping them short and they soon allow'd themselves to be form'd into some sort of order. For this opportune blast of his Chainters, the piper gain'd back the forgiveness of the regiment and was allow'd to take his meals with his old messmates, as if nothing at all had happen'd."*

This is probably the wounded Macdonald who presented himself at Chelsea Hospital five months later.

PRIMARY SOURCES

Airs and Melodies Peculiar to the Highlands of Scotland and the Isles, 1816, Simon Fraser, ed.

Anon., "Anonymous Journal Fragment, 1756," *American Antiquarian Society.*

Anon., *A True and Impartial Account of the Trials of the Rebels at York, upon the Special Commission of Oyer and Terminer and Goal Delivery, begun September 29, 1746, and continued by several Adjournments,* (York, 1746).

"Diary of Captain Edward Wells of Connecticut, 1756," in Earl and Jean Stott, eds.,

Exploring Rogers Island, (Fort Edward, New York, 1986).

Murray, Lord John, Lord John Murray's Papers, *Bagshawe Muniments,* John Rylands Library, University of Manchester.

National Archives, Kew.

WO 12/5478, "Muster Rolls of the 1st Battalion Royal Highlanders."

WO 12/5553, "Muster Rolls of the 2nd Battalion Royal Highlanders."

WO 34/64, Amherst Papers.

WO 120/4 & 6, Chelsea Regimental Registers

National Archives of Scotland

Grant, John, "Journal of Lt John Grant, 2nd Battalion, 42nd Foot," *Register House,* 4/77, [Microfilm].

(Robertson of Kindeace Papers) GD 146/11.

The MacArthur-MacGregor Manuscript., Francis Buisman, ed., (Glasgow, 2001).

Robertson, Lieutenant Alexander, 77th Foot, Selected Correspondence, transcribed by Dr. Scott Stephenson, *Ballindalloch Papers,* Ballindalloch Castle.

SECONDARY SOURCES

Donaldson, William, *The Highland Pipe and Scottish Society,* (Edinburgh, 2000).

Gibson, J. C., *Traditional Gaelic Bagpiping, 1745-1945,* (Kingston-Montréal, 1998).

Irvin, George, *The Art of Robert Griffing: His Journey into the Eastern Frontier,* (Gibsonia, Pennsylvania, 2000).

Livingstone, Alastair, *et al.* (eds.), *No Quarter Given,* (Glasgow, 2001).

MacKay, Angus, *A Collection of Ancient Piobaireachd or Highland Pipe Music,* (Edinburgh, 1838).

MacLeod, R.H., "The MacCrimmons and the '45," *Piping Times,* Vol. 29, No. 6, (March, 1977).

_____, "Drums and Pipes in the Royal Army, 1745," *Piping*

Times, Vol. 32, No. 10, (July, 1980); Vol. 32, No. 12, (September, 1980); Vol. 33, No. 1, (October, 1980).

Murray, David, *Music of the Scottish Regiments*, (Edinburgh, 1994.)

Ramsay, John, of Ochtertyre. "Of the Influence of Poetry and Music upon the Highlands," in Patrick MacDonald, *A Collection of Highland Airs*, (1784).

Sanger, Keith, "Neil McArthur," *Piping Times*, Vol. 38, No. 9, (June 1986).

Turner, James, "*Pallas Armata, 1671*" quoted in, *Scots Guards Standard Settings of Pipe Music*, (Edinburgh, 1954).

Wallace, Col. R. F. H., "*42nd Foot Regimental Routine and Army Administration in North America in 1759*," *JSAHR*, 30, (1952).

PART FOUR

Regimental Muster Rolls
& Returns

The following is a collection of muster rolls & returns from various sources (as annotated) and are presented by seniority of regiment and in chronological order.

42nd Foot (Royal Highlanders)

I. *"Company Return at Lake George Camp - Ticonderoga Oct. 24, 1758"*

Captain: James Murray (wounded)
Lieut: Kenneth Tolmie (detached to engineers).
Lieut: David Milne, (wounded)
Ensign: Charles Menzies
Sergeant: James McNabb
Sergeant: John McAndrews
Sergeant: John Watson
Sergeant: Alexander Cumming
Corporal: John Cumming
Corporal: Jonathan Grant
Corporal: Angus McDonald, Corporal
Corporal: John Stewart
Drummer: Walter McIntyre – Killed-8th July 1758- (probably a piper)
Drummer: Allan Campbell

Privates:

William Anderson
Angus Cameron
William Carmichael
 Hugh Christie
Alexander Cumming
Hugh Fraser
Alexander Fraser
Donald Fraser (1)
Donald Fraser (2)

Killed at Battle of Ticonderoga, 8th July 1758:

John Buchanan
Hugh Cameron
Donald Carr
James Farquharson
Hugh Fraser
Archibald McDonald
James McDonald
William McDonald
Peter McFarlane (2)
James McIntyre
John McKenzie (2)
Dougall McLachlan
Norman McLeodDonald McNeil
Hugh Ross
John Sinclair, died of wounds
Charles Stewart, died of wounds
Donald Stewart, died of wounds
Walter Stewart, died of wounds

II. Roll of Capt James Murray's *"Additional"* Company, November 1758, stationed at Fort Edward, and thus not present at the battle of Ticonderoga.

Sergeant: William Grant
Sergeant: Charles Robinson
Sergeant: John McQueen
Corporal: John Leslie
Corporal: Robert Lachlan
Drummer: Allan Campbell

Privates:

George Bremner
Donald Brown
Duncan Cameron
John Campbell
Donald Conacher
William Cowie
James Douglas
Donald Drummond
James Duncan
Alexander Fraser (1)
Alexander Fraser (2)
William Fife
Robert Grant
Alexander Irvine
James Kennedy
Duncan McAndrew
Donald McDiarmid
Archibald McDonald (1)
Archibald McDonald (2)
Donald McDonald
John McDonald
William McDonald
Peter McFarlane
Alexander McIntosh
Robert McIntosh (1)
Robert McIntosh (2)
William McIntosh
Donald McLean (1)
Donald McLean (2)
Thomas McNab
Alexander McPherson
Donald McRaw
Robert Menzies
William Monroe
John Murray
Alexander Nicholson
Alexander Norrie
Alexander Reed
Alexander Robertson
Angus Robertson
Archibald Robertson
Charles Robertson
Donald Robertson
James Robertson (1)
James Robertson (2)
John Robertson
Peter Robertson
James Scroggie
Alexander Stewart (1)
Alexander Stewart (2)
Alexander Stewart (3)
Robert Stewart
Thomas Stewart
John Wighton (1)
John Wighton (2)

These two rolls were taken from *"Chronicles of the Atholl and Tullibardine Families."* Collected and arranged by John, Seventh Duke of Atholl, K.T., ed., Vol. III, (Ballantyle Press, 1908), 440.

III. *"Return of a Detachment of the 42nd & 77th Regiments that are left at Albany under the command of Lieut. Schaw of the 17th Regt."* September, 1763.

Company	Rank/Name
42nd	
General's	Pte James Macpherson
Col. Reid's	Sgt Alex^r Grant
	Pte Finlay McDonald
	Pte James Fraser
	Pte Hector McWilliam
Capt Murray's	Pte Finlay Grant
Capt Stewart's	Sgt. James McNabb
	Drm^r Donald Fraser
Capt Abercromby's	Pte Alex^r Forbes
Capt Grant's	Corp^l Chas Robertson
	Pte Robt McDonald
	Pte Donald Stewart
	Pte Peter Grant
Capt Graham's	Pte Duncan Munro
	Pte Paul McFarland
Capt Jn Campbell's	Pte Donald McKay
	Drm^r Andrew McEachern
77th	
Maj. Zobell's	Pte Malcolm Macdonald
Capt Clerke's	Drm^r David Davidson
Capt Grant's	Pte John Stewart
Capt Erving's	Pte John McMartin

IV. *Last Muster Roll of the 42nd Foot (RHR) October 25, 1766 – April 24, 1767*
Taken in Philadelphia, 29 April 1767, before its return to Ireland.

Company No. 1
Lieut. Gen. Murray, Col. (Absent with Leave)
Capt-Lieut. Patrick Balneavis
Lieut. James Eddington
James Maclagan, Chaplain
Alex^r Donaldson, Adjutant
Duncan Campbell, Q^r M^r (promoted 3 Sept. 1766)
Charles Graham, Q^r M^r (resigned 3 Sept, 1766)
Alex^r Potts, Surgeon
James Murdoch, Mate
Sgt. James Campbell
Sgt. Colin Smith, (Ft. Pitt)
Cpl. Duncan Mann
Cpl. Roderick McLean

Privates: 18 Present / 12 Absent
30 Total

Company No. 2
Gordon Graham, Lt. Col.
Lieut. George Rigg
Lieut. John McIntosh
Sgt. Leonard McGlasheen
Sgt. Normand McDonald
Cpl. Duncan Cameron, (Ft. Pitt)
Cpl. Duncan Mcgregor, (Ft. Pitt)
Drm^r Donald Fraser, (Fort Pitt)

Privates: 14 Present / 21 Absent
35 Total

Company No. 3
Major John Reid, (New York)
Lieut. George Grant, (Ft. Pitt)
Ens. John Rutherford
Sgt. James Nicolson, (Ft.Pitt)
Sgt. John Ross, (Sick)
Cpl. Alex^r Munroe
Cpl. William Simpson, (Ft. Pitt)
Drm^r Dougal Robinson

Privates: 20 Present /12 Absent
32 Total

Company No. 4
Capt. Thomas Graham (Absent by leave)
Lieut. John Smith (Absent by leave)
Ensn. Peter Herring
Sgt. David Reid
Sgt. Arch'd Fraser
Cpl. John Munro, (on Party)
Cpl. Alex Norrie, (on Party)
Drm^r Alex. Shaw, (on Party)

Privates: 24 Present / 13 Absent
37 Total

Company No. 5
Capt. William Grant
Lt. Charles Grant
Ensn. Thomas Hall
Sgt. Hugh Fraser
Sgt. David Munro
Cpl. John Grant
Cpl. Alex. McDonald

Privates: 31 Present / 6 Absent
37 Total

Company No. 6
Capt. James Murray (Britain)
Lieut. Alex.ʳ· Donaldson
Ensn. Daniel Astle (Britain, Not
  Joined)
Sgt Donald Munro
Sgt. John Smith
Cpl. Nathaniel Manson, (Bedford)
Cpl. Duncan McMartin

Privates: 20 Present / 15 Absent
35 Total

Company No. 7
Capt. William Murray, (Ft. Pitt)
Lieut. Alex.ʳ McKay, (Ft. Pitt)
Lieut. Nathaniel McCulloch
Sgt. Lachlan McLean
Sgt Andrew Smith, (Ft. Pitt)
Cpl. Normand MacLeod, (Ft. Pitt)
Cpl. Allan Stewart
Drmʳ Donald McLean

Privates: 25 Present / 13 Absent
38 Total

Company No. 8
Capt. John Stewart
Lieut. Charles Graham, (Britain)
Ensn. John Peebles, (on Party)
Sgt. Alex. McLean
Sgt. Charles Muir, (on Party)
Cpl. Donald McKay, (on Party)
Cpl. Donald McIntosh, (on Party)

Privates: 26 Present / 8 Absent
 34 Total

Company No. 9
Capt. Thomas Stirling
Lieut. John Robertson, (Absent by
  leave)
Lieut. James Rumsey, (resigned, Aug.
  26, 1766)
Ensn. Richard Nicholls Colden
  (appointed, Aug. 27, 1766)
Sgt. Thomas Leslie
Sgt Alexander Sinclair
Cpl. George McKay
Cpl. Hugh Fraser
Drmr Roderick McDonald
  (Recruiting in Britain)

Privates: 33 Present / 1 Absent
34 Total

Recapitulation
Privates: 211 present (Philadelphia)
101 Absent (Fort Pitt) / 312 Total

**78th Regiment of Foot (Fraser's
Highlanders)**

**I. *A LIST OF THE INVALIDS of
the 78th Regiment Unfit for any
Sort of Duty, September 1763.***

[WO 34/2:f.132], (i.e. Soldiers
unsuitable for drafting into other
regiments upon disbandment).

Col Fraser's Company

Private Murdoch McKenzie

Major Abercrombie's Company

Private Donald McDonald
Private John Anderson
Private Alexander McKay
Private John McIver
Private John MacLeod
Private Donald Ross

Major Campbell's Company

Cpl. John Campbell
Private Duncan Campbell
Private Robert Munro
Private John Kennedy
Private John Ferguson
Private James Lamb
Private Donald Cameron
Private Kenneth McLeod
Private Peter Hill
Private John Clerk

Capt. John McDonald's Company

Private Donald McDonald
Private Donald Stuart
Private John McDonell

Capt. Simon Fraser's Company

Private John McKay
Private Alexander Cormack
Private Hector McNeill
Private Donald Munro

Capt. Hugh Fraser's Company

Private Samuel Cameron
Private Archibald McQueen

Capt. Hugh Cameron's Company

Drummer Donald Gun
Private Alexander Fraser
Private Evan McMillan
Private George Sutherland
Private James Rhind
Private Alexander McDougal
Private John Law
Private Alexander Ramsay
Private John McPhie
Private Donald McAllister
Private John Fraser

Capt. John Fraser's Company

Private Donald McGrower
Private Hugh McFormit
Private John McKenzie

Capt. John Nairn's Company

Sergeant John McKay
Private Alexander Munroe

Private John McDonell
Private James Henderson
Private William Ross

**Capt. Alexander Campbell's
Company**

Private Donald Macpherson
Private Donald Macpherson

**Capt. Archibald Campbell's
Company**

Private Donald Black
Private Lachlan McIntosh
Private David Gollan
Private John Brown
Private John Fraser
Private William Ross

**II. DISBANDMENT MUSTER
ROLL OF 78TH REGIMENT OF
FOOT**
Note: * An asterisk beside a name
indicates one of the 170 NCOs and
men of the 78th Regiment (Fras-
er's Highlanders) discharged in
North America, September 1763.

**The Colonel's Company (The
Hon. Simon Fraser)**

Capt-Lieut: Donald McBain
Lieut: Simon Fraser
Surgeons Mate: Donald. Morrison
Ensign: Malcolm Fraser
*Drum Major: Alexander Kennedy**
*Sergeant: Alexander Fraser **
*Sergeant: Donald Fraser **
*Sergeant: Donald Gray**
*Corporal: Thomas Fraser**
Corporal: John Grant
*Corporal: Thomas Reid**
Drummer: Thomas Gunn

Privates
  William Anderson
  Alexander Cameron
  Alexander Cameron
  Alexander Cameron
  Donald Cameron
  Donald Cameron
  Donald Cameron
  Donald Cameron
  Donald Cameron
  Donald Cameron
  Donald Cameron
  John Cameron
  *Thomas Cameron**
  William Cameron
  William Cameron
  William Cameron
  Duncan Cummins
  *Hugh Forbes**
  William Forbes
  *Alexander Fraser**
  Hugh Fraser
  *John Fraser**

John Fraser
John Fraser
John Fraser
John Fraser
Thomas Fraser
Thomas Fraser
Thomas Fraser
John Gunn
Mary Kennedy
*Thomas Maitland**
Donald McBain
John McBain
Alexander McDonald
Alexander McDonell
Peter McDonell
Ronald McDonell
William McDonald
Peter McGregor
Alexander McKay
Alexander McKay
Colin McKay
Donald McKenzie
Donald McKenzie
Murdoch McKenzie
Evan McPhie
John Reid
*Robert Robertson**
Alexander Ross
Hugh Ross
Ann Simpson
*John Simpson**
Walter Simpson
William Stewart
Donald Thompson

**The First Major's Company
(Major Abercrombie's)**

Major: James Abercrombie
Lieut: John Chisholm
Ensign: Kenneth McCulloch
Sergeant: John Campbell
Sergeant: Duncan McPhie
*Sergeant: Hugh Tulloch**
Corporal: Finlay Fraser
*Corporal: Donald McKenzie**
*Corporal: Allan Shaw**
*Drummer: John McDonell**

Privates
  *John Anderson**
  Neil Beaton
  Donald Cameron
  John Clarke
  Alexander Fraser
  Alexander Fraser
  Charles Fraser
  Donald Fraser
  Donald Fraser
  Duncan Fraser
  *Hugh Fraser**
  Hugh Fraser
  James Fraser
  James Fraser
  John Fraser
  John Fraser
  John Fraser

William Fraser*
David Fullerton
Archibald Henderson
Archibald Henderson
Duncan Kennedy
George McAdam*
Neil McArthur
Evan McBean
Andrew McCulloch
Colin McCulloch
James McCulloch
Jean McCulloch
Donald McDonald*
Donald McDonald
Eliza McDonald
John McDonald
John McDonald
William McGillivrae
Gregor McGregor
Peter McIntyre
Alexander McKay
Alexander McKenzie
Charles McKenzie
Duncan McKenzie
Evan McLachlin*
John McLeod*
Evan McMillan
John McMillan
Alexander McPherson
Angus McPherson
Donald McPhie
Donald Ross
Thomas Ross
Hugh Shaw
John Sumner

The 2nd Major's Company
(John Campbell *Barr Breac's*)

Major: John Campbell
Lieut: James Henderson
Lieut: John McDonell
Chaplain: Robert McPherson
Surgeon: Lachlan McPherson
Sergeant: William Fraser*
Sergeant: John McAllum
Sergeant: George Thompson*
Corporal: Allan Cameron*
Corporal: John Campbell*
Corporal: Duncan McFarlane
Drummer: Donald Black
Drummer: Donald McDonald

Privates

Archibald Buchanan
Alexander Cameron
Angus Cameron*
Donald Cameron
Donald Cameron
Evan Cameron*
Kenneth Cameron
Colin Campbell
Donald Campbell
Duncan Campbell
Mary Campbell
Thomas Campbell
John Clarke

John Duffie
Andrew Ferguson
Duncan Ferguson
John Ferguson
Malcolm Ferguson
Roderick Ferguson
William Fraser
Duncan Gillis
Mary Gillis
John Gray
William Grubb
Colin Henderson
Donald Henderson*
Peter Hill
Donald Innes
John Kennedy*
John Kennedy
James Lamb
John Livingston
Alexander McArthur
Allen McArthur
Donald McArthur
John McArthur
Donald McCulean
Donald McDonald
Allen McDougall
Donald McGillivray*
Donald McIntyre
Duncan McIntyre
James McKenzie
John McKenzie
Kenneth McKenzie*
John McKinnon
Duncan McLachlin
Kenneth McLeod
Malcolm McLeod
Donald McMillan
John McMillan
John McNicol
Lachlan McQuarry
John Munro
Robert Munro
Lachlan Sinclair
Donald Thompson
Donald Thompson

Captain John MacDonell
Lochend's Company

Captain: John Macdonell
Lieut: Alex. Fraser
Lieut: Arch. McAllister
Sergeant: Donald Campbell*
Sergeant:Alex. McDonald*
Sergeant: James Thompson*
Corporal: Donald Fraser*
Corporal: John McMillan
Corporal: Will. Porterfield*
Drummer: Thomas Fraser*
Drummer: James Hamilton*

Privates

Alexander Baine
Andrew Calder
Andrew Caman
Angus Cameron
Donald Cameron

Donald Cameron
Donald Cameron
Duncan Cameron
John Cameron
John Cameron
David Campbell
John Chisholm
Alexander Dunbar
Alexander Ferguson
John Ferguson
John Fisher
Donald Forbes
Hugh Fraser
John Fraser
John Fraser
John Fraser*
William Fraser*
William Gow
Lewis Grant
William Harley
Ranald Johnson
Phanis Knowles
James Lawson
John Livingston
Allan McArthur*
Alexander McCauley
Alexander McDonell
Alexander McDonell
Alexander McDonell
Angus McDonell
Donald McDonell
Ewen McDonell
James McDonell
John McDonell
John McDonell
John McDonell
John McDonell
John McDonell
Samuel McDonell
Arch McDougall
Evan McGillivray*
Peter McGregor
Angus McIntosh
John McIntyre
John McKay
Peter McKay
Alexander McLeod
Betty McMillan
Evan McMillan
Duncan McMillan
Angus McNeil
Alexander Munro
Roderick McNeil
Donald Ross
John McPherson*
Peter Stuart
Neil McPhie
James Thompson
William Mills
Alexander Tolmie
Robert Morris

Captain Alexander McLeod
Balmaneach's Company

Captain: Alexander McLeod

Lieut: Donald Cameron
Lieut: Alexander Fraser
Ensign: Kenneth Stewart
Sergeant: James Carmichael*
Sergeant: James Gordon*
Sergeant: Angus McDonell*
Sergeant: Alex. McNaughton*
Sergeant: James Sinclair*
Corporal: James Carmichael
Corporal: Duncan McArthur
Corporal: Malcolm McNaughton
Drummer: Rory McDonell*
Drummer: Donald Munro

Privates

Neil Brown
Malcolm Cameron
Duncan Campbell*
Finlay Campbell
John Davidson
Angus Eackhorn
John Eackhorn
John Eackhorn
John Fletcher
Donald Fraser
James Fraser
John Gillis
Donald Gillivray
Alex McDonald
Allen McDonald
Allen McDonald
Allan McDonell*
Allan McDonell*
Angus McDonald
Archibald McDonald
Donald McDonald
Donald McDonald
Evan McDonald
John McDonald
John McDonald
John McDonald
Rory McDonald
William McDonald
Donald McIntyre
John McIntyre
John McIver
Donald McKay
Jennet McKay
Finlay McKenzie
Evan McKinnon
Catherine McKirdy
William McKirdy
Dougal McLachlan
John McLean
Nicholas McLean
Rory McLellan
Alexander McLeod
Alexander McLeod
Andrew McLeod
Donald McMillan
John McMillan
Donald McNiel
Donald McNiel
Chas McPherson
Mal McPherson
John McPhie

John McTavish
John Robertson
Robert Ross
Mary Sinclair
Donald Smith
John Stuart
John Stuart

Captain Hugh Cameron's Company

Captain: Hugh Cameron
Lieut: Malcolm Fraser*
Lieut. Robert Menzies
Ensign: James McQueen
Sergeant: Gilbert Anderson*
Sergeant: Allan Cameron*
Sergeant: George McKenzie*
Corporal: Evan Cameron*
Corporal: Roderick Fraser*
Corporal: John Lamb*
Drummer: Duncan McKenzie*

Privates
   John Beaton
   Donald Cameron
   Donald Cameron
   Evan Cameron
   Evan Cameron
   Evan Cameron
   Evan Cameron
   John Cameron
   John Cameron
   John Cameron
   William Cameron
   William Cameron
   Douglas Campbell
   John Campbell
   John Chisholm*
   William Chisholm
   Alexander Fletcher
   Alexander Fraser
   James Fraser
   Jeremiah Fraser
   John Fraser
   John Fraser*
   William Fraser*
   John Gibbon
   Donald Gunn
   Eliza Hunter
   James Hunter
   John Hutchinson
   John Lowe
   Duncan McCraw
   Duncan McCraw
   Alex McDonald
   Duncan McDonell*
   John McDonald
   John McDonald
   John McDonell*
   Mary McDonald
   Robert McDonald
   Alex McDougal
   John McFarlane
   John McGillivrae
   Donald McIntyre

John McIntyre
Alexander McKenzie
Robert McKinn
David McLean*
Duncan McMillan*
Evan McMillan
Evan McMillan
John McPhie
Alexander Murray
William Nichols
Alexander Ramsay
James Rhind
John Ross
George Stuart
George Sutherland*
James Taylor
George Thomson
Donald Williamson

Captain Ranald MacDonell *Keppoch's* Company

Captain: Ranald McDonell
Lieut: Charles Stewart
Ensign: Norman McLeod
Sergeant: Alex. Ferguson*
Sergeant: William Fraser*
Sergeant: Donald Stuart
Corporal: Alex. McDonell*
Corporal: Gregor McGregor
Corporal: Donald McPherson*
Corporal: John Ross*
Drummer: Grigor McGrigor*

Privates
   Evan Black*
   Angus Burke
   Donald Burke
   John Carmichail*
   Miles Carmichail*
   Donald Clarke*
   Edward Davidson*
   John Dunbar
   John Ferguson*
   Alexander Fraser
   Alexander Fraser
   Hugh Fraser
   John Fraser
   Alexander Grant*
   John Grassell
   Peter Grubb*
   John Gunn*
   Donald Irving
   Robert Keith
   Duncan Kennedy
   John Kerr
   John Livingston
   Donald McBean
   Donald McColl
   Evan McColl
   Donald McCrae
   Alexander McDonell
   Angus McDonell
   Angus McDonell
   Angus McDonell
   Archibald McDonell

Archibald McDonell
Donald McDonell
Duncan McGrigor*
John McGregor
Margaret McGregor
Donald McIntosh
Alexander McKay
Alexander McKenzie
Duncan McKenzie
Donald McKinnon
Duncan McKinnon
James McLeod
William McLeod
Angus McNabb
John McNabb
John McNair
Lachlan Mitchell
William Munro
James Ross
John Ross
Duncan Smith
Alexander Stuart
Ann Stuart
Norman Stuart
Alex Sutherland
Donald Sutherland
Donald Sutherland*
James Tavish

Captain John Fraser *Culbokie's* Company

Captain: John Fraser
Sergeant: Alexander Cameron
Sergeant: Alexander Fraser
Sergeant: Malcolm Fraser*
Sergeant: Alexander Kennedy
Sergeant: James McDonell*
Sergeant: Muir Trotter*
Corporal: Benjamin Allen*
Corporal: James Sutherland
Drummer: Thomas Fraser

Privates
   Alexander Cameron
   Alexander Cameron
   Hector Cameron
   Murdoch Cameron
   William Cameron
   John Chisholm
   John Chisholm*
   Kenneth Chisholm
   William Chisholm
   William Chisholm
   John Forbes
   James Forsyth*
   Alexander Fraser
   Donald Fraser
   Hugh Fraser
   John Fraser
   John Fraser
   John Fraser
   John Fraser
   John Fraser*
   Simon Fraser*
   William Fraser

William Fraser
John Innes
James Lawson
Alexander McBain
Duncan McCraw
Donald McDonald*
Neil McDonald
Douglas McDonell
Hugh McDonell
John McDonell
Farquhar McGillvray*
Donald McGregor
Donald McGruer
James McIntosh
John McIntosh
Donald McKay
John McKay
John McKenzie
John McKenzie
Donald McLean
John McLean
Murdoch McLean
William McNabb*
John McPherson
Alexander McTavish
Duncan McTavish
Hugh McTavish
Tavish McTavish
Hugh McTormet
Donald Munro
Catherine Noble
William Noble
James Rioch
William Stewart
John Waters

Captain Archibald Campbell's Company

Captain: Archibald Campbell
Lieut: John Arthur Rose
Ensign: Alexander Campbell
Sergeant: Simon Fraser*
Sergeant: Daniel McAlpin
Sergeant: James Robertson*
Sergeant: John Watson*
Corporal: John Campbell*
Corporal: James Gow
Corporal: Hector Ross*
Drummer: Simon Fraser
Drummer: Daniel McGillivray

Privates
   Roderick Baine
   Donald Black
   James Black
   John Buchanan
   John Browne
   Evan Cameron
   John Cameron
   Angus Campbell
   Donald Campbell
   Donald Campbell
   Duncan Campbell
   James Campbell*
   William Campbell

William Campbell
John Chisholm
Donald Cuthbert*
Angus Fletcher
Alexander Fraser
James Fraser
John Fraser
John Fraser
David Callahan
Donald Gibbon
John Gordon
Alexander Johnston*
James Knight
Alexander McArthur*
John McBain
John McCallum
John McCarter
Duncan McCraw
Alexander McDonell
Donald McDonell
Evan McDonell
Duncan McDougall
John McDougall
Peter McGregor
John McIntosh
John McIntosh
Lachlan McIntosh*
John McKenzie
Roderick McKenzie
Donald McLeod
John McLeod
Catherine McNicol
Duncan McNicol
Duncan McNicol
Alex McPherson
Donald McPherson
John McPherson
John McPherson
Lachlan McPherson
Finlay Munro
Hugh Munro
Catherine Noble
George Noble
John Robertson
William Ross
Arthur Rose
Alexander Smith
William Rose
James Smith
Catherine Ross
James Wright

Captain Alexander Campbell *Aros's* Company

Captain: Alexander Campbell
Ensign: John McPherson
Sergeant: John Fraser*
Sergeant: Edward McPherson*
Sergeant: Duncan Weir*
Corporal: John McCarly
Corporal: Evan McPherson*
Corporal: Neil McPherson
Corporal: Lewis Stuart*
Drummer: John Watson

Privates

Andrew Anderson
John Beaton
Angus Cameron
Duncan Cameron*
John Cameron
John Cameron
Murdoch Cameron*
James Cavanagh
Angus Fraser
Donald Fraser
Donald Fraser
James Fraser*
Robert Fraser
David Gunn
Donald Livingston
Duncan McArthur
Alexander McDonald
Angus McDonald
Angus McDonald
Donald McDonald
Donald McDonald
Lachlan McDonald
Nearow McDonald
John McGillivrae
John McGregor
Malcolm McGregor
John McIntosh
Malcolm McIntyre
John McIver
John McKay*
Robert McKay
Donald McKinnon
Evan McLean
Angus McLeod
Donald McLeod
Evan McLeod
John McLeod
Malcolm McLeod
Peter McNaughton
Donald McPherson
Donald McPherson
James McPherson
James McPherson
John McPherson*
Mary McPherson
Neil McPherson
Thomas McPherson*
Alexander Morton
Alexander Robertson
Alexander Robertson
Donald Robertson
Duncan Robertson
Thomas Ross
William Ross
John Shaw
Robert Shaw
John Smith*
Angus Stuart
Alex. Sutherland
Robert Wilson

Captain John Nairn's Company

Captain: John Nairne*
Lieut: Allen Stewart

Ensign: Charles Burnett
Sergeant: Alexander McDonell
Sergeant: Allan McDonell*
Sergeant: John McKay
Sergeant: Henry Munro
Corporal: William Bruce
Corporal: Donald McKinnon*
Corporal: William Ross*
Drummer: William Bruce*
Drummer: Donald Burke

Privates

William Anderson
Duncan Campbell
Peter Dunbar
James Forbes*
John Fraser
John Fraser
Thomas Fraser
William Ganson
Hugh Graham
Colin Grant
Hugh Grant
William Grant
James Hackney
James Henderson
Donald Kennedy
John McColl
Angus McDonell
Angus McDonell
Angus McDonell
Arnold McDonell
Charles McDonell
Colin McDonell
Donald McDonell
James McDonell
John McDonell
John McDonell
John McDonell
Robert McFarlane
John McGillivray
Donald McIntosh*
Eliza McIntosh
James McIntosh
James McIntosh
Mary McIntosh
Alexander McKay
James McKenzie
Alexander McLeod
John McLeod
Alexander McNabb
William Moore*
Roderick Morrison
Alexander Munro*
Jane Munro
John Munro
William Munro
John Mustard
Malcolm Nicholson
Archibald Robinson
Alexander Ross*
Alexander Ross
John Ross
William Ross
George Strachan
Archibald Stuart*

George Sutherland
William Thompson*
John Turnbull
Donald Walker

Captain Hugh Fraser *Eskadale's* Company

Captain: Hugh Fraser
Lieut: George Fraser
Lieut: James Murray
Sergeant: John Clark*
Sergeant: Alexander Fraser*
Sergeant: Alexander McKay*
Corporal: Alexander Fraser
Corporal: Duncan Forbes*
Corporal: George Geddes*
Corporal: Alexander McDonell
Drummer: Alexander Fraser*
Drummer: John Stuart*

Privates

John Cameron
Alexander Campbell
Peter Campbell*
Peter Croll
George Davidson
Allan Eackhorn
Alexander Ferguson
Alexander Fraser
Donald Fraser
John Fraser
John Fraser*
John Fraser*
David Jackson
Angus Kennedy
John Kennedy
Donald Levache
Alexander McCraw
John McCutchen
Alexander McDonell
Cath McDonald
John McDonell
John McDonell
Robert McDonell
Duncan McIntosh
Farquhar McIntosh
Alexander McIntyre
Angus McIntyre
Evan McKay
John McKay
John McKenzie
John McLachlin
Donald McMaster
Donald McMillan
Murdoch McPherson*
Alexander McPhie
Archibald McQueen
Alexander McTavish
George Miller
John Mitchell
William Nichey
Alexander Patterson
Alexander Rose
Duncan Stuart
John Stuart

Peter Stuart*
Alex Sutherland
John Sutherland*
John Turner

Captain Hugh Montgomerie's Company

Captain: Hugh Montgomerie
Lieut: John Fraser
Ensign: Alexander Fraser
Sergeant: Alexander Fraser
Sergeant: Angus McPherson
Sergeant: Alexander Shaw*
Sergeant: William Watson*
Corporal: John Ferguson*
Corporal: Donald Fraser*
Corporal: Hector Munro*
Drummer: John Provan*

Privates
William Browne
David Buchanan
Isabel Buchanan
Alexander Cameron
Donald Cameron
John Chisholm
Alexander Cormak*
Thomas Davidson*
Martin Ferguson
Alexander Fraser*
Hugh Fraser
John Fraser
William Fraser
James Glass
Lachlan Irving
James Johnston*
Alexander Martin
Hugh McCraw
John McDonell
Roderick McDonell
William McGillivrae
George McKay
John McKay
Roderick McKenzie*

James McQueen*
John McSwaine
David Mitchell
Angus Morrison
Donald Morrison*
Roderick Morrison
Alexander Munro
Donald Munro*
Alexander Provan
John Robertson
Andrew Rose
Donald Ross
John Ross
John Ross*
John Ross
David Saunders
John Smith
John Strachan
Agnes Vass
Nicholas Vass
William Williamson

Captain Alexander Wood's Company

Captain: Alexander Wood
Sergeant: Alexander Fraser*
Sergeant: William Gunn*
Sergeant: Ranald McDonell*
Corporal: John Fraser*
Corporal: John McDonell*
Corporal: Donald McIntyre*
Drummer: Donald McKenzie*

Privates
Donald Cameron
James Crawford*
Angus Gillis
William Graham*
John Kennedy*
Donald McDonald
James McDonell
John McDonell
John McDonell
John McDonell*

Ranald McDonell*
John McDougal
John McIntosh*
Alexander McKenzie*
James McKenzie
Lachlan McKinnon
Angus Morrison

The soldiers shown below were included in 78th Muster Rolls, but not included in separate list of 170 men discharged [NAC Microfilm C-10462 Series, RG4 C2 Vol. 1]:

Private Thomas Cameron*
Private Donald Clark*
Private Alex McDonell*
Private Alex McNab*
Private Angus McDonald*
Private Duncan McCraw*
Private William McNabb*

**Above list prepared by Marie Fraser, Clan Fraser Society of Canada - August 2001.
Please visit her website at www.clanfraser.ca for more details on Fraser Genealogy.**

III. LAND GRANT PETITIONS

Discharged Sergeants of the 78th Foot requesting land grants in Québec, 15 March 1765.

Sgt. James Thompson
Sgt. Hugh Tulloch
Sgt. William Gunn
Sgt. James McDonell
Sgt. John Fraser
Sgt. James Sinclair
Sgt. Alexander Ferguson
Sgt. Alexander Leith
Sgt. Lachlan Smith
Sgt. Donald Fraser

Discharged men of the 78th Foot requesting land grants in Québec, 19 & 31 May 1765.

Corporal Donald McKenivan
Private James Campbell
Private Edward Davidson
Private Thomas Davidson
Private George McAdam
Private Donald Clark
Private John Grant
Private Alexander Cormack
Private Alexander McDonald
Private Ranald McDonald
Private Alexander McNabb
Private Thomas Cameron
Private John Robie
Private Alexander Fraser
Private Angus McDonald
Private Duncan McGraw
Private William McNabb
Private Murdoch Macpherson
Private William McKenzie
Private John Chisholm
Private John Forbes
Private Finlay Monro

Discharged Sergeants & Men requesting land grants in New York Colony, 28 February 1764.

Sergeant Allan Cameron
Sergeant Alexander Fraser
Sergeant Alexander Fraser
Sergeant James Ross

Private John Fraser
Private Donald McIntosh
Private John Anderson
Private Alexander Fraser
Private John McIntosh
Private Findlay McDonald

Private George Sutherland

Facing page, inset: Thomas Mante (1735-1785). Title page from *A History of the Late War in North America* **written by one of the several non-Highland officers who served in the 77th. Mante began his military career in the Marines. He transferred to the 77th Foot while serving ashore as an Assistant Engineer at the Siege of Havana in 1762. Besides his famous history which was published in London in 1772, he wrote several military treatises as well as romantic novels to make ends meet. He died penniless in 1785. (Private Collection).**

A Select & Annotated Bibliography

The books/articles below are divided into four categories. The first lists general books that deal with various aspects of the 42nd, 77th and 78th Regiments of Foot that were common to all three units while serving in North America during the Seven Years' War [SYW] such as dress, weapons, medical services, training, etc. The remaining three sections are more regimental specific and deal with specific battles/campaigns of each regiment or biographies, memoirs, journals or letter collections of their serving regimental officers and/or men.

General

Annand, A. McK. "John Campbell, 4th Earl of Loudoun (1705-1782)," *Journal of the Society for Army Historical Research*, [hereafter *JSAHR*], Vol. 44, (March 1966), pp. 22-24. A short biography of the Highland regiments' first commander-in-chief in North America. Several regimental officers of all three Highland regiments served in Campbell's regiment - Lord Loudoun's Highlanders [64th Foot] - during the War of Austrian Succession [1740-48].

Barnes, R. Money, *The Uniforms & History of The Scottish Regiments: 1625 to the Present Day*, (New York, 1960). An interesting overview of the development of Highland military dress and weapons, with numerous references to the 42nd, 77th and 78th. and line drawings of kit and equipment.

Bouquet, Henri, *The Papers of Colonel Henry Bouquet*, Sylvester E. Stevens, *et al.*, eds., 19 vols. (Harrisburg: Pennsylvania Historical Commission and Works Progress Administration, 1940-1944). Numerous references to the 77th and 42nd as well as letters written by various 42nd and 77th officers. Essential primary source for the Forbes campaign 1758, the battle of Bushy Run [Edge Hill] 1763, and the 1764 Ohio-Muskingum expedition.

Brumwell, Stephen, *Redcoats. The British Soldier and War in the Americas, 1755-1763* (Cambridge and New

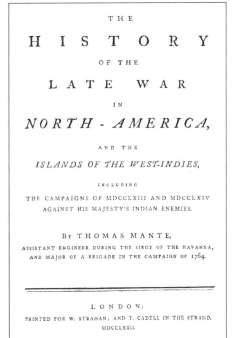

THE

HISTORY

OF THE

LATE WAR

IN

NORTH - AMERICA,

AND THE

ISLANDS OF THE WEST-INDIES,

INCLUDING

THE CAMPAIGNS OF MDCCLXIII AND MDCCLXIV
AGAINST HIS MAJESTY'S INDIAN ENEMIES.

By THOMAS MANTE,

ASSISTANT ENGINEER DURING THE SIEGE OF THE HAVANNA,
AND MAJOR OF A BRIGADE IN THE CAMPAIGN OF 1764.

LONDON:

PRINTED FOR W. STRAHAN; AND T. CADELL IN THE STRAND.
MDCCLXXII.

York, 2002). The best book on the subject to date and contains an excellent chapter on the Highland battalions in North America during the SYW.

Chronicles of the Families of Atholl and Tullibardine: The Manuscripts of the Duke of Atholl, K.T. and of Earl of Home (London, 1891). Though dated, contains many primary source documents pertaining to the 42nd, 77th and 78th Highlanders including letters, muster rolls and biographical notes pertaining to Athollmen.

Clyde, Robert, *From Rebel to Hero: The Image of the Highlander, 1755-1830*. (East Linton, 1995). A scholarly but useful appraisal of how the Highland regiments became an invaluable part of the imperial British army.

Forman, James D., *The Scottish Dirk* (Bloomfield: 1991). This is a fine synthesis of scholars' and arms experts' opinions/observations on the Highlander's fighting dirk.

Fortescue, J.W., *A History of the British Army*, Vol. II (London, 1910), 395. The standard army history, though somewhat dated. Draws heavily upon Stewart for the Highland regiments' participation in North America as well as the American historian, Francis Parkman. See separate entries.

Grant, George, *The New Highland Military Discipline*, (London, [reprint] 1757). An interesting drill manual with excellent plates of a contemporary Highland soldier, written and published in the same year as the raising of the 77th (Montgomery's) and 78th Foot (Fraser's).

Guy, Alan J., *Oeconomy and Discipline: Officership and*

Administration in the British Army, 1714-63, (Manchester, 1985), A comprehensive examination of the inner workings of British regiments in the 18th century.

Hayes, James, "Scottish Officers in the British Army, 1714-63", *Scottish Historical Review*, Vol. 37, (1958), 23-33.

Houlding, John A., *"Fit for Service": The Training of the British Army, 1715-1795*, Oxford, 1981). A scholarly and well-researched book on all aspects of individual and collective training of the British soldier in the 18th century.

Kopperman, Paul E. "Medical Services in the British Army, 1742-1783. *"Journal of the History of Medicine and Allied Sciences*, 34 (October 1979), pp. 428-455. Excellent overview of medical services available to the Highland regiments during SYW.

———————-. "The British High Command and Soldiers' Wives in America, 1755-1783." *JSAHR*, Vol. 60 (Spring 1982), 14-34. Excellent overview on the Army's attitudes towards women in the Highland and other British regiments.

MacBean, William M., ed. *Roster of Saint Andrew's Society of the State of New York with Biographical Data*, 4 vols., (New York, 1911 [privately printed by the Saint Andrew's Society of the State of New York). A good, but at times, incomplete collection of biographical notes on Highland regimental officers who joined the Society during the SYW.

MacLean, John Patterson, *An Historical account of the settlements of Scotch Highlanders in America prior to the peace of 1783; together with notices of Highland regiments and biographical sketches,* (Cleveland, 1900). Some plagiarisation of Stewart but useful information on land settlement by discharged Highland officers and men after the SYW.

MacLennan, Alastair, "Highland Regiments in North America 1756-1783." *Bulletin of the Fort Ticonderoga Museum,* [hereafter *BFTM*], Vol. 12, (September 1966), pp. 118-127. A thinly disguised re-hash of Stewart with some family anecdotes on the 42nd, 77th and 78th. SYW broadsword and dirk depicted in article are now with the National Army Museum weapons collection in Chelsea, UK.

MacLeod, Rev. Walter, ed., *"A List of Persons concerned in The Rebellion transmitted to the commissioners of excise by the several supervisors in Scotland in obedience to a general letter of the 7th May 1746 and a supplementary list with evidences to prove the same",* (Edinburgh, 1890 [reprint, Bruceton Mills, WV, 1999]). Useful for identifying officers of the respective Highland regiments who were out in the '45.

McCulloch, Ian Macpherson & Todish, Tim, *British Light Infantryman in the Seven Years War, North America, 1757-1763, North America,* (Oxford, 2004). An Osprey trade book depicting the everyday life and campaigning of a light infantry soldier featuring Private Robert Kirkwood of the 77th (Montgomery's). Excellent color plates by Steve Noon. See Kirkwood entry in 77th Foot section.

McKillop, Andrew, *"More Fruitful than the Soil": Army, Empire and the Scottish Highlands 1715-1815,* (East Linton, 1999). A scholarly dissertation and detailed discussion of the trends, problems and recruiting of the Highland battalions in the SYW including the 42nd, 77th, and 78th.

Newton, Michael, *We're Indians Sure Enough: The Legacy of the Highlanders in the United States,* (Richmond, 2001). A collection of 18th to 20th century Gaelic songs and poems, some written by, or for, members of the 42nd, 77th and 78th Foot with translations by the author. While historical interpretation and context surrounding the songs is weak, the latter are excellent examples of the Celtic oral tradition during the SYW and give an insight into how the Highland soldier perceived himself and the role he had to play in North America.

Parkman, Francis, *Montcalm and Wolfe*, 2 vols., (London, 1899), Dated but colorful accounts of all the campaigns in which the three Highland Regiments in North America fought..

_____, *History of the Conspiracy of Pontiac,* (New York, 1929). Still one of the best accounts of the events of 1763-65 involving the 77th/42nd at Bushy Run, the 77th and its role in the Paxton Boy riots, the 42nd coping with civil disobedience 1764, the 1764 Ohio Expedition under Bouquet, and Stirling's detachment on the Ohio-Mississippi 1765-66.

Reid, Stuart, and Chappel, Mike, *18th Century Highlanders* (London, 1993). An Osprey trade book with good color plates depicting the various uniforms.

Stewart of Garth, David, *Sketches of the Highlanders of Scotland…,* 2 Vols, (Edinburgh, 1822). The first full length history of the 42nd with small vignette histories of the 77th and 78th Regiments of Foot. Rife with numerous errors such as incorrect dates, locations, names, and casualties. Unfortunately Stewart based this work in large part on anecdotal material collected through interviews, material that subsequent regimental historians have, in many cases, shamelessly plagiarized, and in doing so, have repeated the numerous errors. Unfortunately most internet websites (historical and genealogical) have also directly copied from this 1822 two-volume book and thus too perpetuate all the errors in cyberspace.

Whitelaw, Charles E., "The Origin and Development of the Highland Dirk", *The Transactions of the Glasgow Archaeological Society*, New Series, Vol.V., 1908, 32-42.

42nd Foot

Adams, Paul K. "Colonel Henry Bouquet's Ohio Expedition in 1764." *Pennsylvania History*, 40 (April 1973), pp. 139-147. The Black Watch provided the largest contingent of regulars for this expedition.

Anderson, Niles. *The Battle of Bushy Run*. (Harrisburg, 1966).

_____, "Bushy Run: Decisive Battle in the Wilderness. Pennsylvania and the Indian Rebellion of 1763," *Western Pennsylvania Historical Magazine*, [hereafter *WPHM*] 46 (July 1963), 211-245.

Bascom, Robert O. Bascom, "The Legend of Duncan Campbell," *Proceedings of the New York State Historical Association*, vol. II (1902), pp. 32-38. A short biography of one of the best known Black Watch officers of the SYW, Major Duncan Campbell of Inverawe, immortalized by Robert Louis Stevenson in his poem "Ticonderoga: A Legend of the West Highlands."

Cannon, Richard, *Historical Record of the Forty-Second, or, The Royal Highland Regiment of foot: Containing an account of the formation of six companies of Highlanders in 1729, which were termed "The Black Watch", and were regimented in 1739; and of the subsequent services of the Regiment to 1844.*, (London, 1845). A thinly-disguised re-hash of Stewart's *Sketches*.

Carroon, Robert G., *Broadswords and Bayonets : the journals of the expedition under the command of Captain Thomas Stirling of the 42nd Regiment of Foot, Royal Highland Regiment (the Black Watch) to occupy Fort Chartres in the Illinois Country, August 1765 to January 1766*, (Society of Colonial Wars in the State of Illinois, 1984). A limited edition paperback of two unpublished 18th century Journals by Black Watch officers (one of whom is Thomas Stirling) recounting their 1765-66 expedition down the Ohio and Mississippi Rivers. Biographical notes on Thomas Stirling and others in the Introduction. See also entry on Bradley T. Gericke.

Daudelin, Don. "Numbers and Tactics at Bushy Run.", *WPHM*, 68 (April 1985), 153-180.

Drummond, Lt. Col. M.C.A., "'*Government*' or Black Watch Tartan", *JSAHR*, Vol. 2 (1922), 264-66.

Eaton, H. B. "Lieutenant-General Patrick Sinclair: An Account of His Military Career." *JSAHR*, Vol. 56 (Autumn, Winter 1978), 128-142, 215-232; 57 (Spring 1979), pp. 45-55. A profile on a Black Watch officer who served on the Great Lakes as a naval commander and later as Lt. Governor and superintendent at Michilimackinac.

Embleton, G.A., "The Black Watch at Ticonderoga", *Tradition Magazine*, No. 19.

Forbes, Archibald, *The Black Watch: A record of an historic regiment*, (London: 1910), an unashamed re-hash of Stewart.

Fredericks, Richard B., "The Black Watch at Ticonderoga and Major Duncan Campbell of Inverawe", *Proceedings*, New York State Historical Association, Vol. X., (1911). A good collection of letters, muster rolls, and orderly book excerpts on the 42nd. Some errors and much repetition from *Chronicles of the Families of Atholl & Tullibardine*.

Gericke, Bradley T. *The Black Watch in the Illinois Country: The Stirling Expedition, 1765, Journal of America's Military Past*, Volume XXIV, Number 4 (1998), 5-17. More accessible account of the Stirling expedition of 1765.

Grant, Charles S. "Pontiac's Rebellion and the British Troop Moves of 1763." *Mississippi Valley Historical Review*, 40 (June 1953), pp. 75-88. Good overview.

Haythornthwaite, Phillip J., "The First Highland Regiment," *Military Illustrated*, (December/January 1988) 23-30. A detailed look at the dress, weapons and early history of the 42nd.

John Grant, *Journal of John Grant, 2nd Battalion, 42nd Regiment, covering service from 1758 to 1761*. Register House, Series 4/77. Microfilm. (Original Journal held in Alexander Turnbull Museum in Wellington, New Zealand). Grant served in the 2nd Battalion in Martinique and Guadeloupe before serving alongside the 1st Battalion for the remainder of the SYW.

Gruber, Ira D., *John Peebles' American War - The Diary of a Scottish Grenadier, 1776- 1782* , (Mechanicsburg, PA, 1998) . Grenadier Captain John Peeble's journals of the Revolutionary War with a biographical introduction by Gruber. Peebles served as a "gentleman volunteer" in the 42nd at Bushy Run and was rewarded with an ensigncy for his gallantry during the two-day battle.

Kirkwood, Robert, *"Through So Many Dangers"; Memoirs and Adventures of Robert Kirk, Late of the Royal Highland Regiment*, Ian McCulloch & Tim Todish, eds., (Limerick, 17775 [reprint Fleischmanns, NY, 2004]). The only known memoir of a Highland private soldier who served in North America during the French & Indian War. Kirkwood soldiered initially with the 77th, then transferred to the 42nd on the disbandment of Montgomery's Highlanders. Kirkwood's memoirs include accounts of his capture by the Shawnee at Fort Duquesne, 1758; his participation in Roger's Raid against St. Francis, 1759; fighting at Bushy Run, 1763; and being one of the first Highlanders on the Mississippi with the 42nd's occupation of Fort de Chartres in Illinois.

Linklater, Eric & Andros, *The Black Watch: The History of the Royal Highland Regiment,* (London, c.1962), First half of the book is essentially a re-hash of Stewart, no new scholarship.

Mackay Scobie, Ian, " *'Government' or Black Watch Tartan",* *JSAHR,* Vol. 1, (1922), 154-56.

_____, " *'Government' or Black Watch Tartan",* *JSAHR,* Vol. 2, (1923), 19-21.

McCulloch, Lt. Col. Ian, " *'Like roaring lions breaking from their chains:'* The Battle of Ticonderoga, 8 July 1758" in, *Fighting For Canada: Seven Battles, 1758-1945,* Donald Graves, ed., (Toronto, 2000). Most up-to-date monograph of the Black Watch's tragic but gallant assault during the SYW. Excellent battle maps by Chris Johnson and detailed orders of battle.

_____, *"The Old Squah who should Wear Petticoats":* General James Abercromby at the Battle of Ticonderoga, 1758", Issue 26, *Battlefield Review,* (2003), 39-46. Good overview of the battle with several prints of the Black Watch.

McMicking, Neil, *The Officers of the Black Watch, 1725 to 1937,* (Perth, 1938). An honest attempt to capture all the officers who served from the regiment's inception as the Independent Companies up to the 1950s with their commissioning dates and records of service in one register. While the British Army Lists and extant commissioning lists in the WO were obviously used, numerous errors and duplication have crept in due to the use of other less reliable sources such as Stewart's *Sketches.*

Murray, W.W., "The Black Watch at Ticonderoga,' *Canadian Defense Quarterly,* Vol. 6 (1929), 212-218. Good overview.

"Muster Rolls of the 42nd Foot, October 1763", *War Office* [hereafter *WO*], 12/5478/part 1, f:96.

Ray, Frederick E., Jr, and Frederick P. Todd. "British 42nd (Royal Highland) Regiment of Foot, 1759-1760." *Military Collector and Historian,* 8 (Summer 1956), 42.

Smelser, Marshall, *The Campaign for the Sugar Island, 1759: A Study of Amphibious Warfare,.* (Chapel Hill,

1955). An excellent case study and overview of the Second Battalion, 42nd Foot's first campaign during the 1759 Martinique/Guadeloupe expedition.

Smith, James, *An Account of the Remarkable Occurrences in the Life and Travels of Col James Smith,* (Lexington, 1799 [reprint, Cincinnati; 1907]). Contains first hand account of the civil disturbances encountered by the 42nd Foot against Smith and his "Black Boys" while stationed at Forts Pitt, Ligonier and Bedford, 1764-65.

Stewart of Urrard, Captain James, *Captain James Stewart of Urrard's Orderly Books 1759-1761,* four vols., Black Watch Archives, Balhousie Castle, Scotland.

Waddell, Louis M., ed. "New Light on Bouquet's Ohio Expedition: Nine Days of Thomas Hutchinson's Journal, October 3-October 11, 1764." *WPHM,* 66 (July 1983), pp. 271-279. First-hand account of the 42nd's last major expedition under Col Bouquet during the SYW.

Wallace, Col. R. F. H., "42nd Foot Regimental Routine and Army Administration in North America in 1759," *JSAHR,* 30 (1952).

_____, "The Black Watch in 1761", *The Red Hackle,* 3 Parts, (January/July/October, 1935), pp. 9-10; 18-21; 3-6. Extracts and analysis by a Black Watch officer based on James Stewart of Urrard's Orderly Book [see separate entry].

Westbrook, Nicholas, ed. "'Like Roaring Lions Breaking From their Chains': The Highland Regiment at Ticonderoga", *BFTM,* Vol. XVI, No. 1, (1998), 17-91. An excellent anthology of hither-to unpublished or inaccessible primary source material documenting the service of the 42nd Foot during the 1758 Ticonderoga campaign.

Williams, Edward G., ed., "A Survey of Bouquet's Road, 1764: Samuel Finley's Field Notes." *WPHM,* 66 (April, July, October 1983), pp. 129-168, 237-269, 347-367; 67 (January, April 1984), pp. 33-63, 133-152. The Black Watch on the 1764 Muskingum expedition to chastise the Ohio Indians.

_____, *Bouquet's March to the Ohio: The Forbes Road (from the Original Manuscripts in the William L. Clements Library).* (Pittsburgh, 1975).

_____, "The Orderly Book of Colonel Henry Bouquet's Expedition Against the Ohio Indians, 1764." *WPHM,* 42, ((March, June, September 1959), pp. 9-33, 179-200, 283-302.

_____, "The Orderly Book of Colonel Henry Bouquet's Expedition Against the Ohio Indians, 1764.", *WPHM,* 56, (July, October 1973), pp. 281-316, 383-428; 57 (January 1974), pp. 51-106.

77th Foot

Amherst, Jeffery *et al*, *Amherst Papers: The Southern Sector: Dispatches from South Carolina, Virginia and His Majesty's Superintendent of Indian Affairs*, Edith Mays, ed., (Bowie, MD, 1999). Contains first-hand accounts of the 1760-61 Cherokee expeditions, including letters by Colonel Archibald Montgomery, Lt Col James Grant and Capt Alexander Mackenzie, 77th Foot, as well as casualty and strength returns. Unfortunately most letters have been poorly transcribed from *WO* and *CO* documents according to colleague, Robert Andrews.

Annand, A. McK., "Hugh Montgomerie, 12th Earl of Eglinton, K.T.", *JSAHR*, Vol.39, (1961), 37-40. A short biographical article on the younger cousin of Colonel Archibald Montgomery. Hugh served as a subaltern on the 1760 Cherokee campaign and was with one of the two 77th companies that participated in the recapture of St John's, Newfoundland. He finished the SYW as a captain in the 78th (Fraser's). Includes a good portrait of Hugh in his Fencible regimentals (c.1780) by John Singleton Copley.

Anderson, Niles, *The Battle of Bushy Run*. (Harrisburg, 1966).

_____, "Bushy Run: Decisive Battle in the Wilderness. Pennsylvania and the Indian Rebellion of 1763," *WPHM*, 46 (July 1963), pp. 211-245.

_____, "The General Chooses a Road: The Forbes Campaign of 1758 to Capture Fort Duquesne." *WPHM*, 42 (June, September, December 1959), 109-138, 241-258, 383-401.

Cargill Cole, Richard, *Thomas Mante: Writer, Soldier, Adventurer*, (New York, 1993). A short biography of the enigmatic Lieutenant Thomas Mante, 77th Foot.

Cole, Richard C., "Montgomerie's Cherokee Campaign, 1760: Two Contemporary Views", *The North Carolina Historical Review*, Vol. LXXIV, No.1, (1997), 19-36.

Corkran, David, *The Cherokee Frontier: Conflict & Survival, 1740-1762*, (Norman, OK, 1962). A somewhat biased overview of the 1760-61 expeditions against the Cherokee.

Forbes, John. *Writings of General John Forbes Relating to His Service in North America*. Alfred Proctor James, ed., (Menasha, 1938). Essential primary source documentation for the Forbes campaign of 1758.

_____, *Letters of General John Forbes Relating to the Expedition Against Fort Duquesne in 1758*, Irene Stewart, ed. (Pittsburgh, 1927).

Fyers, E.W.H., "The Loss and Recapture of St John's, Newfoundland in 1762", *JSAHR*, Vol. 11, (1932), 179-

215. Detailed account of the 77th's final battle against the French in the SYW, including officer muster rolls, strength and casualty returns.

Grant, Alastair M., *General James Grant of Ballindalloch, 1720-1806*, (London, 1930). Biography of Major James Grant, 77th Foot, who led the botched raid against Fort Duquesne, 1758 and acted as Col Montgomery's second in command for the 1760 Cherokee expedition.

Greene, Jack P. "The South Carolina Quartering Dispute, 1757-1758." *South Carolina Historical Magazine*, 60 (October 1959), pp. 193-204. A detailed account of the trouble encountered by Colonel Archibald Montgomery and the Highlanders of the 77th Foot on their arrival in Charleston, summer 1757.

Law, W. "The Campaign in Carolina 1760-1761," *Journal of the Royal United Service Institution*, 104 (May 1959), pp. 226-230. An erroneous account of the 77th Montgomery Highlanders' expedition because it draws heavily upon Stewart's "history".

Mante, Thomas, *The History of the Late War in North America, and the Islands of the West Indies, including the Campaigns of MDCCLXIII and MDCCLXIV against His Majesty's Indian Enemies*, (London, 1772). A contemporary history of the SYW by a former officer of the 77th Foot, the result being the best and fullest accounts of the 77th in action in South Carolina, at Bushy Run and the Havana campaign where Mante served as an engineer.

Nelson, Paul David, *General James Grant: Scottish Soldier and Royal Governor of East Florida*, (Gainsville, 1993). Best extant biography of Major James Grant, 77th Foot.

Perry, Captain David. *Recollections of an Old Soldier. The Life of David Perry, A Soldier of the French and Revolutionary Wars*, (Windsor, Vt, 1822). An excellent eyewitness account by a Massachusetts Provincial sergeant of the surprise dawn assault on Signal Hill, 1762, led by Captain Charles Macdonell *Glengarry*, 78th Foot, whose light infantry company comprised elements of recovered men from all three Highland Regiments. The 77th light infantry company commanded by Captain Roderick Mackenzie and a 77th bonnet company commanded by Captain Jock Sinclair formed part of a provisional battalion under the command of Major Patrick Sinclair, 77th.

78th Foot

Chapman, Frederick T., and John R. Elting. "The 78th (Highland) Regiment of Foot, 1757-1763 (Fraser's

Highlanders)." *Military Collector and Historian*, 26 (Spring 1974), 29-30.

Doughty, Arthur G., and G. W. Parmelee. *The Siege of Quebec and the Battle of the Plains of Abraham.*, 6 vols. (Quebec, 1901).

Fraser, Malcolm, "The Capture of Quebec. A Manuscript Journal Relating to the Operations Before Quebec From 8th May, 1759, to 17th May, 1760. Kept by Colonel Malcolm Fraser. Then Lieutenant in the 78th Foot (Fraser's Highlanders)", *JSAHR*, Vol. 18, (1939), 9-22.

Fraser, Marie, "The Old 78th Regiment of Foot", *Clan Fraser Society of Canada Newsletter*, at http://www.clanfraser.ca/78th.htm. Excellent e-zine articles and website including biographical notes on all 78th officers and muster rolls of the companies on their disbandment in 1763.

Harper, Col J.R., *The Fraser Highlanders*, (Montreal, 1979).

_____, *The Old 78th Regiment or Fraser's Highlanders*, (Laval, 1966).

Macleod, Serjeant Donald, *Memoirs of the Life and Gallant Exploits of the Old Highlander, Serjeant Donald Macleod . . .* (London,1791). A somewhat fanciful biographical memoir, ghosted for an old drill sergeant of the 78th.

McCulloch, Lt. Col. Ian, "'*From April Battles and Murray Generals, Good Lord deliver Us!*': The Battle of Sillery, 28 April 1760", in, *More Fighting For Canada: Five Battles, 1760-1944*, Donald Graves, ed., (Toronto, 2004). A detailed battle monograph on the second, bloodier battle fought on the Plains of Abraham six months after the one in which Wolfe was killed, and, in which, the 78th Fraser Highlanders played a key part. Colonel Simon Fraser commanded the left forward brigade. Detailed maps and orders of battle for the battle and the subsequent siege of Quebec.

Milborne, A.J.B., "The Lodge in the 78th Regiment (Fraser's Highlanders)", *Quator Coronati Lodge*, vol. LXV, 19-33. A look at the Freemasons in Fraser's Highlanders and the rest of Wolfe's Army.

Nairn, Captain John, *Nairn's Orderly Book, 1761-62*, (Frederick Mackenzie Papers), National Archives of Canada, Manuscript Group 23, Series K34. Excellent snapshot in time of the 78th Foot's regimental routine, standard operating procedures and administration while garrisoning Quebec city and some of its outlying towns and dependencies.

Hitsman, J. Mackay, "The Assault Landing at Louisbourg, 1758." *Canadian Historical Review*, 35 (December 1954), pp. 314-330. Excellent overview leading up to the assault in which the 78th Foot (Fraser's Highlanders) played a key part.

Knox, John. *An Historical Journal of the Campaigns in North America for the Years 1757, 1758, 1759, and 1760. By Captain John Knox*. Arthur G. Doughty, ed., 3 vols. (Toronto, 1914). Numerous references to the 78th (Fraser's) at Louisbourg and Quebec. Essential primary source book for Cape Breton, 1758 and Quebec campaigns, 1759-60, and includes excerpts of Amherst's *Journals* and extensive casualty and strength returns for all regiments including the 78th Foot.

Wallace, W.S., "Some Notes on Fraser's Highlanders", *Canadian Historical Review*, Vol. 18, pp. 131-140 (1937); see also updated version, "Biography of Officers of the Old 78th Regiment or Fraser's Highlanders," in J.R. Harper, *The Old 78th Regiment or Fraser's Highlanders*, (Laval, 1966).

Index of Scottish Names

Note: This Scottish name index has been provided primarily for genealogists. Actual names highlighted in bold (e.g. **Abercromby** *Glassaugh*, **Captain James**) indicate an extant Register entry in Part One. Page numbers in **bold face** indicate a portrait. Ranks after names reflect the highest rank obtained during the Seven Years' War only. For an officer's subsequent ranks and career progression, see the detailed career summaries included with each entry. While not technically correct (usually reserved to denote the laird), estate and cadet branch names have been placed after some surnames (e.g. **Campbell** *Duneaves*) to help genealogists differentiate the many cadet branches of families that share the same surname. For the interest of clarity, when two individuals with the same family name and surname appear, those without any cadet or estate appellation will appear first, followed by those who do, the latter in alphabetical order. Additionally, some officers in this latter category will also have a bracketed number behind their name which indicates their order of appearance and seniority within their particular regiment to help differentiate them from one another.

Index of Scottish
Place Names

Note: This index of Scottish place names (including estates, institutions, and geographical features) is provided primarily to assist genealogists. For North American and other place names within their historical context, please see Volume I of *Sons of the Mountains*.

Aberarder, 20, 160
Abercairney, 51
Abercherder, 9
Abercorn, 86
Aberdeen, 34
Aberdeenshire, 58
Aberfeldy Green,
Aberuthven, 15
Aboyne, 58
Achalader, 13, 23
Achlyne, 160
Airds, 102
Aldekarn, 9
Amulree, 159
Angus-shire, 19
Appin, 7, 81
Ardchattan, 7, 68
Ardgartan, 9
Ardgour, 69
Ardkinglas, 26, 82
Ardloch, 101, 104-5
Ardnable, 90
Ardoch, 12
Ardrossan, 93
Ardtonish, 102
Argyll, 7, 17, 30-1, 51, 56, 85, 91, 94
Argyllshire, 30, 39, 57, 72, 78, 91,
    99, 105
Arisaig, 154-5
Arkaig, Loch, *see* Lochs
Armady, 91
Aros, 91
Assynt, 101
Atholl, 11-2, 14, 21, 28, 33, 105
Aucharn, 81

Auchatenie, 84
Auchinderrin, 9
Auchterblair, 66
Auldean, 102
Ayrshire, 26, 33, 48, 52, 93

Badenoch, 83, 105-6, 108, 159-60
Balaloan, 46
Balenabie, 68
Balhousie Castle, 10, 51
Ballindalloch, 52
Ballindalloch Castle, 66
Ballimore, 30, 84
Balmeanach, 89
Balmoir, 58
Balnain, 88
Balnagowan, 84
Balmuchie, 96
Balquhain, 98
Balquhidder, 36
Banff, 9
Banffshire, 18
Barbreck (*Barr Breac*), 69, 84, 90
Barcaldine, 7, 22-3, 45, 53, 57, 70
Barra, Isle of, *see* Isles
Barrisdale, 96
Beaulieside, 87
Belladrum, 29
Belmaduthy, 67
Benbecula, Isle of, *see* Isles
Birkenbog, 87
Bishoptoun, 94
Blaich, 13
Blaragie, 108
Bogie, 86

Boisdale, 95
Boleskine, 100, 104
Bonskied, 32, 45
Borlum, Easter, 104
Borrowstoness (Bo'ness), 86
Braemore, 68
Breadalbane, 45, 53
Breakachy, 26, 103
Brolas, 13, 59-60, 69
Bunchgavie, 100, 104

Caithness, 55, 57, 68, 78, 101, 167
Calrossie, 87
Capernoch, 63, 73
Caputh, 14
Carslogie, 82
Castlehill, 95
Castleleathers, 87
Clyne, 55
Coll, Isle of, *see* Isles
Coilsfield, 69, 93
Contullich, 45
Craskie, 70
Craufurdland, 94
Cromarty, 57
Culbeg, 86
Culbokie, 90, 104
Culcairn, 55, 59
Culcherine, 26
Culclachy, 20
Culduthel, 87, 167
Culkin, 65
Culloden, 56, 61, 84-5, 91-2, 94-5,
    99, 103, 106, 153, 168
Culzean, 51

Index of British Units

Note: This index of British military units is divided into three sections: the first reflects the extant regiments during the Seven Years' War followed by two sections containing regiments that only existed before or after the SYW. It should be noted that some officers listed in the Part One registers served in regiments listed in the pre and post SYW sections.

Seven Years' War (1755-1763)

Regular Regiments, Cavalry

2nd Royal North British Dragoons, 51-2, 84, 94
6th Dragoons [Cholmondeley's], 31

Regular Regiments, Guards

3rd Foot Guards [*later* Scots Guards], 3, 10, 11, 15, 80, 98, 164

Regular Regiments, Infantry

1st Foot [The Royal Regiment, *later* Royal Scots], 3, 9, 13, 17, 22, 25, 34, 39-40, 52, 56-8, 69, 79, 83-4, 93, 164
1st Highland Battalion, *see* 77th Foot
2nd Highland Battalion, *see* 78th Foot
2nd Foot [Montagu's], 106-7
3rd Foot [The Buffs], 18-9, 82-3
4th Foot [Duroure's], 25, 58
6th Foot [Guise's, *later* Rufanes], 58
7th Foot [Lord Bertie's], 57, 105
8th Foot [Wolfe's, *later* Webb's], 76
9th Foot [Yorke's], 37, 97-8
10th Foot [Pole's], 20, 94
11th Foot [Bocland's, *later* Grant's], 52-3
12th Foot [Skelton's, *later* Clinton's], 101
13th Foot [Pulteney's, *later* Murray's], 89
15th Foot [Amherst's], 17, 35, 40, 64, 98, 105-6, 158
16th Foot [Handasyd's], 27
17th Foot [Forbes, *later* Monckton's], 9-10
18th Foot [Sebright's], 44

19th Foot [Beauclerk's], 15-6, 63
20th Foot [Cornwallis'], 98
21st Foot [Panmure's, also *"Royal North British Fusiliers"*], 20-1, 37, 62-3, 65, 84
22nd Foot [Whitemore's, *later* Rollo's], 9, 22, 54, 56-7, 83
24th Foot [Cornwallis', *later* Taylor's], 64, 88
26th Foot [Gen. Anstruther's, *"Cameronians"*], 31
27th Foot [*"Enniskillens* or Blakeney's], 14, 16, 76, 79-80, 92
28th Foot [Bragg's], 37
30th Foot [Lord Loudoun's], 39
31st Foot [Gen. Holmes; Oughton's], 28, 58
33rd Foot [Hay's, *later* Lord Walden's], 44, 54
34th Foot [Cavendish's], 14, 22, 42, 44, 97-8
35th Foot [Otway's], 18-9, 45, 54, 57, 99
36th Foot [Lord Robert Manners], 7-8, 51, 63, 68, 80, 104, 108
37th Foot [Stuart's], 63
38th Foot [Dalzell's], 25, 97
39th Foot [Aldercron's, *later* Boyd's], 54, 56
40th Foot [Hopson's, *later* Barrington's, Armiger's], 47, 52-3, 63-5, 73
41st Foot [Parson's, *later* Stirling's], 11-2, 77
42nd Foot [Lord John Murray's; Royal Highland Regiment, *Black Watch*], 1, 3-51, 53, 57, 59-62, 65, 70-2, 75, 77, 81, 83-4, 87, 91, 97-8, 102, 158-60, 165-6, 168

First Battalion, 6, 24, 50
Second Battalion, 4, 6-7, 13-6, 22, 28-36, 40, 42, 46, 49-50, 158-60, 165-6

43rd Foot [Kennedy's], 1, 51-2, 62, 106
44th Foot [Abercromby's], 7, 18-9, 31, 62, 157

Ian M. McCulloch

Lieutenant-Colonel Ian Macpherson McCulloch, CD, is a native of Halifax, Nova Scotia. Educated in Scotland and Switzerland, he holds a degree in Journalism (1977) from Carleton University, Ottawa, and a Master's Degree in War Studies (1996) from the Royal Military College of Canada, Kingston. He joined the Canadian Army in 1977 and has served in a variety of regimental and staff appointments in Canada, USA, and Germany, including an exchange posting with the British Army's Royal Regiment of Fusiliers. Promoted to lieutenant-colonel in 1993, he assumed command of the Black Watch (Royal Highland Regiment) of Canada and in 1996 was appointed Deputy Director of History & Heritage for the Canadian Forces in Ottawa. In 2000, he was posted to Canadian Medical Group Headquarters in Ottawa as a Special Assistant to the Director General Health Services. He is now serving as a NATO senior staff officer at Headquarters Supreme Allied Command Transformation in Norfolk, Virginia.

Ian is an avid military historian specializing in the Seven Years' War in North America and has published numerous articles on that subject in such journals as *Osprey Military Journal, Battlefield Review, Canadian Military History, The Beaver, Canadian Infantry Journal,* and *The Bulletin of the Fort Ticonderoga Museum.* In 1998 he served as a historical consultant for the Seven Years' War episode on CBC's Canada: *A People's History*, and has also appeared on A&E's *Civil War Journal*. An original contributor to *Fighting For Canada: Seven Battles* (Toronto, 2000) with a monograph on the Battle of Ticonderoga, 1758, Ian's most recent projects include a battle study of the bloodiest action ever fought on Canadian soil in the companion volume, *More Fighting for Canada: Five Battles, 1760-1944* (Toronto, 2004) about the Battle of Sillery 1760, outside Quebec; and, authoring a book for Osprey Books (UK) entitled *British Light Infantryman of the Seven Years War, 1756-1763, North America,* (Oxford, 2004) with friend and colleague, Timothy J. Todish. He and Tim have also edited *Through So Many Dangers: The Memoirs and Adventures of Robert Kirk, Late of the Royal Highland Regiment* published in May 2004 by Purple Mountain Press, a reprint of a rare 1775 book, first published in Ireland by a Highland soldier who served with the 42nd and 77th Regiments of Foot in North America, 1757-1767.

Ian is a active member of the Fort Ticonderoga Association and past Chairman of the Interpretation/Education Committee. He lives in Virginia Beach with his wife Susan (a past Deputy Director of the Fort Ticonderoga Museum).